In the Eyes of God

Princeton Theological Monograph Series

K. C. Hanson, Charles M. Collier, D. Christopher Spinks,
Robin Parry, and Rodney Clapp, Series Editors

Recent volumes in the series:

Koo Dong Yun
*The Holy Spirit and Ch'i (Qi):
A Chiological Approach to Pneumatology*

Stanley S. MacLean
*Resurrection, Apocalypse, and the Kingdom of Christ:
The Eschatology of Thomas F. Torrance*

Brian Neil Peterson
*Ezekiel in Context: Ezekiel's Message Understood in Its Historical Setting
of Covenant Curses and Ancient Near Eastern Mythological Motifs*

Amy E. Richter
Enoch and the Gospel of Matthew

Maeve Louise Heaney
Music as Theology: What Music Says about the Word

Eric M. Vail
Creation and Chaos Talk: Charting a Way Forward

David L. Reinhart
*Prayer as Memory: Toward the Comparative Study of Prayer
as Apocalyptic Language and Thought*

Peter D. Neumann
Pentecostal Experience: An Ecumenical Encounter

Ashish J. Naidu
*Transformed in Christ: Christology and the Christian Life
in John Chrysostom*

In the Eyes of God

A Contextual Approach to Biblical Anthropomorphic Metaphors

BRIAN C. HOWELL

◆PICKWICK *Publications* • Eugene, Oregon

IN THE EYES OF GOD
A Contextual Approach to Biblical Anthropomorphic Metaphors

Princeton Theological Monograph Series 192

Copyright © 2013 Brian C. Howell. All rights reserved. Except for brief quotations in critical publications or reviews, no part of this book may be reproduced in any manner without prior written permission from the publisher. Write: Permissions, Wipf and Stock Publishers, 199 W. 8th Ave., Suite 3, Eugene, OR 97401.

Pickwick Publications
An Imprint of Wipf and Stock Publishers
199 W. 8th Ave., Suite 3
Eugene, OR 97401

www.wipfandstock.com

ISBN 13: 978-1-62032-313-7

Cataloguing-in-Publication data:

Howell, Brian C.

In the eyes of God : a contextual Approach to biblical anthropomorphic metaphors / Brian C. Howell.

viii + 300 pp. ; 23 cm. Includes bibliographical references and indexes.

Princeton Theological Monograph Series 192

ISBN 13: 978-1-62032-313-7

1. Metaphor—Religious aspects—Christianity. 2. Bible. O.T. Genesis—Criticism, interpretation, etc. 3. God—Attributes—biblical teaching I. Series. II. Title.

BS1235.52 H59 2013

Manufactured in the U.S.A.

Contents

Acknowledgments / vii

1. Approaching Biblical Anthropomorphic Language / 1
2. Approaching Divine Metaphors / 59
3. Theomorphism / 83
4. Seeing Good and Evil—Genesis 1–3 / 105
5. God, the Sons of God, and the Man of God / 135
6. A View to Judgment—Genesis 11:5 / 165
7. Status and Blessing in the Sight of God —Genesis 16 / 174
8. A Second Look at Sodom—Genesis 18:1—19:29 / 196
9. The Mountain with a View—Genesis 22 / 219
10. Conclusion / 236

Appendix A: Exegesis of Genesis 16:13–14 / 243
Appendix B: The Righteousness of Lot / 251
Appendix C: Testing / 257
Bibliography / 273
Name and Author Index / 281
Scripture Index / 289

Acknowledgments

WRITING A THESIS, I'VE FOUND, IS A VERY REVEALING PROCESS. IT SEEMS to be more about perseverance, hope, and humility than sheer intellectual rigor. Consequently, I have a number of people to thank, not only for insights and suggestions, but for encouragement, and walking alongside me in this journey.

Firstly, I thank Gordon Wenham for seeing me through some dark days, both some of his and some of mine. Your comments have always been insightful and exceedingly helpful. More significantly, however, you modelled for me a life of humble, faithful scholarship and care—one I hope to continue to be molded by the rest of my life.

Thanks to Oliver Crisp for challenging me on broad strokes and asking penetrating and focusing questions. Thanks also for helping me piece these strains of thought together.

Heath Thomas, you were a brother in the trenches, time and again showing me where the ammunition was stored. Thanks for your insights, encouragement, and doing life with us.

Terry Wardlaw and Torsten Uhlig, you both impressed on me a model of scholarship balancing rigorous and thorough research with firm convictions. Moreover, we will not soon forget your faithfulness and kindness and enduring friendship.

Tim Goodwright, I'm not sure how an actor and an aspiring scholar got together, but I am thankful that we did. Thanks for caring about a subject that wasn't your own, and helping me focus and celebrate the task.

Jay and Orene, thanks for letting me sweep your daughter off to faraway lands with funny footballs, visiting us often, and stocking us up from "Home *Sweet* Home."

Pop, so now you know what your prodigal son has been wasting his inheritance on. Thanks for your support in so many ways. Ellen, thanks for your encouragement as well.

Chris, your prayers, visits and attempts at humor have been invaluable to us.

Acknowledgments

Jaylene, Jayden, and Jazmine, you are the loves of my life, and I thank you for bearing with the many days and nights I was holed away with some book or writing up. You are infinitely more valuable to me than what follows, and so I dedicate this work to you.

1

Approaching Biblical Anthropomorphic Language

Does He who planted the ear not hear?
Or the one who formed the eye, not see?
—Ps 94:9

ACCORDING TO BREVARD CHILDS, "NO MODERN THEOLOGICAL ISSUE which presently challenges the church is in more need of serious theological reflection from both biblical, historical, and dogmatic theology than the identity of God whom we worship."[1] This issue is also an ancient one, as we find in the Old Testament. For example, Daniel rebukes the king for honoring false, inanimate "gods," over the God of life. He says, "You have praised the gods of silver and gold, of bronze, iron, wood and stone, which do not see, hear or understand. But the God in whose hand are your life-breath and your ways, you have not glorified"[2] (Dan 5:23b). Hence, God's ability to see, hear, and understand His creation is portrayed as a distinguishing, if not defining, attribute of His identity.

However, this verse, like so many others, speaks of God in a manner that has been viewed as problematic through its history of interpretation—in anthropomorphic terms. Robert Culver defines these: "In theology it means to represent God under the figure of human form and parts—hands, ears, eyes, etc. There is also *anthropopathism*, or representing God as having human passions (emotions) such as pain, fear, hate, mercy, etc., and *anthropopoiesis*, ascribing human actions to God."[3] It is the issue of interpreting these terms, replete through Old and New Testament

---

1. Brevard S. Childs, *Biblical Theology*, 378.

2. Unless otherwise noted, all quotations are from the New American Standard Bible, 1995.

3. Culver, "Anthropomorphism," 1.

descriptions of the deity, which fuels even modern debates such as that of Open or Freewill Theism.[4] Most studies dealing with this issue focus on the iconological representation[5] of God or on the depiction of God as a human,[6] but rarely is this last topic—God's actions[7]—the explicit focus.

Commonly known as "The Problem of Religious Language," or, "The Problem of Naming God," the conundrums these expressions create for interpreters lie between the arenas of linguistics, epistemology, and theology. In terms of linguistics, the issue lies in the capacity for language as *medium* to communicate the correct information about God. Are terms for humans and God used in the same sense, totally differently, or something in between? We must understand in what *sense* human language can

---

4. Open theists such as Clark Pinnock, James Sanders, Greg Boyd, David Basinger, etc., attempt to resolve the traditional Calvinist-Arminian debate by positing a limited sense of divine knowledge. They claim that God does not know the future choices of (indeterminately) free agents, allowing their actions to be truly uncoerced, thus making these agents responsible for their decisions. They base these conclusions primarily upon a reading of anthropomorphic expressions in the Old Testament, such as Genesis 18:21, where God says, "I will go down and see whether or not they [the Sodomites] have all done according to the outcry which has come against them, and if not, I will know." (Cf. also Gen 22:12) The question arises, do such texts indicate that God learns about the future as humans do—as it happens? Questions such as these fuel this study, but we shall restrict our discussion to the interpretation of anthropomorphic language itself, leaving application to issues such as "Open Theism," for future research.

5. See van der Toorn, *The Image and the Book*; Keel, *Symbolism of the Biblical World*.

6. For example, the recent study by Esther J. Hamori focuses on what she calls the *'iš theophany*, where God appears in the form of a man. In her taxonomy, anthropopoiesis seems to fit in a category she calls, "Transcendent Anthropomorphism," where, 'Yahweh is described in anthropomorphic terms, but is not concretely embodied, not explicitly envisioned, and not immanent. Instead, he is portrayed in anthropomorphic terms, but in the heavens . . ." Hamori, "When Gods Were Men," 32–33. However, some of these texts describe God performing human-like actions "on earth" (e.g., Gen 11:5, coming *down* "to see"). As Hamori is focusing on theophanies, her categories may not be the best fit for our current subject. Hence, we prefer to leave the labels in terms of the categories being described, (roles, body parts, feelings, actions), and so opt for Culver's use of terminology.

7. Rather than a subset of anthropomorphism, James Barr sees divine action as a category *sui generis*, "My first point is to make a distinction. . . . These frequent expressions about God's ears or nose, his smelling or whistling, are not seriously anthropomorphisms in the sense of expressions trying to come to grips with the form, the *morphe*, of God. . . . These expressions provide a rich vocabulary for the diversity of the divine activity." Barr, "Theophany and Anthropomorphism in the Old Testament," 31–32. While his point is valid, the common nomenclature for applying the human sphere to God has been "anthropomorphisms," and so we will retain the term.

Approaching Biblical Anthropomorphic Language

be applied to a transcendent God. We seek here to determine the meaning of such language and how it might augment our picture of the biblical God.

Once we determine the sense in which our descriptions of God are to be taken, we are then faced with the question of how we can know what we say is true of God. As Frederick Ferré says, "THE FUNDAMENTAL PROBLEM for users of theological language, as seen by one theological tradition, is the avoidance, on the one hand, of anthropomorphism and, on the other, of agnosticism."[8] If we speak of a divine being in terms originating from our own sphere of life, we risk looking down the well at the proverbial mirror. Conversely, God, as Creator, has traditionally[9] been viewed as transcending His creation, and hence, it is difficult to understand how human (created) language can apply to Him. That is, we must establish a basis upon which we can claim our assertions of God are veridical. Even if we determine the sense in which they are to be taken, how do we know that they even apply accurately to God?

Finally, questions are raised when a biblical reference to God seems to contradict our theological systems.[10] Do we rule the statement out of order as a vestige of earlier, more naive stages of the Bible's development? Is it simply a "manner of speaking" which requires theologically-informed interpretation to keep it in line? For example, Frederick Ferré

---

8. Ferré, *Language, Logic and God*, 67.

9. Those who hold to the process theology of Alfred North Whitehead and Charles Hartshorne claim God is "Becoming" rather than "Being." Hence God incorporates creation into His being, absorbing and growing from the changes within it. This particular form of panentheism eschews the traditional notion of transcendence, which holds that God, as the Uncreated One, is "wholly other" than His creation. John Cooper distinguishes this from classical theism, "In brief, panentheism affirms that although God and the world are ontologically distinct and God transcends the world, the world is 'in' God ontologically. In contrast, classical theism posits an unqualified distinction between God and the world: although intimately related, God and creatures are always and entirely other than one another." Cooper, *Panentheism*, 18. It should be noted that Cooper's treatise reveals many different varieties of panentheism, several of which he deems consonant with orthodoxy, though he personally holds to a classical theism.

10. In view of the hermeneutical circle, we realize that all readers bring *a priori* assumptions to a text, a point often neglected in biblical studies. For instance, we approach these anthropomorphic biblical texts from a rather Arminian-leaning (though not fully Arminian) standpoint, which affects how we view God's actions, the significance and nature of human character and choices, etc. However, the emphasis of this dissertation is on the other half of the circle. That is, ideally, the text should also inform the reader. It is our hope to provide an approach to the text which, while acknowledging the stance of the reader, avoids the pitfalls in which a particular theology can be read *into* a text to the point where the text is not given its full voice.

distinguishes between anthropomorphism and vulgar anthropomorphism (anthropocentrism).[11] He says of the former, "It is, however, not vulgar anthropomorphism, attributing obscene or unworthy traits to the divine. On the contrary, it is precisely by the selection of specific traits acknowledged as eminently worthy that (logically) believers may eliminate the unworthy in connection with the Most High. Without some such positive criterion, as we have seen, anything goes."[12] But how is one to develop such a criterion of which traits are "eminently" worthy?

Previously considered a clear medium of knowledge, an examination of language itself has shown that it has both sense and reference (G. Frege), as well as gathering its meaning within particular *language games* (L. Wittgenstein). Hence, to further establish the nature of this issue and our underlying stances towards it, we too must take a look at how language conveys meaning, its basis for making truth claims about God, and the theological issues involved in the divine-human relationship, if we are able to understand what anthropomorphic language can indicate for us. In the next section, we shall examine the major approaches to the problem of speaking of God in human language, noting the questions which inherently arise. Following this, we shall examine the basis upon which religious language can refer to the divine, and in the final section, we examine how Old Testament theology informs our approach to speaking of the divine.

Approaches to Divine Description

Thomas Aquinas lays out the three main historical approaches to describing the divine in human terms: the *equivocal, univocal, and analogous*. Not necessarily mutually exclusive, theologians have drawn from all of them in attempting to speak of God. In the following section, we will give a short description of each approach, noting the difficulties that arise with each approach. We will also look at an attempt to bridge these difficulties through partial-univocity, and finally, the more recent developments in metaphor theory and various theorists' attempts to use it to fill in the gaps within the *via analogia*.

---

11. Ferré, "In Praise of Anthropomorphism," 203.
12. Ibid., 207.

Equivocation

This approach was adopted by such theologians as John Damascene (674-749), Meister Eckhart (1260-1327) the German mystic preacher, the Jewish theologian Moses Maimonides (1135-1204), and Søren Kierkegaard (1813-55). It is often driven by a theology known as *apophaticism*, which Denys Turner describes,

> It follows from the *unknowability* of God that there is very little that can be *said* about God: or rather, since most theistic religions actually have a great number of things to say about God, what follows from the unknowability of God is that we can have very little idea of what all these things said of God *mean*. And, strictly speaking, that is what "apophaticism" asserts, as one can tell from its Greek etymology: *apophasis*, is a Greek neologism for the breakdown of *speech*, which, in face of the unknowability of God, falls infinitely short of the mark.[13]

Turner further notes, "'Apophaticism' is the same as what the Latin tradition of Christianity called the *via negativa*, 'the negative way.'"[14] This is opposed to *cataphatic* approach, which uses much speech, from many areas of life, to describe God. As Pseudo-Dionysius, a Christian mystic writing in the fifth or sixth century, said,

> What has actually to be said about the Cause of everything is this. Since it is the Cause of all beings, we should posit and ascribe to it all the affirmations we make in regard to beings, and, more appropriately, we should negate all these affirmations, since it surpasses all being. Now we should not conclude that the negations are simply the opposites of the affirmations, but rather that the cause of all is considerably prior to this, beyond privations, beyond every denial, beyond every assertion.[15]

---

13. Denys Turner, *The Darkness of God*, 20.

14. Ibid., 19.

15. Pseudo-Dionysius, *Pseudo-Dionysius*, 136. He goes on to describe Moses' journey up Sinai, "But then he [Moses] breaks free of them, away from what sees and is seen, and he plunges into the truly mysterious darkness of unknowing. Here, renouncing all that the mind may conceive, wrapped entirely in the intangible and the invisible, he belongs completely to him who is beyond everything. Here, being neither oneself nor someone else, one is supremely united to the completely unknown by an inactivity of all knowledge, and knows beyond the mind by knowing nothing." Pseudo-Dionysius, *Pseudo-Dionysius*, 137.

Notably, "This passage directly contradicts a passage from Aristotle, who used identical terminology to argue that negations *are* the opposites of affirmations (*On Interpretation* 17a 31–33). Here at the outset and again at its conclusion (MT 5 1048B 16–21), the treatise refutes the impression that negations can capture the transcendent Cause of all."[16] Rather, he likens this process to, "sculptors who set out to carve a statue. They remove every obstacle to the pure view of the hidden image, and simply by this act of clearing aside they show up the beauty which is hidden."[17] This assumes a particular order, "not all negations concerning God are equally appropriate; the attributes to be negated are arranged in an ascending order of decreasing incongruity, first considering and negating the lowest or most obviously false statements about God and then moving up to deny those that may seem more congruous. Thus the first to be denied are the perceptible attributes . . ."[18]

Thus, the *via negativa* differs from the equivocal approach, where one uses a given term (such as good, wise, loving, shepherding, etc.) in different senses when applied to the human or divine realms. In fact, Maimonides thought that even the negations of these attributions were not fittingly said of God. The idea here is that humans cannot know what God is like directly because they do not have direct access to His transcendent inner being or essence. Hence, human descriptors cannot be transferred wholesale, or in any part, to God, but rather contain different meanings when applied to God than when applied to humans.

Conversely, according to the negative approach, we can say what God is not like, for we know what it is to be human, which He is not. That is, He is neither finite, nor changeable in character, and therefore can be described as infinite, immutable, etc. In equivocal language, things are affirmed of God, but their meanings are left nebulous. One may affirm God to be "good," and yet definitions of "good" are rendered meaningless, as what it means for humans to be good is wholly unrelated to what the term means for God.

The traditional criticism of these views is that there is nothing positively affirmed about God, which is far less than most theologians or people of faith want to say. John Macquarrie says, "If one adhered strictly to the *via negationis*, it is hard to see how the knowledge of God said to be reached in this way could be other than wholly vacuous. It would scarcely

---

16. Pseudo-Dionysius, *Pseudo-Dionysius*, 136 n. 6.
17. Ibid., 138.
18. Ibid., 140 n. 17.

be distinguishable from agnosticism . . . [but] faith is possible only on the basis that God has granted some positive knowledge of himself."[19] In other words, by denying any human limitations or traits to God, one is left somewhat empty-handed in speaking about or directing faith towards such a being. Similarly, affirmations which have no relation to human terms ultimately say nothing intelligible about God.

Secondly, just because God is transcendent does not necessarily define Him as the antithesis of human. It is conceivable that He, though being transcendent, could still have chosen to endow humans with some of His own attributes. Thus, several of these negative ascriptions have been questioned in recent years, such as whether He is atemporal, or perhaps existed before time but entered into it when He created time. However, the *via negativa* obviously continues to influence current conceptions of God, as its descriptors such as infinite, impassible, immutable, etc., representing the lack of finite (e.g., human) passion and change, are commonly used.

Univocity

More recently, process theologians like Charles Hartshorne felt the *via negationis* and *via analogia* (to which we shall return) was unsuccessful and responded: "[theology] is literal, or it is a scandal." Univocity was also espoused in the Middle Ages by John Duns Scotus (1264–1308), who argued that, "since it is clear that meaningful revelation has been given, religious language must consequently be either univocal or based on univocal language."[20] That is, univocal terms are those which can be used as the "middle term" of a syllogism. For example, "All humans are mortal; Socrates is human; therefore, Socrates is mortal—'human' is used univocally as the middle term."[21] Consequently, to contain meaning, figurative language must be reduced to literal (univocal) language. In fact, one modern univocalist, Carl Henry, says, "Unless we have some literal truth about God, no similarity between man and God can in fact be predicated. . . . The alternative to univocal knowledge of God is equivocation and skepticism."[22]

Another modern example of univocity is Thomas V. Morris. He says,

---

19. Macquarrie, *God-Talk*, 26–27.
20. Stiver, *Sign, Symbol and Story*, 20.
21. Ibid.
22. Henry, *God, Revelation, and Authority*, 364.

> But is human language and thought flexible enough for this sort of stretching? I think we have some reason to believe the answer is yes. For consider the fact that in many other realms of human cognitive endeavor, ordinary language successfully bridges the common and the extraordinary, the familiar and the extremely unfamiliar. Well-known examples of this are to be found in such diverse areas as contemporary physics and gourmet wine tasting. We do not have language ready-made for all the discoveries of physicists or all the discriminations of the palate. But we learn to use what we have in novel ways, and do so successfully.[23]

In other words, Morris thinks that ordinary language, as opposed to language with special meanings, can be used to apply to God. Morris goes on to describe our capability of comprehending the divine as rooted in the fact that humans are created in the image of God. Though this presumes significant knowledge of God in order to establish the possibility of knowing God, he claims, "the unavailability of any such noncircular argument for the possibility of theological knowledge would thus not render theology a suspect cognitive enterprise."[24] That is, all such theories of divine knowledge presume *some* knowledge of God.

At first, this approach appears to allow for more understandable speech about God as the terms are thought to carry the same meaning for Him as for humans. However, there is an element of equivocity in Morris' approach. He allows for physicists and others to use words in different ways to cover lexical gaps for newly discovered phenomena. But, is this not using a familiar word with a new meaning, and hence not univocal? Centuries earlier, Aquinas noted similar problems with this approach. Aquinas explains,

> So the words we use of God all express (imperfectly) one and the same thing in God, but do so by way of many different conceptions in us, and so are not synonymous. Words that express the same thing under different aspects have different meanings simply speaking, since words can express things only as we conceive them. This is why such words are not used univocally, [i.e., in exactly the same sense,] of God and of creatures. *Wise* used of a man expresses his wisdom as distinct from his substance, powers, existence and so on; the word, so to speak, delimits that perfection. But when we use it of God we don't want to express anything distinct from his substance, powers and existence:

---

23. Morris, *Our Idea of God*, 24.
24. Ibid., 25.

what that word expresses in God must not be confined by that expression of it but must surpass it.[25]

Hence, because of God's different ontology, words used of him have different meanings than they would when applied to humans.

Philosopher Dan Stiver notes another issue with univocal language, "Part of the problematic behind the traditional univocal approach is the view that only univocal language is properly cognitive language and then that the standards for what is to count as cognitive are raised too high."[26] In this approach, if something is cognitively conceivable, it is thought to be able to be expressed in literal [univocal] language. However, in one contrasting view, Aquinas points to the different aspects in that words convey their meaning, "Words that express the same thing under different aspects have different meanings simply speaking, since words can express things only as we conceive them. This is why such words are not used univocally, [i.e., in exactly the same sense,] of God and of creatures."[27] While some of God's attributes such as tri-unity might be able to be applied in a univocal sense, many others cannot. For instance, the claim that Jesus is the Son of God, does not imply that God had physical sexual relations with a woman. His seeing does not entail having physical eyes. And yet, we are able to understand what these statements are claiming. The problem then, as Ferré puts it is, "If univocal, then language falls into anthropomorphism and cannot be about *God*; if equivocal, then language bereft of its meaning leads to agnosticism and cannot for us be *about* God."[28] Thus we move to the third way, most famously laid out by Thomas Aquinas (1224/5–74) in his *Summa Theologica*, the "way of analogy."

Via Analogia

The *via analogia* seeks a middle road between univocity and equivocity, based on a relationship of similarity that can be found in two primary modes: *attribution* and *proportionality*. With attribution, Aquinas attributed all created qualities to God who, by virtue of creating them, possesses them in a greater way. "Such words apply to God and creatures neither univocally nor equivocally but by what I can analogy (or proportion). This

---

25. St. Thomas Aquinas, *Summa Theologiæ*, 31–32.
26. Stiver, *Sign, Symbol and Story*, 204.
27. St. Thomas Aquinas, *Summa Theologiæ*, 31, I.13.4–5.
28. Ferré, *Language, Logic and God*, 69.

is the way a word like *healthy* applies to organisms (in a primary sense) and to diets (as causing health) or complexions (as displaying it). Whatever we say of God and of creatures we say in virtue of the relation creatures bear to God as to the source and cause in which all their creaturely perfections pre-exist in a more excellent way."[29]

This is not a literal (univocal) meaning, but one that participates in the literal meaning through causation. That is, if the creature possesses some attribute, its Creator must possess it as well, only in an infinitely more perfect way. The usual objection to this is, as Frederick Ferré says, "The analogy of attribution admits of no control."[30] Just because God created them, is God also perfectly and infinitely fluffy, bouncy, fishy, sinister, etc.? Thomas anticipates such a concern and replies that some things such as evil are really non-being, which cannot therefore be attributed to God. Furthermore, he differentiates between the attribute being ascribed to God and the manner in which it is expressed.

> So in using such words of God we must distinguish what they express—goodness, life and the like—from their manner of expressing it. What they express belongs properly, and indeed primarily, to God and only secondarily to creatures. But their manner of expressing it is appropriate only to creatures and inappropriate to God. When a creaturely mode of existence is included in what the word means, as materiality is included in the meaning of *rock*, the word can apply to God only metaphorically, but when the mode is not included in what a word means but affects only its manner of meaning it (as with words like *existent* and *good* and *living*), then the word can apply to God literally.[31]

Hence, for Aquinas, metaphors were not nearly so apt as analogous terms in describing the divine because in mixing material terms and immaterial ones, they participated in the created order, and thus reflected God in an indirect and flawed manner.

A second problem, according to Stiver, is that, "this causal approach makes the terms refer primarily to creatures and not to the Creator, whereas our theological sensibilities incline us to say that these perfections belong primarily to God and not to the creature. We would not want to claim, for example, that humans are 'just' in a primary sense and God

---

29. St. Thomas Aquinas, *Summa Theologiæ*, 32, I.13.5.
30. Ferré, *Language, Logic and God*, 74, in Stiver, *Sign, Symbol and Story*, 25.
31. St. Thomas Aquinas, *Summa Theologiæ*, 31, Part I, 13.3.

is only secondarily 'just.'"[32] Aquinas responds that, "Calling God good or wise doesn't simply mean that he causes wisdom or goodness in creatures, but that he himself possesses these perfections in a more excellent way. As expressing these perfections the words apply first to God and then to creatures (since the perfections derive from God); but because we know creatures first, our words were first devised to describe creatures and so have a manner of expression appropriate only to creatures."[33]

Aquinas' argument ultimately stands upon the cosmological argument which states that God is the cause of all that exists. This is the basis upon which he founds the analogical relationship he claims holds between God and humanity, for he claims that the traits humans have must also be present (in an analogous manner) in their Logical Cause. However, the idea that God is the ultimate cause of the universe is itself a univocal statement. This, as Richard Swinburne notes, renders the *via analogia* contradictory,[34] for it is not founded upon analogy, but requires at least one univocal statement. Furthermore, it is not necessarily true that the Creator possesses the attributes of His creations, or that He does so in a clearly analogous manner. Nor are finite attributes necessarily more "perfect" in their Creator.

Aquinas' second construal of analogy, proportionality, makes an analogy between the creature and a creature's attribute on the one hand,

32. Stiver, *Sign, Symbol and Story*, 26.

33. St. Thomas Aquinas, *Summa Theologiæ*, 32, I.13.6.

34. Swinburne affirms that, like the later medieval scholastics (Duns Scotus, and William of Ockham), "predicates ascribed to God and to creatures, and in general words used inside and outside theology, were used in the same senses." Swinburne, *The Coherence of Theism*, 79. According to Swinburne, Aquinas held, "that we learn all words from their application to mundane objects. In theology we then apply them to an extra-mundane object, God. In such a case the property signified by the predicate, the *res significata*, is the same, but the *modus significandi*, the way in which the predicate signifies the property, or, better, the way in which the property is present in the object of the type in question, differs. Aquinas wants to say that in such a case when we apply a term to an entity of a radically different kind from those by reference to which we originally learnt to use the term, we are using it 'analogically.' He is emphatic that the term is not being used 'equivocally,' that is with a completely different meaning." Swinburne, *The Coherence of Theism*, 74. However, though "Aquinas tried to give a more plausible account of theological language [than either univocity or the *via negativa*] which allowed it to convey substantial information about God, while continuing to emphasize the differences between God and man," Swinburne concludes, "Aquinas did not succeed in providing the *via media* between the earlier account and the Scotist account which, he rightly saw, must be provided." Swinburne, *The Coherence of Theism*, 80.

and God and the similarly named attribute on the other. This assumes that God possesses say, "goodness," in a way appropriate to His nature, just as humans possess "goodness" in a manner commensurate with their being. Stiver notes that this too has its problems:

> As Ferré has pointed out, however, it is not so simple. In a mathematical proportionality, both sides are actually equivalent. So we can say that 2 is to 4 as 8 is to 16 because the relationships are really the *same*. In Aquinas's case, however, the two sides of the comparison are not only materially different, they occur in ontologically different realms of reality. So we should dismiss from the outset the exactitude that comes from the misleading appearance of being a mathematical proportion. In addition, even a mathematical proportion must have three known terms in order to find the fourth. If we know that 2 is to 4 as some x is to 16, we can easily deduce the x as 8. Aquinas's model trades on this fact. His idea is that we can give sense to a predication such as "good" by placing it in equation with three other known terms. For example, good (x) is to God as good is to persons. The problem is that we do not have a way of knowing who God is either. Actually, we have two unknown terms, which means that the proportionality is useless.[35]

Hence, the way of analogy falters in that it has no real (or know-able) basis upon which to stake its claims. Furthermore, it is unclear that the relationship between humans and their traits are indeed analogous to the relationship between similarly named traits and God. As all three of our basic views of religious language have come up against serious objections, we now turn to some attempts to bypass these impasses, including partial-univocity, and metaphor.

Partial-Univocity

William Alston seeks to ground religious speech by establishing a "partial-univocity" for terms applied to God and humans. According to him, "What it is for God to intend something may be, and undoubtedly is, radically different from what it is for a human being to intend something. But this is quite compatible with the basic sense of terms like 'know' and 'intend' holding constant across the divine-human gap."[36] To achieve this,

---

35. Stiver, *Sign, Symbol and Story*, 27.
36. Alston, *Divine Nature and Human Language*, 198.

Approaching Biblical Anthropomorphic Language

Alston takes a functionalist approach to literal language. He contends that predicates, especially those involving action, can be applied to God and humans in a univocal manner. By reducing these terms in meaning to their intentions and results, Alston claims that this leaves their means and mechanisms free to differ according to the nature of their subject (divine or human). For instance, one of the problems with a purely univocal approach has been God's corporeality. As He has no body, it has been difficult for most theologians to envision Him acting in a comparable way with humans. Alston claims, "The core concept of human action is not *movement of one's own body*, but rather *bringing about a change in the world—directly or indirectly—by an act of will, decision, or intention.*"[37] For instance, it is not integral to the statement, "Sam closed the door," that he did it with his hand, by kicking it shut, using the remote control door opener, or asking Sara to do it for him.

In a similar vein, David Aaron, in his *Biblical Ambiguities*, claims that when we don't know whether language is figurative or literal, as with ancient texts, we should take a middle road he terms "functional ascription." As with Alston, he literally ascribes the function, but not the mechanics of the predicate to the subject. Hence, when we say "God is a shield," we mean that he literally functions as a shield, protecting the user, etc., but He is not made of metal or wood and is not strapped onto someone's arm. What these two views have in common is their idea that action verbs can apply to God and humans univocally when properly limited to functions of psychological intent and physical effect rather than the mechanics of their operation.

IRREDUCIBILITY

One of the reasons Alston opts for this approach is that he is interested in what types of statements can be used to make truth claims about the divine. Metaphor is often held to be irreducible to literal speech, presumably imbuing it with the ability to traverse the divine-human gap, as it doesn't require divine terms to carry their usual human meanings. "I would suggest that writers as diverse as Karl Barth, Rudolph Bultmann, I. M. Crombie, I. T. Ramsey, and Ian G. Barbour are in effect treating talk about God as irreducibly metaphorical, though they rarely use the term."[38] Ramsey, for example, speaks of unusual concatenations of terms such as *infinitely*

37. Ibid., 72.
38. Ibid., 19.

loving, where a normal term is paired with an adjective that modifies it in such a way as to take it beyond the normal sense of the term. Thus, when the "penny drops," we see that it is referring to something far beyond normal usage, and irreducible to the sum of its parts.[39]

However, Alston feels metaphors cannot contain propositional statements and thus must be reduced to literal language.

> And he [the speaker] cannot have the property in mind without having a concept of that property. No matter in how inexplicit or inarticulate a fashion he "has it in mind," he will be in possession of at least an equally inexplicit or inarticulate concept. Therefore a statement cannot possess a propositional content unless it is, in principle, possible that a language should contain words that have the meanings required for the literal expression of that content.[40]

Alston contends that to predicate something of God, it must be conceivable. If it is mentally conceivable, then theoretically, it should be accessible to the conceptual ability of other people. Thus it should be reducible to some sort of literal language by which it could be communicated.

The Substitutionary Theory

Alston's idea seems very similar to the Greek tradition of Socrates, Plato, and Aristotle, which shaped some of the medieval and modern ideas about language. They generally held that meaning lies in words, that it is primarily literal or univocal, and that it is "instrumental for thought."[41] For example, "A corollary of Aristotle's approach thus was that the meaning of figurative language can be grasped only if it can be transposed or reduced to literal language. This approach has been called the substitutionary theory of symbolic language because it is based upon the idea that one can 'substitute' a literal term for the figurative."[42] Alston argues that metaphorical language is either irreducible to literal language and therefore too vague to make any definite proposition about the divine, or it is reducible to literal language, and does not help resolve the problem of the difference in divine-human ontology.

---

39. Ian T. Ramsey, *Religious Language*, 19.
40. Alston, *Divine Nature and Human Language*, 29.
41. Stiver, *Sign, Symbol and Story*, 11.
42. Ibid.

Approaching Biblical Anthropomorphic Language

Thus, he turns to his "functionalist"[43] approach whereby the term in question is reduced to its basic function and this sense is "literally applied to the subject." Alston illustrates, "It is obvious that much talk about God is metaphorical. For example:

> The Lord is my shepherd . . .
> The Lord looks down from heaven.

> I believe that it is commonly supposed that metaphors like these are reducible, that it is possible to say in literal terms at least part of what is being said about God metaphorically in these utterances. In saying, 'The Lord is my shepherd' I am saying that God will protect me and see to it that my needs are satisfied; and so on."[44] Thus, Alston feels that when these metaphors are replaced with literal language, only then are they able to make truth-conditional propositions about God.

Problems with Partial Univocity

Alston and Aaron seem to overlook some considerations about the irreducible, contextualized, and revealing/concealing nature of metaphors. As far as Alston's idea that metaphors such as "the Lord is my shepherd" are reducible to literal language, it is the "and so on" he adds to their "literal meaning," which makes them *irreducible,* simply because they have too many entailments to be reduced to one literal statement. Though one can state some of the implications of metaphors in literal language, the point is that they are not reducible to any *one* literal statement and hence the metaphor itself is required to express the multi-valent thought. Furthermore,

---

43. Frederick Ferré also assumes a functionalist approach. He does so based on the purpose of language according to what later became known as speech-act theory. Verficationalists like the early Wittgenstein (*Tractatus Logico-Philosophicus*) and A. J. Ayer (*Language, Truth and Logic*), insisted that language could only have one use—to describe. Thus, if a word did not refer to something which could be "verified" by the senses, then it was considered gibberish. Ayer in particular felt religious language was "nonsense."

However, as Ferré (and others) observed, this is not the only use of language. Language used to command, name, commit, promise, etc., cannot be said to be senseless because it doesn't fall into categorical and verifiable definitions. As Ferré says, "A proposition which is not fully comprehensible need not be *entirely* without significance." Ferré, *Language, Logic and God,* 57. It can gain significance by its function within a communicative context. Or, as Ferré has also claimed, a verb related to the divine nature, which by definition cannot be 'verified' by human experience, can also be reduced to its 'functions' which can then be univocally related to human uses of the verb.

44. Alston, *Divine Nature and Human Language,* 19 n. 3.

Alston seems to contradict himself when he argues that even if one's concept is "inarticulate," that the language, "should contain words" for its literal expression!

More significantly, as Josef Stern observes,

> The fallacy in the argument is, of course, its assumption that all propositional content must be *fully* conceptualized, if it is conceptual at all. In referential propositions, the constituent corresponding to a metaphor may be a bare property for which the speaker possesses no fully conceptualized representation. Nonetheless there is definite reference to, or expression of the property, and there should be a fact of the matter whether *that* property is true of God, even though we may not *know* whether it is.[45]

A philosopher of language at the University of Chicago, Stern has written an insightful treatment of metaphor, *Metaphor in Context*[46] which undergirds much of our approach to anthropomorphic language. We will discuss his work in detail in chapter 2. Here, he alludes to his conception of *de re* metaphors, which act as demonstratives (this, that, etc.). These serve to point to an object (or concept) without exhaustively defining it. Hence, if a metaphor retains the irreducibility necessary to picture a transcendent realm,[47] while retaining the ability to articulate truth-conditional propositions, then there is no need to develop a partial-univocity or a third way between metaphor and literal language.

As for Aaron's middle way between metaphorical and literal usage, he too misconstrues the idea of figurative language. Aaron seems to equate literalness with truth, and metaphor with myth, or falsehood. As we shall see with Stern though, metaphor is simply another manner in which truth-conditional propositions can be asserted. Aaron's middle way of "functional ascription" turns out simply to be metaphorical predication that happens to highlight the function of the term such as shield, while proposing the truth of whether God is indeed like one. Similarly, Alston restricts the meaning of literal speech to terms of intention and function such that a predicate can be used in the same sense for both God and humans. However, both Aaron's functional ascriptions and Alston's "functional language" are so qualified that they no longer count as what

---

45. Stern, *Metaphor in Context*, 193.

46. Ibid.

47. I.e., the ability to refer to the transcendent realm without *reducing* it to that of the finite or human.

we mean by "literal" use. This raises the question, "What do we mean by univocal speech?"

According to linguistics research as early as I. A. Richards, and Max Black, the "literal" use of a term includes all the entailed connotations and experiential connections associated with that term. What Alston does is to create hypothetical logical structures of psychological states which would apply to both realms. "It is not claimed that any human P-predicates ['that distinctively apply to personal agents'] can be applied to God with exactly the same meaning, but it is maintained that more abstract functional concepts can be constructed that will apply equally on both sides of the divide."[48] However, to extract out such obvious human entailments as bodily movement, is to rob the term of some of its key connotative features. For example, as humans are generally not considered telekinetic, they cannot will something to be done and remain in a causative relationship with that entity without some bodily movement. Either to directly act upon the object in question or to communicate with others and act upon it indirectly, requires bodily movement. These movements are part of the conceptual domain of a given human action term.

However, Alston's approach is not without merit. It does serve to establish a significant point of connection between the usage of predicates for God and for humans in their psychological function. This is not to say that human and divine psychology are by any means the same, for Alston reduces these down to basic concepts of intent and will as well, regardless of the differences in human and divine motivations. Alston views his methodology as similar to that of Aquinas, "Thomas, and I agree, thought that it was possible to purify our concepts of knowledge, love, etc., by removing all features that had to do specifically with embodiment, temporality and other creaturely conditions, leaving a distinctive core that can be attributed to God, so far as its content is concerned."[49] What Alston seeks, and what we require in order to make truth claims about God, is a way to draw out certain characteristics in common with human and divine usage without bringing all the entailments of the meaning of one term to bear wholesale upon the other, especially where they might not apply (say due to a difference in corporeality, finitude, and the like).

The primary difficulty with Alston's method is that these concepts are restricted in light of systematic concerns such as timelessness,

---

48. Alston, *Divine Nature and Human Language*, 2.
49. Alston, "Being-Itself and Talk About God," 22.

incorporeality, and what Alston calls the infinity of God.[50] The danger here is that on the one hand, some things like divine timelessness are not necessarily biblical.[51] Whether or not this assumption is correct, timelessness may not be in view within the particular occurrence of an "anthropomorphic" metaphor. This sort of conditioning of the expression runs the risk of not allowing the text its full voice with respect to the nuances of context.

Context

This highlights a problem that Alston ignores in his attempt to draw out a function of certain terms—the role of context. For example, human usage of terms is situated within a context of human action, which requires bodily movement. Thus, to extract the function of the term is no longer to use the term in a literal fashion *within its context of use,* and hence is not univocal. Such a task is better subsumed under metaphor, which gives us what Alston sought—the ability to correlate functions of action across the divine-human gap—while remaining sensitive to the concerns and emphases of a given usage. As we shall see in Stern's treatment, the metaphorical meaning of an expression is determined *in context.* Hence, to return to our earlier example, if the context of Sam parking the car was a garage that contains an automatic door opener, this would indicate his "shutting the door" was by way of the remote, rather than pulling it down by hand or asking someone else to do it. Let us now take a closer look at a more context-sensitive approach.

The Metaphorical Approach

In its earliest treatments, Aristotle introduced metaphor as a form of rhetoric in which one word was *substituted* for another, more literal term. "The effect has been to see metaphor as a mere ornament of language, which enables us to embellish what we know—not to add to what we know."[52] Under this conception, Max Black's famous example of a metaphor, "Man is a wolf," would simply have meant that man was vicious, and nothing more. However, Black followed I. A. Richards, who introduced

---

50. Alston characterizes this as, "the absence of any imperfections and the possession of all perfections Thus among the modes of divine infinity will be omnipotence, omniscience, and perfect goodness." Alston, *Divine Nature and Human Language*, 74.

51. See, for example, Nicholas Wolterstorff, "Unqualified Divine Temporality."

52. Stiver, *Sign, Symbol and Story*, 113.

Approaching Biblical Anthropomorphic Language

the theory that metaphor was cognitive. That is, in the language of the logical positivists, metaphor signified something that related to the real world rather than the realm of the emotions. In this case, "man is a wolf" carries more cognitive information than simply being an "embellished" way of portraying "viciousness." It could carry the ideas of a pack instinct, base behavior, a hunger-driven course of action, preying on the weak, or even being affected by the moon, depending on its context.

Due to these developments, metaphor has been able to provide answers that were lacking in the *via analogia*. Stiver notes, "Aquinas's effort led in the end to the reduction of analogical language to univocal language because thinkers seemed unable to accept the fact that analogy could be understood without being explicitly explained. The interactionist view of metaphor chimes in with the implications of Wittgenstein's work for literal language to show how meaning can reliably occur without being exhaustively specifiable."[53] Some thinkers in the Thomistic tradition such as David Tracy and David Burrell attempt to avoid extensive explanations of analogy in order to avoid such slippage into univocity. They often attempt to appropriate the language of metaphor to explain its function. Burrell notes that even though the exact relationships within analogy cannot be fully explained, like metaphor, they seem to "fit the occasion."[54] Tracy views analogies, "as the perception of irreducible 'similarities-in-difference' between some finite event or reality and ultimate reality."[55]

However, metaphor theorists like Sallie McFague and Janet Soskice argue that analogy does not contain the creative ability of metaphor, in which one thing is perceived in terms of another. McFague says, "One critical difference, . . . between symbolic and metaphorical statements is that the latter always contain the whisper, 'it is *and it is not*.'"[56] Whereas symbols participate in the reality that they depict (e.g., the cross for Christianity), metaphors are usually derived from a conceptual area outside that to which it refers. Thus, though symbols are not *equivalent* to their referents, they are wholly ingrained within the concept of their referents. On the other hand, because metaphors refer via a concept outside of the usual sphere of entailments related to the referent, they are able to point to a reality without using literal language or more directly connected

---

53. Ibid., 119.
54. Burrell, *Analogy and Philosophical Language*, 260.
55. Tracy, *The Analogical Imagination*, 410.
56. McFague, *Metaphorical Theology*, 13.

representation such as symbols. By its very nature, there is an element within the source concept of a metaphor that is not related to the target concept.

This claim supports Aquinas' claim of a third way for religious language, between univocal and equivocal language; but with the help of a newer conceptualization of such figurative language, it avoids the paradoxes into which Aquinas fell. Metaphor can be regarded as making a truth claim, therefore, without being reduced to being a literal truth claim. The inexactitude, or the inability to use it in a syllogism, is recognized without throwing out the truth claim itself.[57]

Metaphors accomplish this by construing one field of reference upon another, and creating what Paul Ricoeur calls "semantic shock,"[58] or a dissonance in meaning. From this dissonance arises new ways of "seeing one thing in terms of another." Some aspects are hidden and others are highlighted, causing us to view the metaphorically expressed term in a new light. Some of the implications of these new understandings of metaphor include the fact that metaphor, "can do more than embellish; it can direct us to what we have never seen before."[59] Unlike Aristotle's substitution theory, metaphors are irreducible to other literal statements. Stiver says, "Rich evocative texts cannot always be replaced by univocal expositions. In other words, a text containing powerful metaphors possesses a virtually inexhaustible fecundity."[60]

However, these new ways of understanding metaphors have not been seen as a complete boon to philosophers. "The ensuing inexactness is precisely what has often bothered philosophers and has led them to prefer univocal language. Their major criticism is that metaphor cannot be used in a syllogism. Such usage results in the fallacy of ambiguity. However, with the work of the later Wittgenstein and others that questioned the 'clarity and distinctness' of univocal language . . . , the way is open to consider metaphor as cognitive, even though inexact and imprecise."[61] It is this ability to represent identifiable cognitive content which gives metaphors the ability to make truth-claims.

However, some philosophers have objected to this due to the imprecision inherent in metaphor. With metaphors, they say, it is difficult to

---

57. Stiver, *Sign, Symbol and Story*, 130.
58. Ricoeur, *From Text to Action*, 173.
59. Stiver, *Sign, Symbol and Story*, 117.
60. Ibid.
61. Ibid., 118.

know just what claim is being made, and hence truth evaluations become impossible. This is where Joseph Stern's theory comes into play. According to him, metaphors represent a semantic usage of language, and hence are rule-governed.[62] Their imprecision—in Stern's vocabulary, non-constancy—is only existent in their theoretical formulae. When they are put into specific contexts, the contextual clues interact with the formulaic meaning (Stern's "metaphorical meaning") to produce precise interpretations. These remain full-bodied, irreducible pictures, but they are identifiable, and hence, are able to make truth claims.

Why is metaphor better than functionalism? Because functionalism seeks to do what metaphors do—highlight one or more aspects of a concept applied to God and humans, while hiding others (corporeality, time markers, etc.). Conversely, metaphor allows the context of the utterance (spoken or written) to determine the parameters of which aspects of the metaphorical ascription are highlighted and which are hidden. Metaphor helps us say something about one realm in terms of another, but in a contextually-sensitive manner. As Brevard Childs observes, this is an important check in the formation of our theology. He says, "The attempt to describe God's identity merely in terms of his acts, apart from his being, is not a serious theological option for either Biblical or Dogmatic theology. The subject matter itself requires that proper theological understanding move from the biblical witness to the reality itself which called forth the witness."[63] Childs here acknowledges the mutually informative role played between (systematic) theology, the text, and the Being to which they refer.

Summary

We have found that all approaches to speaking of God in human language have their problems. Equivocity leaves us saying little or nothing at all about God, and what is said is either meaningless or too ethereal to make Him approachable. Univocity seems unable to overcome transcendence. Even partial-univocity, i.e., reducing things to their functions, lacks an ability to draw out a particular conceptualized statement about God,

---

62. Cf, also, Kittay, *Metaphor*. Though Kittay also proposes a semantic theory of metaphor, as Stern says, "she (apparently by design) does not draw any sharp distinction between speakers' knowledge of language or semantic competence, on the one hand, and their empirical, extralinguistic beliefs and the kinds of skills that enter into their use of language, on the other—what I call 'context.'" Stern, *Metaphor in Context*, 243.

63. Brevard S. Childs, *Biblical Theology*, 370.

relying on systematics to guide its interpretation. Analogy fails due to an undefined relationship between God and humans, either of causation or proportion.

Metaphor alone gives us the ability to capture transcendent qualities without reducing them to either human functions or truths that do not reflect individual biblical contexts. However, the problem remains how any human terms can be applied to God, even metaphorically. To determine this, we must first look at the nature of this relationship.

Traversing the Divine-Human Gap

We have seen that of the ways of speaking of the divine, metaphor seems best suited for dealing with things it cannot fully define. All of these approaches, however, have looked at the issue purely from the standpoint of theory. Next, we need to look at how this issue has been handled in practice. First, we shall look at a theme, ubiquitous throughout most of Jewish and Christian writings—accommodation. In this approach, the *content* of the communication from God about Himself was altered to fit human capacities. Next, we shall look at the philosophy of religious language which wrestles with the *medium* of communication. That is, "what is language and how does it refer?" Finally, we shall glance at several Old Testament theologians who concern themselves with the *process* of communication—both its historical development as well as the direction of its reference.

Accommodated Language

Throughout history many exegetes both in Judaism and Christianity have deemed anthropomorphic expressions to be beneath the dignity of a spiritual Being Who was "completely Other," and sought to explain this sort of scriptural language away. Some, most notably, John Chrysostom, and John Calvin, employed the theory of "accommodation." The latter famously quipped,

> The Anthropomorphite, also who imagined a corporeal God from the fact that Scripture often ascribes to him a mouth, ears, eyes, hands, and feet, are easily refuted. For who even of slight intelligence does not understand that, as nurses commonly do with infants, God is wont in a measure to "lisp" in speaking to us? Thus such forms of speaking do not so much express clearly

what God is like as accommodate the knowledge of him to our slight capacity. To do this he must descend far beneath his loftiness.[64]

Stephen Benin, in his study of the history of this approach, defines this process: "Accommodation/condescension is divine revelation in human terms; that is, divinity adapting and making itself comprehensible to humanity in human terms. It is the adaptation and adjustment of the transcendent to the mundane; it is the fine tuning of divine order."[65] This broad definition was further nuanced in patristic thought into two categories, the positive and the negative. As an example of the latter, Benin says, "The Lord permitted certain ceremonies, such as sacrifices, to keep his people from becoming idolaters, negative accommodation then is both punitive and prophylactic."[66] This sort of accommodative strategy assumes the naivete, stubbornness, or inability of human recipients to comprehend a divine revelation, and consequently requires an adjustment on the part of the divine.

On the other hand,

> Positive accommodation is used in patristic sources when the rise, spread, and triumph of Christianity is being discussed. . . . the Incarnation will be interpreted as the quintessential example of divine accommodation. There is another aspect to positive accommodation; that is, the very act of God recognising the bodily dimension of humanity—part of the creation—and thus a good in itself.[67]

Thus, positive accommodation referred to God's acts to produce or acknowledge good, while the negative was used to prevent or mediate human evil. "The church fathers, influenced by Platonism, and occupied with polemics against Jews, pagans, and schismatics, not surprisingly tended to emphasize negative accommodation at the expense of positive accommodation. Yet as we shall observe, both explanations coexisted."[68]

Benin further comments on Gregory of Nyssa's conception of condescension, "At the heart of the concept of *oi'konomía*, as we have seen 'is the notion of accommodation to circumstance, whether in the daily

64. Calvin, *Institutes*, p21, 1.13.1.
65. Benin, *Footprints of God*, 1.
66. Ibid.
67. Ibid., 1–2.
68. Ibid., 2.

management of an estate, as originally, or in church affairs, or in God's providential concern for his creatures as seen in the Incarnation. It is not the imposition of a rule but the exercise of a function and has properly to do not with compromise but with adjustment.'"[69]

Some of the impetuses Benin observes for this practice included both Jewish and Christian apologetics, and the influence of Greek thought on the early church. For John Chrysostom, the "father of accommodation," it was a means of explaining the Incarnation.

> The true glory and mystery of the Incarnation are made manifest through *sygkatábāsis*, which allowed the divine—with no diminution—to become truly human and expedite the divine redemptive plan . . . *sygkatábāsis*, the stone that others might have overlooked or rejected, became for him, as for no other, the cornerstone of a prodigious hermeneutical edifice. . . . It explained how God became man without demeaning the divinity, thus permitting humanity, on its own level, to behold God. It solved the exegetical problem of the superiority of the "new" law over the Mosaic Code, be it in the practice of virginity or lack of fleshly sacrifices, and demonstrated Christianity's unrivaled prominence over both Judaism and paganism.[70]

For Augustine, however, we see a conception of immutable perfection which drove the practice of accommodation. "Augustine's defense of Christianity, as well as his use of *similitudo*, sprang from neo-Platonic soil. In a universe constantly struggling to become perfect, in which shadowy, imperfect material shapes contended to 'realize' their ideal forms, intelligible to the intellect alone, Augustine's Church endeavored to realize its ideal form."[71] Augustine found adaptability for the immutable God by likening His accommodation to that of prescribing medicine according to the illness. "Medical imagery was highly favored by Augustine, who likened it to divine providence, which is unchanging but able to aid mutable creatures in various ways at diverse times. Divine providence, like medicine, displayed utility and fitness (*aptum*) within the divine dispensation. Thus, the sacrifices commanded of old were fit (*aptum*) for that time, but no longer obtain because another precept that is fit (*aptum*) for this time is now commanded. God knows much better than man what is

---

69. Ibid., 33.
70. Ibid., 70–71.
71. Ibid., 105.

suitably accommodative to each age (*quid cuique tempori accommodated adhibeatur*)."[72]

In medieval times Maimonides (R. Moses ben Maimon, 1135-1204, aka Rambam) and Nachmanides (R. Moses ben Naḥman, 1195-1270, aka Ramban) also strove over accommodation. Maimonides saw this as a reflection of the reader's capacity for wisdom. According to Benin, the Rambam, "proposes pedagogy as the reason the sages employed parables; to stimulate the wise and confound fools; a practice he would also employ in the *Guide*."[73] He also takes this as a matter of intelligence of the reader:

> To understand a proverb, and a figure; the words of the wise, and their dark sayings [Prov. 1:6], and because of this our Sages, peace to them, spoke about divine matters in riddle form. Thus it is proper for a person who happens to come across one of their statements, which he thinks is opposed to reason, not to attribute the deficiency to those statements, but to attribute the deficiency to his own intellect. And when he sees one of their parables whose literal meaning is far from his understanding, it is proper for him to be much grieved that he did not understand the issue so that all true statements became extremely distant [to his understanding]. For the intellects of men are as different as differences of temperament, and as the temperament of one man is better and closer to the mean than the temperament of another man, so too, will be the intellect of another man. There is no doubt that the intellect of one who knows a sublime matter is not as the intellect of one who does not know that matter, for the one is like an intellect *in actu* and the other an intellect *in potentia*.[74]

For example, Maimonides, attributes sacrifice as a pedagogical measure to bring the children of Israel, so influenced by Egyptian and Sabian practices, into worship of the one true God. By altering the direction of the worship, but not the means, they were effectively brought out of paganism into the one true faith, even if the residue of sacrificial offerings remained.

To the contrary, Naḥmanides argues against Maimonides' position on condescension. He says, "The Rabbi [Maimonides] wrote in the *Guide* that the reason for the sacrifices is because the Egyptians and the Chaldeans . . . always used to worship the herd and the flock. These are his

72. Ibid., 111.
73. Ibid., 149.
74. Ibid., 148-49, from Introduction to *Commentary on the Mishnah*, 35-37. Cf. *Introduction* to the first part of the *Guide*, 10-14.

words, and he expounded them lengthily. They are utter nonsense.... God forbid that these rituals should have no other purpose and intention, save the elimination of idolatrous opinions from the minds of fools."[75] He further asks why, "did Noah sacrifice when there was neither one Sabian nor one Egyptian in the whole world? How could anyone attribute sacrifice to them?"[76] Thus, Maimonides' reasoning for accommodation appears to rest on shaky ground.[77]

Calvin, the reformer, attributed the need for accommodation to human *captus* or capacity. Jon Balserak boils this reason down to a fourfold division of God's reasons for accommodation.

> God accommodates,
> *first* to human being[sic] as creatures
> *secondly* to human beings as sinners
> *thirdly* to Israel as a primitive nation
> and *fourthly* to human beings as either the wicked or the godly.[78]

Hence, God spoke in human terms which, though not fully in accord with His own Being, were suitable for communicating with a compromised human capacity. Calvin's concern was, "not so much our concern to know who he [God] is in himself, as what he wills to be toward us."[79] He too sees God as required to stoop to human understanding, but in more of a generic, rather than historic evolutionary manner. That is, all humans require this condescension, rather than simply the "primitive" Israelites.

Calvin's position was primarily theologically driven. Paul Helm explains,

> According to Calvin, God as he is in himself has an unaltered and an unalterable plan formed in eternity. God as he seems

---

75. Benin, *Footprints of God*, 163, from Naḥmanides' commentary on Leviticus 1:9.

76. Ibid., 163.

77. According to Benin, Gersonides (Levi ben Gerson, 1288-1334), the Ralbag, adds to this argument, "unlike Maimonides, who saw sacrifices as commandments of second intention, for Ralbag they are of primary intention. Sacrifices were commanded to help establish prophecy." Benin, *Footprints of God*, 165. As seen in Num 23:3, Ralbag sees prophecy as facilitated by sacrifice. "Sacrifices help isolate the intellect and better facilitate the mantic art. The immolation of the animal is equated with the dominance of form over matter—the intellect over the body. Sacrifices were not an accommodation to puerile Israel, but a vehicle to accomplish prophecy." Benin, *Footprints of God*, 166.

78. Balserak, *Divinity Compromised*, 54.

79. Benin, *Footprints of God*, 188.

to us "repents." So in order to understand such divine repentance in a way that is consistent with God having an unaltered plan it must be purged of its usual associations of displeasure, especially displeasure with the self, of fluctuation in mood or temper, and of ignorance that are intrinsic features of human repentance. The word "repentance" is nevertheless appropriately used, according to Calvin, because God's actions change over time. He does A at one time and not-A at a later time, but in doing so he does not change his mind. So when the language of repentance is ascribed to God it is not ascribed with full literalness. In other words, the language of repentance when ascribed to God does not carry with it exactly the same semantic value that it has when ascribed to human beings, but it is nevertheless appropriate language to use of God because it carries some of that value. In God's case the meaning of such terms is controlled or modified by a core of metaphysical truths about God, such as his immutability and his omniscience, which comprise his unchangeable nature and will.[80]

Hence, when, in Genesis 3:21, it said that God fashioned garments of animal skin for Adam and Eve, Calvin reinterprets this as God showing the couple how to make them, rather than doing it Himself. He, "treats all references to God's remembering, resting, repenting, returning, sleeping, yearning, smelling, seeing, wondering, laughing, speaking and using spears and bucklers' as accommodation."[81] Calvin sought to preserve a high sense of the sovereignty of God by abrogating these expressions.

Issues with Accommodation

However, there are several points to be made against this sort of reading. Firstly, some of the apologetics used by early church fathers against Judaism leave the doctrine of accommodation in dubious light. For example John Chrysostom argued that images were forbidden because of the Jews propensity for idolatry. Balserak comments,

> [Chrysostom held that] These restrictions no longer apply to Christians, . . . because Christians are no longer prone to idolatry for they are spiritually mature and not Jewish "children," referring to Paul's argument from the end of Galatians 3. Thus, John

---

80. Helm, *John Calvin's Ideas*, 188–89.

81. Benin, *Footprints of God*, 191, quoted from H. Jackson Forstman, *Word and Spirit, Calvin's Doctrine of Biblical Authority*, (Stanford, 1962) 115, and 164 nn. 50–61.

> employs accommodation to argue for a plainly-contentious conclusion which many Christians, living before and after John, would argue vehemently against, and yet his argument is cogent and possesses at the very least a *prima facie* plausibility. He relies upon the themes set out in Galatians 3, as do many who employ accommodation.... It is this kind of volatility or unpredictability that is sometimes present in, or connected, to accommodation and makes it such a potentially unstable concept.[82]

Thus, accommodation, as with many approaches, evidences a proclivity for use that can be blinded by other agendas. This inconsistency can also be found in Calvin who attempts to explain an omnipotent God's use of angels to accomplish His work in Pss 91:11–12; 34:7. He says:

> The God found in Calvin's treatment of accommodation in relation to the angels is being viewed, by Calvin, as the omnipotent God who has all power, majesty and authority. By contrast, the God described in Calvin's examination of the Old Testament case laws is a God who must draft legislation to fit a variety of circumstances and must, therefore, temper that legislation to the people and circumstances in which it will have to operate.[83]

So, we see that Calvin uses different pictures of God to suit different situations. However, Balserak finds that this is related to Calvin's exposition. "It is hard not to conclude that this tension appears in the reformer's thought by design (as it were).... So, for instance, in his treatment of Old Testament case laws, Calvin often stresses God's inability and the frustrating of the divine will by the Jews even though it is not by any means essential to the interpreting of the text that he do so."[84] For example, Calvin asserts that in Exod 21:1–6 the concession God makes, "is to be reckoned amongst the others which God tolerated on account of the people's hardness of heart, because it could hardly be remedied."[85] Hence, when Calvin must explain a divine concession in Old Testament law, the problem of the Israelites' hardness of heart is simply insurmountable, requiring God to modify His law. However, when explaining God's use of angels to accomplish His purposes, His will is eternal, unchanging and absolutely undefeatable. Though misuse of an approach does not preclude the possibility of its proper employment, it does point to the need for a principled application.

82. Balserak, *Divinity Compromised*, 18–19.
83. Ibid., 189.
84. Ibid.
85. Ibid., quoted from *Ioannis Calvini Opera* 24: 650.

Approaching Biblical Anthropomorphic Language

In addition, some forms of accommodation imply hints of deception in God's character. Though Calvin would not concede such an element within God, others who used this approach to the biblical text did. For example:

> Gregory [of Nazianzus, one of the Cappadocian fathers] raises yet another aspect of this method of salvation; did not God use deceit (*ăpatē*)? After all, the devil was confronted not with pure divinity but divinity wrapped in a human envelope; is that not fraud and deception (*a'patē tís ĕstí tro pon tína kaì paralōgismós*)? Gregory's answer is that the Lord was just, in that each got his due, and wise, because justice was not perverted. Yet, he does acknowledge, rather surprisingly, that God's design (*ĕpínoia*) did contain a certain deceptive character (*ăpatē*); however, it not only brought salvation to man, but benefited the devil as well, for the process leads to the ultimate eradication of evil. Gregory likens the process to patients who may be angry with their doctors for painful treatments, but are thankful after they are cured.[86]

This raises the question of whether the utilization of accommodation, though often conformed to the theological tenets and polemics of the day, appears to contradict the nature of God who cannot lie (Num 23:19, Titus 1:2, Heb 6:18). That is, attributing the idea that God says one thing but really means another seems to contradict the principle that He cannot lie.[87] Is this method of explaining the rather human descriptions of a transcendent deity truly available to a God of this character, or is this very description yet another 'accommodation' to human understanding?

Divine Hiddenness

Thirdly, there is the issue of knowledge of divine accommodation itself. David Aaron asks,

---

86. Benin, *Footprints of God*, 50.

87. There is the broader idea of accommodation in which say, the incarnation of Christ is claimed to be the ultimate accommodation to humanity. And yet, this revelation of God not only hid things from the eyes of those not willing to believe, but at the same time revealed the fullness of God to those who would. Hence, this sort of revelatory act only counts as accommodation with respect to a particular group of people, whereas its more general use applies to all humanity. It is this sense, in which God is, as Calvin suggests, 'lisping,' which implies a certain duplicity in God's revelation. How He reveals Himself, according to accommodation is not how He truly is. Hence, we find in this hints of deception, even if for a good cause.

> If humans cannot accommodate ideas about or descriptions of the deity except through figurative forms of speech, how does the human intellect manage to perceive what it is that it is supposed to describe? Hardly an original question, this is a basic problem in the history of philosophy and theology, epistemological in nature. My contention is that Bible scholars rather uncritically project postbiblical conceptualizations of language and transcendence upon the Bible, all the while assuming that the ancients recognized the same philosophical problems that occupy us. For the most part, the Bible lacks explicit statements that might confirm that the ancients understood there to be these "limits" to the powers of language, not to mention the disjunction between our perceptions and our ability to express them directly and literally.[88]

Not only is it difficult to see how we could come to the understanding *that* some language is accommodated, but Aaron asks how the writers would have come to any knowledge of God at all if it were accommodated. It is hard to envision how humans could know a transcendent God outside of His revelatory acts. If those acts are accommodated, upon what basis would humans become aware of this fact? Balserak also questions Calvin's bold statements on this matter.

> Exactly how Calvin, or anyone for that matter, can believe that he can know the mind of God in these matters to the extent of knowing God's purposes and motives is not clear. On some occasions, of course, they are divinely revealed (see, for instance, Ex. 13:17). Yet on others, Calvin feels confident in asserting them despite God's silence.[89]

Hence, accommodation runs into problems in acquiring a separate source in which to measure the accommodation of a particular biblical statement. As there is no other means of establishing God's identity other than His revelation, there is no means to measure His revelation as either straightforwardly literal or accommodated.

The problem comes to a head when Calvin selects appropriate entailments of anthropomorphic terms strictly[90] according to theological

---

88. Aaron, *Biblical Ambiguities*, 35.

89. Balserak, *Divinity Compromised*, 101.

90. All exegetes come to a text with theological bias. We simply are emphasizing that Calvin, at least, orders his application in order to preserve his theological convictions to the extent that some aspects of the text become marginalized. A more balanced approach would allow the text to inform the theology as well, and would be

criteria, which often overlook the textual criteria. For example, Helm holds that, "One reason why Calvin thought that language about divine repentance is an accommodation to our understanding but that of God foreseeing is not is that such foreseeing coheres with his 'core theism', particularly his emphasis upon God's eternity and immutability, whereas the ascription of repentance to God doesn't."[91] Thus, Calvin's exegesis of such texts is theologically-driven to the point of muting the individual senses of the terms. He seeks to preserve a sense of changelessness about God, for which he must nuance terms that, like repentance, would connote change if applied to humans.[92]

Not only does Calvin seek to preserve a sense of immutability in God, but also an unchangeable will.

> For Calvin, God is not an unknowable *noumenon* or substrate. Indeed, the reasons that Calvin gives for the language of accommodation have surprisingly little to do with the limitations of human knowledge. They have at least as much to do with what Calvin considers to be the "torpor" of the human mind, and particularly with the need for God to achieve certain ends in the lives of those to whom he makes himself known in these ways.[93]

---

more consistent in the application of accommodation.

91. Helm, *John Calvin's Ideas*, 193.

92. "His overall position seems to be something like this: Given that God, the eternal God, has not only decreed the course of history but has himself acted in history, in particular in dialogue with his ancient people Israel, such divine actions can only be understood and, more particularly, can only be responded to, when they are taken to be the actions of a person who is himself in time and who therefore appears to change or vary in his action. More than this, if men and women who are themselves in time are to respond to God, then he must represent himself to them as one to whom response is possible, as one who acts and reacts in time. . . . For Calvin, only on such an understanding of divine activity is the divine-human interaction that is at the heart of biblical revelation, and particularly at the heart of the Old Testament narrative passages, possible. So it is a logical point, rather than a pragmatic or pedagogic point, that is (195) at the centre of Calvin's remarks about divine accommodation. A logically necessary condition of dialogue between people, or between God and humankind, is that the partners in the dialogue should act and react in time, or appear to do so. If dialogue with God is to be real dialogue, then God's language about himself cannot be restricted to characterizing himself as eternal and immutable, even though his nature and purposes are eternal and immutable, but he must accommodate himself to speak in ways that are characteristic of and essential to persons in dialogue with each other." Ibid., 194–95.

93. Ibid., 193–94.

In other words, Calvin sees God as presenting Himself in the ways that He does in order to bring about His will, such as a successful test of Hezekiah's faith in 2 Kings 20:1–11. Though God promises Hezekiah he will die, upon Hezekiah's prayer, God grants him fifteen more years to live. Accommodationists see this as a case where God knew all along what Hezekiah's response would be and contend that thus, God never really changed. God simply accommodated himself to Hezekiah by *appearing* to threaten his life, though He never intended to take it.

One problem with this view is that it rules out any possible conditions for God's change of mind. What exactly would the biblical text have to say to prove that God changes His mind? As with Hezekiah, it describes Him as changing His stance towards those who repent, and occasionally those who haven't (Hos 11:8–9). Though 1 Samuel 15 claims God won't change His mind, it twice claims He has (vv. 11 and 35). God made a command in verse 2, "Set your house in order, for you shall die and not live." Clearly this does not happen, as Hezekiah pleads for his life and God grants him fifteen more years (v. 6). Even if this was an implicitly conditional statement as Helm claims,[94] this involves change. God had to take one stance towards Hezekiah in order for the test to be genuine, and, upon his reaction (which happened to be a faithful one), God takes another.

A further problem is that an explanation of accommodation does not seem consonant with the context. Helm and others argue that God doesn't really intend for Hezekiah to die because He knows He will plead for his life. But, we may ask what is the imagined "condition" for Hezekiah to keep his life—"if he will plead with God"? This is not mentioned in any of the versions of the story (2 Kgs 20:1–11; Isa 38:1–8; 2 Chr 32:24–25). Furthermore, no version of this narrative mentions Hezekiah as in need of repentance before he falls ill. 2 Chr 32:25 mentions pride, but only *after* he is healed. So, though some would argue that God did not change here, it is unclear exactly what God is attempting to do by this supposed case of accommodating to Hezekiah.

Finally, it seems that accommodation can mute the sense of the text. Though accommodation would seek to explain away an expression such as "God forgets," let us look at an example from Nicholas of Lyra, who interprets Gen 8:1, "One is said to forget someone when he will not free him from present difficulties though he is able to; and one is said to remember him when he begins to help him."[95] Here, Nicholas is doing something

---

94. Calvin, *Institutes*, 198.

95. Balserak, *Divinity Compromised*, 100, quoted from Nicholas of Lyra, *Biblia*

similar to our approach. He recognizes that the idiom "to forget" can mean other things than simple lack of cognitive ability to recall, even with human subjects. Hence, this term does not speak to whether or not God loses the ability to recall information, requiring a theological explanation via accommodation, but rather it highlights God's focus during the flood.

Thus, we find that the approach of subsuming anthropomorphic language under divine accommodative practices lacks a consistent principle for its usage and conception,[96] often resulting in a flattening of the text. Finally, we find that this practice actually tends to mute the import of at least some texts by subjugating metaphors for God to theological concerns which may or may not be in view within a particular biblical context.

What we propose in this book is that anthropomorphic texts be treated under a particular type of accommodated language—metaphor. This, however, is not in contrast with veridical language, but is another means of expressing truth which allows for the differences between divine and human realities. Unlike some interpreters' use of the concept, God does not accommodate by saying one thing and meaning another. Rather, He accommodates by revealing things through metaphors which give us fuller and more accurate pictures of what He is like, whilst retaining the flexibility to hide those elements that either do not correspond to human life, or that He has simply chosen not to reveal about the workings of His inner being.

Thus, because of its multi-valent and pictorial nature, metaphor becomes a vehicle for expositing rather than concealing divine truth. Through Josef Stern's conception of metaphor, we are able to chasten our application of accommodation by seeking clues to a metaphor's meaning in its individual context of use. Thus, there is at least some check upon the importing of theological notions, which all interpreters bring to the text, into the text. Furthermore, this allows a metaphor to speak more vividly within the themes and comparisons being made in a given text, rather than being reduced to one static meaning, read paradigmatically across all texts.

Sacra cum glossis, interlineari & Ordinaria, Nicolai Lyrani Postilla & Moralitatibus, Burgensis Additionibus, Lugduni: ex officina G. Trechsel, 1545, 1, fol. 54.

96. This practice does not seem to be stated in Scripture save for the concept of the law being an accommodation to the people's heart conditions. (Matt 19:8, Mark 10:5) This however, is not the same as an accommodation to one's intellectual capacity. This accommodation is not regarding an ability to apprehend *descriptions of God*, but to faithfully obey the covenant.

However, there remains the problem of reference. Though we have found metaphor to be a more chastened account of accommodating divine revelation, there is no guarantee that such language truly or accurately reflects God. In order to see how human metaphorical language about God can correspond to His transcendent being, we turn to Nicholas Wolterstorff.

God Speaks: Divine Discourse and Speech Act Theory

To speak of God, we require a way that, as Karl Barth observed,[97] begins with Him. However, Barth's *analogia gratiae,* by which God causes human language to accurately refer to Him, seems a bit heuristic in that it does not explain how human language refers to God or in what sense it refers. Wolterstorff's explanation, conversely, begins with similar premise of Divine initiative in communication, but allows us to speak intelligibly of Him by dealing in the only sort of language we know, that rooted in the human context.

Nicholas Wolterstorff attempts to bridge this impasse of divine reference through the eponymous concept of his book *Divine Discourse.* Divine discourse has often been subsumed under the rubric of revelation, because divine speech was assumed to be impossible due to God's presumed lack of a body. Maimonides says in his *Guide of the Perplexed*:

> Since . . . all these acts are only performed by means of bodily organs, all these organs are figuratively ascribed to Him: those by means of which local motion takes place—I mean the feet and their soles; those by means of which hearing, seeing, and smelling come about—that is, the ear, the eye, and the nose; those by means of which speech and the matter of speech are produced—that is, the mouth, the tongue, and the voice. . . . To sum up all this: God, may He be exalted above every deficiency, has had bodily organs ascribed to Him in order that His acts should be indicated by this means. And those particular acts

---

97. In speaking of God, Barth correctly sets out a top-down case, beginning with God and His revelation to humanity in order to speak accurately of Him. However, he sees human language as a broken entity, which cannot in itself refer to God. He says, "What we can represent to ourselves lies in the sphere of our own existence, and of existence generally, as distinct from God. . . . If we do know about God as the Creator, it is neither wholly nor partially because we have a prior knowledge of something that resembles creation. It is only because it has been given to us by God's revelation to know him, and what we previously thought we knew about originators and causes is contested and converted and transformed." Barth, *The Doctrine of God*, 76–77.

are figuratively ascribed to Him in order to indicate a certain perfection, which is not identical with the particular act mentioned. . . . Action and speech are ascribed to God so that an overflow proceeding from Him should thereby be indicated . . . organs of speech [are] mentioned with a view to indicating the overflow of the intellect toward the prophets . . .[98]

This view is also found in contemporary writers, as in Sandra M. Schneider's *The Revelatory Text*:

Despite the widespread insistence to the contrary that biblical fundamentalism represents, it seems evident that word of God or divine discourse cannot be taken literally. First, words . . . are the intelligible physical sounds emitted by the vocal apparatus (or some substitute for that apparatus) of a rational creature or, by extension, some auditory or visual representation of those utterances. Language, in other words, is a human phenomenon rooted in our corporeality as well as in our discursive mode of intellection and as such cannot be predicated of pure spirit . . .[99]

However, Wolterstorff counters,

One response to this argument of Maimonides and Schneider is that they have just overlooked some things—overlooked, for example, the possibility that God might cause soundings-out or inscribings of words even though God has no body. But what I want to do in the chapters which follow is pursue what seems to me a much more interesting line of thought, one suggested by that position in contemporary philosophy of language commonly known as speech-action theory.[100]

Wolterstorff utilizes Speech-Act Theory[101] to demonstrate how a text can be human and yet divine. He does this by distinguishing revelation

98. Moses Maimonides, *The Guide of the Perplexed*, tr. by Shlomo Pines (Chicago: University of Chicago Press, 1963), I, 46 [pp. 99–100], in Nicolas Wolterstorff, *Divine Discourse*, 7, see footnote 5, p 297. Similarly, Wolterstorff notes that Maimonides' view of God's commanding in Genesis at creation merely means that God "willed" or "wanted." (See Maimonides, *Guide*, 159).

99. Schneider, *The Revelatory Text*, 27–29. Wolterstorff compares this to Karl Barth, who, in His *Church Dogmatics* (I/I, P.132), says that, "God's Word means that God speaks. Speaking is not a 'symbol.'" In Nicolas Wolterstorff, *Divine Discourse*, 10, 11, and note 6 on pp. 296–97.

100. Nicolas Wolterstorff, *Divine Discourse*, 11.

101. This theory has made a significant impact upon the philosophy of language since its initial articulation in Austin, *How to Do Things with Words*. Other works

from discourse. In discourse, one assumes a particular *stance* toward what one is saying, whereas in revelation, knowledge of something hidden is simply unveiled. This is true whether or not the revelation is transitive or intransitive (if it results in the recipient's gain in knowledge), and whether or not it is manifestational or propositional (whether it is embodied or not). This distinction is derived from Speech-Act theory, in which the propositional content of what is said is called the *locution*, and the act of uttering this content the *locutionary act*. The stance toward this content or what is being done *by means of* the locutionary act is called the *illocution*, and the effect of this illocution called the *perlocution*. It is through these distinctions that Wolterstorff dethrones the issue of epistemology (though not done away with by any means), which he claims has been a primary focus for Western philosophy and theology.[102] This preoccupation is what has led most commentary on divine speech to be on revelation rather than discourse. It is this implication in particular which provides insight in dealing with anthropomorphic language.

If the primary issue is no longer how we know what God has said, that is, revelation, then it becomes what God is *doing* by saying something. In the case of anthropomorphic language, God may be asserting that He is a king, or commanding submission to His rule. He may be claiming to have eyes, or promising that nothing escapes His attention and care. He may be asserting that He can be moved by a worshiper's petition, or insisting on the freedom to change His mind. No longer are these terms, whether roles, body parts, or actions, etc., to be seen as compromised language due to the nature of revelation. That is, the assumption that God must "condescend" to human language in order to reveal Himself to humans is no longer the point. It is what He is saying *by means of* the human authors.

Wolterstorff essentially views Scripture as an "appropriated" speech act in which God commandeers the speech of the prophets, psalmists, scribes and chroniclers,[103] and thereby says things by means of these human writers' locutionary and illocutionary acts.[104] That is, God takes both

---

influenced by Austin include, Searle, *Speech Acts*, Alston, *Illocutionary Acts and Sentence Meaning*, and Nicolas Wolterstorff, *Divine Discourse*.

102. Nicolas Wolterstorff, *Divine Discourse*, 36.

103. Presumably, this would include redactors and 'schools' such as the hypothetical Deuteronomistic or Isaianic schools. Thus, the issue of the texts' creation is also side-stepped, as the important issue becomes God's appropriation of the text.

104. Similarly, Kevin Vanhoozer says, "The basic insight is that the Bible is not simply a deposit of revelation but one of God's 'mighty acts'—a mighty *communicative* act, to be exact." Vanhoozer, *The Drama of Doctrine*, 48. See also his *First Theology:*

Approaching Biblical Anthropomorphic Language

what they said and their intention in saying it, and uses either the content alone or both of these as the locution of His own speech acts.

To explain how God could speak through the fully human, i.e., uncoerced and free speech of a human author, Wolterstorff discusses several options, all of which fall under the category of *double-agency discourse*. In these situations, say where a personal assistant is employed to draft a letter for her supervisor, it follows that this letter is appropriated for use by the supervisor. This is true whether it was dictated, or created by the personal assistant and simply signed by the supervisor. This requires the authority of the supervisor to be exercised via the discourse (even if written) of the personal assistant. Furthermore, this can be effected through *deputized discourse*. In this case, one person is authorized to speak on behalf of the other, as in the case of an ambassador. Here, the content of the discourse is completely up to the style and nature of the ambassador, but the aim and goals of the message is defined by the country's head of state. Finally, we have the case of *appropriated discourse*, where one agent's discourse is appropriated to serve as the expression or command or explanation, etc., of another. This is the case when one speaker refers to another's words in a manner to say, "My sentiments exactly," or when someone quotes another person.

> What is appropriated in these new cases is not the text produced by someone else but *the speech of someone else*—this, even though the speech may not [sic] been supervised and will not have been deputized by oneself. In the case of the ambassador, the deputy, the prophet—that is, in the case of deputized, in-the-name-of speech—there may or may not be double-discourse. Here there is inherently double-discourse.[105]

The actual words spoken or written, the locution, has an original purpose in its use, its illocution, but when appropriated by another, may serve that second agent's potentially wholly different illocution.

Hence, God's illocution, or what He is doing by appropriating the human speech, may or may not match that of the prophet or psalmist or chronicler. For instance, when the prophet Jonah warns the people of Ninevah, "forty days and this city will perish," he was saying so as a promise. However, God was appropriating Jonah's speech (as well as dictating it), using it as a conditional promise—a threat, if you will. That is, in appropriating Jonah's words, God was not only making them His own

---

God, Scripture, and Hermeneutics, chap. 5.

105. Nicolas Wolterstorff, *Divine Discourse*, 52.

locution, but using them as His illocution. In co-opting Jonah's words, He was performing the act of warning the Ninevites. This can be seen in the difference between the prophet and God's view of the outcome (the perlocution). Whereas Jonah expected a Sodom-like annihilation (and was greatly disappointed!), God's perlocutionary act (of turning the Ninevites from their sin) was accomplished.

A further distinction clarifies how Wolterstorff sees this as affecting the reading of a biblical text. That is, whereas authoring a text is one way of presenting discourse, such as where the prophets speak in the name of or on behalf of the Lord, the psalms and other types of literature are *presented* to their addressees. That is, the words of the Psalmist, for example, obviously are not a direct address from God, as they are being addressed *to* Him. However, they can be appropriated as God's thoughts and then presented in this function. It is in this way that Wolterstorff establishes a double discourse—an illocutionary appropriation of another's illocutionary discourse. God appropriates the language of the Psalms, which was spoken or written as an act of worship. He uses it then to reveal Himself and speak to His audience.

So, if God uses human discourse, whether by dictation (prophets), deputizing, or appropriating their entire speech acts, what are we to say about anthropomorphic language contained therein which He thus applies to Himself? Wolterstorff says,

> A good deal of the human discourse was not literal. In such cases, the phenomenon in question, of God speaking tropically where the human writer spoke literally, does not arise. For example, I take it as beyond doubt that the human writers were speaking metaphorically when they spoke of the eyes and ears and limbs of God. But what about their application of the language of emotions to God? Were they speaking literally then? I rather think they were. If so, then if we follow the tradition of the church in insisting that such language about God must be construed metaphorically, we do have a case of the human author using the sentence literally whereas God uses it metaphorically.[106]

Hence, if human writers were being metaphorical, then God also could be. However, if the human authors were ascribing human traits to God in a literal fashion, God could be using metaphorical speech in His appropriation of their speech.

---

106. Wolterstorff, *Divine Discourse*, 211.

If the biblical text is an instance of God appropriating human speech, we need not concern ourselves with its appropriateness, as He has deemed it so by His choice to use it. More than this, God's appropriation of such language to describe and reveal Himself becomes the basis upon which we can claim the validity of biblical language with regard to His nature. As we said earlier, there is no *biblical* indication that the nature of divine and human language is any different, and so there is no compelling reason to assume all (self) references to God must necessarily be invalid on the basis of human finitude, whether in nature, experience or knowledge. It applies to God because He applies it to Himself.

This does not, however, render all biblical divine references to be literal. Rather, the particular metaphorical entailments of a given biblical reference to God are determined by the metaphor's individual context, not simply due to its human origin. What we are concerned with here is the ability of biblical statements, made through human agency, to refer to God. What we have seen is that the language itself is a suitable vehicle and that by divine appropriation, human language can indeed be used to refer accurately to God. What this language actually says about Him, and how we go about interpreting it is another issue, one we will discuss in chapter 3.

Summary

To a certain extent we agree with Barth that created beings, such as humans, can only know what a transcendent Creator reveals of Himself. And yet as we have seen with Wolterstorff, Speech-Act theory provides us with a model whereby the brokenness in finite human language is overcome through divine appropriation of human speech acts. This allows terms we understand from human contexts to be used of God, for He has applied this (biblical) language to Himself. However, it remains to be seen what is actually being said about God, for the speech being arrogated is informed by human usage, which due to differences in ontology, would not seem to be univocal when used by the creature and Creator. In short, though God has appropriated the speech, how He uses it for His own speech acts regarding Himself is yet to be determined. In what way does God connect the human terms used of Him with Himself? To further delineate this, we now look at the treatment of anthropomorphism within Old Testament theology. We seek to discern how biblical language has been interpreted regarding its reference to the divine, in terms more commonly associated with the "human."

Anthropomorphism in Old Testament Theology

As Barth rightly observes, no claim about God can be veridical unless grounded within God Himself. However, the need remains for a way to speak in comprehensible human terms (Bultmann), without redefining our subject matter (Tillich, Macquarrie). In Wolterstorff, we find a way forward in the appropriations of human speech by God Himself. This assumption, of course, has not always informed approaches to Old Testament theology. In the following we shall examine various giants of the field, to better understand how their approaches to anthropomorphic language affected their interpretation.

History of Religions and Divine Personhood

In his *Theology of the Old Testament,* Walther Eichrodt suggests that anthropomorphic terms were primitive attempts to counterbalance the pantheistic deifications of nature in surrounding cultures and deistic, philosophical grounds of God's being with the personal nature of Israel's God. Eichrodt assesses the Old Testament's depiction of deity as having defects, primarily based on the history-of-religions approach, which finds behind some of the earlier Hebrew texts a more primitive concept of God, focused on His personal nature. Rather than attributing little or no real value to these expressions, Eichrodt acknowledges their substance as deriving from pagan religion: "here [is] a parallel to the manner in which paganism speaks of its personified natural forces. To hush up what there is in common with heathen ways of thought is merely to gloss over the facts, and to obscure the individuality of Israelite religious faith."[107] So, Eichrodt sees anthropomorphic descriptions of God as essentially putting a face on the unapproachable entity that was God.

However, he also finds safeguards against the excessive humanization of God.

> Definite provision was made to counter any excessive deviation in the direction of subjecting God to human limitations. This was achieved primarily through the experience of *the infinite superiority of the divine nature* to all merely human attributes

---

107. Eichrodt, "Theology of the Old Testament," 211.

and capacities—an experience which marks every encounter with the divine in the Old Testament. Nowhere, not even in the remarkable familiarity of the descriptions in the patriarchal narratives, is there any trace of that companionable equality of God and man which is so characteristic not only of the Greek stories of the gods, but also of the Indian and many of the Babylonian and Egyptian myths. The plain fact of God's superiority to everything human is brought out so clearly throughout the Old Testament that even many Christians never notice the very definite defects in its picture of God."[108]

An infinite nature safeguarded against humanization because, "The possessor of this highest form of life can obviously not be bound by the limitations which circumscribe human personality."[109] As evidence, Eichrodt cites God's lack of sleeping (Ps 121:4), his eyes not being like mankind's (Job 10:4f.) and that he can search beyond outward impressions and view the heart (1 Sam 16:7; Pss 44:22; 139:23). Eichrodt founds this notion of God's "inexhaustible life which has no need of human service,"[110] on the occurrences of *ḥay yhwh* "As Yahweh lives," in oaths and elsewhere to confirm the fundamental nature of God's being. His main concern, however, seems to be the protection of God's freedom. "The transcendence of God is not maintained in an abstract fashion or with strict logic even in this instance; but there is a deliberate intention of eliminating the danger that the Deity might be limited to a particular place or made available to man's control in a physical way."[111] Thus, for Eichrodt, anthropomorphic expressions serve to make God approachable, whilst statements of His transcendent nature protect against the limitations of overhumanization.

However, Eichrodt also equates these biblical descriptions of God's physical modes of living and self-manifestation as cultural limitations, even flaws, in the conception of God.

> There can be no doubt that among the great mass of the people, and especially in the earlier period, the deity was frequently conceived as restricted to physical modes of living and self-manifestation. They understood the anthropomorphic expressions in a

---

108. Ibid., 213.
109. Ibid., 214.
110. Ibid., 213.
111. Ibid., 214.

quite literal and concrete way, and so managed to acquire a most inadequate conception of the divine supremacy.[112]

In following the history-of-religions approach to Old Testament theology, Eichrodt seems to view anthropomorphic expressions attributed to the deity as primarily an early stage of development. The function of these terms was to emphasize the personality of God, much in the same way the pagan religions had done in their worship of natural phenomena. Though the prophets retained some of this language, they began to balance it with statements of God's character extrapolated from, yet amplified beyond human abilities. Motivated by piety, they sought to protect God's reliability through a stress on His transcendence, yet one mixed with anthropomorphic expressions of His immanence. In the priestly school, the pendulum swung completely to the transcendent pole, attempting to correct earlier naïve conceptions with philosophically "correct" ones. Thus, the text is a mixture of layers and stages in the theological development of Israel's concept of God which mark His personality, reliability, and otherness. However, Eichrodt sees the anthropomorphic expressions as carryovers from pagan religion, used to emphasize God's approachability, and yet inaccurate and even defective in their description of God (in) Himself.

Similarly, R. E. Clements finds the primary purpose of anthropomorphism as the portrayal of divine personality because though, "with severe restraint as to the more physical aspects that might be associated with such personality, . . . it enables the emotional and intellectual aspects of his nature to be vigorously presented. Hence the most telling and moving pictures of the relationship between God and his people are those which draw upon the realm of human relationships."[113] Clements illustrates this with both father-son and husband-wife pictures of divine-human relationships in the Old Testament. Thus, for Clements, despite being early in the development of Israel's theology, anthropomorphisms represent genuine expressions of God's nature. However, they are limited in their analogical function to expressing His moral, emotional, and intellectual aspects.

One problem with the history-of-religions approach as noted by Horst Dietrich Preuss is that evidence of the earlier stages of development seem to span all of the periods of the development of the Old Testament. Against Eichrodt, Preuss does not see anthropomorphic language in Scripture as being progressively tamed. "Anthropomorphisms are found not only in the older texts of the Old Testament, so that one might be able

112. Ibid., 211.
113. Clements, "Old Testament Theology: A Fresh Approach," 60.

Approaching Biblical Anthropomorphic Language

to say that these are the undigested remnants from a period that still possessed little theological clarity, but also, as the evidence shows, even from later periods. For example, one finds these anthropomorphic statements even in Deutero-Isaiah, which also presents a 'theoretical monotheism.'"[114] He also cites 2 Chr 6:40, a post-exilic text mentioning God's ear, to dispel notions of late "corrective" treatments. For Preuss, the human terms in which God is spoken of are evidence of His desire be related to by humans. "The anthropomorphisms are evidence of the inadequacy of human speech about God, but they also bear witness to the living relation to Him that compels the faithful to speak of Him."[115]

Preuss labels passages as anthropomorphisms due to contradictions found in Scripture:

> That the Old Testament anthropomorphisms ought not to be taken purely and simply as declarative statements but also already can develop a tendency toward metaphor is shown in the fact that often opposite statements can coexist. Thus, while YHWH is "sorry" in Gen 6:6, this is contested elsewhere (Num. 23:19; 1 Sam. 15:29; and Jer. 4:28; cf. Mal. 3:6). . . . Also, YHWH sees (Ps 94:7); however, he does not see with human eyes (Job 10:4f.). YHWH's heart recoils within him because of compassion, while at the same time he is God and not a human being (Hos 11:8f.). . . . He is simply the living God and wants to be taken seriously as such. He wishes to be near human beings, elects them to exist in community with him, comes to the world (E. Jüngel), and therefore assumes already in the Old Testament a human form (Phil. 2:7). Old Testament anthropomorphisms consequently deal with God as a you (personal), as a "person," with God's community with human beings, with God in human language, with an event between God and human beings, and not with divine characteristics in and of themselves. God acts humanly, not in spite of, but rather on the strength of his divine status. He is near and far (Jer. 23:23).[116]

Thus, for Preuss, contradictory language about God is evidence that the human language is being used to speak of superhuman realities. Furthermore, divine characteristics are only spoken of within relationships. Anthropomorphic language in the Old Testament then, is merely

---

114. Preuss, *Old Testament Theology*, 244–45.

115. Ibid., 347 n. 762.

116. Ibid., 246. According to note 769, this is from C. K. H. Miskotte, *Wenn die Götter schweigen* (1963), 139.

a reflection of God's dealings with humans, on *their* terms (language, expressions, senses, feelings, time) and not an indication of His own reality. Preuss comments,

> It is only seldom that one finds in the Old Testament statements about the nature or the characteristics of God, and when such occur, they concern, not the nature of God in and of itself or his absolute being, and so forth (also not in Exod 3:14), but rather his relationship to human beings. Characteristics of God are mentioned, not because God in and of himself is thus and so, but because he does or did this or that, behaves or behaved in this way or in that manner, and he shows or showed thereby something of his own nature.[117]

This being said, Preuss also shrinks from applying philosophical concepts to God. "While there are inferences that may be drawn from the Old Testament's understanding of the nature of God, one would be careful about the use of later philosophical, theological categories of thought to set forth the Old Testament's view of reality (e.g., 'aseity')."[118]

Thus, Preuss diverges from Eichrodt, and Clements, (and Rendtorff), in that anthropomorphic language is no longer a by-product of the evolution of Old Testament religious beliefs. Rather it is an intentional balancing mechanism seen in both early and later texts which is necessary for humans to speak of God. This is evidenced by the contradictory statements of God's nature in Scripture which reflect not God's reality, but His relationships to humans. Thus, Preuss views anthropomorphic expressions as both necessary for communicating God's relationship to humans via His acts, but not reflective of God's inner being. But this leads us to ask how these acts of God should be construed, to which we now turn.

Acts of God

Though Eichrodt and Clements view anthropomorphic language as a by-product of the evolution of Israelite religion, Preuss' observation that this language is found in earlier and later texts points to another solution. Brevard Childs locates the "condescension" of a transcendent God to humanity not in His use of conformative language, but in God's *acts* described therein. "The biblical language of depicting God in human form is not an unfortunate accommodation to human limitation, but a truthful

---

117. Preuss, *Old Testament Theology*, 239.
118. Ibid., 239.

reflection of the free decision of God to identify with his creation in human form and yet to remain God."[119] This shift is significant in its view of the text as accurately depicting God's actions. However, Childs tempers this saying God acts not of His nature, but of His will.[120] This means that He is not required to act in the (human?) manner in which He does, but makes the sovereign choice to do so.

Similarly, instead of abstract ontological categories, Walter Brueggemann observes in Israel's "testimony" about God an emphasis on active engagement, a context of human relationship, and a parameter of text for the character of Yahweh. He says, "This focus on sentences signifies that Israel is characteristically concerned with the action of God—the concrete, specific action of God—and not God's character, nature, being, or attributes, except as those are evidenced in concrete actions. This focus on verbs, moreover, commits us in profound ways to a *narrative* portrayal of Yahweh, in which Yahweh is the one who is said to have done these deeds."[121] Brueggemann's approach to the biblical witness of God attempts to sidestep philosophical intrusions by removing God's essence from the scope of the biblical text.

Consequently, Brueggemann finds Israel's God to be primarily known in terms of relationship rather than theological definition. That is, He is known more in what He does than for who He is. He acknowledges the presence of direct statements of God's nature, but reserves pride of place for the more prolific narrative ascriptions. "To be sure, Israel offers more reflective statements concerning the character of Yahweh (as in Exod 34:6–7). My urging, however, is that these statements are of another order and likely derive from these verbal affirmations that I take to be more elemental."[122] This reveals what he sees as the Old Testament's primary *modus operandi*—situating theological truth in narrative rather than propositional statements. Among these embedded descriptions of God, he lists verbs (creating, promising, delivering, commanding, and blessing), adjectives (faithful ['ĕmet] and loving [ḥesed]) and nouns depicting roles (judge, king, and father).

---

119. Childs, *Biblical Theology*, 358.

120. This could conceivably be reconciled as Paul Fiddes does, [*The Creative Suffering of God*, 67], by arguing (following Barth) that God's fundamental nature actually is freedom. Thus, "how God chooses to be" is thereafter, of necessity, how He is within His own being. If He chooses to do things that humans also do, that is His prerogative.

121. Brueggemann, *Theology of the Old Testament*, 145.

122. Ibid., 179.

In the Eyes of God

Just as Brueggemann demands that critical interpretation not attempt to discover a true history behind the text, he also says, "theological interpretation does not go behind this witness with questions of ontology, wondering 'what is real.' What is real, so our 'verdict' is, what these witnesses say is real. Nothing more historical or ontological is available. But this mode of 'knowing' finds such a claim to be adequate."[123]

The ubiquitous theme of the "cry" ($s^e\bar{a}q\bar{a}h$) also underscores the significance of Yahweh's textual limitations. "The reality of nullity causes a profound renegotiation of Yahweh's sovereignty vis-à-vis Yahweh's pathos-filled fidelity."[124] Alluding to Patrick D. Miller's *They Cried to the Lord*,[125] Brueggemann says, "'Cry' is the core theme of the Psalter." Then he adds, "given Exod. 2:23–25, it is perhaps the core theme of Israel's life in the world."[126] According to Elie Wiesel, rabbinic teaching stipulates, "So long as he [the human] cries, he can hope his father [God] will hear him. If he stops, he is lost . . ."[127] Thus, the human party is dependent on the cry. But, so too is Yahweh, for, "that is how Yahweh was moved to enact Yahweh's powerful verbs in the first place (Exod 2:23–25)."[128] The risk Yahweh runs is seen in Psalm 88 where, "the accusation turns to threat against Yahweh in the rhetorical questions of vv. 10–12. If Yahweh allows the death of the speaker, Yahweh will lose a witness to Yahweh's *ḥesed*. There will be no speech on earth, among the living, of Yahweh's steadfast love or faithfulness or wonders or saving help. *The loss of the speaker will cause Yahweh to lose the speech on which Yahweh's reality in the world depends.* [Ital. original]"[129]

For Brueggemann, Yahweh's reality is limited to that of the text and the community in which it is received and lived out. Thus, the descriptions of His acts there are to be taken literally, as these consist of a witness essential to His reality. As this witness is primarily in verbs of action rather than essence, so Yahweh is defined primarily in terms of action.

---

123. Ibid., 206.

124. Ibid., 558.

125. Patrick D. Miller, *They Cried to the Lord: The Form and Theology of Biblical Prayer*. Minneapolis, MN: Fortress, 1994.

126. Brueggemann, *Theology of the Old Testament*, 399 n. 37.

127. Elie Wiesel, *All Rivers Run to the Sea: Memoirs*. New York: Knopf, 1995, 275, in Brueggemann, *Theology of the Old Testament*, 399 n. 37.

128. Brueggemann, *Theology of the Old Testament*, 399.

129. Ibid., 398.

Approaching Biblical Anthropomorphic Language

Anthropomorphic language is used to avoid speaking of God's essence, but conversely, according to Brueggemann, to establish his reality.

John Goldingay, however, finds an anthropomorphism indicative of more going on *within* Yahweh. For example, when God *looks*, this indicates an awareness, impetus, and responsibility within Him. Goldingay illustrates, "Having listened, 'God looked at the Israelites' (Ex 2:25). 'I really have seen the affliction of my people who are in Egypt' (Ex 3:7; cf. Ex 3:9). The first stage in a response is that God looks at what is going on. The reality of God's seeing is also repeated: The cry causes God to look."[130] For Goldingay, this anthropomorphic expression indicates not simply an action *toward*, but a true interaction *with* people. "Sight confirms that the facts are what the cry says they are (cf. Gen 18:21) and makes more inevitable the further response of action. . . . Seeing, like hearing, is not merely the means of receiving information but the stimulus for acting on it."[131] This interaction has implications for God's own being,

> Looking means God now bears the burden of knowledge. That, too, has to be more than merely cognitive. Knowledge, recognition or acknowledgment is a key theme in the story of Israel's deliverance, for integral to this story is Israel and Egypt's coming to acknowledge Yhwh. . . . God is not such a transcendent being as to be exalted above engagement with people. That does not mean God suffers with the people in the sense of sharing their suffering, any more than the king does. Knowing/acknowledging Israel's pains does not in itself imply personal experience of them. It does mean God gets involved with their suffering. Insofar as knowing is more than an intellectual matter, it is more directly a matter of the will than the feelings. Acknowledging the reality of Israel's affliction is a start to taking action to change things."[132] (Contra Fretheim, *Exodus*, 60.)[133]

Though apparently lending theological substance to Yahweh's perceptions, Goldingay recoils from viewing God's knowing as emotional or experiential. As with Childs, it is more than just a cognitive issue, God's knowledge is a "matter of the will." By "knowing" of Israel's plight, God implies that He intends to do something about it. And yet, in Hos 11, Goldingay finds God moved by sympathy, "Ephraim is the child Yhwh

---

130. Goldingay, *Old Testament Theology: Israel's Gospel*, 301.
131. Ibid., 301–2.
132. Ibid., 302.
133. Ibid., 302 n. 40.

delights in, the one who stirs up feelings inside Yhwh, the one for whom Yhwh feels a consuming compassion (*rachamim*, the word for the womb; cf. Jer 31:20). That is the reason Yhwh cannot finally throw this unresponsive son out of the house."[134]

Hence, Goldingay views these anthropomorphisms as carrying consequence for the narrative, and occasionally containing implications for God's inner life. Sight, for example, becomes not simply information gathering, but signifies the impetus upon which Yahweh acts as well as the burden of knowledge of His people's plight.

Finally, Rolf Rendtorff attempts to set out a fresh look at the Old Testament through the lens of the canon. However, he adheres to the conclusion of a history-of-religions approach when dealing with anthropomorphisms. He equates anthropomorphic language to the development of stages, "a large proportion of the statements about God are highly graphic, 'anthropomorphic,' one might say. This applies, though certainly in very different ways, to all areas of Old Testament literature. (Criticism of the anthropomorphism of biblical language is an element of the criticism of biblical religion as a whole; so in the context of the representation of biblical statements it has no meaningful function, cf. *EKL*,[135] 1559.)"[136]

He illustrates the biblical use of these terms by pointing out how many of God's activities come from "secular" human usage.

> Creative verbs come from, "the realm of handiwork," and "the adoption of battle motifs from neighboring religions (Isa 51.9 etc.). . . . But it is also clear that the verbs utilized in relation to Yhwh's fighting and gaining victory are meant metaphorically, to describe the power and strength of the creator God. To that extent they do not express anything fundamentally different from other verbs that instead of God's fighting describe his creative speaking (Ps 33.6, 9 etc.) There are various ways of expressing something that can only be described in vague terms. And there are not other means of expression available for use than concrete graphic depiction using terms from the human realm.[137]

Rendtorff interprets anthropomorphic images as having singular, practical considerations, such as "fighting" representing God's "power" or "strength." Furthermore, anthropomorphisms are at the same time a

---

134. Ibid., 305.
135. EKL is *Evangelisches Kirchenlexikon*, 3rd ed.
136. Rendtorff, *The Canonical Hebrew Bible*, 610.
137. Ibid.

Approaching Biblical Anthropomorphic Language

holdover from other religions and a concession to the paucity of human language, but not a means of depicting realities within God Himself.

Following Brueggemann, Rendtorff classifies statements about God as verbal, nominal, and adjectival. Anthropomorphisms are simply reflections of how humans experience God, and not indicative of God's inner life.

> Each of the shapes that God assumes in the metaphors displays quite particular characteristic traits. In biblical discourse these become God's qualities: for instance, when we read that God is angry, this means that humans experience God as angry, or more precisely, they experience something that they understand, or try to understand, as God's anger. Thus particular adjectives, "qualifiers" in English, become statements about the behaviour and the nature of God. But it is evident that none of the designations of the qualities can quite comprehend and embrace God's "nature." In the case of metaphors in nominal expressions it has emerged clearly that they can only ever comprehend and represent a partial aspect of the nature of God. The same applies to the adjectives too; unlike the nouns, however, they can occur in association with other terms and so contemplate and illuminate God's nature from various angles.[138]

Thus, for Rendtorff, anthropomorphisms indicate elements of early more naïve and occasionally non-Israelite traditions, and are reducible to other statements. Furthermore, they simply reflect human "experience" of God, and do not reflect the "inner" life of God.

Summary

The observations made by all of the commentators on implications of anthropomorphic language, and specifically divine perception, are only hampered by some of their initial assumptions. Eichrodt, Clements, and Rendtorff presume a history-of-religions approach which relegates the use of human-oriented terms for God to an earlier, more naïve time. This affects their understanding of how the text comments on itself, the direction and existence of analogical language, and ultimately, the understanding of the inspiration of the biblical text.

To their credit, their insights on God's personality as a rationale for the abiding worth of anthropomorphic language are still helpful. The

---

138. Ibid., 622.

aspects of divine personality set Him far above nature worship or rationalistic philosophy by casting Him as transcendent and yet approachable. However, this approach implies that there is something hollow and strained about anthropomorphic texts. According to Clements,

> In many instances the anthropomorphic way in which God's being and actions are described seems to border on the creaturely and the naïve. Thus when he is said to 'walk' (cf. Gen 3.8), to "laugh" (cf. Ps 2.4), and even to "pant" and "groan" (cf. Isa 42.14), the analogical function of such language seems clearly to be stretched. It is evident in the later parts of the Old Testament literature that a serious effort has been made to tone down some of this language and to describe God's actions in a more restrained manner. . . .Yet it is never seriously given up, nor indeed could it be if the ascription of personality to God, which is so essential a part of the Old Testament understanding of him, was to be retained.[139]

Though Eichrodt, Clements, and Rendtorff see these anthropomorphic descriptions of God and His actions as establishing His personality, the proof for this is lacking; Walking, laughing, and groaning do not necessarily indicate the presence of personality. Hyenas can be said to laugh, dogs cry, and yet these supposedly "anthropomorphic" terms are being applied to animals, in which personality is not really present. The same applies with the presence of facial features; eyes and ears do not guarantee the presence of personhood. Only when given a particular context can these terms say *what sort* of personality one has. What is it that one person laughs at compared to another? What makes them groan? Does their walking indicate a peaceful, unhurried demeanor, a contemplative spirit, a desire to be in community with others who are walking, or ambivalence—walking when one should run? Thus, the interpretations of anthropomorphism seen in these authors seem incomplete. In fact, rather than being explanatory, the act of ascribing personality to God could itself be considered anthropomorphic.

If, as Preuss claims, humans are only able to recognize the presence of their own qualities in other beings, or the lack thereof, then how can we determine whether anthropomorphisms are inconsistent with divine reality, or not? Eichrodt offers the presence of superhuman traits and Preuss the existence of opposites to establish the metaphorical sense of divine anthropomorphisms. However, the possession of superhuman traits does

---

139. Clements, "Old Testament Theology: A Fresh Approach," 58–59.

Approaching Biblical Anthropomorphic Language

not exclude the ability to act in normal human fashion. Just because God can traverse[140] the vast reaches of the cosmos unassisted does not mean He cannot assume a form and walk (Gen 3:8). Clement's pairs of opposites (God is sorry, but doesn't repent, etc.) are also misleading, as some of the "opposites" to God's anthropomorphic traits are merely opposed to humanity's *sinful nature*, and not human ability. God sees, but doesn't see as *sinful* man, who looks on the outside appearance (1 Sam 16:7—Consider the injunction for Samuel to see otherwise.). Thus, the possession of supernatural ability by itself is not necessarily key to the interpretation of anthropomorphic language in a given context.[141] In order to discern what God is saying of Himself in appropriating human language, we require more than a simple contrasting of God's potential with his action. We also need more than a *carte blanche* imposition of the theme of God's "personality" or "approachability." We require a more nuanced and context-sensitive approach to the text.

Furthermore, this discussion raises the issue of how the canon comments on itself. Does it, according to the history-of-religions approach, contain mistaken notions, or strained exaggerations, which required subsequent correction? Does progressive revelation invalidate earlier texts? Does the nature of a canonical approach dictate that all parts are equally and simultaneously true? (e.g. the "anthropomorphic" descriptions of God seeking knowledge through testing in Gen 22:1, or the number of innocent in Sodom and Gomorrah in Gen 18:20–21, versus the all-knowing God of Ps 139 or Isa 44–45).

Inspiration and Revelation

Part of the problem surrounding anthropomorphic language has to do with the issue of how the Hebrew Scriptures came into being. Both Eichrodt and Brueggemann, though typically at opposite ends of the spectrum, both seem to view the Scriptures solely as human products. Eichrodt implies that Israelite authors were trying to say something about their conception of deity that was both parallel to and yet significantly different from that of the surrounding pagan cultures. Hence, they couched God in human terms, to imply personality and yet applied superhuman traits. Brueggemann speaks of Israel's testimony and countertestimony to

---

140. Even this may be metaphorical, as even the heavens (read space) cannot contain Him (2 Chr 2:6).

141. This is especially so if the supernatural ability is not being highlighted in the given text.

Yahweh's existence, but never allows Yahweh to take the stand Himself. He claims that, "the outcome [of historical critical approaches that often ran contrary to the theological claims of the text] is a 'history of religion' that not only resists theological metanarrative, but resists any notion of Yahweh as an agent in Israel's life."[142] However, in an effort to split the difference between skepticism and fideism, Brueggemann is left with a God who affects Israel, but is embodied only in the text and Israel's practice. He protests that Yahweh is not therefore controlled by the readers, because, "such self-deceptions, however, are acts of serious disregard of the text in its daring specificity. The daring, maddeningly deconstructive temper of the text keeps its central character elusive and refuses to make Yahweh available in ways that violate Yahweh's odd character."[143] However, if the text is as enigmatic as Brueggemann asserts, so daringly elusive of any readerly manipulation, it would seem to be a prime candidate for divine involvement in its authorship as well.

As Childs observes, Israel did not come up with these traditions through clever innovation, but by revelation. If the communities of faith that affirmed these documents as authoritative did so because of a belief in their inspiration, there are significant implications for our reading of biblical anthropomorphic language. First of all, the scriptures change from biographical to autobiographical. There is a *prima facie* assumption within the text that what is written is not merely human description of God, but divine self-description transmitted through[144] human agents. Regardless of one's theory of *how* inspiration works, there remains at least some level of divine instigation and quality control of the message. Thus, canonically speaking, anthropomorphisms are not *simply* borrowings from pagan nature religions, nor *simply* human attempts to color in a more correct, but sterile (and still human) philosophical concept of God. Though part of the creation of the text may have involved these things, the texts are ultimately, by nature of their appropriation by the divine, self-revelations,

142. Brueggemann, *Theology of the Old Testament*, 727. Note 5 says, "To refer to 'Yahweh as agent' reintroduces the whole vexed issue of a 'God who acts.' For a review of the issue, see Thomas F. Tracy, *God, Action, and Embodiment* (Grand Rapids: Eerdmans, 1984)."

143. Brueggemann, *Theology of the Old Testament*, 574.

144. Or, alternately, appropriated from those of human agents. Wolterstorff actually proposes both, according to the type of literature. That is, prophetic words may include direct quotes the prophets heard from God (Thus saith the LORD) Indeed, the "ten words" were presumed to be written directly by God's own hand (Exod 31:18). Narratives and wisdom literature, on the other hand, may include more appropriated speech.

Approaching Biblical Anthropomorphic Language

and therefore not correctives, but assertions. This is not to say that all scriptural God-language is literal. It is, of course, mediated by the nature and style of language itself. God can be said to use metaphors as well as literal speech. The point is that scriptural language is not *necessarily* inappropriate in its God-talk, simply because it came through human agency.

The assumption that anthropomorphic language is early and naïve language in the evolution of the text entails a rather negative perspective on the ability of earlier peoples to handle issues of transcendence and immanence. As Eichrodt and others would have it, they were fooled into thinking God was basically a large human (von Rad). The view that the Israelites were thus naïve, was widely held in the early church (Origen, Athanasius, the Cappadocians, etc.) and even by the Reformers (Luther and Calvin) as they attempted to defend Christianity's break from Judaism. In explaining why the sacrificial system was no longer needed, they continually appealed to the primitive nature of the early Israelites who could not handle the truth of Christ directly.[145]

However, this sort of approach brings a severe prejudice to the text, either against ancients or against Jews, both of which seem unwarranted. We have no reason to believe that these large groups of people were categorically less intelligent than the people of our own day. Approaches informed or heuristically propped up by such means tend to mute the meaning of the text. Anthropomorphic texts are systematically labelled as early or influenced by earlier rather than later thought, despite Preuss's (and Clements!) observations that this language pervades the entire corpus of the Old Testament. They are then treated as a sort of second-class language which contains less truth-value than other more "philosophically correct" statements concerning divine omniscience, omnipotence, life, or personhood. This seems to reflect an unfounded cultural bias upon the part of these interpreters. For example, at which point did the Israelites "get wise" to their naïve anthropomorphic notions? What is it that definitively makes the approach of one age better than that of another? These questions go largely unanswered.

It becomes evident that assumptions about metaphorical language steer the interpretation of the text. For some authors, anthropomorphic metaphors are reducible to one proposition across their occurrences in the text. For example, a metaphor such as God's seeing, is equated with a sign of personhood (Eichrodt) or God's justice (Rendtorff). However, as is readily shown, this cannot be the case. When God sees His creation as good in Gen 1:31, there is no legal or judicial context which would

---

145. For this, see our earlier discussion under the heading "accommodation."

53

construe this as an expression of God's justice. Such interpretations overlook the role God's sight might play within such a context. Is it one of witness, or one of fair judgment (e.g., seeing through false testimony), one of empathy for the victim, or appreciation of beauty? For this we need a better understanding of how these metaphors for God function, so we may grasp more of the picture that they are giving us of the biblical God.

This illustrates the necessity for an *irreducible* approach to interpreting anthropomorphic metaphors for God. Brueggemann and Childs see the acts of God as defining who He is, and from this stems the need to define these acts more specifically. However, Brueggemann restrains the implications of divine acts to the text itself, and does not allow them to refer to a Being outside the text. This we find untenable if they represent Israel's witness, for a witness by its very nature, points to something *outside* itself.

Thus, a theological view of anthropomorphic language depends on a view of the nature of the text. If the text was completely a human product, anthropomorphic terms can be seen as early, naïve projections of personality onto a deity which were later emended by philosophically more correct conceptions. If language itself is solely of human origin, then, as Preuss says, all God-talk is to some degree analogical, and to that degree, inaccurate. However, if the biblical text is an appropriated divine speech act, then its message takes on new possibilities for describing the divine. If language is divine (as well as human) in nature[146] then Scripture is capable of effectively depicting the divine reality. Anthropomorphic expressions then, do not merely lend a human face to an abstract Deity, but are able in some degree to describe His fundamental acts and nature.

Our Approach

In approaching the question of biblical anthropomorphic language, we discerned three main areas of discussion, all of which focus on how we communicate across the divine-human divide. First, there was the issue of the meaning of terms when applied to the respective realms. We have seen that of the main ways of speaking of God, the metaphorical allows the most flexibility to apply contextually-relevant elements of a term to God without making the statement univocal. Univocity fails on the grounds

---

146. That is, if language is a medium used equally by the deity and humans, as per our earlier discussion. Furthermore, though language is shaped and influenced by human conceptions, these too can be appropriated into divine speech, and hence, lent credibility in their ability to accurately depict the divine.

that God is transcendent and His ways are not those of humans, and neither is His nature. Thus, terms cannot apply to God in the same way they do to people. Some approaches, such as process theology, end up redefining God's difference from His creation in order to preserve the ability to speak univocally of Him, but this contrasts sharply with the biblical picture of God[147] and church tradition. Equivocity does not fail so much in its application as in its ability to say anything significant of God, as the human and divine use of a given term are utterly unrelated. The *via negationis* leads to an agnosticism about who God is and the *via eminentia*[148] does little better at defining such a Being in accessible terms.

The *via analogia* also falls down on the fact that the nature of the analogy is uncertain. It either falls back into univocity in attributional analogy, by predicating the Creator's attribute on the basis of that of the creatures, or in proportion, it seeks to make an attribute such as "goodness" relevant to God's nature in the way that it is related to human nature. This fails because we don't know God's nature by another means in order to establish what 'goodness' is to Him. We only possess one side of the equation—the human one.

Metaphor, however, allows us to readdress this issue by attributing some elements of an attribute to God and hiding others, say, the physical mechanics. Furthermore, as Stern's methodology claims, we are able to point to the quality without exhaustively defining it. Though metaphors leave some elements of God's nature unexplained, they are a way forward—one with the ability to refer to a transcendent being, to do so accurately, and yet to say more about who He is than who He is not.

The second issue involved the nature of transmission of knowledge between the transcendent realm of God and that of humans. Traditional approaches to such accommodation, seek to explain away anthropomorphic language by taking it as univocal speech, but disconnect this from referring to God's internal reality. We found this approach in tension with

---

147. The Old Testament is replete with depictions of God which distinguish His nature from that of mankind (cf. Num 23:19; Hos 11:9). Isa 44, for example, describes Him as the only God, distinct from things made with hands, Who in fact was the One who formed (created) Israel. There is no sense of God's Being as ontologically entwined with that of creation. In fact, Gen 6:5 speaks of how His Spirit will not dwell with mankind, primarily due to their sin. Thus, panentheism, while clever, does not seem to agree with the *prima facie* sense of the biblical text.

148. "The medieval and traditional notion of *analogia eminentiae*, of working from the lower to the higher, may address issues of intelligibility, provided that it is not transformed into an ontology that transposes the transcendence of God into what Aquinas seeks to avoid, namely a projected anthropomorphic construct." Thiselton, *A Concise Encyclopedia of the Philosophy of Religion*, "Analogy," 8.

the honest character of God as portrayed in the biblical text, as well as muting the force of His depiction in the text. Traditional accommodation also assumed knowledge of God that was contradictory to the text, without establishing the source of this knowledge. Thus, we found accommodation requiring a more chastened and principled approach—one which we found metaphor filled quite well.

To establish the referentiality of these metaphors for God, we turned to the appropriated Speech Acts proposed by Wolterstorff. In this theory, God co-opts the discourse of human authors, with varying levels of control, and makes it His own. Whether through dictation to a prophet, or even more distant acts of putting His stamp upon a text, He appropriates this as second-order discourse. In this manner, we find *humanly*-generated texts can serve as divine discourse. Thus, the assertions made therein are grounded in the authority of the divine as Barth sought to do, and yet overcome any "brokenness" in human language through Divine sanctioning of it.

However, our third question now arises—"How do we know which elements of a concept are transferable to the divine and which are not?" Here we did a survey of Old Testament theologians and found varying results. Eichrodt, Clements and Rendtorff followed the history-of-religions school, considering anthropomorphic language to be a vestige of earlier Israelite religion. Though they were seeking to answer different questions than those that concern us here, the implications of their diachronic approach to Israelite religion effectively relegates anthropomorphic language to a vestige of earlier, more naive notions of God, rather than the later, more philosophically "correct" versions. They attempted to explain this by subsuming these terms under an assertion by the Israelite authors of the 'personhood' of God. However, we found this unsatisfactory, as several anthropomorphisms were not necessarily personal (cf. eyes, ears, etc.), and as Preuss observed, were not necessarily early texts. Furthermore, these again took no account of contextual factors. While Brueggemann took great stock in the context, He also ended up confining God to the text, and hence does not help us in bridging a true transcendent-immanent divide. Childs, though laying more importance upon anthropomorphic expressions, falls back upon the tendency to reduce them to indicating no more than the "personhood" and "living" nature of God.

As we shall explore in more depth in chapter 3, the biblical text itself provides a means of discerning this relationship between humanity and the deity. According to the *theomorphic* nature of Old Testament anthropology, humans are defined in terms of the divine, as the "image of

Approaching Biblical Anthropomorphic Language

God" (Gen 1:26). Accordingly, the divine itself, is defined, not in terms of humanity, but within the context of the interaction with humanity. This is similar to the functionalism of Alston, Aaron, and Ferré, in that the function of a given term is transferred without the *modus operandi*. The major difference lies in the fact that this function is defined in context and neither as universal constants, nor according to pre-conceived theological systems. As Childs observes, the nature of theology is that it must be drawn from the text.

Hence, we ground our approach to "anthropomorphic" language upon three legs—the biblical depiction of the divine-human relationship, divine Speech Acts, and context-sensitive metaphorical interpretation. The upshot of the theomorphic depiction of humanity in the Bible is that there is a spectrum of meaning within any given divine predicate that is neither located exclusively within the human, nor the divine realms. Rather, this semantic field ranges from the "natural" to the "supernatural," with both God and humans potentially capable, with some concessions, of action involving elements of both ends of the spectrum. Admittedly, the natural is most closely and often associated with humans and the supernatural with God, but the fact that these denotations can be transferred to divine and human subjects demonstrates that the nature of the action is derived as much from its context as its actor. The implications of this are that, rather than establishing fixed definitions for verbs associated with the divine, and applying them to the text, we must derive the definitions from the individual contexts of usage.

Secondly, the capability of anthropomorphic language to accurately refer to the divine is founded on Wolterstorff's conception of a divine Speech Act. Within Wolterstorff's economy, whether or not the human writers wrote from direct revelation, their language was appropriated by the Divine Author behind the canon, who applied their writings to Himself. Thus, it is not human knowledge, but divine second-order discourse which makes the language veridical. The discourse is grounded in God's act and thus accurate, and the language is comprehensible because it is human. However, this does not mean that all of scripture speaks univocally of God. This takes us to our third leg, that of context-sensitive metaphorical interpretation.

In the next chapter, we take our own linguistic turn, looking at how metaphors work, and how they might serve to describe the characteristics a transcendent God would possess. We will also examine the extent to which metaphors may or may not be able to make truth-claims. The question in view, then, is how do we know what it means for God to do something, say, "to see," in the first place? In short, we don't—at least not fully. Rather, we know some of its functions within a particular context, which is why, in a given context of a divine metaphor such as "seeing," a semantic concept of metaphor allows us to highlight entailments from that domain while hiding others. It accomplishes all this without having to exhaustively define a predicate for which we do not know the mechanics. Thus, we can point to God's action, partially delineating its functions within a particular context, and thus derive a paradigm for human action within that context based upon the divine.[149]

Having looked at how metaphors derive and convey their meanings, we then turn to the issue of the direction of metaphorical transfer. The biblical text provides us with a model for this—the theomorphic portrayal of humanity. We shall look at the nature of this relationship and its implications for our exegesis of the text.

Finally, we provide a test case of anthropopoeisis—God's action—which is closely connected to His identity. We will focus upon divine sight, a term both prominent and significant in its import, and we will examine how our understanding of the theomorphic relationship and the metaphors that it utilizes play out in the biblical text. For reasons of space, as well as keeping close parallels in literary genre, we will limit this study to the book of Genesis, and to the proto-history (chp. 1–11) and Abrahamic narratives (12–25), focusing on instances of divine sight (Heb. *rā'ā*). We shall compare them with other applications of the same and related terms, human and non-human, noting how they comment on each other. What we hope to show is that by a proper understanding of the mechanics of a metaphor, we will be better able to discern the content and manner of their reference to God, both as truth-conditional propositions, and actions informed and shaped by the context of biblical narrative. This approach, based on a more flexible notion of the semantic domains of verbs and their applications, can provide a interpretive stance that is both more sensitive to the motifs, genre, and thrust of a given narrative, and more reflective of the biblical conception of the divine-human relationship.

---

149. We should note that there are verbs which are not applied to both God and humans, such as *bara'*, "to create" (Gen 1:1ff.). In such cases, the meaning of the verb is still derived from context, but there is no redefining of human usage based on relationship with the divine.

2

Approaching Divine Metaphors

IN THE PREVIOUS CHAPTER WE SAID THAT METAPHORS PROVIDE US WITH a manner of speaking of God that is neither too human in its univocity, too nebulous in equivocity, too ungrounded as with analogy, while being both functional and context-sensitive. We now take a closer look at how metaphors convey information, the type of information they bear, and their ability to make truth-conditional propositions. As we shall see, these factors directly impact subsequent interpretations of the Bible, including its descriptions of God.

Initially, we consider the manner in which metaphors convey meaning. For this we find the conceptual framing in Cognitive Linguistics and Conceptual Blending Theory most helpful. These theories outline the type of information we can expect to derive from a metaphors such as those found in anthropomorphic language, and how this is conveyed. However, we find that this theory is lacking in areas such as the effect of context, so we turn to the context-sensitive semantic approach to metaphor developed by Josef Stern.[1] Both his concepts of metaphorical character and *de re* metaphors assist us greatly in taking into consideration the unique contexts of anthropomorphic expressions as well as their transcendent target domain—God. Stern also helps us understand the truth-conditioned nature of statements metaphors are able to make, and hence the nature of the assertions anthropomorphic language can make of the deity.

---

1. Josef Stern is currently Professor in the Department of Philosophy and the Committee on Jewish Studies at the University of Chicago. His monographs include Stern, *Metaphor in Context* and *Problems and Parables of Law: Maimonides and Nahmanides on Reasons for the Commandments (ta'amei Ha-mitzvot)*.

How Metaphors Convey Meaning: Conceptual Domains

If biblical anthropomorphisms constitute metaphors in which human terms are applied to the divine, then it is important to understand how these metaphors function in order to understand what is being said of God. For much of Western history, metaphor had taken a cue from Aristotle's *Rhetoric*, in relegating metaphor as an ornament of speech which did not convey propositional truth. One of the first to challenge this notion was I. A. Richards.[2] He demonstrated in his "interanimation of words," that concepts in metaphors impinge upon one another to create new thoughts. Following Richards, Max Black developed an *interaction* theory of metaphor whereby the two subjects in a metaphor, the source and target concepts, transform each other. In his famous example, "Man is a wolf," the concept of man is made more savage, while wolf is somewhat personified. In so doing, he demonstrated that at least part of the metaphorical process was cognitive and not simply ornamental as Aristotle had contended. Black said, "Suppose we try to state cognitive content in 'plain language.' Up to a point we may succeed. . . . But the set of literal statements so obtained will not have the same power to inform and enlighten as the original. . . . [T]he loss in such cases is a loss in cognitive content. . . . [The plain language version] fails to be a translation because it fails to give the insight that the metaphor did."[3]

Initially driven by psychological research on cognitive processes, George Lakoff reconfigured metaphors as primarily *cognitive* rather than purely *linguistic* phenomena. That is, noting the similarities in subject area and meaning transfer in similar linguistic expressions of metaphors, he postulated that there are entire cognitive concepts around which humans organize meaning. "In the traditional view, linguistic meaning is divorced from the human conceptual system and encyclopedic knowledge that speakers of a language share."[4]

Lakoff and Johnson, however, approach definitions in a uniquely *experiential* manner. Whereas traditional definitions of objects or concepts are in terms of essential properties, cognitive linguists claim that their non-objectivist approach defines things by the manner in which they are encountered in typical human experience (e.g., in terms of birth/death, heat/cold, growth, gravitational orientation, movement, etc.). "On the

---

2. Richards, *The Philosophy of Rhetoric*.
3. Black, "Models and Metaphors," 46.
4. Kövecses, *Metaphor*, 200.

Approaching Divine Metaphors

standard objectivist view, we can understand (and hence define) an object entirely in terms of a *set* of its *inherent* properties. But, as we have just seen, at least some of the properties that characterize our concept of an object are *interactional*. In addition, the properties do not merely form a *set* but rather a *structured gestalt*, with dimensions that emerge naturally from our experience."[5] For example, though a "dog" can be traditionally defined in terms of its salient features, such as carnivorous, four-legged, barking, mammal, etc., some examples of dogs do not fit this mold, and yet are still readily recognized as dogs. Barkless Basenji, three-legged, or cartoon canines could still be recognized as dogs. So, for any given concept, these *experiential gestalts* are comprised not of a Tarskian[6] list of requisite defining characteristics, but of all *subjective* human experiences involving that concept. Lakoff claims that these conceptual gestalts (or *domains*) are then metaphorically applied to each other in order to understand one conceptual realm in terms of another.

Typically, these conceptual domains are viewed as empirically grounded in human sensory-motor experience. Empirically-grounded networks of meaning [source domain] are applied to more abstract networks of meaning, [target domain] creating a conceptual metaphor (which Lakoff denotes through the use of small caps). For example, in Lakoff's system, the saying, "to be *in love*" is metaphorical, whereas "the groceries are *in the bag*" is not. According to Lakoff, humans transfer the physical experience of 'being in' something to the abstract notion of love. This experience metaphorically lends structure to the more abstract experience of feelings such as "love."

Lakoff locates conceptual metaphors such as AN ABSTRACT CONCEPT IS A CONTAINER behind the metaphorical linguistic expression (e.g., being "in love"), controlling and guiding its formation and interpretation. He contrasts this with the traditional position which postulates homonymy when a single morpheme seems to have multiple meanings.

> Similarly, it would say that all of the concepts for *in* or *up* are not ways of understanding concepts partly in terms of spatial orientation but, rather, are independent concepts related by similarity. On this view, it would be an accident that most of the pairs of concepts that exhibit "similarities" happen to consist of one relatively concrete concept and one relatively abstract

---

5. Lakoff and Johnson, *Metaphors We Live By*, 122.

6. From, "The Concept of Truth in Formalized Languages," in Tarski, *Logic, Semantics, and Metamathematics*.

> concept. . . . In our account the concrete concept is being used to understand the more abstract concept; in theirs, there would be no reason for there to be more similarities between an abstract and a concrete concept than between two abstract concepts or two concrete concepts.[7]

Taking our case in point, that of God performing some act, Cognitive Linguists would assert that this is a case of people using the empirical human experience of the act to structure the abstract idea of the divine act. Pierre Van Hecke illustrates cognitive theory's approach with respect to biblical metaphors:

> The essence of metaphor, according to cognitive linguistics, is that we make use of our knowledge of one conceptual domain (the source) in order to gain new understanding of a second, non-related domain (the target). When we call God our shepherd, we thus make use of our knowledge of the conceptual domain of pastoralism to form our understanding of the relation between God and man. We do so by mapping the elements (e.g., "shepherd," "sheep") and relations (e.g., "to guard") from our source domain unto the target domain, with the purpose of structuring our knowledge of that target domain in a new and insightful manner.[8]

In contrast, Cognitive Linguists say that traditional, "definitions for a concept are seen as characterizing the things that are inherent in the concept itself. We, on the other hand, are concerned with how human beings get a handle on the concept—how they understand it and function in terms of it. Madness and journeys give us handles on the concept of love, and food gives us a handle on the concept of an idea."[9] That is, humans conceptually structure love in terms of being "madly in love" or ideas in terms of "digesting an idea." This is helpful for our understanding of anthropomorphic metaphors, in that instead of transferring a fixed definition of (human) repentance in its entirety onto God, only select elements of the "human" source domain of a term need to be transferred to the target domain of God. Hence, for Lakoff, God's repenting would not necessarily have required Him to have done something wrong, but could involve several of the other associations with the term, such as a change in His course of action.

7. Lakoff and Johnson, *Metaphors We Live By*, 112–13.
8. Van Hecke, "Conceptual Blending," 219.
9. Lakoff and Johnson, *Metaphors We Live By*, 116.

Metaphorical Processing

One of the important issues for anthropomorphic language is knowing which entailments are transferred from the human conceptual realm to the divine. William Croft and D. Alan Cruse observe the, "deceptively simple [problem] of how best to describe a particular metaphorical mapping."[10] They note that though Lakoff and Johnson (1980) observe "conceptual metaphors" such as AN ARGUMENT/THEORY IS A BUILDING behind linguistic metaphors such as "He built his argument on shaky ground, so it came tumbling down," or, "Her reasoning was well-founded," some metaphorical entailments would not fit this:

a. Is that the basement of your theory?
b. That line of reasoning has no plumbing.
c. This theory has French windows.[11]

Croft and Cruse feel this suggests, "That the metaphor should be formulated more concisely, that is, using less schematic source and target domains, in such a way that the metaphorical mapping is valid for the concepts in the source and target domains. Clausner and Croft propose the more specific formulation THE CONVINCINGNESS OF AN ARGUMENT IS THE STRUCTURAL INTEGRITY OF A BUILDING."[12] Clausner and Croft argue that this is more "productive" in that all expressions based on it function more fully in their entailments. Sometimes, too general a conceptual metaphor can be replaced with multiple specific ones.

Furthermore, one needs to determine which structure is retained between the two conceptual domains. In order to facilitate this, "Lakoff proposes the Invariance Hypothesis as a constraint on metaphorical mapping (Lakoff 1990:54): Invariance Hypothesis: Metaphorical mappings preserve the cognitive topology (that is, image-schematic structure) of the source domain."[13] Basically, this limits the number of metaphorical entailments one can apply to the target by keeping the structure and nature of the source intact. For example, we are able to describe a concept like life by applying to it the structure of a journey (having a beginning, middle, and an end), but though we can turn around and retrace steps in a journey, many life choices cannot be changed.[14] This hypothesis would basically

---

10. Croft and Cruse, *Cognitive Linguistics*, 198.
11. Ibid.
12. Ibid., 198–99.
13. Ibid., 201.
14. Kövecses, *Metaphor*, 103.

impact our anthropomorphic metaphors by stipulating that the structure of the human source domain would be retained when applying it to the divine.

While this is helpful, it raises questions concerning pre-existent structures in the target domain (in our case, God). However, there are also restrictions to metaphorical mappings that originate in the target. Turner proposes an important constraint on the Invariance Hypothesis: "In metaphor, we are constrained not to violate the image-schematic structure of the target; this entails that we are constrained not to violate whatever image-schematic structure may be possessed by non-image components of the target."[15] These restrictions serve to preserve important aspects of a target's structure. Croft and Cruse explain:

> Lakoff calls these "target domain overrides" (1993: 216), and illustrates them with *give a kick* and *give and idea*. When you give someone a kick, the person does not "have" the kick afterward, and when you give someone an idea, you still 'have' the idea. The target domain of transfer of energy or force does not allow that energy to continue to exist after the transmission event, hence that metaphorical entailment does not hold. Likewise, the target domain of knowledge does not imply that knowledge transmitted is lost: that metaphorical entailment does not hold either.[16]

Similarly, if one were to ascribe the idea of "walking" to God (Gen 3:8), God would not be "tired" afterwards, or have dirty feet, etc. Croft and Cruse observe that this creates some serious questions for the nature of conceptual metaphors and the mapping of their entailments and structures.

> The Invariance Hypothesis and the target domain override raise a fundamental issue about conceptual metaphors: why do they exist in the first place? If the target domain has image-schematic structure already, which can override the metaphor, then why do we have metaphors? Likewise, if we can isolate image-schematic structure, or construct highly schematic metaphors such as ORGANIZATION IS PHYSICAL STRUCTURE, is it not simply a highly schematic conceptual structure that is instantiated in both source and target domains? If so, then is it really a metaphorical mapping, or simply an instantiation of the image-schematic conceptual structure in two different cognitive domains? (This

---

15. Turner "Aspects of the invariance hypothesis." *Cognitive Linguistics* 1990, 1, 252, in Croft and Cruse, *Cognitive Linguistics*, 201.

16. Croft and Cruse, *Cognitive Linguistics*, 201.

latter view has been propounded by Glucksberg [2001] and Jackendoff and Aaron [1991:328–30].)[17]

Lakoff and Johnson, however, attempt to deal with this in two ways: incomplete structure in target domains, and asymmetry between source and target domains.

> Although target domains of metaphors are structured, they are not fully so: 'they are not clearly enough delineated in their own terms to satisfy the purposes of our day-to-day functioning' (Lakoff and Johnson 1980: 118). Thus, target domains lack at least some (image-schematic) structure. Lakoff and Johnson argue that the linking of otherwise independent conceptual domains by metaphor in fact *creates* similarity.[18]

For example, for the metaphor IDEAS ARE FOOD, "The concept of swallowing food is independent of the metaphor, but the concept of swallowing ideas arises only by virtue of the metaphor (Lakoff and Johnson 1980: 147–48)."[19]

In addition to structure, there is an issue with direction of metaphorical transfer. Lakoff defends the existence of conceptual metaphors based on his observation of, "an asymmetry between source domain and target domain. For example, love is expressed in terms of journeys, but journeys are not expressed in terms of love (Lakoff and Johnson 1980:108). If image-schematic structure were simply a highly schematic concept subsuming the corresponding concepts in the source and target domains, then one would expect metaphorical mappings to go in either direction; but they do not. Even when it appears that there is a bidirectional metaphorical mapping, Lakoff and Turner argue that the two mappings are different."[20] For example, PEOPLE ARE MACHINES tends to map the parts and breakability of machines, but for MACHINES ARE PEOPLE, it is the will and desire of humans that is mapped. Similarly, it might be argued that when God is being mapped as a person, it is will, desire, and purposes, personhood, etc., that is mapped, but not the selfishness, greed, violence, and finitude of humanity.

However, Croft and Cruse observe that, "These two counterarguments are persuasive; but they also imply that the Invariance Hypothesis

17. Croft and Cruse, *Cognitive Linguistics*, 201.
18. Ibid., 202.
19. Ibid.
20. Ibid.

and the target domain override captures only part of the nature of metaphorical mappings, and perhaps not the most important part."[21] For example,

> It is likely that a far richer structure than simply compatible image-schemas is brought into the target domain from the source domain. It also suggests that Lakoff and Johnson's first counterargument—the target domain lacks (image-schematic) structure that is added by the metaphorical mapping from the source domain—makes too sharp a distinction between target domain structure and mapped source domain structure. It implies a minimum of interaction between the target domain structure (already there) and the source domain structure (filling in for the absence of target domain structure). Instead, many metaphor theorists argue for a more interactive relationship between source and target domain structure, involving something like a "fusion" or "superimposition" of structure from both domains (Jackendoff and Aaron 1991:334; they also cite Black's [1979] "interaction" and Ricoeur's [1978] "reverberation"). Jackendoff and Aaron suggest that the source domain concepts are transformed as well in being metaphorically applied to the target domain (ibid.). It is this intuition that blending theory attempts to capture (see 8.3.3). This interactive relationship of course strengthens the first counter-argument: the metaphor brings much more than extra image-schematic structure to the target domain.[22]

This idea is important for interpreting anthropomorphic language because it stipulates that the metaphor is not simply unidirectional. We would not simply be reading human concepts *in toto* upon the divine. Rather, what is *lacking* in the target (divine) structure is filled in with material from that of the source (human) structure.

Conceptual-Blending Theory

A more recent development in Cognitive Linguistics seeks to ameliorate some of these pitfalls with regard to conceptual transfer is the Conceptual Blending Theory of Joseph E. Grady. The difference between it and the "classical" cognitive approach is that, "according to this 'blending' approach, metaphor cannot fully be understood if regarded as a simple

21. Ibid.
22. Ibid., 203.

mapping operation between two domains. Rather, in each metaphor, at least four spaces are at work. The two central spaces roughly correspond to the source and target domain as defined in the 'classical' cognitive theory. It is important to note that these 'spaces' are packets of conceptual knowledge, which may contain much more information than what is explicitly put into words in the metaphor."[23] These extra spaces are the "generic space" and the "blend." The generic space is where the common elements of the source and target are located. The more innovative space, however, is the blend, where entailments from both source and target interact and sometimes merge. Van Hecke explains its significance, "The reason for discerning this blend is the important observation that metaphorical expressions sometimes 'display emergent structure—that is, implications that don't appear to originate in either the source or target domain.'"[24]

Van Hecke illustrates,

> One of the standard examples in Blending Theory makes clear what is meant by these emergent implications. If we speak of "digging a financial grave," we relate the domain of GRAVEDIGGING to that of FINANCIAL (MIS)MANAGEMENT. The meaning and the implications of the metaphorical expression "digging a financial grave" are of a blended nature, however, and do not emerge directly from one of the two central input-spaces: digging a grave is usually a conscious and intentional activity, whereas digging your financial grave is not. Moreover, even though digging a grave does not cause death, digging your financial grave will eventually cause your financial "death." Examples like these show that metaphor can contain implications that pertain in none of the input spaces and only emerge in the course of the metaphorical process itself. For this reason, it is justified to define this new emergent structure as a separate blended space.[25]

Though this theory is more specific about the nature of the conceptual transfer than Cognitive Linguistics, there are some problems with it as well. Croft and Cruse note,

> One important factor that is missing from the BT account [Blending Theory of Grady et al., 1996] is . . . the openness of mapping

---

23. Van Hecke, "Conceptual Blending," 220.

24. Ibid., 221, citing S. Coulson, *Semantic Leaps. Frame-Shifts and Conceptual Blending in Meaning Construction*, Cambridge: Cambridge University, 2001.

25. Van Hecke, "Conceptual Blending," 221–22.

between the source and target domains: the correspondences simply cannot be enumerated. This point is well illustrated by ... "A myriad of ugly, dark thoughts clung to my reason and dug in with their claws." ... Perhaps the "seeing as" account of blending [Stern 1999] is the most illuminating suggested so far, except that it is not really explicit enough.[26]

Furthermore, there seem to be problems in determining which factors are chosen to "blend" in a metaphor. "The correspondences between domains in a novel metaphor are also subject to construal, and in a sense are created by the metaphor, rather than being preexisting. This aspect of novel metaphor is not recognized in either CMT [Conceptual Metaphor Theory—Lakoff] or BT [Blending Theory—Grady et al. 1996]. There is an element of context sensitivity in the BT model, in that the features that enter into the input spaces are constructed on-line. However, no account of how the features are selected is offered."[27] Hence, the random selection of features tends to weaken the impact of Cognitive linguistics as a truth indicator, and emphasize its relativity and arbitrary nature.

Summary

How does Cognitive Linguistics inform our approach to anthropomorphic language? First, by denying Tarskian "list" models for the designation of an object, they have opened the way to viewing God not against a theologically defined set of truth-conditions, such as "omniscient, impassible, etc.," but as how He was humanly experienced. Secondly, Cognitive Linguistics conceives of metaphors as the interaction of entire conceptual domains consisting of all human relationships to the term, rather than literary definitions. All or part of one conceptual domain may be highlighted and other parts hidden. Hence, in applying typically "human" concepts to the divine, the more corporeal aspects can be hidden while other more functional aspects are highlighted.

Though Cognitive Linguistics provides helpful understandings of conceptual schemas as the proper content of individual terms, we have found its approach ultimately unsatisfying. It lacks specification on which structures to retain in the source and target. Furthermore, because it is a cognitive theory, it fails to address the issue of context. Though Conceptual

---

26. Croft and Cruse, *Cognitive Linguistics*, 209.
27. Ibid.

Blending adds an element of this, it too is unable to specify which elements should be blended or to what degree.

However, we are still left with the problem of determining what the language does say. Equipped with the conceptual domains rather than Tarskian definitions of words, we will seek to look at how metaphors are used in context. To help with this program, we turn to an approach that emphasizes the influence of context on transferred entailments. As Croft and Cruse note,

> Stern (1999) makes the lack of context sensitivity the major plank of his critique of Lakoff. He argues that the aspects of a source domain that are relevant to a target domain are heavily dependent not only on the domains themselves, but on the whole context of the utterance, even of the discourse, and that any model that depends on fixed structures in the mind is doomed to failure. He points out that every context structures domains that are invoked in it in a characteristic way, in terms of what is salient and what is backgrounded, patterns of inference, and expressive or attitudinal factors.[28]

As we will see, Josef Stern's approach is also primarily referential, but it contains semantic, and thus propositional content, allowing biblical metaphors to be truth-conditional statements about God.

Armed with the understanding of metaphors as the transfer of conceptual domains, we are able to see how human conceptual areas might transfer to the divine, despite their ontological differences. Metaphors highlight some entailments and hide others, which could be employed to emphasize functional elements and cover issues of non-corporeality in God. However, we now turn toward the issue of metaphorical determination. In what way shall we determine whether or not a given assertion about the deity is metaphorical or literal?

Metaphorical Determination

This raises the question of discerning whether or not a particular expression is a metaphor. Croft and Cruse, for example, take issue with Lakoff et al's view of metaphor recognition. "Lakoff is very much against the view that an essential property of a metaphorical expression is deviance. Basically, Lakoff asks how something so widespread and natural as metaphor

28. Ibid., 210.

can possibly be described as deviant."[29] Rather, Lakoff, in viewing metaphors as reflective of human cognitive processes rather than literary functions, sees metaphors inherent in nearly any abstract concept. However, contrary to Lakoff's contentions, Croft and Cruse distinguish between the pragmatic *use* of a metaphor, which is indeed a normal practice, and the interpretive strategy required by them, which 'deviates' from that of literal language. They conclude, "It is not obvious how a metaphor can function if there is nothing perceptibly odd whatsoever about its literal construal (Eco 1996 gives a concise account of this argument)."[30]

However, though many commentators determine metaphoricity simply on the basis of a *failed* literal reading, Stern argues that this too, cannot be the case, for there are many twice-true metaphors, such as "no man is an island," which are true both literally and metaphorically. Furthermore, the knowledge that a statement is a metaphor does not tell us how it functions. For instance, he cites the metaphors, 'Juliet is the sun," and "Achilles is the sun." Each contains the same structure and failed literal reading, neither of which determine the nature of the metaphor. Namely, the sun could refer to Juliet as an object of worship, a source of light and strength, etc., while for Achilles, it might speak of his ferocity in battle. Rather, along with Davidson, Stern finds that metaphorical meaning and use are two different entities.

For Stern this "knowledge *that*" metaphor is not well-defined, partly because it is not solely semantic—it is also pragmatic. "On my view, recognition of a metaphor—the knowledge *that* an utterance is to be interpreted metaphorically—is a matter of recognizing that an utterance is a token of one rather than another type, where the types are individuated (in part) by their respective meanings (or characters)."[31] In short, one must know the possible types of semantic tokens an expression can have and then the context of usage determines which type it is, whether literal, metaphorical, and what part of the expression is metaphorical. In the end, Stern defines metaphors in terms of context-dependency. "This is the sense in which that content is *literal—of the letter*: of the word in isolation from its containing schema or context. Literal meaning is atomistic, unlike metaphorical interpretation, which, if not holistic, always depends on its containing context."[32]

29. Ibid., 206.
30. Croft and Cruse, *Cognitive Linguistics*, 207.
31. Stern, *Metaphor in Context*, 245.
32. Ibid., 317.

Approaching Divine Metaphors

Secondly, deciding whether or not something is indeed metaphorical not only considers initial, failed, *prima facie* readings of an expression, but involves balancing several factors and a discernment of the *best* interpretation. Stern illustrates this with several statements that could be taken either literally or metaphorically, and can work either way, often with an intention to be taken literally.

> Consider Lakoff et al.'s examples of the non-metaphorical: *sentences* (.e., types) such as "the balloon went up" or "the cat is on the mat." Yet it is obvious that even these "literal" sentences or expressions can, in some context with a little imagination, be used metaphorically. T. S. Eliot might have continued his famous depiction of fog as a cat with "the cat is on the mat" or we might summarize the impact of a stock market run on a vulnerable economy with "the balloon went up."[33]

He concludes, "Contra Lakoff et al., there are no *expressions* (types) per se that are either metaphorical or nonmetaphorical."[34] Rather, it is all in how they are *used*.

Hence, in our approach to anthropomorphic language, we must pay attention to the use of these terms rather than the simple "literal" meanings. In our case, divine usage of "human" terms generally necessitates a metaphorical reading more on the basis of a lack of perceived structure within the divine realm, requiring this to be supplemented from the human conceptual domain of the term in question.

One advantage of seeing metaphors as particular usages of expressions is that it looks at the greater context in which a statement is placed to determine its usage. There may be times when, in say, the context of the naming of a newly discovered solar system whose star was dubbed "Juliet," that "Juliet is the sun" could be quite literal. The advantage of Stern's system is not only that metaphors are seen pragmatically and not atomistically, but also, their continuity between contexts can be observed. Stern explains how metaphorical meaning can change from context to context through the concept of metaphorical character.

Context Sensitivity and Metaphorical Character

Upon determining that an expression is indeed metaphorical, it is necessary to determine its meaning. This problem can be illustrated by

33. Ibid., 179.
34. Ibid.

examining a Cognitive Linguistic interpretation of a biblical passage. Zoltan Kövecses sees conceptual metaphors as the mechanism behind dream interpretation in the Bible.

> How was Joseph able to interpret the dream [of Pharaoh in Genesis 41]? How did he know that it was about years and time? The reason is that he was aware of a metaphor that has been with us ever since biblical times: TIMES ARE MOVING OBJECTS . . . ACHIEVING A PURPOSE IS EATING. This explains why we have cows and ears of corn in the dream. These were typical foods eaten at the time. Finally, Joseph relied on the metaphor RESOURCES ARE FOOD. By combining these conceptual metaphors, Joseph could arrive at the correct interpretation. What this example shows is that much of the interpretation of dreams depends on everyday conceptual metaphors. In other words, dreams realize particular combinations of metaphors.[35]

As this example demonstrates, there are some other pitfalls in applying a cognitive linguistic program to biblical exegesis, primarily in the area of context sensitivity. Kövecses seems to overlook the biblical explanation, that it was God who specifically enabled Joseph to interpret the dream correctly, rather than being simply a natural human cognitive process. (Gen 41:16, 25) If this was merely a matter of natural human cognition, how did Joseph know these were the same event described twice, rather than two separate famines? How did he know to use those particular conceptual metaphors? What Kövecses ignores is not how humans conceptualize as with the interpretation of time and resources, but how these are being used. Here, they are used not to interpret the dream itself, but to explicate the interpretation.

Josef Stern provides us with a contextually-sensitive approach to determine the meaning of metaphors. Primarily, he sees them as functioning similarly to demonstratives, i.e., as elements of utterances within a communicative event. Demonstratives such as "this" or "that" are words whose meaning is not determined lexically, but by the context of their utterance. Assuming the purpose of the utterance is to communicate, the metaphor is therefore infused with this purpose. To accomplish this, he adopts David Kaplan's distinction between the *character* and *content* of a demonstrative and applies it to metaphors.

> Content is (roughly) what we have been calling the interpretation of a metaphor: what the metaphor says, its propositional

---

35. Kövecses, *Metaphor*, 61.

component, or truth-condition(al factor). So, just as the content of a (singular) demonstrative is an object or individual, the content of a (predicative) metaphor is (something like) a property. Character roughly corresponds to the (linguistic) meaning of an expression: a rule known by speakers as part of their linguistic competence that determines the content of the expression in each context of utterance (like the rule for "I" that each of its utterances has its individual utterer as its content). Both demonstratives and metaphors have *nonconstant* characters: characters that determine different contents in different contexts.[36]

On Stern's account, a "metaphorical meaning," "is the rule that determines its content for each context, that is, its character."[37] Following Max Black[38] and Paul Ricoeur,[39] the unit of such "metaphorical meanings" is a whole sentence and like Lakoff, it involves entire conceptual networks rather than singular definitions. "But none of this changes the fact that *what* is interpreted metaphorically in a context may be a proper constituent within the sentence."[40] In other words, Stern is arguing for a *semantic* interpretation of metaphor, or one where the metaphorical interpretation *depends* on the literal.

> But metaphor does not fit neatly into the standard classification of ambiguities, which suggests that a metaphorical interpretation is not *simply* an additional sense of an ambiguous expression. Consider the *idiosyncratic* ambiguity exemplified by words like "ear" (used of corn and of the bodily organ) or "corn" (used of the vegetable and the growth on the foot). Their different senses are mutually independent in that knowledge of one does not require knowledge of the other, whereas knowledge of the metaphorical interpretation(s) of an expression does require knowledge of its literal interpretation (in whatever exact way).[41]

---

36. Ibid., 16.
37. Ibid.
38. See Max Black, *Models and Metaphors*.
39. Ricoeur says, "It is as syntagma that the metaphorical statement must be considered if it is true that the meaning-effect results from a certain interaction of the words within the sentence." Ricoeur, *Rule of Metaphor*, 76. By this, he means that the semantic influence of other words in the sentence upon each other dictate that only as a conceptual unit, the sentence, can a metaphor be evaluated and understood.
40. Stern, *Metaphor in Context*, 22.
41. Ibid., 74.

Stern approaches this by dividing a metaphor into two parts: its character and its content. "The character of a metaphor is nonconstant,"[42] which means it determines different *contents* according to its varying contexts. Just as the indexical "I" has different referents depending on who utters it, so metaphors vary in their content according to their context.

Stern designates this relationship between a metaphor's character and its particular content in a given context as "Mthat[Φ]." "Mthat" represents the non-constant character of the metaphor, which functions similarly to the rule for the indexical "I" mentioned above. The variable "Φ" denotes the (specific) metaphorically interpreted expression in a given context. To continue with Stern's analogy with indexicals, in the context of Jesus saying, "I thirst," the content of the indexical "I" is determined to be Jesus. The meaning of "I" without this context is more like a principle of "the one speaking." Similarly, Stern claims that the "character of 'Mthat[Φ]' is a function from the set of contexts (or the set of relevant contextual parameters) to a set of (sets of) properties rather than to a set of individuals."[43] For Stern, this 'knowledge *of*' metaphor is the "specifically semantic competence that underlies our ability to interpret a metaphor."[44] So, just as we know how the indexical "I" functions so that we can understand its specific content in a particular usage, so too, metaphors have a rule of "character" that determines how they will function, what they can entail, and how they will refer in a given instance. That is, we establish the character of a metaphor semantically and the content of a metaphor contextually. The particular instantiation of a metaphor is determined from the text, but how the character of the metaphor functions is dependent on its potential contexts of use, including the particular application to which it is made. The "meaning" of a metaphor is a set of rules about its application which, considered on its own, is non-constant (like the rule for the indexical "I" which refers to an undetermined speaker), but in any given instance contains specific truth-conditional propositions.[45]

The difference between a metaphor and its metaphorical character can be seen in comparing two statements which have the same referent, but refer to it differently. Frege uses the example of the "morning star" and the "evening star." Both refer to the planet Venus, but the manner in which

42. Ibid., 105.
43. Ibid., 107.
44. Ibid.
45. Similarly, the indexical becomes determined when we know the speaker, such as the case, "*John* said, 'I am here.'"

Approaching Divine Metaphors

they refer is different. He calls the manner in which one refers to an object as the "sense." Ricoeur expounds on this saying, "a referent may have many senses, but a sense only one referent, hence, 'the reference of 'evening star' would be the same as that of 'morning star,' but not the sense.'"[46] This manner of referring is represented by Stern's 'metaphorical character.' It is this sort of information which Stern argues is missing from a literal paraphrase of a metaphor's content. Though we might say, "Phil is an eel," can be summarized by the statement, "Phil is stealthy," the character of the metaphorical statement Mthat ["is an eel"] is missing from the paraphrase "is stealthy."[47] It is this frame of reference the metaphor gives to any given content (e.g., Phil, or John, or Sue) in a given context which consists of the metaphorical meaning.

God Seeing

Let us illustrate Stern's approach using our test case of divine "seeing." As divine character presumes both omniscience and an epistemology not requisite of physical visual apparatus or stimulus, Stern would find this statement to be a metaphorical usage.[48] Stern would formulate the statement, "God 'sees' X," as, "God Mthat['sees'] X," indicating that "sees" has a metaphorical character that changes with its given context. Thus, we cannot interpret this as meaning something like, "God is cognizant," for this reductive "paraphrase" misses the *character*-istic information being given in the statement. The metaphorical usage of "seeing" (Heb. *r'h*) may connote many other things besides cognition, including affirming worth, attending something or someone, witnessing, discerning guilt, etc. The particular content of the metaphor is then determined by the specific context of the utterance, "God sees X." Thus, Stern establishes a flexible (non-constant) rule in which metaphors are interpreted according to their respective contexts, and not as *quid-pro-quo* substitutions for literal statements.[49]

---

46. Ricoeur, *Rule of Metaphor*, 217.
47. Stern, *Metaphor in Context*, 274.
48. This is his 'knowledge *that*' metaphor. Stern, *Metaphor in Context*, 3.
49. Incidentally, neither could a metaphor be substituted for a literal statement in a specific literary context. This is because it includes a metaphorical means of referral, which invariably includes more information than a literal statement. As with Stern's example of Phil on the previous page, to call him an "eel" instead of just "stealthy" puts a pejorative slant on Phil's behavior.

Truth-Conditionedness

Stern's program not only addresses context sensitivity in determining metaphors and their meanings, but also their ability to convey truth. Because it has commonly been understood that they cannot be replaced by a single literal statement, it has often been concluded that metaphors cannot make identifiable propositions upon which truth or falsity can be determined.

This aspect of metaphors is essential to our study of anthropomorphic language. Although we have founded the ability of biblical texts to reference the transcendent deity upon Wolterstorff's divine speech acts, we still must understand the nature of the human speech being appropriated. Only upon determining whether or not a given anthropomorphic expression can make a claim about God, can we know what it is God then asserts of Himself.

Hence, we shall now examine both the implications of irreducibility, and a common confusion between the literal and actual.

Irreducibility

In *The Language of Symbolism: Biblical Theology, Semantics and Exegesis*, Pierre Grelot casts biblical anthropomorphic statements as a reflection of a particular doctrinal view. For example, he says,

> It is self-evident to suggest that God "sees," but even this is actually an understatement, since God, by his very nature, sees everything, unlike the idols, who "have eyes but do not see," in the words of the classic taunt that appears in Ps 115:5 and elsewhere. Nevertheless, the ancient biblical traditions make use of this verb as an anthropomorphism to highlight God's omniscience. Thus we read in Gen 11:5, God "came down to see" what people were doing in building the tower of Babel (cf. Gen 18:21). We encounter the same thing in some of the stories in Exodus (e.g., Exod 2:25; 3:7, 9; 4:31). In other cases, God himself says, "I have seen this people" (Deut 9:13). The psalmists frequently implore God to see their condition: although we usually translate the underlying Hebrew word as "consider" in these contexts, it is the same verb *ra'ah*: "See my affliction and my trouble" (Ps 25:18).[50]

However, Grelot's conclusions are less than self-evident. For example, in his own example of Psalm 25, "see" does not highlight God's omniscience.

---

50. Grelot, *The Language of Symbolism*, 152–53.

Approaching Divine Metaphors

If it did, there would be no need to use it in the imperative. It would simply be a fact, "*You see* my affliction . . ." Rather, in this instance, it is a plea for God's attention and care for the Psalmist, which fact must at least *seem* in doubt. In another passage he cites, Gen 18:20–21, omniscience is far from view:

And the LORD said,

> The outcry of Sodom and Gomorrah is indeed great, and their sin is very serious. I will go down now, and see if they have all done according to its outcry, which has come to Me; and if not, I will know.

On the surface, this usage actually seems to contradict God's omniscience! What it highlights, as will be discussed later, is God's legal function as a witness. Grelot's conclusions exemplify the problem of trying to reduce metaphors to a single literal statement, and that across its many usages.

But if a metaphor has infinite potential "meanings," how can it be a truth-conditional statement? With incalculable numbers of entailments mappable from the source domain to the target domain, there would seem to be no discernible content upon which to make a truth-valued judgment. Returning to Max Black's example "Man is a wolf," because "wolf" can have various entailments such as viciousness, pack-mentality, wildness, hunting, and so on. It becomes impossible to say specifically what is being asserted, and thus assigned a truth-value, (i.e., to say whether the statement is true or false). The accusation against semantic theories of metaphor such as Stern's is that if metaphor is a linguistic phenomenon, it is difficult to see how it can contain truth-conditional meaning and not simply poetic flourish.

Stern counters that the problem lies in misreading of these open-ended lists of metaphorical entailments. "What the 'and so on' signals is a *potential* for a different or additional interpretation that, by hypothesis, no *actual* interpretation can capture or exhaust."[51] He demonstrates how, though a given metaphor might have infinite number of interpretations,

> *in* each respective context, the interpretation, or content, of the metaphor is finite and fixed. The conditions under which the utterance is true or false in that context are determinate and finite. If we know the context set and our literal vocabulary is rich enough, it even ought to be possible for us to state the content

---

51. Stern, *Metaphor in Context*, 269.

finitistically.⁵² Hence this kind of limitlessness of metaphorical interpretation neither conflicts with the finitistic requirements of a semantics (as Davidson seems to argue)⁵³ nor requires a different kind of truth or content sui generis to metaphor (as Cavell suggests).⁵⁴

Furthermore, "the *appearance* is that utterances containing metaphors, no different from exclusively literal utterances, make assertions that are judged true or false. But if they are truth-valued, they must have truth-conditions or content. The burden of argument therefore falls on those who deny that this appearance is reality."⁵⁵

Stern explains the misconception that irreducible metaphors cannot be truth-conditional,

> The fallacy in the argument is, of course, its assumption that all propositional content must be *fully* conceptualized, if it is conceptual at all. In referential propositions, the constituent corresponding to a metaphor may be a bare property for which the speaker possesses no fully conceptualized representation. Nonetheless there is definite reference to, or expression of, the property, and there should be a fact of the matter whether *that* property is true of God, even though we may not *know* whether it is.⁵⁶

Stern argues that, "given the transcendence of the deity, . . . we can't really fully understand the nature of those divine properties."⁵⁷ He concludes that, "propositions about divine properties are, then, paradigms of beliefs or thoughts that we incompletely understand, (or even completely fail to understand), that is, of not fully conceptualized beliefs or thoughts. Nonetheless, through the context-sensitive mechanisms of metaphor, we can 'point' to those properties despite our conceptual deficiencies."⁵⁸

Stern calls these incompletely defined properties, *de re* propositions. These are, "properties that, despite our lack of concepts, theologians appear to believe we can identify or reidentify (if only in context) on

---

52. I.e., in finite terms.

53. Davidson argues that metaphors only have their literal meaning. This is why they are deemed to have a truth-conditional factor, but that, for him, is always false.

54. Stern, *Metaphor in Context*, 268–69.

55. Ibid., 132–33.

56. Ibid., 193.

57. Ibid., 194.

58. Ibid.

Approaching Divine Metaphors

different occasions."⁵⁹ In other words, metaphors, like demonstratives, can contain reference to properties that cannot be fully articulated by language used literally. Still, they bear truth-conditional content discernible within context. Stern exemplifies this with the issue of God's seeing:

> Although divine properties are properties true of God, not all metaphorically expressed propositions containing divine properties need be propositions *about* God. Consider the biblical verse, "There will you worship gods made by human hands out of wood and stone, gods that neither see nor hear, neither eat nor smell" (Deut 4,29) [*sic*- 4,28].⁶⁰ Although this verse is true under its literal interpretation, the great medieval Jewish Talmudist, mystic, and biblical commentator R. Moses Nahmanides argued that what are denied of the false gods in this verse—that is, the properties expressed by "seeing," "hearing," and "eating"— are the properties expressed by these predicates when they are interpreted metaphorically as applied to God, say, in a sentence like "God sees" or "God eats [your sacrificial offerings]." For Nahmanides, then, we can meaningfully speak of the *same* property truly attributed to God and denied of false gods. But such a divine property is not purely conceptualized, not fully understood, and it is assumed that there is no literal expression for it. To generate the proposition, we need, then a context of interpretation in which we hold certain presuppositions about God, even though the (negated atomic) proposition itself predicates the divine property of something other than God.⁶¹

Stern later expresses the fact that metaphors can carry this *de re* knowledge of underdeveloped concepts to imply more knowledge, in this case of God, and to restrict its discovery to those who seek it (As with parables, Matt 13:10–11). "In sum: The specifically contextual orientation of a metaphor enables it both to extend our powers of expression and to restrict the reception of their contents."⁶²

Consequently, we see that these metaphorical usages of "sight" still represent truth-conditional events. God either did or did not see that His creation was good, or that Noah was righteous. This is where Stern's method is helpful. Whilst pointing to an event or a state-of-affairs in

---

59. Ibid.
60. Thanks to my friend Gary Hoag for this correction of Stern's reference.
61. Stern, *Metaphor in Context*, 194.
62. Ibid., 196.

the manner of demonstratives, Stern's conception of metaphor does not require a fully-detailed explanation of what is referenced by a metaphor. Hence, a biblical metaphor such as 'seeing' can point to a transcendent divine attribute without explaining its mechanisms.

Literal vs. Actual

Stern illustrates a common misconception that often causes metaphors to be assumed as non-truth-conditional statements. "Some writers take 'literally' to mean actually,' and then use this assumption to argue that metaphors, not being literally true, are also not (indeed cannot be) actually true."[63] However, Stern explains, "what is 'actually' true is simply a proposition that is true in the actual world, namely, the circumstances of the context in which the utterance is performed. Contraries of the actual are the merely possible and the contrafactual."[64] In contrast with this, "The distinction between the metaphorical and the literal, on the other hand, is a distinction between two kinds of interpretations or uses of language, not between kinds of truth, or between the circumstances in which what is said is true or false."[65] Hence, metaphors should be approached as a mode of expression that can still convey truth-conditioned propositional statements. Thus, the difference between the literal and metaphorical is not whether they refer to actual states of being or realities, but *how* they refer.

This distinction between literal and real is the main problem with an approach such as David Aaron's. Aaron contends that phrases like God is sun, God is army, and God is shield are not metaphorical. This is because, "(1) *real* actions, not figurative ones, are required of God as established by the context; and (2) there is no incongruity or anomaly implied by the predicational statements. While the appositional phrases do not convey ontological identity via reductionism, ontological identity is *not* the only alternative we have to metaphorical meaning."[66] He assumes that because these expressions represent real actions they must be literal. This confusion leads him to develop a compromised approach he calls 'functional ascription' which predicates the function of the metaphor, but not the ontological implications of the statement taken literally. However, this solution only attempts to do on a limited scale what metaphors do, even

63. Ibid., 304.
64. Ibid.
65. Ibid.
66. Aaron, *Biblical Ambiguities*, 59.

as statements of what is actual—highlight and transfer some entailments from the source concept to the target, whilst hiding others.

While Aaron conflates the nature of referring statement with the reality of its referent, He nonetheless makes a relevant point—metaphorical concepts such as "God is shield," though untrue in a literal sense (God is not a piece of wood/metal with a handle), are true in what they assert through the medium of the metaphor—that God actually protects people from insults and even physical attacks of His people's enemies.

We have seen that like literal statements, metaphors can make truth-conditional assertions, only in a different manner. Although metaphors allow for many different entailments, each instantiation of a metaphor is limited by its context and given specific content. It is this content which is asserted as true or false, even though the same metaphor has many other potential meanings in other contexts. In the following chapters, we will proceed to examine how this works out in biblical contexts.

Conclusion

We have sought to answer several questions regarding biblical anthropomorphic language, including whether or not it constitutes metaphorical language, how it might function to ascribe things to a transcendent being, and its capacity to make truth-claims. Van Hecke explains the benefit of Cognitive Linguistics as the idea of the interaction of conceptual domains. "Cognitive linguistics has convincingly argued that metaphor is not the substitution of one word for another, but the interaction between conceptual units (domains or spaces). For the analysis of biblical metaphor, this means that in order to understand a metaphor, one should gain insight in these conceptual structures with their constituent elements and relations."[67] This approach both augments the amount of data that metaphors can ascribe to God, as well as allowing elements of a particular concept to remain hidden and essentially unapplied to God. The most obvious benefit here is to allow the corporeal elements of a metaphorical source domain to remain "hidden" with respect to their divine target.

However, as we have seen, this process must be informed by context. Under Stern's conception of metaphors, the object (in this case, "seeing") is pointed to without being exhaustively defined or explained. The effect of this is that there is some reality about God or His actions to which these metaphors point, but which is not reducible to literal paraphrases. Rather,

---

67. Van Hecke, "Conceptual Blending," 230.

metaphors describe how God uses sight in a given situation. They have a metaphorical character Mthat "sees" [Φ], which is God's seeing in instance [Φ]. That is, God's seeing becomes a function of the context of that particular occasion, rather than a statically defined expression. It can mean different things in each context, though all limited by its character. In one situation, it may indicate a judgment, or an act of valuation, whereas in another it may refer simply to affirmation or awareness. In no instance is this exhaustively defined, nor its mechanics described, but the act is designated, nonetheless.

Finally, these expressions point to divine realities through distinct usages of familiar terms, which are undefined as to their mechanisms. This, however, by no means denigrates their ability to reference reality. As Croft and Cruse put it, "In short, the ordinary appearance is that utterances of sentences that contain metaphors are truth-valued, express propositions, and can be used to make assertions (or other speech acts that presuppose assertion)."[68]

One element of metaphorical workings that we did not conclude is the direction of conceptual transfer. We discussed how there needed to be restraints upon which structures, the source or the target's, were allowed to guide the entailments which then constitute the meaning of the metaphor. In our present case, this is the issue of whether the human structure of a given predicate would govern the entailments being applied to God, or whether divine structures would govern this process. It is this issue which constitutes our next chapter.

---

68. Croft and Cruse, *Cognitive Linguistics*, 24.

3

Theomorphism

At this point, it is important to note how the problem of direction of transference within a metaphor impacts anthropomorphic language. Whilst the theories of Lakoff and Grady propose a transference from the source to the target domain, in biblical anthropomorphic language it becomes difficult to discern which is which. The traditional approach involved a transfer of human concepts to the divine, often resulting in either a mundane univocity, or a need for accommodating the language to the point of rendering it equivocal with respect to the divine. But, as we have seen, this need not be the case. In this chapter, we turn to a point of biblical theology to inform our linguistic approach to the process of interpreting biblical metaphors. We shall examine the biblical basis for this claim, the divine-human relationship itself, the nature of primary and secondary senses of a term, and how this informs our method for interpreting human language when applied to God.

In his magisterial theology, Gerhard von Rad observes a critical concept concerning the direction of allusion in metaphors within the Hebrew Bible. He says,

> Israel conceived even Jahweh himself as having human form. But the way of putting it which we use runs in precisely the wrong direction according to Old Testament ideas, for, according to the ideas of Jahwism, it cannot be said that Israel regarded God anthropomorphically, but the reverse, that she considered man as theomorphic.[1]

Oddly, the implications of this idea, though picked up by several subsequent writers, such as Abraham Heschel and Brevard Childs, have rarely been carried through in Old Testament theology or the philosophy of religious language. They are at least two-fold, respecting humanity and deity.

---

1. Von Rad, *Old Testament Theology*, 145.

With the former, as has been observed, humans are derived from and defined in terms of the divine. "Rather than accommodating God to the level of the human or raising human characteristics to the nth degree, the human is seen to be fashioned in the likeness of God. Hence, the human is seen in theomorphic terms, rather than God in anthropomorphic terms."[2]

As to the latter, the fact that man is described in *theomorphic* language, has repercussions for understanding the actions and traits ascribed to God. Centuries earlier, Aquinas noted, "Our knowledge of God is derived from the perfections which flow from him to creatures, which perfections are in God in a more eminent way than in creatures."[3] For example, as Abraham Heschel notes, "God's unconditional concern for justice is not an anthropomorphism. Rather, man's concern for justice is a theomorphism. Human reason, a feeble reflection, reminder, and intimation of the infinite wisdom deciphered in God's creation, is not the form after which our concept of God's wisdom is modeled."[4] Thus, the fact that humans are created as the image of God, provides an ontological basis for understanding a transcendent and otherwise incomprehensible being. This, however, leaves us with the question of how to understand divine attributes and in turn, human ones. In the next section, we take a look at the relationship between how God and humans are described in the Bible.

Natural Versus Supernatural Traits

Instead of extrapolating from known human nature, i.e., casting God as human-like but to the nth degree,[5] humans are described as essentially, very God-like (Gen 1:26; 3:22; 11:6; Pss 8:5; 82:6). The differences stem initially from their created status, as they are not everlasting or imbued with the same creative powers as God. However, many of the differences are primarily reflections of human transgression against the divine.[6]

---

2. Ibid., 11.
3. Aquinas, *Summa Theologica*, 1.q.1 3a. 3.
4. Heschel, *The Prophets*, II, 51–52.
5. The *via eminentia*, seeks to understand divine virtues as primary, and not derived from their human namesakes.
6. This is not to impute human finitude and brokenness to God, for God is also described as never sinning (Deut 32:4) and often in infinite terms (e.g., the everlasting God, Gen 21:33).

Humans abilities are curtailed, in terms of lifespan, language, and access to the divine, and thus become even further limited in scope and authority.[7]

While God's traits may not derive from human characteristics, they need not mute "anthropomorphic" expressions of Him and His activity either. He is bound neither by the finite human usage of these terms nor His infinite nature, for He is free to act in any manner—divine or human—as he desires. Not only should He not be limited by human uses of these terms, but neither should our idea of the difference between God and man be based on a *human* idea of perfection.[8] Heschel acknowledges, "Sight, because of its being a faculty of man, is not to be denied to God. Yet, there is an absolute difference between the sight and the thought of God and the sight and the thought of man," which essentially gives, "new meaning to borrowed words. The prophets had to use anthropomorphic language in order to convey His nonanthropomorphic Being."[9] In other words, human

---

7. Humanity was barred from the intimate fellowship with God in the garden (3:22–23), had their lifespan curtailed (Gen 6:3), and became "confused" (Heb. *bālal*) in their languages. All of these things happened in response to sin, but reflect the innate power residing in humanity which needed to be curbed lest it be used to bring about even greater destruction and independence from God. Some of the results of the sin affect humanities' relationship with creation as well as the Creator. Consider, for example, what Adam might have been able to do agriculturally, before the ground was "cursed" on account of his "fall" (Gen 3:17). Cain too, was cursed such that the ground would no longer yield its fruit to him (Gen 4:12).

8. However, this does not mean God is not perfect at all as His work and His law are said to be so (*tammîm*), implying their source is as well. My thanks to Professor Gordon Wenham for this insight. Heschel's point here is to note that the conception of perfection often predicated of God (i.e., that He does not "act" or "feel") is not necessarily a biblical one. For example, Thomas Weinandy generally argues that God is "Pure Act." Weinandy, *Does God Suffer?* That is, His *esse* and *essentia*, or Being and Essence are one and the same, as opposed to humans, whose being is different from their relations/actions. God *is* one pure act of love towards the world which is mitigated by human stances toward Him. If they rebel, they experience that love as wrath, if they obey, as blessing. This model becomes problematic, however, with issues of mercy, where a human deserves wrath, but God expresses mercy instead. The experience of God by the human in these cases is not dictated by the human's stance, but by God's sovereign choice. This choice is not automatic, however, for He does not show mercy *carte blanche*. Rather, He says, "I will be gracious to whom I will be gracious, and I will show compassion upon whom I will show compassion" (Exod 33:19). Hence, the model of divine perfection entailing divine simplicity (that God has no parts) seems to contradict the presentation of His actions in Scripture, where they are not shaped solely by human action. Furthermore, it seems illogical to us to construe attributes such as goodness, justice, love, etc., as the same, or that the divine Being is the same as His acting, and hence we opt for a model we find more consonant with His representation in the biblical texts—that He is an Agent distinct from His individual acts.

9. Heschel, *The Prophets, II*, 56.

faculties are not necessarily inapplicable to the divine. Rather, the divine attribute is distinct from the human. However, as we shall see, there is more continuity than Heschel indicates in the idea of transferability of these characteristics.

Notably, God is not being defined in human terms, but giving new meaning to the terms themselves. It is not that God cannot see, because that is a human thing to do, but rather that He sees in a more profound way—and one in which He can enable humans to do as well. For these purposes then, it is better to distinguish between "natural" and "supernatural" senses of anthropomorphic metaphors such as "seeing," rather than "divine" and "human." Though God may not see as a man sees (Job 10:4; 1 Sam 16:7), this doesn't mean He abdicates the act of seeing altogether in light of an infinite attribute such as omniscience. His seeing is more than a facade of "personality" on a faceless philosophical entity. Rather, acts such as "seeing" are His prerogative[10] and the intentional exercising of His faculties in relationship to mankind. They are also commensurate with His nature as a God who sees and hears (Gen 16:11, 13; 22:14). As Goldingay observed, the very acts of hearing or seeing, more than simple information gathering, can indicate a desire for relationship and often carry real theological implications such as the burden of knowledge in a covenantal relationship.

Childs explores the effects of theomorphism by engaging Terrence Fretheim's *The Suffering of God*, who

> makes the case for understanding a biblical metaphor as not merely emotive language, but "reality depicting" (7) . . . Fretheim offers as a hermeneutical guide for interpreting the anthropomorphic metaphors the establishing of a balance between the depiction of God within Israel's story and generalizations which the community made in rendering coherence to its tradition. The goal is to prevent the reading of the imagery against the metaphorical grain (8).[11]

In other words, the assertions of the text are tempered, but neither nullified nor muted by the community of faith in which it is received.

---

10. I am physically stronger than my son, (at this writing!), but that does not mean I must use all of my strength when I wrestle with him. Similarly, God may choose to perform actions that are not reflective of the extent of His abilities, and may do so for His express purposes. These self-limited acts should not then be ruled out of the realm of interpretation within a biblical narrative.

11. Childs, *Biblical Theology*, 356.

Theomorphism

Childs sees this approach as analogous to his own, but differs from some of Fretheim's applications.

> Fretheim assumes that a biblical metaphor always arises from the projection of human experience to a depiction of the divine. If the enterprise involved was one of describing the development of language in general, perhaps Fretheim's position could be partially defended, but the theological problem of understanding the function of metaphor within the Bible is far more complex.... From the perspective of the Bible God's identity is primary and human response is secondary. It is a truism of the history-of-religions that man forms God in his own image. However, according to Israel's scriptures this is blasphemy. God, not man, is the only creator.[12]

The primary nature of God in the Old Testament demands that ideas such as justice, love, mercy, grace, compassion, forgiveness, etc., are not transferred from the human realm, but defined by the divine realm. Picking up this theme, Aquinas says,

> We have to consider two things, therefore, in the words we use to attribute perfections to God, firstly the perfections themselves that are signified—goodness, life, and the like—and secondly the way in which they are signified. So far as the perfections signified are concerned the words are used literally of God, and in fact more appropriately than they are of creatures, for these perfections belong primarily to God and only secondarily to others.[13]

But, we are compelled to ask, how can this be? Are not the biblical words human words? Childs explains, "The point is that the Bible functions in such a way that such terms as 'father' and 'king' gain their theological content from the character of God, who continues to be worshipped in the conventions of language which believers have always understood as inadequate for rendering the full divine reality."[14] Childs acknowledges that the content of theological predicates is ultimately derived from the divine rather than the human realm, which in turn renders the usual connotations of these terms according to human usage inadequate. Von Rad adds,

> The meaning of the many human descriptions of God in the Old Testament is not to bring God from afar to a level like that

---

12. Childs, *Biblical Theology*, 356–57.
13. Aquinas, *Summa Theologica*, 1a, 13.3, trans. Herbert McCabe. See also 1a, 13.6.
14. Childs, "Canonical Context," 40.

> of a man. The human likeness is not a humanization. And these descriptions were never thought of that way except in unfair polemic. Rather they are to make God accessible to man. . . . They present God as a person. They avoid the error of making God a static, unconcerned, abstract idea, or an inflexible principle. God is person, full of will, to be found in active discussion, prepared for his communication, open to the impact of human sin and supplication of human prayer and the weeping over human guilt; in a word, God is a living God (L. Köhler, Theologie des A.T., 6.).[15]

Von Rad sees these terms as simply conveying God's personhood and thereby making him more accessible to His worshipers. Bruce Baloian seems to concur, saying,

> The ascription of passion or human characteristics to God allowed Israel to authenticate human existence. The texts that describe his action or passion demonstrate his intense involvement in the world of human beings (1 Sam 25:29) and therefore the validation of human experience in history. They also imbue the human person with significance. They indicate that Israel perceived meaning and intentionality in their personal existence because foundational to reality was a sentient, willing, passionate, and relationally-accessible Person.[16]

However, there are a few problems with this view. Firstly, how can human beings "validate" their own existence? If they first attribute human characteristics to God and then compare their lives to Him, have they not made themselves their own measure? Despite Baloian's attempts to incorporate a real experience of God as the basis of Israelite theology, he ends up leaving God, the non-human Being, effectively out of the equation. However, if one eliminates the term "human characteristics," Baloian's points retain some merit. Human existence is authenticated, given validation and significance, meaning and intentionality, based on its relationship with its Creator. But according to the biblical view, God *precedes* human existence, experience, and description (Gen 1:26–27). As Ulrich Mauser suggests, due to humanity's creation in[17] the image of God, this defined human life as well. "The priestly writers perceived in Israel's cult and demeanor the

15. Von Rad, *Genesis*, 114.
16. Baloian, "Anthropomorphism."
17. With D. J. A. Clines, we prefer the translation "*as* the image of God," treating the preposition as a *bet essentiae*. See Clines, "The Image of God in Man." However, Mauser uses both the expressions "in" and "as" the image.

Theomorphism

historical and concrete actualization of the destiny given to human life from its origin in God. The image of God is, then, not a description of the given of human nature in and of itself, but an outflow of the conscious and life-shaping bond to God."[18] God's identifying characteristics anticipate and thus define human existence. God can only validate that which He defines.

Secondly, in ascribing the effect of these metaphorical terms as a stand-in for the "personhood" or "accessibility" of the divine, both Childs and von Rad seem to found their explanations upon reductionist views of metaphor. However, as we demonstrated earlier, metaphors by nature are *irreducible*. Thus, these metaphors must function more significantly than painting a human mask on God (though the ascription of personality itself is also made implicit).

It seems then, that those divine actions which have human counterparts can function paradigmatically for them. For example, as Heschel argues, "The statements about pathos are not a compromise—ways of accommodating higher meanings to the lower level of human understanding. They are rather the accommodation of words to higher meanings."[19] Not only are these things not derived from the human realm, but, "The conception of selfless pathos, synthesizing morality as a supreme, impartial demand and as the object of personal preoccupation and ultimate concern, consists of human ingredients and a superhuman *Gestalt*. Absolute selflessness and mysteriously undeserved love are more akin to the divine than to the human. And if these are characteristics of human nature, then man is endowed with attributes of the divine."[20] As Heschel observes, the things said of God simply are not true of humankind generally. And yet, they are within the scope of possibility. Humans can conceive of such uncharacteristically-human attributes as compassion and justice, even if they do not practice them personally.

Biblical Distinctions between God and Humanity

However, the objection is often raised in discussions of anthropomorphic language, that divine actions are categorically different from human ones. To justify this view, several passages are often cited which emphasize not simply the transcendent nature of God, but the specific areas in which

18. Mauser, "God in Human Form," 93.
19. Heschel, *The Prophets, II*, 51.
20. Ibid.

He differs from humanity. Based on these passages, it is then concluded that anthropomorphic expressions cannot be literally true, and so other means are sought to explain their presence in the text. However, rather than dismissing the truth-value of anthropomorphic metaphors, a closer look at the *nature* of the differences between God and man being highlighted lends insight into what sort of assertions anthropomorphisms can make about God.

In Hos 11:7–9, Yahweh's people are insistent on turning from Him, but instead of responding to their sin by His wrath, His compassion takes over.

> So My people are bent on turning from Me. Though they call them to *the One* on high, None at all exalts *Him*. How can I give you up, O Ephraim? How can I surrender you, O Israel? How can I make you like Admah? How can I treat you like Zeboiim? My heart is turned over within Me, All My compassions are kindled. I will not execute My fierce anger; I will not destroy Ephraim again. For I am God and not man, the Holy One in your midst, And I will not come in wrath.

Here, we see that though God is different from humans, the difference being highlighted in this passage is not in terms of superhuman ability, but *choice*. God is unlike humans in His decision to show compassion where wrath was due. As their independence from their Creator severs them from the ground of their own worth, humans are left to uphold or establish it on their own. Thus an injustice perceived against them typically demands a defense of their offended honor. However, the nature of the difference is not that between the created vs. the Uncreated, but a voluntary and *humanly* conceivable choice. As Eduard LaB. Cherbonnier says, "This difference between God and man is not a difference 'in principle.' It is merely *de facto*—a difference which God means eventually to overcome."[21]

Similarly, compare also the ways and thoughts of the wicked and of God in Isa 55:7–9.

> Let the wicked forsake his way And the unrighteous man his thoughts; And let him return to the LORD, And He will have compassion on him, And to our God, For He will abundantly

---

21. Cherbonnier, "The Logic of Biblical Anthropomorphism," 188. Though Cherbonnier may use this in service of Mormon theology, where men are seen to become gods, he does not do so in this article. The biblical texts never claim divinity as an end for humanity, but rather ridicule such folly (cf. Isa 14:14–15). Nevertheless, they do adjure people to be *like* God in character (Lev 11:44–45, 19:2, 20:7, 26, etc.).

pardon. "For My thoughts are not your thoughts, Nor are your ways My ways," declares the LORD. "For *as* the heavens are higher than the earth, So are My ways higher than your ways And My thoughts than your thoughts."

Though God's ways and thoughts are higher than those of the wicked, the implication is that the wicked should turn from their ways and adopt His. In other words, the difference between the divine nature and human in this particular instance is in moral character, not ontology. It is humanity's sinful character which causes them to react with wrath at offenses, but it was certainly within the realm of possibility for them to do other than they do, for they are held responsible for such sinful reactions. That is, they are accounted wicked not on their created ontological status, but upon their (mis)use of their faculties. Hence, the difference highlighted here is not simply one which derives from the transcendent nature of God, but upon mankind's choice to follow their own selfish ways over God's—a choice that can be reversed.

In fact, we see that God can enable men to have His compassion (Gen 43:14; 1 Kgs 8:50; 2 Chr 30:9; Neh 1:11; Pss 72:13, cf. vs 1; 119:77; Jer 42:12; Dan 1:9). Compassion is one of Yahweh's self-defined attributes (Exod 33:19), and His compassion seems to be the source of that of others. Though people may have compassion on their children (Isa 49:15, Ps 103:13), they are unable to have this on their enemies, save by God's intervention. It has the unique quality of being undeserved (Hos 2:23). Humans, however are still expected to show compassion (Zech 7:9).[22] Hence, divine compassion, though it originates in God, is not a concept to which humans have no access, nor something that they cannot understand, at least in part, except via the limitations of human language. Rather, it is something expected of them. The difference is that humans do not *naturally* practice compassion in the manner in which Yahweh does. However, He can enable them to do so.

Similar things can be said of verses that have been used to claim intractable differences between God and humans. Isaiah 31:3 says,

> Now the Egyptians are men and not God, And their horses are flesh and not spirit; So the LORD will stretch out His hand, and he who helps will stumble and he who is helped will fall, and all of them will come to an end together.

---

22. Micah 6:8 and Job 6:14 both demonstrate that compassion was expected of humans.

This verse clearly differentiates between the power of God and humans (and horses, for that matter) to deliver, attributing this to the distinction between spiritual and corporeal beings. Isa 40:18 also speaks of the difference in power between God and man (cf. 40:25–26), but also of His omniscience (22, 27) and his imperviousness to fatigue (28).

However, just as God does not grow tired or weary, He may also become the source of this same strength for humans who trust in Him (vv. 28–31). Once again, we find the nature of the difference between divine and human terms is not a simple case of the transcendent vs. the immanent. Though some attributes definitely lie in that category (such as God's creation and rule over the universe) others (such as strength, will, wisdom, endurance, etc.) are qualities that God and humans share in ways that, though significantly different, are directly comparable and occasionally transferable. For example, though God's supernatural immunity from fatigue differs from humanity's natural susceptibility, according to Isa 40:28–31, humans can actually be infused by God's own power to endure.

It should be noted, of course, that humans are not *naturally* or *intrinsically* endowed with divine attributes. Their manifestation only comes from a symptotic participation in the divine, where God enables humans to act with His endurance, or His wisdom, or to see as He does, and yet humans never "become" divine themselves.[23] In addition to their dependency upon this symbiotic[24] relationship, humans also differ from God in other ways. As Cherbonnier says, "At two decisive points the Creator-God establishes his superiority over all creation, mankind included. First, He can do things that mere man can never do. He alone can confer existence.... Secondly, the superiority of the Creator to his creatures consists of his 'eternity.'"[25] He can live forever, while they need not. They exist

---

23. Cf. Isa 40:28–31; Exod 31:3; and I Sam 16:7; Num 22:31; 2 Kgs 6:17, etc. There is a common theological distinction between partaking in the divine *nature*, as opposed to the divine *essence*. Biblically speaking, humans can partake in the former, thus exhibiting traits of the divine, but not the latter, in which they themselves would become deities (cf. Deut 4:35, 39; Isa 45:5, 14, 21, 22; Heb 6:4; 1 Pet 1:4).

24. More specifically, we mean a commensally symbiotic relationship as opposed to a mutually symbiotic one. This is a relationship in which one party benefits, but the other party is neither harmed nor in need of this relationship, as when a bird lives in a tree. Similarly, humans would greatly benefit from divine empowering, but God is not in need of this arrangement.

25. One wonders if Cherbonnier means here "everlastingness." Eternity usually implies a state of timelessness, whereas "everlasting" indicates activity in time, and yet spanning the duration of time. See Wolterstorff, "Unqualified Divine Temporality," and his "God Everlasting."

only at his pleasure.... In short, the relation of the Creator to his creation is not that of logical disjunction, but the 'existential' relation of sovereignty."[26] However, despite the differences, God participates in categories of being and acting which are common to humans, and thus is not logically ruled out of these types of descriptions. Rather, He is sovereign over these areas, defining them by His own being rather than by human terms.

Summary

The point of this discussion is not to imply that the biblical texts equate humanity and God, for clearly, they take pains to distinguish the two. Rather, it is to elucidate the nature of this difference that turns out not to be homogeneous across all categories. Whereas God's creation and control of the universe is incomparable to man's power, and remains in a category all its own, (creation *ex nihilo,* etc.), no one claims that this is an anthropomorphic description. However, many other abilities predicated of God are either expected of humanity, and thus at least conceivable along the same lines, or are transferable from God to humanity.

This highlights the directional difference of von Rad's idea of theomorphism. Though some traits are unique to God, many are seen as *potentially* available to humans. The point of this is to say that for any given attribute ascribed to God in the Bible, it is important not to consider it as empty or fallacious talk simply because it seems anthropomorphic, but to compare how it is being used in its context and the manner and degree to which it becomes paradigmatic of the human application of the term. While God remains divine, humans reported to have encountered Him are often changed to become more like Him.[27]

We have established that *ontologically speaking,* the direction of transfer of meaning actually goes from the divine to the human. We have also seen that many terms are used of both God and humans, and yet not only in their respective modes. Sometimes humans are enabled to function beyond their own "natural" capabilities, both morally and otherwise. Similarly, God can be said to act in a manner less than His "supernatural"

---

26. Cherbonnier, "The Logic of Biblical Anthropomorphism," 203.

27. When humans are divinely "enabled," they nevertheless do not become "divine." Note all of the character flaws in those said to have been so empowered: e.g., Noah's drunkenness, Abraham's lying, Jacob's deception, Moses' dishonoring of Yahweh, David's adultery, Solomon's idolatry, Elijah's cowardice, etc. Though there are a few characters whose flaws seem to go unmentioned (Samuel, Daniel, etc.), there is never a clear implication that any of these characters attained divinity.

capability would involve, if He decides the situation so warrants. This is a far cry from humans projecting their own traits upon the divine. However, as human language is developed around human usage of terms, what we still need to know is how to discern the sense of the divine which in turn sets the bar for humanity. To do this, we consider primary and derivative senses of terms.

Primary and Derivative Senses

To better understand the relationship between a term used for God and humans, Roger White talks of primary and derivative senses. He defines a primary sense as the sense presupposed by other senses. "When we say one sense is primary and another secondary, we are saying that to explain the secondary sense one must necessarily bring into one's account the notion signified by the word in the primary sense."[28] Hence, to comprehend what it means for humans to be "good," we must first understand what it means for God to be good.

White illustrates, "So that one could not explain the notion of a healthy climate without bringing in the notion of what it was for a man to be healthy: a healthy climate is precisely one which promotes health in an animal."[29] That is, rather than mere predications that can be applied in a more or less eminent manner to an object, White is arguing that a primary sense is *integral* to understanding the secondary sense. In our case, the biblical text would be arguing that understanding divine sight is in some way *integral* to the understanding of human sight.

White says,

> I argued that, contrary to many of our immediate intuitions, the primary sense of a large number of the words we use predicatively is not to be found in their use in making predications about everyday empirical objects, but rather in their use to allude to an idea or standard of comparison to which those objects in some way approximate. I suggested that this was in particular true of almost all the words at stake in the doctrine of the divine attributes, and further that there it was true that it was by no means a necessary condition of our having understood

---

28. Roger White, "Notes on Analogical Predication," 201.
29. Ibid.

the sense of the word that we should be able to spell out what in fact such an ideal would be like.[30]

Though this sounds like a neo-Platonic sense of ideal "forms," White distinguishes the two. He describes the problem with Plato's system saying,

> In his later dialogues, Plato was himself to see many of the grave difficulties involved in positing an ideal object that was φ and nothing but φ, but did not take the further step of seeing that his quest for a point of comparison by means of which we could see whether everyday objects did or did not approximate to being φ was not a quest for an object that was perfectly φ, but for an account of the primary sense of a word where in that primary sense it was not in the first instance predicated directly of anything at all, not even an ideal form.[31]

As an example, White takes the idea of kingship. In comparing notions of it within Shakespeare's *Antony and Cleopatra* and Eisenstein's *Ivan the Terrible*, he notes that human power is often lauded for eschewing morals in order to attain one's goal (The end justifies the means?). In contrast, Christ's kingship refuses this dodge of ethical issues and, taking the authorities head on, He suffers at their hands in order to bring about a new type of rule. "He [Jesus] established His solidarity with all despairing, sinning, lonely men, with all human failure, by refusing to acknowledge the absolute nature of the need to evade their condition if possible, but to relativize it to the will of Him who sent Him."[32] Hence, when we speak of Kingship, we speak of Christ's as its primary sense. White explains,

> It is in this strange overcoming of death, darkness, things which are not—by not evading them, but undergoing them in their full depths, that He establishes His Kingdom. And when we say neither Caesar, Pilate, Caiaphas, nor Ivan, nor their masters, death and violence, are Lords, but Jesus alone is Lord, we, however dimly we perceive what we are saying, affirm a finality to His kingship, which makes it appropriate for us to reserve the word "King" for Him and Him who sent Him, alone, and if we continue to use the word 'king' of the kings among the Gentiles, we see that we are now constrained to say that it is this latter sense of kingship which is the derivative one—that this kingship is only the regency for the conditions and constraints of this world

30. Ibid., 221–22.
31. Ibid., 223.
32. Ibid., 220.

that they treated as absolute, but which He treated with sovereign disdain by comparison with the will of His Father.[33]

This view is in accord with Barth's idea of the need for divine revelation in order to know not only God, but ourselves in relationship to Him. "Barth transforms our apprehension of an entire complex of theological questions by simply challenging the assumption that we know what being φ really is in independence of divine revelation, to learn there what truly constitutes being φ, being prepared to take this to extremes that may appear paradoxical and yet which can almost invariably be given a good and profound sense."[34] In fact, "Barth has argued with great subtlety in his doctrine of the Image of God in man for the theological possibility of our language containing words that in their full sense may only be used to describe God."[35] What this means is that, although human language initially gains its meaning from human usage, it is only fully comprehended when its divine referents are understood.

There remain two considerations. First of all, even if we grant divine epithets primary status, are they not still couched in human language? How is it that we can know the primary and thus the secondary aspects of any given predicate? Initially, of course, we only know the meaning of a given predicate within its context of human usage. When speaking of divine attributes, however, there is, of necessity, a lexical and epistemological gap. This is where Stern's approach to *de re* metaphors is helpful. When we cannot define something, the most we can do is to point to it, which is what Stern enables us to do. His "metaphorical character" does not define these attributes of God, but allows us to refer to them in an ambiguous state. Thus, instead of developing a definition of some divine attribute that can be applied in all instances, his metaphorical "character," allows us to "point" at this "primary" sense of the term without defining it for each of its instantiations. However, he takes us further by allowing us to flesh out the content of these metaphors, in a given context. Hence, we can speak more definitively of God's seeing *within* the Noah narrative, or the creation narrative (chap 1), or the Sodom pericope. It is in this manner that the secondary sense of the term is then linked to the primary *within* its own context of use.

This is not odd in itself, for human usage of a term is contextually-determined as well. If I see a "cat," we only know what these words

---

33. Ibid., 220–21.
34. Ibid., 224.
35. Ibid., 225.

essentially entail by knowing the context. If I'm in a pet store, it may refer to the calico I'm intending to buy, but if I'm at a jazz club, it could refer to the saxophonist leading the band. Similarly, we are able to determine the nature of divine attributes as primary, only within their context of use.

The additional step we need to take, however, is to compare the contextualized usage of the divine action/attribute with that of the human in the same context. It is here where the hermeneutical circle is completed. Beginning with human language understood in human contexts, we move to divine referents by means of *de re* metaphors which point at the action/attribute. These are further delineated within a particular context. This contextualized usage is used as a sample or instantiation of the primary sense of the term. This divine usage is then reflected back upon typical human usage in a paradigmatic relationship, lending new perspective to the human term. Thus, by virtue of God's appropriation of human language in His self-revelation in the Scriptures, we are able to begin with humanly understood terms to gain a limited and contextually-bound comprehension of these terms applied to the divine realm.

The second consideration is that in this book, we are not dealing with "attributes." Rather, what Barth and Aquinas, according to White, do with the "perfections," we are doing with "actions" of God. These too, take their primary sense in God and secondary in humanity, according to the concept of the image of God.

Perhaps we can clarify this idea of theomorphic description by saying that the biblical writers attempted not to define God in human terms, but to define humanity on divine terms. That is, as human beings are the images of God (Gen 1:28, 9:6), they are not their own measure. Rather, their actions and character are wholly defined in terms of how they reflect God's actions and character (e.g., "Be holy for I am holy," Lev. 11:44, 19:2, 20:7, 26).

In fact, the biblical writers did not define God at all, leaving much of the *mysterium tremendum* all the more evident. They did not describe the mechanics of how God does things, like seeing across cosmic distances, but merely stated that He does. How could such an undefined notion become paradigmatic for humans as His images? Paul Ricoeur helpfully observes that in denoting something metaphorically, one actually, in part, reverses the denotation.

> For a painted figure to possess greyness is to say that it is an *example* of greyness; but to say that this, here, is an example of greyness is to say that greyness *as such* applies to . . . this

97

> thing, hence denotes it. Accordingly the denotation relation is reversed. The picture denotes what it describes; but the colour grey is denoted by the predicate "grey." If, then, to possess is to exemplify, possession differs from reference only as to its direction. The term symmetrical in this context to "label" is "sample" (for instance, a sample of fabric). The sample "possesses" the characteristics (colour, texture, etc.) designated by the label. It is denoted by that which it exemplifies; . . . predicates are labels in verbal systems.[36]

Though the biblical text does not often explicitly define its predications of God, it overflows with samples. These are what we have to understand the attributes and actions of God, and thus measure those of humanity.

God's Sight

For purposes of illustration, to say "God sees" is to predicate something of him, but also to give an example, or in Ricoeur's terms, a sample, of that very predicate. Thus, in stating that God sees, we do more than claim something of God, we claim something of "seeing." Many of these are acts that only God is able to do. With seeing, for instance, the description is not meant to make a rough approximation of God's activity using inadequate and inappropriate analogies through finite human language, but to refine the concept itself in terms of divine exemplification. Rather than defining God's sight, detailing how it functions and delimiting its parameters, these expressions effectively sample it by its usage. This usage can vary from context to context, alternately as value judgments (Gen 1:4ff.; 16:13), ethical ones (Gen 11, 18), the perception of inner realities (Gen 22; 1 Sam 16), spiritual ones (2 Kgs 6:17), legal witnessing (Gen 18:21, cf. Isa 43:10; 44:8), displaying compassion (Gen 29; Exod 2:23–25; 3:7–9), or seeing the future (Isa 44). These categories are not merely human ones taken superlatively, but distinctly divine in their scope, object, and effect. And yet, it remains possible for these applications to be imbued to the human.

Let us look at some of these "samples" of divine sight and their implications for human sight. We will initially look at 1 Sam 16:7, examining the explicit nature of the difference between divine and human sight, as well as the implied transference of these abilities. Next we will look at

---

36. Ricoeur, *Rule of Metaphor*, 234.

Theomorphism

Num 22:31 and 2 Kgs 6:1, exploring a spiritual sense of divine sight. These are distinct in that human sight is augmented here by the divine.

According to the Heart (1 Samuel 16:7)

Though God is able to "see" things humans cannot see on their own, He often sees things they simply don't choose to see. 1 Samuel 16:7b says,

> God *sees* not as man sees, for man looks according to the eyes, but the LORD looks according to the heart.[37]

This does not merely denote the difference in the object of the sight,[38] but in the mode of seeing—"according to the heart." More important for our discussion is the first part of the verse, in which the LORD commands Samuel, "Do not look (אַל־תַּבֵּט) at his appearance or at the height of his stature, because I have rejected him." Though in verse 6, Samuel had seen (*rā'ā*) the stature of David's elder brother Eliab and mistaken it for God's anointing, even David is described in glowing terms (v. 12). Yet, it is a man after God's own heart whom Samuel is to see and anoint (1 Sam 13:14).[39] Thus, divine sight is not merely human sight *par excellence*, for no amount of visual examination of a person's appearance will allow proper judgments of one's character and destiny.

We find here that though God doesn't see as man does, man occasionally sees (at least partially) as God does. Notably, Samuel is called upon to use his sight differently. He is to choose not on the basis of appearance, but regardless of it, as both candidates mentioned held impressive physical features. Rather, he was to depend on God's sight (cf. v. 12 with v. 7).

Thus, divine sight is not exclusively a transcendent phenomenon, but something that humans are to image. Neither God nor man physically looks upon the incorporeal entity of the "heart," but both are to judge

---

37. The mode of sight is emphasized in the Hebrew by placing the ל preposition before eyes and heart. Thus, it actually says that man looks *according to the eyes* (הָאָדָם יִרְאֶה לַעֵינַיִם) but the LORD sees *according to the heart* (וַיהוָה יִרְאֶה לַלֵּבָב).

38. NIV, NASB, translate "man looks . . . *at* the outward appearance," whereas KJV, RSV, ESV have "*on* the outward appearance."

39. 1 Samuel 13:14 "But now your kingdom shall not endure. The LORD has sought out for Himself a man after His own heart, and the LORD has appointed him as ruler over His people, because you have not kept what the LORD commanded you."(NASB, 1995) Note that the Hebrew says, (בִּקֵּשׁ יְהוָה לוֹ אִישׁ כִּלְבָבוֹ), literally, "The LORD *sought* for Himself a man *according to His heart*." Though the verb is different, it only represents a pointed search for the man to be Israel's next king, whose results are revealed in 16:7.

according[40] to it. This "sight" is metaphorical for both humans and God, in that it refers to discernment and not merely visual recognition. And yet, as both human and divine "seeing" require acts of giving attention toward an object, weighing characters and attitudes, and ultimately, making a judgment, they represent historical, real-world actions.

Spiritual perception (Numbers 22:31; 2 Kings 6:17)

The episode in 1 Sam 16 does not explicitly say Samuel saw with God's eyes, but only that his use of typical human sight was condemned and further judgment instructed to be made upon other bases. However, other pericopes shed more light on this phenomenon. In Num 22:31, the LORD is said to have opened Balaam's eyes to see the angel who was about to kill him, and whom the donkey he was riding had seen. It was not that the angel appeared (niph. of *rā'â*), but that LORD affects Balaam's ability to perceive. Likewise, He "opens" (*pātaḥ*) the donkey's mouth and she tells Balaam what she had seen. Balaam's eyes are then "uncovered" (*gālâ*) by the LORD, and he admits that he had sinned—"because *he did not know* the angel was standing to meet him." Apparently this lack of knowledge, resulting from the lack of perception, along with his resultant beating of the donkey, consisted of an offense against God. And yet it is only the change in Balaam's perception that makes him aware of all this. Balaam is empowered (his eyes "opened") to become aware of the spiritual reality of the situation and not just the physical one.

Similarly, in 2 Kings 6:17, we see a case where sight is given a paradigm in the biblical text through God's appropriation of it. Elisha asks that the eyes of his servant be opened. He is then enabled by the LORD to see the chariot armies of God all around him:

> And *the LORD opened the youth's eyes*, and he saw, and behold, the mountain was full of horses and chariots of fire surrounding Elisha." (emphasis mine)

The salient feature here is that Elisha had already seen this reality, as he already knew that there were more warriors with them, in this case spiritual ones, than in the enemy camp. (v. 16) Ironically, the next verse (v. 18) has him asking God to strike the enemy armies with blindness. This is not necessarily physical blindness, but lack of discernment, since Elisha

---

40. The Hebrew preposition ל is used in this case to indicate "according to." If the instrument of sight had been indicated, the preposition would have been ב "with" the eyes. (Cf. Ps 91:8, Isa 52:8, etc.)

Theomorphism

proceeds to lead them to the king whom they are seeking, only into the midst of the city, and thus into his power. It is this that they realize when they are "unblinded" (v. 20).

So, in both the episodes with Balaam and Elisha, we see God enabling and disabling sight. This, however, is not normal vision, but a recognition of the presence of spiritual beings and the true identity of physical ones. It is metaphorical in that it is not the typical use of sight, (their eyes had to be "opened"), but appears to be reflective of a reality within the text (recognition of the angels or hosts).

Not only these rather unusual episodes, but many more speak of Yahweh causing people to see or to be blind, including His own people. This becomes a major theme in Isaiah, where God commissions Isaiah saying,

> Go, and tell this people: "Keep on listening, but do not perceive; keep on looking, but do not understand." Render the hearts of this people insensitive, their ears dull, and their eyes dim, otherwise they might see with their eyes, hear with their ears, understand with their hearts, and return and be healed. (Isa 6:9–10)

This is in order for the people not to respond to God in order that they may receive their punishment. This too, is not a physical blindness or deafness, but one concerning the perception of spiritual truth.[41]

From these examples, we see that divine sight is not derived from human, but something that has its own qualities. It involves perception of spiritual realities such as angels and God Himself, as well as intangible things such as the character of people. One could argue that this is simply applying a human term to what God is doing, except for the fact that humans are then enabled, and sometimes expected, to do this same action. It is a metaphorical usage, then, not in the sense of applying a human term to the divine, but in applying one typically used of the physical realm to that of the spiritual for both God and humans.

Metaphor *De Re*

What we propose is that this "divine sight" is a phenomenon, a way of interacting with creation, entirely distinct from normal sight, which takes

---

41. Cf. Deuteronomy 28:29, 31, 32, 34. Here the curse for idolatry is that the Israelites will, "grope as a blind man at noon" and yet they will be driven mad, "by what they see." The blindness caused by the curse is spiritual, not physical.

upon many different forms.[42] As humans have no term for this, for it is not natural for them, the metaphor of sight is being used in a catachretical manner, to fill the lexical gap. This is where Stern's *de re*[43] metaphors are helpful. He distinguishes between referring *de dicto* and *de re* where the former is a reference using, "a purely conceptualized individuating representation, where we express it by using vocabulary in our linguistic, or conceptual, repertoire that is determinately true or false of arbitrary things without depending on features of its context of application."[44] *De Re*, on the other hand, is a reference that expresses a, "property only by way of a sample that we demonstrate in context or by way of applying the property to a particular object in a context, without knowing, and perhaps even without there being in the language, a label or concept for that property."[45] It refers, in the manner of a demonstrative, without defining the referent semantically. Sight, as a metaphor, has a metaphorical character which, combined with its content in a given context, determines its meaning. With Samuel, in the context of anointing a king, divine sight refers to a specific ability to read the character of a person. This is especially pertinent considering the fact that Saul, the former and failed king, had been described as,

> a choice and handsome *man*, and there was not a more handsome person than he among the sons of Israel; from his shoulders and up he was taller than any of the people. (1 Kgs 9:2)

Obviously, an impressive physical appearance did not make for a good king. Furthermore, the eventual king, David, is actually described as no less attractive.

> Now he was ruddy, with beautiful eyes and a handsome appearance. And the LORD said, "Arise, anoint him; for this is he." (1 Sam 16:12b)

Hence, physical appearance could not *distinguish* between the faithful and unfaithful kings.

In the context of Elisha facing an enemy army, this sight takes on the meaning of perceiving the spiritual realities, in this case (angelic?) armies.

---

42. In the examples just mentioned, 1 Sam 16:7 referred more to a discernment, whereas 2 Kings and Numbers to an apprehension of the presence of spiritual beings.

43. A term he borrows from Tyler Burge, "Belief De Re." *Journal of Philosophy* 74 (1977) 338–62.

44. Stern, *Metaphor in Context*, 188.

45. Ibid.

Similarly, with a wayward prophet like Balaam, this ability can also be used to perceive spiritual beings coming against oneself. When confronting the idolatrous audience of the prophet Isaiah, this sight can mean a discernment of truth and the divine will, or lack thereof. In each case, the exact mechanics of such sight are left unspecified, except that God Himself enables or disables it. In terms of metaphor theories, this means the entailments of sight involving their mechanics are backgrounded or hidden, whereas other aspects—such as their objects and sources—are foregrounded. What Stern helps us see is that this metaphor of divine sight, though generally undefined, is delimited by the character of the metaphor, and thus semantically determined in each individual context.

Conclusion

In sum, biblical anthropomorphisms are metaphorical, but not strictly derived from the human arena. Because humans are created as the image of God, there is an ontological basis for their descriptors to refer and refer accurately to God. They describe God in a supernatural sense of these terms, and yet one in which humans have potential to access. Thus, it is misleading to speak of these attributes and actions as drawn from the human realm and somewhat naively applied to God. Rather, the concepts, originally understood from their employment in the human realm, are applied to God *metaphorically* in such a way as to "point" to the divine attribute or action, without fully defining it. Their meaning is then further delineated according to its contextualized usage or sampling (Ricoeur). This then becomes paradigmatic for human behavior, *in that context*, and sheds new light on how human behavior is then seen (e.g., kingship). Biblically speaking, these concepts originate in the divine sphere and are occasionally applied to humans.

For human beings to be defined in terms of God means that the traits used to describe them do double duty. We found that the differences between humans and God as described in the more definitive statements in the Bible (e.g., 1 Sam 16:7) were not usually found to be that of the transcendent versus the immanent. Rather, they were matters of character and choice, which lent to the idea that in certain cases, both humans and God could potentially act in similar manners. This said, there are verbs and attributes assigned to God in the Bible for which there is no human counterpart, but these do not consist of anthropomorphisms (or theomorphisms for that matter). What we do find in the terms that are predicated of both God and humans is that often, there is a natural and supernatural sense of the term. These can, at times, be used of either humans or God, though with special limitations. For example, humans are not able to function supernaturally unassisted. And yet this assistance is offered. Conversely, God can function in "natural" ways if He so chooses. Often here, though, the mechanics of these "natural" functions are different for God than for corporeal humans, and yet they function similarly *within* the narrative.

What this means, however, is that as these traits are not derived from their human counterparts, they cannot be defined once and for all, but must be defined according to their context. Hence, by appealing to Stern's approach, we are able to point to the attribute, or in our case, action, using the metaphor, but cannot spell out its meaning except in individual contexts. When these are examined, we are then able to outline the entailments that this action has in this particular instance. In so doing, we are also able to reflect back upon the human traits in the passage, noting their similarities and differences with respect to the divine. In this manner, the biblical narratives do not define God in terms of humanity, but seek to redefine, or at least reevaluate humanity, in terms of the One in whose image, it claims, they are made.

4

Seeing Good and Evil—Genesis 1–3

IN THE PREVIOUS CHAPTER, WE FOUND THAT ACCORDING TO THE BIBLIcal text, mankind is actually in a theomorphic relationship with God. This effectively casts the human sense of terms as the derivative one, with the divine sense being primary. Hence, the divine sense cannot be determined from the human, as the human is dependent upon the divine. Rather, this must be gleaned from its context of usage—something Josef Stern's approach is uniquely suited to do. In his conception, metaphors (*de re*) can point to objects without fully defining them. Rather, their content is determined, like that of the indexical "I", according to its individual context of usage. Hence, in our attempt to bring this to bear on biblical metaphors for divine action, we should expect to see the same metaphor change in meaning, emphasis or nuance according to its context. Furthermore, this meaning *in context* should function paradigmatically with regard to the human application of the term.

In the following chapters, we will examine the occasions of divine sight, noting the objects, vantage points, intersection with main themes, and effects of the sight in the narrative. Furthermore we will compare and contrast this with human use of sight within the pericope, particularly noting both changes in meaning or function for "sight" (Heb. *rā'ah*), and its relationship to the human sense of the term.

Quite often in the Old Testament, God is said to see something or someone. In Genesis alone, such a phrase occurs seven times in just the first chapter, with other instances at 2:19; 6:5, 12; 7:1; 9:16; 11:5; 16:13; 18:21; 22:8, 14; 29:31–32 and 32:25. John Sailhamer says, "In light of such an emphasis at the beginning of the book, it is hardly accidental that throughout Genesis and the Pentateuch the activity of 'seeing' is continually at the center of he author's conception of God."[1] However, though the

---

1. Sailhamer, *The Pentateuch as Narrative*, 87.

In the Eyes of God

Hebrew verb *rā'â*, ("to see")[2] is common, in some cases, like Gen 22:14, it is occasionally translated in a manner strikingly different from the vast majority of its occasions—"provide."[3] We ask whether such renditions constitute fair translations within the context, or heuristic solutions based on views of anthropomorphic language which render such terms meaningless in their usual denotations.

Not only is the translation of the Hebrew verb affected, but the vital comparisons within the text are often overlooked. Take for instance, the interplay with seeing and naming that happens between the first two chapters. Initially God sees and names, but after creating man, God sees

---

2. Among other verbs related to sight, "שׁקף" "to look down" is only found with an ambiguous reference to God. In 18:16, the three "men" with whom Abraham has been eating get up and look down towards Sodom. However, there is some confusion about who is actually doing the "looking down." In verse 16, the "men" (הָאֲנָשִׁים) look down, but the very next verse begins a separation between the LORD and his two companions, as He delivers a monologue that is either self-talk or private discussion regarding whether or not He should let Abraham in on His plans. (In either case the verbs are in the singular, both the introductory "And the LORD said," [17, 20], and the first person singular verbs within His speech "Shall I hide," "what I will do," [17]; "I have chosen" [18], "I will go down," "I will see," "I will know" [21]. These verbs would exclude the other two men from being part of their subject.) In 18:20–21 it seems that the LORD Himself is planning to give a closer inspection of Sodom's activities to determine the extent of their sin. However, in 18:22, the men (הָאֲנָשִׁים) depart for Sodom, whilst the LORD remains with Abraham. Hence, it is unclear that the verb (שׁקף) in 18:16 necessarily includes the LORD Himself.

There may, however, be a link with this verb in Ps 14:2 where many allusions are made to Gen 18. In each case, God (or the men) look(s) down (שׁקף) on humans in order "to see" (ראה) the moral nature of their actions. The same phrase is used of Abraham in 19:28 as he too looks down on Sodom observing the smoke rising up after its judgment. This verb seems to have a much more physical denotation, as in both cases, the parties are upon a hill looking down towards the plain (lit. the "face") of Sodom. The other occurrence in Genesis is in 26:8, which has Abimelech looking out through a window at Isaac caressing his wife Rebeqah.

Another verb, "נבט," 'to gaze' also has primarily physical denotations. In Gen 15:5, Abraham is commanded to gaze into the night sky and count the stars, an exercise compared with the numbering of his promised descendants. In chapter 19, the men/angels command Lot not to look back at Sodom (19:17), which his wife subsequently does (26). However, this verb is not used of God in Genesis.

The verb, "נכר," "to recognise," is also not used of God in Genesis, as with "חזה," "to see (in a vision)." However, a noun form is used in 15:1, when the LORD appears to Abram "in a vision," "בַּמַּחֲזֶה." As neither of these verbs is used of God "recognizing" or "seeing in a vision," we will exclude these from our analysis, except to note that these are not things predicated of God in Genesis.

3. (22:8, 14 NASB, NIV, RSV, KJV, NRSV, ESV, NLT. However, cf. KJV and JPS, "It will be seen" (v14), JPS and Tanakh, "Where there is vision." cf also. 1 Sam 16:17)

what man names—is this a relinquishing of some degree of authority? If God's seeing is more than a superfluous and naive attempt to portray Him as personal and living, then more significance should be attributed to the actions that are shared by God and man.

This is not to say such terms are univocal in their meaning. Often how they are used constitutes a significant thrust within a narrative and serves to highlight the differences between God and mankind, such as how God and people see good and evil (Gen 3:5, 22). There are further contrasts to be made between how the "sons of God" view the world differently from their Father, and how Noah is seen by God and his son Ham.

In this chapter we will look at the creation and the fall, examining the active[4] use of the verb "to see" (rā'ā) with respect to God. In order to illustrate Stern's contextually-sensitive approach, we will look at the entailments derived in each occurrence of this metaphor throughout Genesis. As these change, we expect the meaning of the metaphor to change. To observe this, we will primarily focus on the descriptions of God as the subject of the seeing, the nature of the objects that He sees, and the impact of His sight within the narrative. Secondly, we will examine the interpretation of seeing with respect to other characters in the story to elucidate the relationship between divine sight and that of other beings (i.e., human, angelic, etc.). From this we hope to illuminate the need for a context-sensitive approach to anthropomorphic metaphors in determining their various meanings, relation to "human" terms, and significance within a narrative. Ultimately, we aim to show that the interpretation of such metaphors is integral to the development of the primary themes in the book of Genesis.

Creation and the Fall— Genesis 1:4, 10, 12, 18, 21, 25, 31

"And God saw . . . that it was good."

Form

As mentioned above, this refrain constitutes an "approval formula," repeated seven times in the first chapter. However, there are some variations in its occurrence. Though one might expect it once per day, on day

---

4. We will omit the instances when the niphal or passive sense of the verb is applied to God, which generally carries the sense of "to appear" or "be seen." This represents a focus on encounter rather than divine perception vs. human perception.

two, when God creates the sky (heavens), there is no mention of Him seeing it as good. The LXX supplies the phrase, but this is almost certainly a harmonization.[5] Interestingly, however, the MT has two mentions of God's "seeing that it was good" on day three—first after dry land is formed and secondly after it sprouts vegetation (v. 10, 12). Similarly, on the sixth day, God sees that the animal life is good before "seeing all that He had made" was "very good." The following chart highlights the themes of the objects created, how they were viewed, and separation functions:

Day	Object Created	Result of Seeing
1	Light	that it was good
2	Sky	
3	Dry Land	that it was good
	Vegetation	that it was good
4	Cosmic Entities	that it was good
5	Fish and Fowl	that it was good
6	Land animals	that it was good
	All He had made (now including humans)	and behold it was very good

This structure reveals a parallel with twin visions of goodness at the end of each half of the creation sequence. Day three concludes the first half with the creation of the environments specific to mankind, including his initial source of food, while day six sees a two-fold creation of land creatures and mankind. The lack of such a vision of goodness on day two may be due to the nature of the creation, the sky not being a particularly visible entity,[6] but also the fact that it, along with the seas, serves merely

---

5. Verse 12 (day 3) Hamilton says, "Only in connection with this second day is the phrase 'and God saw how beautiful it was' absent in the MT. LXX has the phrase, probably artificially and for the sake of consistency. It is unlikely that the LXX represents an earliest form of the Hebrew text. The omission of the phrase in v. 8 may indicate that the author viewed the creation of the vault as only a preliminary stage to the emergence of dry land in v. 10, and thus he reserved the phrase until its most appropriate time." Hamilton, *The Book of Genesis*, 124. Wenham notes that the LXX's inclusion of "it was good" mars the sevenfold repetition of the phrase. Wenham, *Genesis 1–15*, 4.

6. This use of שׁמים (heavens) refers to that between the waters upon the (sur)face of the earth and that above its atmosphere, or the sky. Though we say the sky is blue, this is actually a result of the refraction of light through earth's atmosphere, which makes it appear visible to those on its surface. Technically, however, it is not the air itself which is being viewed. Furthermore, within the creation narrative in Gen 1, the perspective is that of God looking *at* the earth which He has made. Hence, there is

as a backdrop for the fish and fowl, whilst the other initial days include entities such as light and vegetation, which are more than mere containers waiting for their filling. In any case, this asymmetry is counterbalanced by the separation motif which occurs twice in the first half and only once in the second, separating light and darkness, the waters above/below the heavens, and marking units of time.

From this brief examination of the form we see that God sees each part of creation after He creates it, save the sky. Furthermore we find a structure where the entity viewed is mentioned only in the first and last instances, whilst the evaluative formula is present each time, the last time, with special emphasis.

Interpretation of "Seeing"

The verb "to see," as we shall see, has been translated in disparate manners. For instance, Gordon Wenham observes that God's "seeing" in Gen 1:4f. is part of the "approval formula" or "formula of appreciation."[7] In this sense, he compares the formulaic aspects of this refrain with its complements such as God's dividing (Heb. *bādāl*), finding these elements to be flexible in their order. He also compares this to an artist's admiration of his work, apparently emphasizing the aesthetic qualities of what God sees.

Claus Westermann highlights the idea that God's sight acknowledges the value of the work. He says, "The procedure itself is quite clear: a craftsman has completed a work, he looks at it and finds that it is a success or judges that it is good. The Hebrew sentence includes the 'finding' or 'judging,' in the act of looking," and furthermore, "The light is good simply because God regards it as good; the light and its goodness cannot be separated from God's attentive regard."[8]

Seeing, for Westermann, is a metaphor for a value judgment that functions as a catalyst for the response of the creation to the creator. He notes, "an event in the Old Testament, is always an event in the community; it has no meaning unless it happens for someone or something. It is proper therefore to acknowledge anything that happens and to express thereby that the work is good or not good for someone or something."[9] It is

---

nothing to see when looking at the sky, as it is backgrounded with the surface of the planet itself.

7. Wenham, *Genesis 1–15*, 18.
8. Westermann, *Genesis 1–11*, 113.
9. Ibid., 165–66.

this phenomena, acts in community requiring praise, which Westermann sees as operative in the pericope of Creation. "Every work of humanity requires not only reward, but also acknowledgement; so too with the works of God. What he does for his people arouses praise and the Old Testament is full of praise of his mighty acts. The same must be true for God's work of creation."[10] In addition, this refrain of God's seeing functions as a link to His praise. "God's regard, which recognizes that what he has done is good, provides here the clearest link between the account of creation and the praise of the creator. The praise of the creator is a continuation of the recognition by the creator."[11] Thus, God's creation of the world and subsequent seeing of it as good establishes an initial pattern of good works followed by praise, which later His people, and indeed all of creation, are to echo back to Him.[12]

Though Kenneth Matthews does not comment directly on "seeing," he says, "'Good' as a double entendre indicates that God as Judge of the universe distinguishes between what is morally 'good' and morally evil (e.g., the tree of 'good and evil,' 2:17; 3:5). There is in the biblical understanding of the universe an inherent moral factor that cannot be divorced from the proper order of things."[13] Furthermore, he states, The divine evaluation that the light was 'good' (*tôb*) indicates that God is Judge, as well as Landlord, who evaluates the consequences of his creative word (1:10, 12, 18, 21, 25, 31)."[14] Hence, Matthews views God's act of seeing here as an act of evaluation of the intrinsic moral value of His creation.

John Hartley says,

> God saw that the light was good, thereby making a qualitative judgment about what he had created (also vv. 10, 12, 18, 21, 25, 31). While usually a word carries only one nuance in any given occurrence, "good" in this account is a loaded term. It carries four implications: (a) What came into being functioned precisely as God had purposed. (b) That which had just been created contributed to the wellbeing of the created order. (c) The new creation had aesthetic

---

10. Ibid., 166.
11. Ibid., 113.
12. Ibid., 166. Cf. Pss 19:1–6; 145:4, 6–7, 9–10; 148:1–14.
13. Matthews, *Genesis 1:1—11:26*, 147.
14. Ibid., 146.

qualities—that is, it was pleasing and beautiful—and (d) it had moral force, advancing righteousness on earth (Job 38:12–13).[15]

So Hartley interprets "God's seeing" here as a "qualitative judgment" on creation.

Bruce Waltke interprets, "God's seeing that the light is good," as, "a metaphor for God's spiritual perception."[16] John Sailhamer has suggested that this is an instance of light 'appearing', and refers only to the land of Israel.[17] However, as Waltke observes, *r'h* does not mean "appear" in the Qal stem.[18] Hence, Waltke views this term as a metaphor for God's spiritual discernment, rather than observing a localized (or generalized) physical phenomenon.

However, Waltke boils this metaphor down to the simple propositional statement, "God creates." He says,

> One of the key ways in which the text distances itself from a bare-facts retelling of the events of creation is its metaphorical language. As soon as we talk about God in heaven, we are in a realm that can only be represented by earthly figures. The narrator must use metaphor and anthropomorphic language so that the reader can comprehend. When the text says that God said, commanded, called and saw, are we to understand that God has vocal cords, lips, and eyes? Obviously this language is anthropomorphic, representational of the truth that God creates.[19]

In a note, Waltke adds, "Young . . . clearly recognizes the anthropomorphic language here: 'It is certainly true that God did not speak with physical organs of speech nor did he utter words in the Hebrew language.'"[20] Waltke has boiled the "metaphors" of God seeing, speaking, etc., down to "the truth that God creates." But, is that really all that is being described in Genesis 1? What is it that requires such anthropomorphic terms for human readers to "comprehend"? Why did the author not stop at verse 1 where the actual verb "to create" (*bāra'*) is used?

So then, we have encountered various ways of interpreting the verb "to see" in this first chapter of Genesis. While Waltke sees these verbs as

15. Hartley, *Genesis*, 44.
16. Waltke, *Genesis*, 61.
17. Sailhamer, *Genesis Unbound*, 47–59.
18. Waltke, *Genesis*, 59 n. 21.
19. Ibid., 77.
20. Waltke, *Genesis*, 77 n. 90. Young quoted from E. J. Young, *Studies in Genesis 1*. Philadelphia: Presbyterian & Reformed, 1973, 55–56.

anthropomorphic metaphors for God's creative work, Hartley sees them as evaluations. Matthews counts them as moral judgments, while Westermann views them as the beginning of a praise cycle. Finally, Wenham regards them as signifying the enjoyment of aesthetic and other qualities within God's work. How do we sift through these significantly differing, though perhaps not fully incompatible, solutions?

Essentially, we seek to understand how God's seeing *functions* in the narrative, apart from systematic theological issues such as omniscience. To do so, we will look at the entailments associated with God's seeing that seem to be highlighted in the context and those that are not. With Stern, we will avoid placing fixed definitions upon this usage of the verb "to see," preferring to examine its character in the specific context through its entailments such as its object, and effects, etc. Finally, we will compare this with human sight in closely related passages to detect similarities and differences in the usage of the verb "to see" (*rāʾâ*).

Object of Sight

Firstly, we may note that in each instance *rʾh* occurs in Genesis 1, God is said to have "seen" something He *created*. We have here neither mere self-reflection, nor the viewing of some pre-existent primordial chaos. Wenham observes, "It may be noted that light, not darkness is noted as good: God is, as it were, prejudiced in favor of light."[21] So, in some basic manner, the verb deals with the interaction between the uncreated One, and His creation.

But what was it that God viewed in His creation? Did He "see" the objects that He had created, their separation from each other, or the state of affairs—that they were good? According to Victor Hamilton, regarding the separation of the light and darkness in verse 4, "The major difference between this work of separation and the other two in Genesis 1 is that here the pronouncement of God's benedictional statement—*God saw how beautiful the light was*—precedes the separation. In vv. 6–8 and 14–19 this sentence of evaluation follows the separation. Thus it is the light itself that is *beautiful* (or good, Heb. *tôb*), not the creation per se of time into units of light and darkness."[22] At least here, it is the light itself as an object, and not simply the act of separating it from the darkness, that is found to be good by God. However, as with the gathering of the waters and the dry land

21. Wenham, *Genesis 1–15*, 18.
22. Hamilton, *The Book of Genesis*, 120.

(vv. 9–10), the separation of light and darkness is part of what defines the entity God sees. The last occurrence in verse 31 says, "And God saw all that He had made, and behold, it was 'very good' (*ṭôb meʾōd*)." Not only does this statement summarize the whole of creation as opposed to just one act, but it adds the emphasis that the collective whole is greater than the parts. So, it appears that God saw not only the individual entities he had made, but also their distinctiveness from each other, as well as the entire matrix of creation in its interelatedness and wholeness.[23]

Kî ṭôb

In discussing the object(s) of God's sight in Gen 1, we come upon a difficult expression in the Hebrew—*kî ṭôb*, often translated, "that it was good." However, there are other uses of the *kî* clause which lead J. L. Kugel to advocate an adverbial use of the phrase. He says,

> The refrain of the first chapter of Genesis thus has nothing to do with seeing, still less with seeing "that it was good." The phrase *wayyar' 'ĕlōhîm kî ṭôb* means simply, "And God was most pleased." It is noteworthy that each time this refrain occurs it comes at the end of a series of actions: construed as an adjective or stative verb, *ṭôb* has no clear referent, and translators are forced into the ambiguous 'it was good.' But for such an idea one would more likely expect *kî ṭôb ʿāśâ (cf. Gen* 40:16 *kî ṭôb pātar).* In our case, therefore, it seems better to construe *kî ṭôb* adverbially and understand the idea to be, as in Eccl 3:13 above, that of taking pleasure in one's work. However, even where there is a clear possible referent, as in Gen 1:4, *wayyar' 'ĕlōhîm 'et hā'ôr kî ṭôb*, it might be better to translate, 'And God was very pleased with the light.' A similar use of the expression with a[sic] object might be Gen 49:15—*wayyar' mĕnuḥâ kî ṭôb wĕ'et hā'āreṣ kî nā'ēmâ* which would mean, "and he was very pleased with (the) place . . ."[24]

---

23. R. Bultmann comments on God's summary view of creation, "On the previous days the words *that it was good* were applied in specific detail; now *God saw* EVERYTHING *that He had made*, the creation in its totality, and He perceived that not only were the details, taken separately, good, but that each one harmonized with the rest, hence the whole was not just *good*, but *very good*. An analogy might be found in an artist who, having completed his masterpiece, steps back a little and surveys his handiwork with delight, for both in detail and in its entirety it had emerged perfect from His hand." Quoted in Cassuto, *A Commentary on the Book of Genesis*, 59.

24. Kugel, "The Adverbial Use of *Kî ṭôb*," 435.

In the Eyes of God

However, in reviewing Kugel's article, J. Gerald Janzen finds several things amiss. For example, Kugel takes the formulaic statement in 1:4 which has an object, the light, in light of the middle five elliptical statements of the approval formula, which omit the direct reference to an object. Janzen observes, "Kugel does discuss 1:4, but only in the light of conclusions drawn from analysis of the middle five. Rhetorically such an analysis is backward. Where we have longer and shorter forms of a refrain, and the shorter form is enclosed between opening and concluding longer forms, surely the latter provide the basis for interpretation of the former, and not the other way around."[25] Hence, one should look at the middle expressions of the formula as elliptically shortened forms of the longer beginning and concluding expressions. These have a clear object for the verb "to see" (v. 4, "the light," and v. 31, "all that He had made."). This implies that the middle cases elliptically referred to God seeing what He had just made, and that He saw, "that (it) was good." As Janzen concludes,

> Surely in such a series the interpretation must go all one way or the other. But then what of 1:31? Is there any way (not to mention the "clear possible referent" in *'et kōl 'ăšer 'āsâ*) that we can construe *wĕhinnēh ṭôb mĕ'ōd* adverbially? I think not. Surely this concluding instance of the refrain dispells [sic] all doubt concerning the impropriety of Kugel's proposal for the refrain as a series.[26]

In fact, as Janzen observes, the reference of *kîṭôb* is unambiguous whether taken adverbially (as with Kugel) or as an adjective or stative verb. "Kugel wants to translate the refrain 'and God was most pleased.' Pleased with what, we may ask? What is the source or occasion or object of God's great pleasure? Kugel does not say."[27] Janzen answers that it is, "the immediately concluded action to which *ṭôb* clearly refers . . . ," and thus, "one is at a loss to see how the construal of *kîṭôb* bears on the question of clarity of referral, since *that* question remains the same no matter how *kîṭôb* is construed."[28]

Secondly, an ambiguous reading is not necessarily grammatically improper. Janzen asks, "Is absolute grammatical unambiguousness a universal feature of proper usage? Is it not often the case, in literary (especially poetic) texts that the correct construal of a text that displays several

25. Janzen, "Kugel's Adverbial *Kî ṭôb*," 105.
26. Ibid., 106.
27. Ibid., 105.
28. Ibid.

possibilities is implicit from the general context of usage and from closely related usages?"²⁹ For the expression *kîṭôb* to be more open-ended in its referring is to allow it to speak.

Finally, Janzen answers the examples Kugel cites for support from other Genesis texts, such as the case in Gen 40:16 where Joseph has just interpreted the cupbearer's dream with a positive outcome.³⁰

> This focus is rhetorically nuanced by the verb which follows *kîṭôb*—he sees that Joseph has *interpreted* positively, and is indifferent to Joseph's *plea*. (It is unlikely that *kîṭôb* here is to be taken intensively—as though the baker waited to see *how* good the interpretation was before speaking up. He waited rather to see whether the interpretation—not the act but the content—was auspicious or ominous. Seeing that it was auspicious he sought an interpretation of his own dream, with, so to speak, unlooked-for results.)³¹

Though the verb, "*pātar* functions to specify the focus of the baker's attention upon one specific part of Joseph's speech to the exclusion of another . . . in Genesis 1 there is no need to specify, since the referent is the whole of the preceding divine action."³²

Having similarly dismissed an adverbial use of *kîṭôb*, Hamilton elects for the intensive usage in Gen 1, "*how* beautiful.³³" However, it would

---

29. Ibid., 100.

30. Janzen explains how other verbs combined with *kîṭôb* do not use it adverbially. He says, "Kugel wishes to insist that for the conventional reading 'one would more likely expect *kîṭôb 'āṣâ* (cf. Gen 40:16 *kîṭôb pātar*).' . . . Why not take the *kîṭôb* here as modifying the preceding verb, and render 'and the chief baker was delighted with the interpretation'? On Kugel's premises that would seem plausible. But in Gen 3:6 the phrase, though just possibly adverbial considered by itself, surely must be taken as syntactically co-ordinate with the following *kî-*clause (*kîṭôb hā'eṣ lĕma'ăkāl/kî ta'wâ hû' la'ĕnîm*). Likewise in Gen 6:2 *wayyir'û . . . kîṭôbōt hēnnâ*, and in Exod 2:2 *wattēre' 'ōtô kîṭô hû'*, we have further evidence of non-adverbial *rā'â + kîṭôb*; i.e., evidence of a usage conveying the sense either of seeing *that* something is good or of seeing *how* good it is. As such, they go to support Kugel's non-adverbial (sic!) construal of *kîṭôb* in Gen 40:16." J. Gerald Janzen, "Kugel's Adverbial *Kî ṭôb*," 105–6.

31. Ibid., 106.

32. Ibid.

33. Cf. Albright, "The Refrain 'And God saw ki tob' in Genesis." Albright alternately translates some passages as "And God saw, how good it was," and others, "And God saw, that it was very good." As Westermann concludes, "The procedure in itself is quite clear: a craftsman has completed a work, he looks at it and finds that it is a success or judges that it is good. The Hebrew sentence includes the 'finding' or 'judging' in the act of looking." Westermann, *Genesis 1–11*, 113.

seem to be the fact of creation's goodness that is in view, not its degree (e.g., What would creation be seen as "better" or "more beautiful" than?). This is similar to the progression in 3:6 where the list of three facts constitutes the reasons why the woman ate the forbidden fruit, not their degree.

Thus, we see that God's sight involves not only the created entities, their distinction from each other, and their dynamic as an inter-related whole, but that God sees in creation an innate sense of goodness. This goodness, in the absence of other objects of comparison, can only consist of a reflection of God's own creative expertise.

Nature of Sight

Secondly, we observe that the instruments of God's vision are not mentioned. Unlike human characters in Genesis, such as Abram and Isaac (13:14; 18:2; 22:4; 24:63), God does not "lift up His eyes" to see.[34] In fact, nowhere in the Hebrew Bible is this expression employed with God as its subject.[35] While many passages speak of God's eyes, the organs with which He sees are not an emphasis here. Rather, it is *the object* of His seeing which is emphasized through the *kî* clause. Paul Joüon notes, "With the *verba sentiendi* (= 'verbs of sense perception'), especially with רָאָה *to see* and יָדַע *to know*, there is often anticipation of the subject; Gn 1.4 וַיַּרְא אלהים אֶת־הָאוֹר כִּי־טוֹב *God saw that the light was good*; again with רָאָה: Gn 6.2; 12.14; 13.10; 49.15; Ex 2.2; Ec 2.24; 8.17."[36]

Notably, God is not said to see anything until *after* light is created. However, this does not indicate God requires light to see, as the Psalmist says, "Even the darkness is not dark to Thee, and the night is as bright as the day. Darkness and light are alike *to Thee*" (Ps 139:12 NASB). And yet, God is said to see it, and that it was good. There is no mention of how He

---

34. Though, this idiom always signifies something important is about to occur or be presented. Wenham says, "The pair of verbs 'look up and see' indicates that what he sees will prove very significant." Wenham, *Genesis 16–50*, 45.

35. In most cases where this verb is used, there seems to be something of great importance about to be observed by the character in question. For example, when Rebekah is on her way to Isaac, in Gen 24:64, she lifts up her eyes and we are given a glimpse of her first vision of her new husband. In Gen 13:10 Lot sees the land he will live in, foreshadowing the destruction in 18–19, whilst God shows Abram the land his descendants will inherit in verse 14. Perhaps this is one reason for its absence of use in relation to the deity, as there is no news of which He is suddenly made aware. My thanks to Professor Wenham for this insight.

36. Joüon, *A Grammar of Biblical Hebrew*, 591, §158d.

sees³⁷ nor if this vision is obstructed, skewed, from a distance, etc. It is simply stated that God saw, regardless of method. However, *rā'ā* can also be employed as a metaphor for mental evaluation of a state of affairs, (as it is "seeing that . . ." [*wayyar'* . . . *kî*]). Is this the case, or is it simply that God *perceived* the light?

Whether eyes are unnecessary or just unmentioned, we still need to know what it means to say God *saw* these things as good. If God's sight is not physical sensing, is it purely cognitive? Often, the verb *rā'āh* as with the English "to see," can simply indicate a mental state³⁸ (e.g., "I see your point."). However, in Gen 1:4 and 31, we find alterations to the "approval" formula, where the object of God's seeing is inserted into the middle of the statement, (v. 4, "And God saw *the light*, that it was good"; v. 31, "And God saw *all that He had made*, and behold it was very good"). At least in these two cases, the text seems to emphasize an act of perception on God's part, and not simply a cognitive assessment of the light/all creation. We see this primarily in the use of the direct object marker and its object preceding the *kî* clause, yielding, "God saw *the light*, that it was good." Presumably, if the author had desired to comment merely on God's mental assessment of the situation, he could have put this within the *kî* clause. (God saw *that the light was good*).³⁹ The same applies for the summary statement in v. 31—'God saw all that He had made, and behold, it was very good.'

A further key, found in this same verse, is the particle, "Behold!" This often overlooked expression holds significance for us because it emphasizes the perspective being highlighted. As Adele Berlin observes, "Often a statement of perception includes the word *hinneh* (הנה), which is known to sometimes mark the perception of a character as distinct from that of the narrator." She gives the example of Gen 24:63 which says,

---

37. Other texts, in fact, do speak of His eyes, (Ps 33:18, 32:8, 34:15, Job 36:7), though these could simply be metaphorical expressions for His ability to see, rather than attributions of physical organs. In the present narrative, however, the effects of God's actions are highlighted, but their *modus operandi* is not.

38. Koehler and Baumgartner, *HALOT*, s.v. "ראה."

39. According to Koehler and Baumgartner, "After verbs of seeing, hearing, saying, noticing, believing, remembering, forgetting and of joy or regretting, it [כִּי] introduces the subordinate clause: that Gn 1₁₀ 1K 21₁₅ Jb 36₁₀ Gn 22₁₂ Ex 4₅ Ju 9₂ Jb 35₁₅ Is 14₂₉ Gn 6₆." Koehler and Baumgartner, *HALOT*, s.v. "כִּי" B. 5. Similarly, according to Joüon, the subject of the *kî* clause is often the object of *r'h*. Joüon, *A Grammar of Biblical Hebrew*, s.v. "כִּי" §157d.

> Isaac went out to meditate in the field toward evening; and he lifted up his eyes and looked, and behold, camels were coming (NASB).

Berlin comments, "The Bible could have said here, as it does elsewhere, 'He saw *that* there were camels coming', but that would have given a view external to Isaac. The present form is more dramatic. I think it functions in much the same way as interior monologue (see below), to internalize the viewpoint; it provides a kind of interior vision." Similarly, in Gen 1:31, we have God surveying all of creation, and suddenly we get a glimpse of His "interior vision." As God surveys all of His handiwork, suddenly the goodness, not simply of each part, but of the entire integrated system comes into view. The whole is found greater than the sum of its parts. Thus, the implied author is not only using repetition to highlight the importance of God's seeing, but also helping the reader to "see things through God's eyes." In this passage, God doesn't simply think that creation is very good, He *senses* it as a reflection of Himself. As Wenham puts it, "God the great artist is pictured admiring his handiwork. This account of creation is a hymn to the creator: creation itself bears witness to the greatness and goodness of God."[40]

Blessing

Occasionally, it is helpful to delineate what entailments are *not* involved in a particular context for a metaphor. One such common entailment for God's sight, is that God's face and eyes are equated with blessing, and even used in blessing formulas (e.g., the Aaronic blessing in Num 6:23–27). However, Hamilton observes of the fifth day of creation, "The recipient of God's first blessing in the Bible is not man—that must wait until v. 28—but fish and fowl. Quite evidently, the essence of God's blessing is the capacity to be fertile, to reproduce oneself. Everything thus far in the created order has received God's inspection. To that is now added God's blessing."[41] This is significant, as God is already said to have seen the light, the dry land, the vegetation, and the cosmic entities. God's seeing is therefore not equivalent to blessing in this passage, and remains a separate act. Though they are "seen" by God, the environments do not reproduce, and though the vegetation is commanded to do so, it is not "blessed," despite its goodness

---

40. Wenham, *Genesis 1–15*, 18.
41. Hamilton, *The Book of Genesis*, 131.

Seeing Good and Evil—Genesis 1-3

being seen by God. So, though divine seeing is metaphorical, it is not simply a euphemism for another act such as blessing.

Summary of Genesis 1

What we have discovered is that in Gen 1, God's seeing concerns objects (e.g., light) as well as states of affairs (e.g., that it was good). How He sees is not specified, but the fact that He sees is stressed through repetition and by giving us a "look" through God's eyes. Furthermore, His seeing does not seem to be simply a metaphor for blessing or creating. What we find is a separate act, used of most days of creation but not all, and not directly linked to these other actions. What does seem to be involved is a general interaction with creation in the form of evaluation and enjoyment. This has the effect of establishing that creation, as it was made, in part and *in toto*, innately reflects the goodness of God in His creativity.[42] Furthermore, it sets forth the motif that God's work originally brings Him joy, a theme which resurfaces in the flood story (cf. 6:6-7). This sight certainly differs from human vision, at least in its scope. It apparently extends to all of creation (v. 31) and can take all this in view simultaneously. However, it remains similar in function to human sight in that it also involves an interaction with creation, as opposed to *a priori* or intuitively derived types of knowledge.[43] Often, too, a similar enjoyment of God's own goodness is expressed within it.

We might also note that both human and divine sight in the Bible, whether physical interaction or mental assessment, seem to imply *real* actions. However they might function, they are described as significant events in the sequence of the narrative. They cannot be ruled out of existence simply due to their use of metaphorical speech. Rather, the metaphorical character itself, in this case, God Mthat *sees* [Φ], is concretized by its specific instantiation in Gen 1, namely, [that it (creation) was good].

---

42. Wenham says, "Primarily ["good"] draws attention to an object's quality and fitness for its purpose. But the Hebrew term as used by the Israelites is more closely related to the mind and opinion of God than is the English word. God is preeminently the one who is good, and his goodness is reflected in his works (Ps 100:5; cf. I. Höver-Johag, *TDOT* 5:296-317; H. J. Stoebe, *THWAT* 1:652-64). Wenham, *Genesis 1-15*, 18.

43. It does not, however, rule these sorts of knowledge out of the theological picture of God. The first chapter of Genesis simply makes a limited claim about one sort of knowledge God has which involves His interaction with creation. This picture obviously must be augmented with other statements made in the rest of the Hebrew Bible to gain a complete picture.

This, according to Stern, still comprises a truth-conditioned statement, as either God did or did not see creation, "that it was good." Even though the nature of God's seeing is not permanently delineated for all cases, in this context it appears to consist of an interaction with its objects (cf. "Behold") rather than simple *a priori* knowledge, and an assessment of their quality.

However, if Stern's theory proves correct, we would expect to see significant differences of meaning and entailments in different uses of a particular metaphor. If God Mthat *sees* [Φ] is non-constant in meaning, due to its context-dependency, then the expression "God sees" will not always include the idea of aesthetic appreciation. Therefore, we must continue our examination of this verb with respect to God in Genesis to observe its flexible character. In chapter 2 we find God again seeing creation, but this time He is observing the actions of one of His creatures, rather than the result of His own actions.

A View to Naming—Genesis 2:19

> *So out of the ground the LORD God formed every beast of the field and every bird of the sky and brought them to the man to see what he would call them. And whatever the man called the living being, that was its name.*

Following the spate of formulaic accounts of God's seeing in Genesis 1, we now find Him "seeing" what man would call each creature. Using Stern's approach, we find that this constitutes a different usage of the term "seeing" when applied to God, as it differs in content from the previous chapter, though with the same metaphorical character (Mthat "seeing"[Φ]). In the following we will attempt to shed further light upon the metaphorical character of this phrase.

Seeing and Naming

In the previous verse (2:18), we find the first instance in Genesis where God states that something is not good. While formerly, God "saw" the value of each of His creative works, now He simply pronounces it "not good," without any mention of seeing it. In Genesis one, everything God created possessed an innate sense of "goodness," which He Himself observed. In the second chapter, it is His statement, rather than an act of perception, which establishes the positive or negative value of parts of creation, in this

Seeing Good and Evil—Genesis 1–3

case, Adam's aloneness. Perception, if any, is only implied. Hence, "seeing" plays a different role here than observation and enjoyment.

This change in emphasis can also be seen in the order in which events transpire. In the first chapter, God speaks some things into being,[44] observes their goodness, and then names them. In the second chapter God speaks what should not be, stating its lack of goodness, and then observes what the man, not He, names the creatures. Unlike the first chapter of Genesis, seeing does not perform a personal evaluative or pleasure-giving (receiving?) role with respect to God.

Transferral of Authority

In chapter 2, the content of the metaphor changes in that though God is still the subject, the object of His seeing is now the actions of another creature, rather than the direct result of His own. The text does not indicate any foreknowledge or influence on God's part of what Adam will choose to name the creatures, but this naming serves a different function in the narrative.

Though this chapter is often seen as generated by a different hand from chapter 1 (J as opposed to P), it seems a fruitless task to speculate upon the different *Sitz im Leben* for the generation of these two chapters as both utilise this same anthropomorphic language which is often cited as an early phenomenon (Eichrodt, etc.). Rather, we should look at the final form of the text to understand how the editor of the tradition viewed the pericopes as interacting.[45] In chapter 1, for instance, God has given the man dominion over the animals (1:28). Gerhard von Rad asserted that, "name-giving in the ancient Orient was primarily an exercise of sovereignty, of command."[46] Gordon Ramsey has convincingly demonstrated that naming is not necessarily a sign of authority[47] (Cf. Hagar naming

---

44. In verses 3, 9, 11, 15, 25, there is a confirmation of the newly formed existence of the entity immediately after God has said, "Let there be . . ." This is most often seen in the formula, "and it was so." In other cases, this formula is omitted and it is said that God made (אשׂה) v. 7, or God created (ברא) vv. 21, 27, possibly implying that God did not verbally call these things into being.

45. This will be our approach throughout the rest of the chapters as well.

46. Von Rad, *Genesis*, 83.

47. In fact, Ramsey notes that only in cases of kings bestowing new names [Joseph in Egypt (Gen 41:45), Eliakim and Mattaniah by kings of Egypt and Babylon respectively (2 Kgs 23:34; 24:17)], and "warriors conquering certain areas and naming them after themselves," does naming possibly indicate authority. Still, "In each of these cases it is the fact that the place is named after some individual that constitutes the claim

God Gen 16:13, and Isaac naming wells whose authority he is abdicating Gen 26:17–21). In fact, Ramsey says, "If the act of naming signifies anything about the name-giver, it is the quality of *discernment*."[48] Thus, "When *hā'ādām* names the animals, it is more appropriate to understand this as an act of his *discerning* something about these creatures—an essence which had already been established by God."[49] If this is the case, then God's naming in chapter 1, as well as the man's in chapter 2 refer to the discernment of qualities innate to the object being viewed. This would seem to be in line with the idea that God evaluates things according to their created purpose, as well as working well with the man's search for a suitable partner. Ramsey argues against naming being determinative of the recipient's nature, "When *hā'ādām* names the animals, it is more appropriate to understand this as an act of his *discerning* something about these creatures—an essence which had already been established by God. (If naming constituted the power to determine the essence of the creatures, why could *hā'ādām* not dictate the characteristics essential to enable one of the animals to be the *'ēzer kĕnegdô*?)"[50]

This interpretation, however, would render God's "seeing" as superfluous in the passage. Ramsey seems to conflate naming as an exercise of authority with naming as a determining creative act. He admits that there are passages where naming includes a claim of authority over another being. As God presumably knew the character of the animals He had created, does He watch the man name them merely to see if he agrees with God's own assessment?

There are some similarities between royal naming and this occasion. In its context within the canon, chapter 1 gives humanity the divine injunction to rule (*radah*) over the animals (vv 26, 28). God then commands the couple to "subdue" (*kabaš*) the earth. In the majority of its usage, this refers to the subjugation of a people, whether in war (Num 32:22, 29; Josh 18:1; 2 Sam 8:11; 1 Chr 22:18; 2 Chr 9:18), or in slavery (Neh 5:5; Jer 34:11, 16).[51]

---

of dominion." G. W. Ramsey, "Is Name-Giving an Act of Domination in Genesis 2:23 and Elsewhere?" 32.

48. Ibid., 34.

49. Ibid., 34–35.

50. Ibid.

51. The other instances represent similar actions such as Haman seen as "assaulting" Esther (Esth 7:8). There is a connotation of trampling underfoot when God subdues or tramples the iniquities of the people (Micah 7:19) and when the people of Zion "trample" on the sling stones (Zeph 9:15). All of these remain closely related

Seeing Good and Evil—Genesis 1–3

While this "rule" of humans over the animals was verbally commanded in chapter 1 (1:28), the beginning of its implementation is embodied in God's seeing in chapter 2. Thus, the rather passive role of God "seeing" what the man would name the animals is tantamount to His handing authority over the beasts to his vassal. This transfer of authority is underscored when 2:19 says, "and whatever he called it, that was its name."

Contextual considerations: Knowledge of Good and Evil

It is significant that the event of seeing is placed after 2:16–17, where God commands the man regarding the tree of the knowledge of good and evil. This juxtaposition connects the knowledge bound up in the forbidden fruit—the prerogative of deciding what is good and what is evil[52]—with authority. For instance, we see that in 1:4, after God "saw the light, that it was good," He separates it from darkness and then names it. God observes the goodness of the light, distinguishes it from its opposite, and demonstrates His authority over it by naming it. In contrast, in chapter 2, God forbids the man to eat from the tree of the knowledge of good and evil, yet extends to him the privilege of naming his fellow creatures. Compare the following sequences:

Chapter 1	Chapter 2
God *sees* the goodness of creation	God forbids man from independently acquiring knowledge of good/evil
God *names* the creation	God sees man *name* the creatures

The two main actions of seeing and naming are realigned with respect to goodness. From this we see that God gives man jurisdiction over the animals, and yet this authority is explicitly excluded from the act of valuation—deeming them good or evil. His authority in naming the creatures merely extends to his relationship with them, not to their ultimate value.

---

to the idea of subjection and the idea of someone exerting power over someone or something else.

52. See Excursus: The Knowledge of Good and Evil.

Relational Evaluation

This sequence of the man naming the animals seems odd in the context of searching for a suitable helper. In fact, we find in 2:20 that a helper is not found for the man. (lit. "for Adam, he did not find a helper corresponding to him" וּלְאָדָם לֹא־מָצָא עֵזֶר כְּנֶגְדּוֹ). The subject of this clause is unclear, for it is never stated that either the man or God were searching for anything. It was not simply that Adam didn't find the helper, as if he didn't look hard enough, or wisely enough, which would have been easy enough to say. But here, God Himself would seem to be included in the verb, as He is observing the whole situation (v. 19), brings the creatures to the man, and does this all after stating His intention to make a corresponding helper for the man (2:18). In fact, the parallel phrases in 18 and 20 would seem to indicate that God was the subject of both.

18b: אֶעֱשֶׂה־לּוֹ עֵזֶר כְּנֶגְדּוֹ:

"I will make for him a helper corresponding to him."

20b: וּלְאָדָם לֹא־מָצָא עֵזֶר כְּנֶגְדּוֹ

"But for the[53] man, He did not find a helper corresponding to him."

It seems that implied in God's "seeing what man would name the creatures," was an evaluation of the relationship between them, rather than their intrinsic value, as in chapter 1. Apparently, the (non)suitability of the creatures for the man is appraised in the names that Adam gives them. Like him, all of the other creatures are created from the ground, (2:7, 19). But unlike them, God has personally "breathed the spirit of life into his nostrils."[54] Thus, he requires something more for his partner. It is only when God intervenes and creates woman *from the man*,[55] that a being cor-

---

53. BHS notes indicate this should be read with the article, "the man." Hess finds the first definitive use of Adam in 5:1–3, while all previous instances, either articular or inarticular functioning similar to the Akkadian logogram *lú* (man, human being) Hess, "Splitting the Adam."

54. Note, other beings seem to have this *nephesh hayyah* (7:2), but none have it personally breathed into them by God. Furthermore, woman would then have been made not from inanimate dirt, but from a creature who already had the "breath of life" in him. All this serves to connect the woman with the man as unique from other creatures and seen as a unified whole.

55. Notably, woman is the only creature not directly created from the ground. This appears later in the punishment directed at the man in 3:19—"By the sweat of your face You will eat bread, Till you return to the ground [*'adamah*], Because from it you

responding (*knegdo*) for the man is found (cf. 2:18, 22). She too is named by the man, but uniquely, as she is, "flesh of my flesh and bone of my bones." His quest is finished because she "corresponds to him," as only one who is equal in substance can. As the two are considered "one flesh" (v. 24), man's "helper" is considered equally part of him.

In light of this, it would seem that God's seeing what man calls the creatures also carries the sense of evaluating the "goodness" or "appropriateness" of the relationships between the creatures. God sees this in Adam's naming, and perhaps the man does as well. God sees the man name them with names that do not reflect his own substance. Hence, He creates a new being from the man, and presumably continues watching as the man names her "Woman—for out of man she was taken." The name and the helper fit perfectly.

Hence, whilst in the first chapter God's seeing played more of a role of evaluation and an expression of God's enjoyment of the innate quality of His work, in chapter 2, it signifies a transferal of authority to the man. All trace of the previous enjoyment is absent here. God too, had noticed something was amiss, both in Adam's aloneness, and also in the fact that He Himself did not find an appropriate complement to the man among what He had already created. However, in watching the man name, He evaluates the relations between creatures, and as He will many times in the future, intervenes to make them right. We find then, that God's "seeing" represents an interaction with His creation, for in "seeing" the actions of another He essentially takes a more passive role, allowing the man to act in a similar manner to the way He had in the previous chapter—exercising authority over part of creation (i.e., God names the day and night, v. 3). At the same time, God exercises His wisdom in establishing the man's peer relations.

Summary

Hence, we see that the content of the metaphor of God "seeing" changes in this particular context, and yet, the character is still that of an interaction between God and His creation, based on God's visual observation of it. In the context of the creation of the universe (Gen 1) God's seeing was not only evaluative of the worth of His creation, separately and as a whole, but also stressed the enjoyment God took in His creation and the reflection of His own character within it. The objects of the seeing were

---

were taken; For you are dust, And to dust you shall return."

the varying pieces of His creation, their goodness, and their nature as a collective whole.

In the second chapter of Genesis, the context is still creative, but more specifically concerns the lack of a mate for fulfilling God's procreative purpose for man (cf. 1:28). The object of God's seeing is now an act of one of His creatures, which highlights the limited sense of authority with which God invests the man. This use of seeing implies a transfer of authority from God to the man in that part of what God had done is now done by the man. However, this is only partial, in that man is not allowed to determine the value of creation. Furthermore, God's sight is an evaluation of (non)corresponding relationships, prompting His creation of woman. Both of these things are described as real events within the narrative and not simply states of affairs, further indicating the truth-conditioned nature of this statement concerning God's sight.

This contrast in the usage and entailments of the verb for sight in the first two chapters reflects Stern's idea that metaphorical character is nonconstant. It's meaning, like demonstratives such as "this" or indexicals such as "now" is dependent upon its context of usage. In the first chapter it reflected the evaluation of creation and expressed a personal delight of the Creator in His creativity. Chapter 2 found the verb functioning to transfer a limited sense of authority to humanity. Chapter 1 found God seeing everything as innately good, whereas chapter 2 finds the relationships between man and animals as "not good"—at least for the purposes of partnership and fulfilling God's procreative decrees.

Having examined the differing contexts of God's seeing in the first two chapters, let us now turn to the third chapter, which provides our first direct contrast with divine sight in the form of human sight. The comparison with divine sight is especially apt here, as the human couples' eyes are "opened" and they become *like God*, (3:5, 7, 22) knowing good and evil. In the following, we shall look at the nature of human sight, its objects, and how it becomes like God in order to discern the differences and similarities with divine sight.

Seeing Good and Evil—Genesis 3:6

> *When the woman saw that the tree was good for food, and that it was a delight to the eyes, and that the tree was desirable to make one wise, she took from its fruit and ate; and she gave also to her husband with her, and he ate.*

Contrast with Divine Sight

Initially, human sight finds similarity with divine sight in that it sees goodness in creation. The man sees the suitability of his wife for her created purpose as his partner.[56] However, when the woman encounters the serpent, we find a new sense of vision. Von Rad describes it as a, "rush through an entire scale of emotions. 'Good for food,' that is the coarsely sensual aspect; 'a delight to the eyes,' that is the finer, more aesthetic stimulus; and 'desired to make one wise,' that is the highest and decisive enticement (cf. 1 John 2:16, 'the lust of the flesh and the lust of the eyes and the pride of life')."[57]

Unlike God, the woman uses her physical organs ("it was a delight to the *eyes*"), and, instead of merely finding the fruit good, a strain of doubt creeps into her thinking. As Wenham observes, as she continues to see, she also begins to covet, for the verbs describing what she saw are related to the tenth commandment. "'Delight,' תאוה and 'desirable,' נחמד, are from roots meaning 'to covet' (Deut 5:21; cf. Exod 20:17)."[58] So, this usage has something in common with the act of God seeing in chapter 1 in that both appreciate the innate goodness and beauty of creation. However, it contrasts with this use of divine sight not only in the manner in which the woman sees, but also in that her sight is tainted by the motives which lay behind it.

Nature of Vision

Upon eating the fruit, the woman and the man, having their eyes "opened," gain the knowledge of good and evil (cf. 3:22). But, as most commentators observe, it is their nakedness of which they become aware, an ignorance that had previously caused them no shame (2:25). This realization is underscored with the oft-cited word-play on the nakedness (*ʿērōm*) of the couple and the "craftiness" (*ʿārûm*) of the serpent (3:1) The woman employs her vision, not in response to a creative act, but to a lie given by the serpent. Genesis 3, then, tells of the introduction of an "aversion to

---

56. Genesis 2:23. Cf. the use of *happaʿam*—(now, finally, etc.) to underscore the excitement of the man at this new creature made suitable for him in a way nothing else in creation was.

57. von Rad, *Genesis*, 90.

58. Wenham, *Genesis 1–15*, 75.

(human) nakedness" as *a deviant perspective*, and not a created norm.⁵⁹ Combined with the covetous nature of the woman's sight discussed earlier, we begin to create a picture of human sight. Its corruption seems to be in two arenas, in the motives behind it and the manner in which it is used to evaluate things and states such as nakedness. But, the fact that it is corrupted at all implies that it was not created with such defects. Let us examine the change in sight to gather more insight on its differences with divine sight.

A New View: the Opening of the Eyes

In reviewing the serpent's strategy of seduction, Moberly says the couple is promised that, "(a) their eyes will be opened, an expression which elsewhere in the Old Testament has positive connotations of a new God-given quality of perception (e.g., Gen 21:19, 2 Kgs. 6:17, 20); (b) they will be like God who knows good and evil, and this too picks up one of the positive fundamentals of Old Testament faith, that human nature finds its fulfilment in the imitation of God (so e.g., Gen 1:26–28; Lev. 19:2). So the serpent is offering a prospect that is in principle entirely good and desirable."⁶⁰ It is this different nature of seeing that is relevant to our discussion. In 3:22 God acknowledges that, "the man has become like one of Us, knowing good and evil." If this has come about through the "opening of their eyes,"

---

59. This is against Moberly's view (Moberly, "Did the Serpent Get It Right?") that nakedness was always shunned in Hebrew society. However, J. Collins writes, "Moberly, 'Did the serpent get it right,' 8–9, suggests that this is actually something positive, since 'the dislike of nakedness is never considered something negative or sinful in the Old Testament.' This assumes too many things: first, that the passage is not about a particular event whose consequences all humans receive; second, that the text *reflects*, 'Hebrew outlook' as opposed to trying to *shape* that outlook. Since the action of clothing themselves is in contrast to the unashamed nakedness of 2:25, it is appropriate to find here evidence of a change in their condition. Further, this would be the *origin* of the importance of clothing oneself for subsequent time. Also, as many commentators point out, the fact that their next reaction is to hide in the bushes at the sound of the Lord's approach (verse 8) is evidence of a bad conscience. Westermann, 253, objects to such reasoning: 'these words express directly neither a consciousness of guilt nor a fear that results from it. Had J wanted to say that, he would have said it clearly and unequivocally.' But this is an insistence on *telling* rather than *showing*, contrary to the Hebrew narrative style! Further, he says, the couple hide because of their 'fear of being naked before,'; but what else is this but a bad conscience? And surely this misses the point of the stark contrast with 2:25." Collins, "What Happened to Adam and Eve?" 30, note 61.

60. Moberly, "Did the Serpent Get It Right?" 7.

has human sight then become divine? In what way? And further, has it done so through rebellion?

To answer these questions, we must take a closer look at the nature of this perception. Whilst we agree that the phrase "their eyes will be opened" does indicate a new "quality of perception" elsewhere in the OT, it seems that the key element here is that it is not *God-given*. In both the pericopes Moberly cites—Hagar in the wilderness and Elisha and his servant at Samaria—it is God Himself who causes Hagar to see the well and the lad to see the horses and chariots of fire. In Eden, however, it was the fruit that the man and woman take *on their own* which facilitates the new sight. In fact, in all other cases, God is behind the opening of human eyes in the OT (cf. Num 22:31 and 2 Kgs 4:35; Ps 35:21; and Isa 35:5).

Furthermore, the "opening of the eyes" is typically a positive thing.[61] That is, either the person is physically blind and then healed (Ps 146:8), or they are unaware of something of importance and are made aware of it (2 Kgs 6:17–20; Isa 35:5; 42:7). In contrast, the "opening" of the eyes in Gen 3 consists of a unique usage, where it is obtained by the human couple in rebellion against God rather than as a result of His beneficence or answer to prayer, and results in a negative view of what was once pronounced "good" (cf. 1:31).

Actions Mimic Creator

Wenham sees the key to understanding "eye opening" as lying in the woman's mimicry of the divine actions. In trying to become divine, the woman oversteps the bounds of creaturely behavior. "Actions hitherto characteristic of the creator are now ascribed to the woman. She 'saw *that* the tree was *good*,' clearly echoing the refrain of Gen 1, 'God saw . . . that it was good.'"[62]

---

61. D. J. A. Clines says, "In the Gen. iii narrative we find that after Adam and Eve had eaten the fruit of the tree of knowledge 'their eyes were opened' (*watti-paqahnâ 'ênê šenêhem*, iii 7). *Pāqah 'ênayim* often means 'to open the eyes after sleep', but sometimes metaphorically 'to cause someone to become aware of something' by means of supernatural insight: e.g., God opened Hagar's eyes, Gen. xxi 19; Elisha prays to God to open the eyes of the young man to see the mountain full of horses and chariots of fire (2 Kings vi 17). In this sense the phrase is exactly equivalent to *gillâ 'ênayim* as in Num. xxii 31: Yahweh opened (*wayegal*) the eyes of Balaam and he saw the angel of Yahweh on the path. With this we may compare 'Open thou my eyes that I may behold wondrous things out of thy law' (Ps. cxix 18). The law of Yahweh as a light to the eyes is thus compared to the fruit of the tree which brought knowledge (*wayyēdeʿû*, Gen. iii 7) through the opening of the eyes." Clines, "The Tree of Knowledge," 11.

62. Wenham, *Genesis 1–15*, 75.

This aping of God, along with taking the fruit as God had taken the man's rib, and fashioning fig leaves, as God fashioned everything, leads Wenham to conclude, "The human pair are shown usurping divine prerogatives as well as explicitly disobeying God's express word."[63] Moberly casts this as a sort of moral independence.[64] "If one allows the context of the Genesis story itself to be the decisive factor in determining the details of the story, it would appear most likely that 'knowledge of good and evil' signifies *moral autonomy*, that is the adoption of a stance whereby one decides right and wrong for oneself rather than in obedience to divine Torah."[65]

However, whilst it is certainly the case that the couple disobeyed the word of the LORD God, it is not immediately clear that this amounted to trespassing upon the domain of the divine. Only in the mouth of the wily serpent does the text hint that God would not want them to become like Himself in "knowing good and evil." Can a voice from such a character be trusted to represent divine designs? In other texts, such a phrase designates an age of accountability (Deut 1:39; Isa 7:14). It could well have been that the man and woman were designed to gain such knowledge through different means, such as fellowship with God Himself. The prohibition on the fruit did not indicate that wisdom itself was forbidden, but that avenues to gaining it outside God's provenance were forbidden.

Viewpoint

This difference in *viewpoint* is crucial to the entire pericope. Von Rad illustrates this in the ancient definition of good and evil.

> For the ancients, the good was not just an idea: the good was what had a good effect; as a result, in this context "good and evil" should be understood more as what is "beneficial" and "salutary" on the one hand and "detrimental," "damaging" on the other. So the serpent holds out less the prospect of an extension of the capacity for knowledge than the independence that enables a man to decide for himself what will help him or hinder him. This is something completely new in that as a result man leaves the protection of divine providence.[66]

---

63. Ibid.
64. For further discussion, see Appendix: The Knowledge of Good and Evil
65. Moberly, "Did the Serpent Get It Right?" 24.
66. von Rad, *Genesis*, 89.

So, when their eyes are opened, "For the first time, in their shame they detect something like a rift that can be traced to the depths of their being . . . which governs the whole being of man from the lowest level of his corporeality."[67] The couple goes from no knowledge of their naked state (innocent eyes) to knowledge with shame (tainted eyes).[68] What the couple had formerly known in trust as a given good, they now see as a weakness and vulnerability. This demonstrates the changeable nature of human vision in the pericope.

Hamilton, following von Rad, characterizes this element, "von Rad is quite correct when he says that 'the serpent's insinuation is the possibility of an extension of human existence beyond the limits set for it by God at creation, an increase of life not only in the sense of pure intellectual enrichment but also familiarity with and power over, mysteries that lie beyond man.'"[69] However, there is more involved in the temptation than simply the possibility of gaining mastery over realms not initially placed under their authority.

In addition to the negative view of this newly acquired "vision" displayed in the couple's reaction, we find another clue to its nature *before* the woman takes the fruit. In the promise of wisdom the woman finds a deficiency in herself. The woman is faced not simply with the differences between her and God, but also the implication that she should be other than she is. Seeing the fruit as "profitable to make one wise"[70] necessarily implies that she is not.[71] This newly borrowed worldview insinuates that

---

67. Ibid., 91.

68. This perhaps implies there might have been a third, unexplored option, that of being enabled by God, (not the forbidden fruit), to see things like their nakedness, yet, as in chapter one, with His eyes—as good (*tob*).

69. Hamilton, *The Book of Genesis*, 190, quoting von Rad, *Genesis*, 89.

70. The verb (*lehaskil*) is in the causative stem (hiphil) yielding, "to cause to be wise." Wenham says, "In the woman's eyes, the forbidden tree is now like the other trees. It was also 'desirable to give one insight.' This is preferable to the 'desirable to look at' of Vg, S, Gunkel, and Skinner, who, prompted by 2:9, would ascribe a rare, if not unparalleled, meaning to השכיל, which otherwise has to do with understanding." Wenham, *Genesis 1–15*, 75.

71. Not merely a state of affairs such as the man's aloneness, this is something intrinsic to her being. This differs from the first two enticements she finds to eat the fruit (v. 6). Though seeing fruit as edible might make one hungry, and seeing its beauty might strike one with awe, neither implies a defect in the one seeing it. One simply satisfies the hunger or enjoys the vision of beauty, both of which were in plentiful supply in the garden. These descriptions simply imply that there was nothing physically ominous about the fruit itself. It is the potential to gain divine wisdom that changes the woman's outlook not just on the fruit, but herself.

In the Eyes of God

she requires something her Creator has not provided for her. Consequently, her worth begins to be measured on a different scale from her divinely created purpose, and focuses on being fully autonomous and equal with God (at least in knowledge).

We can also see this element in the woman's reaction to being caught. W. Lee Humphreys comments on her reply to God's questions,

> "The snake tricked me," she says, rather than "The Snake made me or forced me." She seems to acknowledge that she entered into the Snake's way of seeing things as she examined them for herself, and thus acknowledges her role in the outcome. Indirectly Yahweh God appears to acknowledge her acknowledgement by not prefacing his next words to her with "because you did this . . ." or "because you listened . . ." as he does for the Snake and the Man.[72]

So, one of the distinctions between divine and human seeing here is that humans can "buy" into other ways of seeing the world. Furthermore, this mode of seeing the world shifts the foundations of human valuation, both of the world and of themselves. This contrasts with the divine sight we saw in chapter 1, which seemed to detect an innate value within creation, according to its created purpose.

Conclusion

In the text, we have an explicit comparison between God and humans. In Gen 3:5, the tempter dangles the proverbial carrot in front of the couple, insinuating that they too can be like God in their knowing, specifically in having their eyes "opened." Moreover, he implies that God does not desire this to come about ("*For God knows that . . .*") and has laid down the law for this purpose. This is obviously a metaphorical usage of "opening the eyes" in that in verse 6, the woman sees that the fruit of the forbidden tree is good for food, and aesthetically pleasing. All of this she discerns with her physical eyes ("וְכִי תַאֲוָה־הוּא לָעֵינַיִם" "and that it was a delight to the *eyes*"). However, here we have the woman using sight in both a physical and mental capacity. She sees the tree and its beauty, but as seen with the *kî* clause (*that it was profitable to make one wise*) she also *perceives* its utility for her purposes. This function of sight is often noted but rarely contrasted with that of God. In the first chapter of Genesis, for example, we see that God sees the goodness in each thing He creates, but not for any

---

72. Humphreys, *The Character of God in the Book of Genesis*, 47.

Seeing Good and Evil—Genesis 1–3

mentioned personal gain. He sees light, for example, simply as good in its own right (1:4 "וַיַּרְא אֱלֹהִים אֶת־הָאוֹר כִּי־טוֹב," "And God saw the light, that *it was* good").

The couple's new sight actually begins to be manifested *before* the temptation, and seems to have the effect of placing its *subject* in a poor light. That is, the object, whether fruit or the state of nakedness, does not change in its value, (i.e., its created purpose), but in how it is valued by the one seeing it. It is their eyes which have changed. What was originally viewed for its innate worth according to its created function is now viewed in relation to a diminished sense of adequacy and self-worth on the part of the one seeing. This seems also to have been manifested not only in the actual transgression of God's command, but in the adoption of the view the serpent lays out, including possibilities for the future, denial of God's words, and the perception of deficiency and need within themselves.

In what sense is this like God? As Wenham, Moberly, Hamilton, and von Rad observe, the couple has now taken on the responsibility of *determining* good and evil. This is not an ontological consideration but a perspectival one. Here begins the diffusion of truth. Whereas God sees innate and corporate goodness according to created purposes, and even enjoys this, the couple see a secondary or utilitarian goodness which centers upon their own perception of need. Whereas they could initially detect the former, (cf. the man's view of the creation of the woman), this is supplanted by the adoption of the view of the serpent.

Hence, in these first three chapters, we find the uses of divine sight to substantially differ. Initially, we find a "God's eye" view of creation's innate goodness, both piecemeal and collectively. This usage entails an interaction with creation, as the objects of sight are emphasized (in 4, and 31, and by ellipsis in the rest), putting this out of the realm of simple cognition. In chapter 2, sight acts as a signal of the transfer of God's authority, as the object is now the action of the man. Furthermore, there is an evaluation of creaturely relationships, which is subsequently acted upon. In none of these cases is omniscience necessarily entailed, and yet distinct interplay with the created objects of sight is highlighted. This shows that sight as a metaphor must be interpreted according to its context. Furthermore, the contrast with human sight in chapter 3 shows it to be initially like divine sight in its appreciation of the goodness in creation, and yet susceptible to a more self-centered utilitarian ethic.[73] In this, we see that rather than

---

73. By "utilitarian ethic," we are primarily referring to the sense in which the woman saw value in the tree (and its fruit) in terms of its potential to further her

utterly distinct, there is some overlap in the sense of human and divine action.

---

own ends- of becoming "wise." (Gen 3:6) This provides both a distinct parallel and contrast with God's own sight in Genesis 1, where God also sees value in creation. This is similar to the woman's seeing, in that God also values creation according to its suitability for fulfilling His purposes. But this is because an object's created purpose is also in line with, if not identical to, God's purpose. The contrast lies in the fact that here, the woman's purposes are at odds with those of the Creator (Gen 2:17, 3:3), and thus her estimation of the tree no longer rests on its created purpose.

5

God, the Sons of God, and the Man of God

Genesis 6:2, 5, 12; 7:1; 9:16

A SIMILAR THEME OF DIVINE SIGHT RUNS THROUGH THE FLOOD NARRAtive.[1] Both prominent and key to the story's structure, it provides us yet another contrast—that of the "sons of God." This particular usage holds special interest due to the non-corporeal nature of these beings. Additionally, the many echoes throughout this pericope drawn from earlier texts give us further insight into the nature of divine sight. In the following, we shall examine the nature of the vision of the "sons of God" (6:2), contrasting it with that of God Himself (6:5, 7:1). Then we shall look at a different instances of divine sight seen in the covenant made between God and Noah involving the rainbow (9:16). Then we have another contrast with divine sight—that of Noah's son Ham (9:22). For all of these occasions of 'seeing,' we shall compare their meaning in context, involving the seer, scope/object, nature, and narrative purpose/effect. From this we hope to further draw out the full range of meaning of divine sight as it is used and defined in this context, noting its similarities and differences with the sight of other beings.

The "Sons of God"—Genesis 6:2

> *The sons of God saw that the daughters of man were good.*
> *And they took as their wives any they chose.*

---

1. The Flood narrative is often divided into two versions, one by J, and one by the P source, but the lines of such division are heavily debated as is the division itself. As such, this is beyond the scope of this study, and we will focus on the final form of the text to ascertain the usage of the anthropomorphic expressions of divine sight.

In the Eyes of God

Form

God's "seeing" forms a key part of the structure in the first part of Gen 6, forming an inclusio with His other actions based on His view of mankind as a whole and Noah in particular. Wenham observes the structure of Gen 6:1–8 and finds: "The contents of 6:1–8 are arranged in a rough palistrophe:

> A The LORD sees mankind, 6:5
>   B The LORD regrets, 6:6
>   C The LORD says "I shall wipe out," 6:7
>   B' because I regret
> A' The LORD sees Noah, 6:8[2]

Wenham also demonstrates a parallel in the introduction to the Flood narrative, contrasting the sight of the "sons of god" with that of the LORD Himself.

> The sons of god   see ...   the daughters ... are good
>
> The LORD   sees   the thoughts   are evil[3]

From this, we observe not only that divine sight is a key motif in this pericope, but also that the difference in *how* God sees things conveys His unique values. As divine beings and part of God's council (cf. Job 1:6; 2:1; 38:7), the "sons of God"[4] comprise an interesting parallel, for their use

---

2. Wenham, *Genesis 1–15*, 136.

3. Ibid., 137.

4. There are three main views on the identity of the "sons of God(s)" in Gen 6:1–4. The Sethite view purports that this was a the godly line of Seth who then intermarried the godless line of Cain. (Though compare the reverse theory by Eslinger, "A Contextual Identification".) Evidence for this is severely lacking in the text, and furthermore, this does not explain the race of Nephilim. Another view, such as that of Meredith Kline, holds these to be despotic human kings (Kline, "Divine Kingship"). However, this view also runs into the same problems as the first, as well as that "daughters of *men*" is a generic group, especially in light of the use of *'adam* (men) in 6:1, 3. The third view is the so-called "angel" view, of which Wenham says, "The 'angel' interpretation is at once the oldest view and that of most modern commentators. It is assumed in the earliest Jewish exegesis (e.g., the books of 1 Enoch 6:2ff.; Jubilees 5:1), LXX, Philo (*De Gigant* 2:358), Josephus (*Ant.* 1.31) and the Dead Sea Scrolls (1 QapGen 2:1; CD 2:17–19). The NT (2 Pet 2:4, Jude 6,7) and the earliest Christian writers (e.g., Justin, Irenaeus, Clement of Alexandria, Tertullian, Origen) also take this line." Wenham, *Genesis 1–15*, 139. This not only has the advantage of more attestation, but it fits both with the interpretation of *'adam* and explains the Nephilim. Other views espouse nearly the same concept, preferring gods (Westermann, *Genesis 1–11*, 372) or semi-divine beings akin to Gilgamesh (Clines, "The Significance of the 'Sons of God' Episode"). It

God, the Sons of God, and the Man of God

of sight cannot be ruled any less "anthropomorphic" than that of God Himself. Thus they provide something of a common denominator, and yet their sight is set in stark contrast with His. We shall now investigate the object of the "sons of God's" sight—the daughters of men—and how they are viewed, to further delineate the background against which God's sight is contrasted.

Rebellion in Heaven, Subterfuge on Earth

Why would the "sons of God" desire human marriages? Westermann suggests an insurgency on the part of the sons of God. "We might suggest then that there lay behind 6:3 a version of the story that has been deliberately obscured, according to which the sons of the gods, like Prometheus, took the part of humankind by marrying the daughters of men, aspired to raise the status of the human race and so forced the creator to intervene."[5] Clines opts for a very human and violent interpretation of their progeny, the Nephilim,[6] but nothing in their behavior is specifically reprimanded. They are simply "warriors" (*gibborim*) and "men of name." Neither description is explicitly condemned in the text. Rather, there seems to be greater promise of explanation in their ancestry. If, as part of a divine rebellion, these Nephilim were created not simply to dominate, but to unite a divided rebellion against God, then their purpose is in their lineage, not just their behavior.

In this case, the story in Genesis 6 would represent the ambition of spiritual beings to corrupt the purpose of God. As Hamilton says, "This story, with this approach [that the sons of God were divine beings], supplies another illustration of such transgression, albeit in the opposite direction. Here the divine or angelic world illegitimately impinges on the human world."[7] According to Clines, the result of the creation of their hybrid race is an offence against God's image.[8] "We find a satanic parody of the idea of the image of God in man. Far from God being present on earth in the person of man as his kingly representative exercising benign

---

is with the view that the "sons of God" are divine beings, that we shall proceed with our exegesis.

5. Westermann, *Genesis 1-11*, 374.

6. Clines sees them as men either sired by divine beings or merely viewed as divine by other men as with kings like Gilgamesh.

7. Hamilton, *The Book of Genesis*, 263.

8. Clines posits a synthetic view of the sons of God as human rulers seen to be divine. Thus his conception of the Nephilim is that of both divine and human despots.

dominion over the lower orders of creation, we now have the presence of the divine on earth in a form that utterly misrepresents God through its exercise of royal violence and despotic authority over other humans."[9] Hence, this act of divine-human procreation was a strike at the heart of the nature of this image.

However, this theory of rebellion runs into two problems: the withdrawal of the spirit of God and the punishment of humans. God's response is rather nebulous in verse 3, "My Spirit will not dwell (יָדוֹן)[10] with mankind forever, because he is flesh (*basar*)." As man's corporeality is hardly a new fact (Gen 2:21, 23, 24), it cannot by itself explain the withdrawal of God's Spirit.[11]

Furthermore, as the Nephilim also existed afterwards (6:4), this removal cannot simply have been to prove their mortality. As David Petersen observes, "Longevity *per se* is no problem in the primeval history, especially for the Priestly writer. And for the Yahwist in Gen 6:1–4, the issue is surely whether or not this mutant strain of humanity will live *'ôlām* [forever], not simply whether they will live a long time."[12] A further

---

9. Clines, "The Significance of the 'Sons of God' Episode," 37.

10. Kraeling derives the Hebrew (יָדוֹן) from the verb (דִּין) "to contend, judge." Kraeling, "The Significance and Origin of Gen. 6:1–4." He claims the vocalization with the holem is similar to verbs "conjugated after the manner of יָבוֹא *yābhō*, יָאוֹר *yāʾōr*," which Cassuto finds, "are not particularly satisfactory." Cassuto, *A Commentary on the Book of Genesis*, 295. However, Cassuto finds a significant amount of cognate evidence that this could mean "remain," in which case, the idea is that God's Spirit cannot indwell His corrupted image. Whereas Cassuto finds this to be the "spirit of life," we see read this more as God's own Spirit (cf. von Rad, *Genesis*, 115), which, though absent within mankind will still enable his life.

11. Hans Walter Wolff observes that, "Even in the Old Testament *b*[*asar*, 'flesh']. does not only mean the powerlessness of the mortal creature but also the feebleness of his faithfulness and obedience to the will of God." Wolff, *Anthropology*, 31. Furthermore, in the *Theological Dictionary of the Old Testament*, N. P. Bratsiotis says specifically of Gen 6:3, "It cannot be denied that in this passage sin is intimately connected with *basar*, and that it is also used to denote the ethical aspect of man, in spite of the cosmic dualism between *ruach yhvh*, 'the spirit of Yahweh,' and *basar* (which is here par. to *'adham*, 'man'). Moreover, it can be maintained with certainty that *basar* as a designation of man (so esp. in Ps. 56:5[4]; 78:39; as well as *kol basar*), and especially as an antithesis to God (so Jer. 17:5; Job 10:4; 2 Ch. 32:8), not only emphasizes all the characteristics of *basar* that have been mentioned, but also reflects its ethical inadequacy and inclination to sin as well as its physical nature." Botterweck, *TDOT*, s.v. "בָּשָׂר." Hence, here in Gen 6, it is mankind's physical nature which is contrasted with God's Spirit, but his ethical weakness. Because man as flesh, is *sinful and rebellious* in nature, God's Spirit will no longer abide with him.

12. Petersen, "Yahweh and the Organization of the Cosmos," 50–51.

complication lies in the fact that it seems this withdrawing would indeed limit human lifespan—but to nothing at all! As Job 34:14–15 indicates, the removal of God's Spirit would result in the immediate death of humanity, not merely decrease his days. If this had been the sum effect of the withdrawal of God's Spirit, flood waters would not have been necessary.

THE PUNISHMENT OF THE INNOCENT?

However, this raises another question—the one most often posited against the theory that the sons of God are divine beings: why are humans punished for acts of the sons of God?[13] Hre Kio sees the guilt of the sons of God confirmed in intertextual allusions about "taking women." "[In] other passages such as Genesis 12.10–20, and 2 Samuel 11, the contexts show that seeing and taking women is automatically condemned."[14] He adds, "In the context we see a situation where humankind was being punished for the sins of 'the sons of God.' The crucial question is: If it was angels who were the ones to blame, why was the judgment of God not directed against them? . . . The guilty ones were those who came from above; the women seemed to have been doing nothing except being beautiful."[15]

However, discerning the actual wrong committed here is more difficult than it would seem at first. Though some commentators feel this amounts to rape, Cassuto notes, "*And they took them wives* is simply the usual expression for legal marriage. The passage contains not a single word . . . alluding to rape or adultery or any act against the LORD's will."[16] Some of these arguments simply confuse "taking wives" with "taking other men's wives." For instance, Wenham observes, "Westermann argues that the parallells in 12:10–20 and 2 Sam 11 show that seeing and taking a woman is automatically condemned, and such a condemnation may be inferred here. But again his conclusion is unjustified. The Pharaoh and David were condemned because they committed adultery with other men's wives;

---

13. E.g., Clines says, "The principal objection to this identification is that it is far from clear in the present context why mankind as a whole should be subjected to the divine threat of verse 3 for the sin of such non-human beings; the 'daughters of men' can hardly have been regarded as culpable (though their beauty [verse 2] was the antecedent condition), since they were taken by force." Clines, "The Significance of the 'Sons of God' Episode," 34. In fact, however, this question holds whether the sons of God are human or divine, for why should the innocent suffer at the hands of human tyrants any more than those of divine beings?

14. Kio, "Revisiting 'the Sons of God,'" 235.

15. Ibid., 235.

16. Cassuto, *A Commentary on the Book of Genesis*, 294.

there is no hint of that here."[17] Hamilton adds, "When indiscriminate rape is described some verb like 'forced' (2 Sam. 13:14) is necessary. Furthermore, in the OT (Gen 36:2; 2 Sam 1:20, 24; Isa 3:16) *benōt* ('daughters') followed by a gentilic or a place name normally designates those who are eligible for marriage, another indication that we are dealing here with marriage rather than rape."[18]

There are other instances of the combination, "saw, . . . took" that involve illicit sexual union. One is the rape of Tamar (2 Sam 13), and the other that of Dinah (Gen 34). In his treatment of the latter, Robin Parry compares the two and finds, "We have seen that the very language used to describe the crime ('saw . . . took, lay, shamed') carries with it a negative evaluation of what happened. This leaves us in no doubt as to the narrator's stance on the crime."[19] However, unlike these stories, Gen 6 contains no mention of "defiling" (טמא), "shaming" (ענה), or "playing the fool (in Israel)." Although the Hebrew (נָשִׁים) can mean simply "women," it also commonly refers to "wives." As we previously mentioned, the emphasis in the chapter was on the bearing of children (v. 1, 4). The sons of God "go into" (יָבֹאוּ) the daughters of men, who "bear them children" (וְיָלְדוּ לָהֶם). This is not rampant or mass rape, but an event in the course of the multiplication of the human race. All of these elements of the story testify to the consensual nature of the relationship.

Hence, this passage is not portraying the "sons of God" as forcing themselves on "the daughters of men." In which case, the silence on the part of the women and their fathers speaks a bit louder. If they had been subjected to injustice, why does their distress go unmentioned, and the exploits of their progeny become highlighted?

If, however, the divine enemies of God have unified themselves with His images, then the evacuation of God's spirit begins to make sense. It intimates that mankind was "sleeping with the enemy" (Gen 2:24 "and the two shall become one flesh" [*basar*]), and hence was unfit to "sheath" (Heb. דין)[20] the divine Spirit. Rather, the "daughters of men" were in league

---

17. Wenham, *Genesis 1–15*, 141.

18. Hamilton, *The Book of Genesis*, 265.

19. Parry, *Old Testament Story and Christian Ethics*, 149. However, Parry notes that, "In Hebrew there is no technical term for rape so clearly all the terms used to describe this act (לקח את, שכב, ענה, טמא, נבלה עשה בישראל) can be used in non-rape situations." Parry, *Old Testament Story and Christian Ethics*, 143. In Gen 34, it is a collocation of these terms which merits the charge of rape. In Gen 6, there simply is no such context.

20. E. A. Speiser, argues against the conclusion of E. Kraeling for positing, "an

with the "sons of God." Not only they, but their fathers were as well, as they would have participated in the marriages. As there was no protest before God, no outcry (cf. Gen 18:20; Exod 3:7), there is an implied consent. They sought, as Westermann explains, "the elevation of the *genus humanum* as a group by super-men or semi-gods who were the fruit of the union of gods and women."[21] Hence, their act constitutes treason against God's ultimate purpose—that His Spirit would indwell those made as His images. This explains the condemnation of humanity in the flood, not for the acts of divine beings, but for being accomplices to them.

Thus, we propose that the withdrawal of God's Spirit represents a distancing of God's person from humanity as a result of their extreme corruption. Instead of seeking to fulfil their creation purpose as divine images, they have sought to become divine themselves, first through the fruit in the garden and now through divine intermarriage. Their rebellious ways make them unsuitable for their intended fellowship with Him. However, as God is not so quick to give up on His plans (Isa 55:11), He extends

---

underlying *dwn* in the sense of 'contend, strive,' without adequate linguistic justification. The required vocalization in that case would have had to be *yādūn*." Speiser, "YDWN, Gen. 6:3," 126 n. 5. Speiser opts for a connection with Akkadian *dinānu*. However, he too makes arbitrary shifts in the pointing of the vowels, from *yādōn* to *yādon*. (Cf. also Ronald Hendel who posits the Akkadian root *dnn* (fortress or stronghold), citing a place name "Dannah" in Josh 15:49. Hendel, "Of Demigods and the Deluge," 15, note 10.) Speiser connects this specifically with Akkadian *dinānu*, and even attests this in, "some of the old rabbinical sources and certain of the later writers versed in that material already operated with the same idea of 'shield, protect' in dealing with the form *yādon*. They based this on the occurrences of a nominal form containing the consonants *ndn*, which is found in the Aramaic portion of Daniel (7 15 , significantly in association with *ruūḥī*, just as in the passage before us) and in 1 Chron 21 27. The indicated sense in both instances is that of 'sheath,' which serves to protect the sword and could be used metaphorically, it was felt, as a symbol of protection for mankind." Speiser, "Ydwn, Gen 6:3," 127–28. Speiser then construes God as saying, "My Spirit will no longer shield the ungodly." However, this doesn't seem to fit with the following phrase, "nevertheless his days will be 120 years." If God is unsheathing humanity from His protection and delivering them to the flood, then why the 120 years? Others argue for a grace period (Keil, König, and Kidner). Though Speiser takes it as protection for mankind, a sheath is also a housing, similar to how the image functioned for the deity. As all we have are nominal forms, it is conceivable the verb is passive "to be sheathed." Thus, Yahweh is referring to humanity's role as a sheath for His Spirit. Thus it reads, "My Spirit will no longer be sheathed by (note the *bet* preposition in construct with *ha'adam*) mankind, for he is but flesh." This in turn explains the next phrase, "Nevertheless his days shall be 120 years." Though God is withdrawing His Spirit, he will not cause the immediate annihilation of mankind, but has set a limit on their life, despite the absence of His Spirit.

21. Westermann, *Genesis 1–11*, 369.

a grace period for human life to continue, not just before the flood, but to exist at all without His Spirit's immediate and constant presence.

The Sight of the Sons of God

What does all this say about the sight of the sons of God? Westermann says, "it is the beauty, not the sons of the gods and their action, that sets events in motion."[22] He compares this with similar plots in Gen 12:10–20 and 2 Sam 11f., where beauty seems to be the impetus for the taking of the women. But why is the beauty of the women the deciding factor?[23] If, as we have found, the sons of God are bent on the corruption of humans as divine images. But, how does this color their "divine sight" when they observe the "daughters of men" (Gen 6:2)?

An oft-overlooked, but distinct parallel with chapter 3 provides some answers.[24] Wenham notes, "The sequence of 'saw . . . good . . . took' parallels most closely the terminology in 3:6 and suggests the sinfulness of the action of the sons of God. When the woman saw and took, she transgressed a boundary set by the LORD."[25] Furthermore, in both chapters 3 and 6, we find a woman being used by a non-human being (if not divine), to instigate rebellion against God. This pattern is an unmistakable allusion to the motif of sin and rebellion against God in chapter 3, and it thus applies this perspective to the actions of the sons of God.

Not only similar in action, the parallel in 3:15 illuminates the motives of the sons of God for looking at and taking the daughters of men. Often referred to as the *proto-evangelium*, Yahweh makes a promise,

> And I will put enmity between you and the woman, and between your seed and her seed; He shall bruise you on the head, and you shall bruise him on the heel. (NASB)

---

22. Ibid., 372.

23. For instance, though angelic beings are only ever referred to as male, their taking of human form is obviously not their natural state. Hence, there remains some question of the gender of these beings. This is all the more relevant for our present story, as these beings focus solely on the daughters of men and not the sons. Either they truly are male in nature, or, they are focused on the 'seed of the woman' through which the divine promise is to be fulfilled, or perhaps, both.

24. But, cf., Budde, "War Genesis 6:1–4 ursprünglich mit der Sintflut verbunden?" *ZAW*, IX (1889), 135ff. Also cited in Kraeling, "The Significance and Origin of Gen. 6:1–4."

25. Wenham, *Genesis 1–15*, 141.

God, the Sons of God, and the Man of God

Hamilton observes, "Note the prominence given to these pronouns, which in the Hebrew text precede the verb for added emphasis: *'as for it*, it shall . . .,' and *'as for you*, you shall . . .'"[26] The subject of the third clause is highlighted in the same way that the subject of the final clause (you—the serpent) is. Whether or not this was messianic is highly debated, but there is clearly something significant going on here with respect to God's plans for the future of mankind. The nature of God's curse on the serpent says something relevant to the purpose of the "sons of God" in chapter 6, which may illuminate for us their "seeing" of the 'daughters of men.

The Curse

First, the serpent is cursed, "more than all cattle." What is the significance of this? We know that in chapter 1, cattle and creeping things are made in the same day as man, but he is given authority over them (1:26). This is due to his creation as the image of God. This same authority is reiterated in chapter 2 as Adam names all of the creatures, beginning specifically with "all cattle" (*lekol habbehēmāh*, 2:20). So in chapter 3, by ranking the serpent below the cattle, God is actually emphasizing his subjection to the man, over whom he had formerly attempted (quite successfully) to exert power through deception.

Furthermore, though God punishes both the man and the woman according to their gender-specific assignments (man being assigned to till the garden, and woman to aid the command to be fruitful and multiply), they nonetheless escape any sense of a curse. Rather, there is an oddly placed statement after their punishments. Adam names his wife Eve, the "mother of all living." They have just been punished for rebelling against God, and yet Eve is honored with a name proclaiming the fulfillment of one of the couple's original divine commands—to be fruitful and multiply (Gen 1:28). More interesting, however, is that Adam is never called the "father of all living." Neither is *his* seed mentioned at all, much less with respect to the serpent. Something to do with the continuation of life and the fulfillment of divine commands lies with the woman, not the man.

It is not mere coincidence that the serpent speaks with the woman and not the man. It is also significant that part of its curse contains a prophecy whereby the *seed of the woman*, and not the man or humanity in general, will crush its head. This serpent, whether intended as a purely mythical creature or a historical being, represents the influx of evil and

---

26. Hamilton, *The Book of Genesis*, 197.

rebellion within the ordered cosmos which God creates. Though its initial ploy is successful in spreading rebellion, the curse upon the serpent spells its ultimate demise ("He will crush your head"). It is thus reasonable to assume that the "seed of the woman," represents God's answer to the rebellion sparked by the serpent. In part, it displays God's commitment to the couple, and especially the woman. Though she was initially the one deceived, God not only re-instates the woman with respect to her divinely created purpose, but reaffirms her role[27] and employs it in the ultimate struggle against the serpent. She may have lost this battle, but she will play a key role in winning the ultimate one.

Similarly, progeny is key to the present story, which begins, "Now it came about, when mankind began to multiply upon the face of the earth, and daughters were born to them . . ."). Though not quite as explicitly, this emphasis is also repeated in the remainder of Genesis. For example, Sarah's seed (as opposed to Abraham's) is highlighted in chapters 16 and 21. Furthermore, it is Tamar's role in continuing the line that is emphasized, over Judah and his sons (cf. Ruth 4:12; 1 Chr 2:4; Matt. 1:3). Thus, we find the seed of the woman an important motif in Genesis. By controlling or altering the seed of the woman, in this case, the "daughters of men,"[28] the "sons of God," sought to interfere with God's plan for creation.

If the actions of the sons of God are portrayed in the same self-serving light as that of the woman in chapter 3, in the order of their actions (saw, . . . good, . . . took), then their actions are similar attempts to circumvent the divine order laid out in creation. In fact, they, like the woman, see a created object, "the daughters of men," as "good."[29] But though both saw

---

27. This is not to say that a woman's role is solely to bear children. These are simply roles highlighted in the text which emphasize her unique capability with respect to the man. Carol Meyers makes a strong argument that Genesis 3:16, written with the context of entering Canaan in view, might have simply indicated a differing balance between the gender roles rather than mere pain in childbirth or subjugation to men. For a culture to survive in the hill country, men needed to work (the sometimes distant) fields, whereas women needed to both bear children and help with the horticulture and viticulture closer to the domiciles. Hence, the statement indicates that women will increase in both their work load and bearing of children. Men will increase their workload with respect to women. Meyers, "Gender Roles and Genesis 3:16 Revisited"; Meyers, *Discovering Eve*. In any case, the woman in Genesis 3 is endowed with the same commands, (Do not eat of the fruit of the tree of the knowledge of good and evil, Be fruitful and multiply, rule over all the creatures of the earth, etc.) and status as God's image as is the man.

28. For a similar motif in the NT, see Rev 12:12–17.

29. Van Gemeren says, "I agree with the traditional translation of 'beautiful' instead of 'good.' The quality of moral goodness is not in view. The word 'good is a shortened

God, the Sons of God, and the Man of God

goodness within the object of their desire, this does not fully explain their sight.

Whereas the woman in chapter 3 saw the fruit was good to eat and a delight to the eyes, it was the promise of gaining knowledge like that of God, that of good and evil, which clinched the deal for her. Similarly, the sons of God see the beauty of the daughters of men, but their ultimate motive does not consist in lust as Westermann and others[30] would have it. They seek not just beauty, but to control the seed of the woman, which explains the emphasis on the progeny created by these relationships (6:1, 4). In so doing, they seek to pervert the seed[31] of the woman, and in part, they succeed, much as the human couple does earlier in acquiring the knowledge of good and evil. The hybrid race of the Nephilim, and their relations, the Anakim and Rephaim, ultimately serve as enemies of the people of God. Their significance endures, as they become a symbolic barrier to the Promised Land, and are eventually overcome by Moses, Joshua, and Caleb, (Josh 15:14) whose annihilation of the majority of them including King Og of Bashan, is much celebrated. (Deut 3:11; 29:7; 31:4; Josh 12:4; 13:12; Neh 9:22; Pss 135:11; 136:18, etc.). Later, a remnant are eradicated by David and his mighty men (2 Sam 21:16, 18, 20, 22; 1 Chr 20:4, 6, 8).

---

form of the idiom 'good in appearance.'" van Gemeren, "The Sons of God," 331. However, when the beauty of a person (usually female) is specifically in view, the term יָפֶה is most often used (cf. Gen 12:11, 14; 29:17) or alternately (טֹבַת מַרְאֶה) "good in appearance." (Gen 24:16; 26:7; 2 Sam 11:2; Esth 1:11; 2:2,3) Hence, while certainly possible (cf. Exod 2:2 (baby Moses), Judg 15:2 (Samson's fiancee's sister), 1 Kgs 20:3, though this last example possibly refers just to the sons, meaning "best"), it is not as probable that the phrase in Gen 6:2 (טוב, "good") refers simply to the beauty of the "daughters of men." The "goodness" of the women, or lack thereof, is key to the plot, for it partially explains the subsequent punishment of mankind. Furthermore, as we shall see later, this word has multiple connotations in this context: that of physical, moral and utilitarian good. As we have shown, there was no connotation of rape, nor even necessarily of lust.

30. For example, Waltke adds, "They are driven by lust, not spiritual discernment." Waltke, *Genesis*, 117.

31. Meredith Kline explains why the Nephilim were the product of the marriages: "We must agree with the judgment expressed by Dillmann: 'That the Nephilim were the fruits of those marriages is certainly the meaning, and is also clearly evident from [sic] אֲשֶׁר יָבֹאוּ וג׳.' For if the author's intention had been to say nothing more than that the Nephilim-Gibborim were contemporary with the marriages mentioned, he would have simply referred to those marriages in language similar to or even identical with that in verse 2. But his reference to the conjugal act and to childbearing finds justification only if he is describing the origin of the Nephilim-Gibborim." Kline, "Divine Kingship," 190.

So, based on the similarity between the motives and actions of the sons of God and Eve, we conclude that in "seeing the daughters of men" as good, the sons of God do not simply lust after their beauty, but see the women with an ulterior self-serving motive of rebellion and control. Secondly, the emphasis on their progeny, far from explaining the flood, actually points back to Gen 3:15 and the battle between the seed of the serpent and that of the woman. By uniting their seed to that of the woman[32] the sons of God sought to unify the parties set at enmity with one another and undermine the word of judgment (and hope) that God had pronounced. As we have shown, the 'daughters of men (and their fathers) were complicit in this act, which is tantamount to treason against their Creator. Hence, their punishment is not for the sins of the $b^e n\hat{e}$ $h\bar{a}\bar{e}l\hat{o}h\hat{i}m$, but for their own freely chosen roles in the rebellion. All of this resulted in the withdrawal of the divine Spirit from humanity.

Summary

The "sons of God" were divine beings, members of the divine council, who had forfeited their rank as divine messengers. As with the woman who followed her eyes to the fruit, they followed theirs to the daughters of men in rebellion against God. Both saw their object as good, but primarily in a utilitarian sense. The daughters served the purposes of these beings, just as the fruit had been seen as good for Eve's purposes in chapter 3, "to make one wise." However, whereas the woman seems not to have seen the evil present in her situation, the sons of God actually used the corruption of the daughters of men in an attempt to undermine the redemptive plan of God through the "seed of the woman." This can be seen in the lack of rape language and the implicit consent in the silence of both the daughters and their fathers regarding the marriages. Furthermore, the emphasis on their progeny's status and exploits implicates the daughters of men as collaborators in this plot to undermine God's purposes for them as divine images. As with the woman in chapter 3, this alternate "divine sight" thus involves both mental awareness of the good of the daughters of men, but viewed primarily as a means to personal ends.

Hence, we see that the metaphor of divine sight requires specific knowledge of the context in order to determine its entailments. Here, the identity of the divine "seers," as well as their motives and ends played a

---

32. This is as opposed to the man. Goddess and male intercourse was also prominent in the ANE.

God, the Sons of God, and the Man of God

decisive role in determining the nature of their sight. Though seemingly comprehensive in scope, ("daughters of *men*"; "*whomever* they chose"), their sight is superficial and utilitarian. Though how they see remains unmentioned, the emphasis is clearly on their motives. Unlike chapter 1, their apprehension of good is not for enjoyment of its innate value, but to undermine the redemptive plan of God in the seed of the woman. In the rest of the chapter, we shall see contrasts both between the sons of God and God, and within the sight of God itself, giving us a yet fuller picture of the varying meanings of the expression, "God saw."

The Wickedness of Men and Righteousness of Noah—Gen 6:5, 12; 7:1

Genesis 6:5

> Then the LORD saw that the wickedness of man was great on the earth, and that every intent of the thoughts of his heart was only evil continually.

DIVINE PERSPECTIVE

In a passage directly juxtaposed with the sons of God in verses 1-4, we find God Himself holding a quite different view of things. Matthews calls God's seeing here, "an intentional mimicry of the sons of God,"[33] in that whereas they see good, God sees evil. This further contrasts with His own previous view of creation as "very good" (1:31). John Sailhamer says this accents the change in the object of God's sight before and after the fall.

> In a tragic reversal of his portrayal of the sense of God "seeing" the "good" in Creation, the author subsequently returns to the notion of God's "seeing" at the opening of the account of the Flood. Here too the biblical God is the God who "sees," but at that point in the narrative, after the Fall, God no longer "saw" the "good," but rather he "saw that human evil was great

33. Matthews, *Genesis 1:1—11:26*, 340. Matthews explains that, "the wording in vv.2 and 5 contrasts this deplorable scene with the pristine setting of creation. God 'saw' his creation and evaluated his handiwork as 'very good' (*tôb meōd*), (1:31), but here the sons of God have taken the 'good' ('beautiful') and defiled it. This is reinforced by the play between man's 'great (*rabbâ*) wickedness' (v. 5) and human 'increase in number' (*lārōb*; v. 2)" (ibid., 340).

147

upon the land" (6:5). The verbal parallels suggest that the author intends the two narratives to contrast the state of humanity before and after the Fall.[34]

In the following, we shall look at the function of God's seeing in terms of action, duration, and object, while comparing it with that of the sons of God.

Wenham comments that the expression, "'The LORD saw' is used in other passages to introduce a decisive divine intervention (6:12; 29:31; Exod 2:25; 3:4; 4:31, etc.)."[35] Thus, God's seeing is indicative of a critical moment in the narrative. God's sight provides not only the introduction of His action in causing the flood, but gives an alternate view of the situation.

However, Cassuto says, "The word *saw* does not denote sudden perception but the consideration of a state of affairs that had long been in existence, and on account of which a decision has to be taken. Compare xxx 1: *When Rachel* saw *that she bore Jacob no children, etc.; ibid. v. 9: When Leah* saw *that she had ceased bearing children, etc.; l 15: When Joseph's brothers saw that their father was dead, etc.*"[36] Here, Cassuto casts God's sight into the cognitive realm of "considering," rather than of action, as with Wenham. In support of his conclusion, we note that the expressions "every intent" (וְכָל־יֵצֶר) and "continually" (כָּל־הַיּוֹם) demonstrate that this was an assessment of the situation over some period of time.

However, these views need not be mutually exclusive, as it is common practice for the Old Testament writers to express situations that occurred over long stretches of time, only to hit the highlights of a change in that situation. For example, in Exod 2:23 and 25, we find God "hearing," "seeing," and "taking notice" of the plight of the Hebrews in slavery in Egypt. However, this bondage had transpired over several hundred years (Exod 12:30, cf. Gen 15:13). The mention of it, on the other hand, marks the occasion of His intervention (Exod 3:8, 10). The expression of God's viewing of the situation thus may contain not only an awareness over time, but can also be specifically mentioned as a motive for His impending incursion into the situation. In our present context in Gen 6:5, it appears that both these implications are involved. Hence, divine sight in this context implies awareness, interaction with creation, and the impetus for the critical timing of God's action.

---

34. Sailhamer, *The Pentateuch as Narrative*, 88.
35. Wenham, *Genesis 1–15*, 143–44.
36. Cassuto, *A Commentary on the Book of Genesis*, 302.

God, the Sons of God, and the Man of God

Object of God's Sight

As we discussed earlier, the emphasis in Gen 1 was on the object God had created and the fact of its goodness. In chapter 6, like chapter 2, His focus is on the acts of His creatures, but here it focuses on their evil. Secondly, though it was simply the man's naming which God watched in chapter 2, here we have an explicit reference to his thoughts. The second *kî* clause states,

וְכָל־יֵצֶר מַחְשְׁבֹת לִבּוֹ רַק רַע כָּל־הַיּוֹם:

And all the inclinations of the thoughts of his heart were only evil all day (long).

This is the ultimate antithesis to the *kîṭôb mᵉʾōd* "that it was very good" in Gen 1:31. Not just "very evil," but "*only* evil." The extent, duration, and depth of human depravity is emphasized here. We have noted earlier that the sons of God saw that the daughters of man were *ṭôb* "good, beautiful." The contrast between what God sees and what the sons of God see highlights the superficiality of their vision.

Despite their beauty, the daughters of men, would certainly have been included in the generic "mankind" (*hāʾādām*) of Gen 6:5, and were therefore as evil as their fathers and brothers. Furthermore, they, along with their fathers who presumably gave their consent to these marriages,[37] were accomplices to these illicit unions. Thus, the vision of the *sons of God* acts much more like that of the woman in chapter 3, who saw the tree was "*good* for food," a "delight to the *eyes*," and "desirable to *make one* wise"[38] (emphases added). It is a utilitarian view of the world which evaluates the goodness of the object for one's own purposes without measuring its value *sui generis*. Blinded by their ambition, the sons of God overlooked (or even used!) the wickedness of the hearts and minds of the daughters of men in their effort to thwart the plans of God (3:15).

---

37. As we have stated, the terms for marriage here are the typical ones. Rape would have required a verb of force to be used. Thus, we can only assume these unions were mutually agreeable.

38. Although objects of the woman's sight in Gen 3:6 differs in that each follows a *lamed* preposition ("for" food, "to" the eyes, "in order to" make one wise), the verbal parallels with 6:2 make a clear allusion to utilitarian purpose highlighted there. It would be highly uncharacteristic Hebrew to say, 'the sons of God saw that the daughters of men were good (*ṭôb*) for (*lamed preposition*) intercourse, or "for making offspring." Rather, this is implied in the context where they immediately take wives for themselves, and in 6:4, have offspring.

In contrast, God appears to measure mankind by setting their created purpose against their current intentions. Whereas originally mankind was included in the "very good" of creation, designed to multiply (רבה), filling (מלא) and subduing it, He now finds them multiplying evil (רַבָּה רָעַת), and filling (מלא) the earth with violence (6:5, 11). Created to "rule" (1:26, 28) over creation, they now live by the rule of violence. Though God had formerly done the "taking" with mankind by placing him in the garden and taking the rib and fashioning the woman, so called because she was "taken from man" (כִּי מֵאִישׁ לֻקֳחָה־זֹּאת), we now find the "sons of God" doing the taking (לקח) of the daughters of men. The actions and intents of God have been mimicked and thoroughly corrupted by both the sons of God and their cohorts-in-crime, humanity. Thus, the use of divine sight here stresses the polar differences in *how* God viewed things as well (evil as opposed to good) as what He viewed (the hearts rather than appearances or utility).

Genesis 6:12

> *God looked on the earth, and behold, it was corrupt; for all flesh had corrupted their way upon the earth.*

Hamilton characterizes these accounts of God's sight saying,

> These two verses present the analysis of the narrator (v. 11) and of God (v. 12). Both are in agreement that the earth is polluted and in an irremediable situation. Note that God's analysis is prefaced by *God viewed . . . and indeed*, or "God saw, and behold. . . ." This construction appears a number of times in Genesis, and it frequently designates something that is not expected, something surprising (see 8:13; 18:2; 19:28; 22:13; 24:63; 26:8; 29:2; 31:2, 10; 33:1; 37:25; 40:6; 42:27; only in 1:31 is the element of surprise lacking). If this nuance applies here as well, then further support is found for the reason behind God's grief and pain. That is, the earth's contamination caught him by surprise.[39]

This view of God's sight implies that He learns about creation through His sight, a view that would seem to stand in contradiction with many systematic views of God's omniscience and foreknowledge.

However, many of Hamilton's cited parallels don't necessarily entail divine "surprise." They include both human perception, which would be

---

39. Hamilton, *The Book of Genesis*, 278.

God, the Sons of God, and the Man of God

limited in space and time, and incidents of divine perception which simply don't imply suddenness or shock. For example, in Gen 19:28, Abraham sees the result of God's judgment on Sodom and Gomorrah, but he has been warned of it (18:17), and certainly seems to expect it from his debate about how many righteous it would take for God to spare it (18:23–33). In Gen 29:2, the flocks of sheep are hardly unexpected around a well. Additionally, as we have seen in Gen 1:31, the *behold,* is more likely a change of point of view.

This can be further explicated by an interesting parallel between 6:12 and the previous verse. Verse 11 speaks of the earth as corrupt "before God" (לפני האלהים), and explains that this was because it was "filled with violence." Verse 12 initially resumes the narrative description of God's action, "And God looked at the earth," but then shifts to His personal viewpoint after the *hinnēh,* "And behold, it was corrupt, as all flesh had corrupted its way upon the earth." Not only was the earth corrupt, but it was so because all flesh had corrupted its way. This is similar to 6:5, as we had noted that God's gauge for creation is to measure it against its created purpose. It is this way that has now been corrupted by the creatures themselves. Creatures have chosen to live outside their initial mandates and domains. By shifting to a "God's-eye" view (in a quite literal sense!), we see not only the relationship between the two parties, but how God measures the difference.

In verse 13, we find more of God's viewpoint on what He has seen as He relates His intentions to Noah,

> Then God said to Noah, "The end of all flesh has come before Me; for the earth is filled with violence because of them; and behold, I am about to destroy them with the earth."

The object of God's sight here is also "the end of all flesh." His seeing here entails not merely the violence itself, but also the projected result of this course of events and the realization of what He needs to do in response. It is an analysis not only of a state of being but of a *trajectory.* The corruption of all flesh was not going to improve or gravitate back toward its created purpose.

As we have shown, several indicators in the flood story establish the "corruption" as taking place over a long period of time. Thus, surprise at the event itself does not seem to be involved. Rather, the reader is meant to see things through a character's point of view, enhancing the impact of the development of events, even though expected. Though God knew of the corruption as seen by its comprehensive nature (6:12, "all flesh") and time-bound markers (6:5, "all day"), its reality still seems to impact Him deeply, moving Him to dreadful action.

Not only do we find God's sight to be illuminating for His own measure of the situation, but as Hamilton has astutely observed, "The novel element in God's analysis, as distinct from that of the narrator, is that *all flesh* had gone awry. In some OT passages 'all flesh' specifically indicates human beings (e.g., Jer 25:31). But in view of the fact that elsewhere in the Flood story 'all flesh' includes both animals and people (6:17, 19; 7:15, 16, 21; 8:17), it is most likely all-inclusive in 6:12."[40] The cancer of rebellion introduced in the garden has now spread beyond humanity and into its environment. This is perhaps another reason why God's creation project must be scuttled and re-established after the flood. Here, He grants man a new authority over the animals which includes the right to eat them (9:3). This, however, is restricted as well in order to honor the life God has given each creature (9:4). The fear he puts in the animals (9:2) represents a fundamental alienation of mankind from his environment, though designed to prevent it from overwhelming him through its acquired nature of violence. So, God's sight in 6:12 is not only comprehensive and future-focused, but perceptive of the nature of both mankind and animals.

In sum, God's view in Gen 6:12 of all creation includes an entire system of order which is all too quickly unravelling. First there is a transgression against a seemingly innocuous restriction, then murder, polygamy, pride, and finally widespread violence, godlessness, and occultic intercourse. His seeing involves not only the current state of creation, but its future development, and further embodies the response required of Him. While not necessarily containing any element of surprise, there is a sense of the deep impact which the object of His sight has upon Him, indicating the closely-bound nature of His interaction with creation. Finally, it includes the ability to perceive the nature of creation, in this case, a corrupt and inherently violent one. Whilst some of these entailments are shared with the human use of sight, such as the objects of sight impacting the viewer, clearly God's viewpoint is more comprehensive, and far-reaching in this instance. He evaluates creation not only upon current action, but against its created purpose and its ultimate end.

---

40. Hamilton, *The Book of Genesis*, 179.

God, the Sons of God, and the Man of God

Genesis 7:1

> Then the LORD said to Noah, "Enter the ark, you and all your household, for you I have seen righteous before Me in this generation."

Again, we are seeking to examine the entailments of the use of divine sight in each instance it occurs in Genesis. We seek to note the differences in these occasions of the metaphor to highlight how the meaning changes according to its context. We've seen that divine sight can have in view either a state of being over a long period of time (6:5), or a progression or hypothetical trajectory (6:12–13). It can focus on the nature of a thing compared with its creative purpose and mandate, or contrast with that of another being. It can also indicate strong reaction within God Himself. In this next instance, we find the precision of divine sight highlighted, along with a function of acknowledgment and fulfillment.

One difference in this instance of seeing is the verb tense, as Waltke notes, "The Hebrew literally reads, 'I have seen,' forming a striking contrast with 6:5,12."[41] In 6:5 and 12, God's actions have been narrated, and hence, His seeing has been designated in the imperfect (with *waw* consecutive) and translated, "And God saw." In 7:1, however, we find God describing His own act of seeing to Noah, and hence the perfect first person, "I have seen." So, when God "sees" (saw) Noah as righteous (cf. 6:8, 7:1), the question arises, does that mean He observes Noah's pre-existent condition and on this merit grants him salvation, or does God's seeing function as evidence of a previously-determined election? Hamilton comments,

> Translations that render the second half of the verse "for I have found that you are righteous" are wide of the mark. Such a translation would give the (false) impression that Noah's obedience in building the ark is the immediate reason for his salvation, and thus produce a works-righteousness emphasis. If the writer had wanted to make that point in 7:1, he would have used either the verb *māṣā'*, "to find," or *yāda'*, "to know," as in Gen 22:12, and thus turn 7:1 into a recognition statement (*Erkenntnisaussage*). He could have accomplished that same purpose by using this structure: *rā'îtî kî ṣaddîq 'attâ lepānay*, "I have seen that you are righteous before me" (verb plus *kî* plus direct object). But here we

---

41. Waltke, *Genesis*, 137.

have a verb plus two direct objects: *I have seen you, a righteous person.*[42]

Hamilton views God's seeing here as neither declarative nor causative. "We rule out the possibility that this is a declarative statement ('I have seen that [or I declare that] you are a righteous person') on the grounds that there is no evidence that 'see' plus pronominal direct object ('you') plus attribute ('righteous') can mean 'declare/pronounce A to be B.' Nor is it a causative statement ('I have seen you because you are righteous'), for the indirect accusative of cause is almost nonexistent in the Hebrew Bible."[43]

Rather, Hamilton, like W. M. Clark, views this case of seeing as that of "royal election," when compared with texts like 1 Sam 16:1 and 1 Sam 10:17, the election of David and Saul, respectively. He claims this function of the verb has parallels with Gen 7:1b for the following reasons:

> 1) a first person statement by Yahweh with *r'h*. 2) "For me" compares to "before me").[sic] 3) "From (*b*) his sons" introduces the idea crucial to election, that the elected entity is chosen out of others). It recalls the "in 9*b*) this generation" of Gen vii 1b. 4) Other coincidental similarities include the preceding imperative and the introduction with *kî*. 5) The differences are attributable to the difference in addressee: in Samuel the person addressed is not the person elected. Also, there could be no mention of the person who has been chosen as this is first to be revealed in the following ceremony. Nevertheless, there is implicit a second object.). 6) David's kingship is prospective and the present account is not meant to replace the story of David's actual enthronement. Election and taking of office could be two chronologically distinct elements of royal ritual in ancient Judah."[44]

Hence, Clark's parallel of Noah and David finds God's seeing in both cases as an expression of His election of them, not based on merit (what He sees) but on grace (how He chooses to see).

However, Wenham observes a significant structural context in Genesis for these phrases concerning divine sight, "'Because you I have seen are righteous in this generation" clearly points back to 6:9 (P), for the same

42. Hamilton, *The Book of Genesis*, 286.

43. Ibid. GKC 117h According to Gesenius, "*verba sentienti* may take a second object, generally in the form of a participle or adjective and necessarily indeterminate, to define more exactly the action or state in which the object is perceived." ' Gesenius, *Gesenius' Hebrew Grammar*, 117h.

44. Clark, "The Righteousness of Noah," 275.

words 'righteous' and 'generation/contemporaries' appear."[45] Wenham explains the implications of this structure,

> W. M. Clark's attempt (*VT* 21 [1971] 261–80) to prove that in 7:1 Noah's righteousness is prospective, not actual, does not suit the present context of 7:1. Nor is he justified in arguing that "I have seen" refers to royal election ideology; cf. I Sam 16:1. In context 'I have seen' echoes "God saw ... the earth was ... ruined' (6:12), so that there is a long-range chiasmus between 6:9, 11, and 6:12 and 7:1, viz.:
>
>> 6:9 Noah was righteous ... among his contemporaries
>> 6:11 The earth was ruined
>>> 6:12 God saw the earth was ruined
>>> 7:1 The LORD said ... "you I have seen are righteous in this generation."[46]

This form not only sets up Noah as previously righteous as the reason for finding God's favor, but it illuminates the causal interplay in God's own vision. In each case, that of Noah and the earth, the state of affairs is established, and then God sees them and acknowledges them. Since He was "grieved" over this state of affairs (6:6), it seems improbable that God would have intentionally 'elected' this to come about. Rather, God's "seeing" of the world parallels that of Noah (being in immediate proximity), and lends support to God's "seeing" of Noah being non-elective. God acts upon what He sees in order to bring its current state to fruition. The world that is ruined (vv. 11, 12 "שָׁחַת"), He destroys (v. 13 "שָׁחַת"). The man that is rightly-related to Him, He saves through the flood (7:1 "Enter the ark, for you alone I have seen to be righteous before Me"), and establishes a covenant with him, thereby committing Himself to the relationship. The emphasis here is neither on Noah's merit, for there is no mention of his acts or words, nor is it on a causative sense of God's grace, but rather its precision. God sees the single, blameless individual amongst an entire world full of violent and rebellious people, a theme revisited on a smaller scale in Genesis 18. His sight here demonstrates a theme of appraising the individual despite the actions of the community (cf. Exod 32, Num 14:30, 38; 16:22ff.; Josh 7:1, Ezek 18).

Thus, this instance of God's seeing contains several distinctions from those that have come before. Hamilton notes, "This particular verse

---

45. Wenham, *Genesis 1–15*, 176.
46. Ibid.

contrasts with 6:5 and 6:12, two other places where God 'saw' something. There wickedness and corruption on the earth, but here he sees one righteous person on the earth."[47] Whereas many of the cases included a comprehensive look at creation (1:31; 6:5, 12), this instance has God seeing the exception to the rest of creation. It thereby highlights the precision of God's sight, both in sensory terms and appraisal. Not a causative term, God's sight acts as a passive reception of creation. God doesn't make Noah righteous by seeing him but rather takes notice of his righteousness. The proverbial "needle in a haystack" was not glossed over by the overwhelming flood of corruption, but righteousness was found in its midst.

Hence, God's sight is again not a substitute for omniscience, as it sets a foundation for God's action (commanding Noah to get in the ark) upon God's perception of creation (Noah's righteousness). Here it highlights a particular individual's righteousness, demonstrating that God does not use broad brush strokes in His dealings with creation. Sight here entails His attention to detail as well as an acknowledgment of uniqueness in Noah. Though the world is corrupt, God still sees Noah.

The Rainbow Connection

Genesis 9:16

> *When the bow is in the cloud, then I will look upon it, to remember the everlasting covenant between God and every living creature of all flesh that is on the earth.*

After the flood, we find God "looking" at the bow as a covenantal reminder. This "bow," will be in the clouds that God will bring over the earth (v. 14) and will "be seen." The Hebrew construction does not indicate to whom it will appear, but the distinct implication is that God will cause it to be seen. Not only will it be in the cloud that *He* brings over the earth, but also it is *His* bow over which He is presumably in control (v. 13). Furthermore, the fact that God says it will "be seen," and will be a "sign of the covenant" (אוֹת־הַבְּרִית), connotes that both He and the "living beings" upon the earth with whom He is covenanting, will see this sign.

What is this sign? Many (Wellhausen, Gunkel, von Rad, etc.) take the bow (הַקֶּשֶׁת) as being an instrument of war, for which the term can stand. However, Lawrence Turner observes how the "bow," rather than

---

47. Hamilton, *The Book of Genesis*, 286.

God, the Sons of God, and the Man of God

a "war-bow" is simply a sign of the covenant concerning the firmament. God promises never to allow the firmament to be removed from its protective function against the waters over the earth which threaten to become a *mabbul* or flood. Hence the sign is put in the firmament (*rāqiʿa*) as a reminder.[48] Furthermore, Westermann says, "B. Jacob says correctly that ..., where the word means 'rainbow,' בענן is always added (also Ezek 1:28)."[49]

Notably, God says He will "see to remember" (verse 16. וּרְאִיתִיהָ לִזְכֹּר). As in Exod 12:13 at the Passover, God sets up (or instructs to be set up) signs not simply for people, but for His own reminders. In Exodus it is blood on the door frame, here a bow in the cloud. Hamilton interprets this, "The point is made, as unequivocally as possible, that God's promises are entirely believable. His words are totally trustworthy. He backs up his word with an act to eliminate even the possibility of forgetfulness. One need not worry that God is capable of stooping to prevarication. He stands by his word."[50] The assumption is that God should not need a reminder. However, the Hebrew Bible contains pleas that God not forget (1 Sam 1:11; Pss 10:12; 74:19, 23. Cf. also Heb 6:10). It also contains promises that He will not forget :

> Isa 49:15 Can a woman forget her nursing child And have no compassion on the son of her womb? Even these may forget, but I will not forget you.

הֲתִשְׁכַּח אִשָּׁה עוּלָהּ מֵרַחֵם בֶּן־בִּטְנָהּ גַּם־אֵלֶּה תִשְׁכַּחְנָה וְאָנֹכִי לֹא אֶשְׁכָּחֵךְ:

> Ps 9:12 For He who requires blood remembers them; He does not forget the cry of the afflicted.

כִּי־דֹרֵשׁ דָּמִים אוֹתָם זָכָר לֹא־שָׁכַח צַעֲקַת (עֲנִיִּים) [עֲנָוִים]:

So, if God promises not to forget, what can it mean for God to "see to remember"? It is difficult to discern, as this collocation of "see" (ראה) and "to remember," (לזכר) is found only here in the Hebrew Bible. However, it may be noted that in each of the above cases, the beneficiary of God's commitment not to forget is a covenant partner—the "people of God." Even in Ps 9, there is an allusion to those who sing God's praises in the gates of the "daughter of Zion" (9:14). Many times in the Old Testament people are adjured "not to forget" either God or His covenant (e.g., Deut

---

48. Lawrence A. Turner, "The Rainbow as the Sign of the Covenant," 124.
49. Westermann, *Genesis 1–11*, 473.
50. Hamilton, *The Book of Genesis*, 319.

8:19 states that the penalty for forgetting such a covenant is death. Deut 4:9, 23; 6:12; 8:11; 2 Kgs 7:38; adjure Israel not to forget her covenant or her God. Lam. 5:20 goes so far as to accuse God of forgetting His covenant partner, though she is in the wrong.

Hamilton observes concerning the Passover sign of blood on the door posts that "God is certainly in no need of external evidence about the identity of the occupants of each house. "Still, the blood, like the bow in Genesis 9, is a sign which God observes, and upon seeing it he is moved to a certain course of action."[51]

Remembering, then, is not simply recalling. It is an intentional[52] act of reorientation. It involves acting in light of past events and relationships in lieu of current ones. For example, Deut 4:31 says,

> For the LORD your God is a compassionate God; He will not fail you nor destroy you nor forget the covenant with your fathers which He swore to them.

God will not forget His covenants, but the manner of putting it here implies that He will intentionally look upon the sign of His covenant, and act in accordance with it. Whether the world becomes corrupt again or not, God will be diligent to look upon this sign and observe His promise. Hence, we find God's 'seeing' here to carry a sense of intentionality and careful commitment to act in a certain way. God not only sees the rainbow, but He sees the world in its light.

Looking to Offend

Genesis 9:22

> *Ham, the father of Canaan, saw the nakedness of his father, and told his two brothers outside.*

Placed in such close proximity to God's looking on the rainbow to remember the covenant, we find a very sharply contrasting use of vision by Noah's son Ham. Here he looks on his father's nakedness and then publicizes it to his brothers. His brothers respond by *not looking* at their father's nakedness, and taking extreme precautions not to do so as they cover their

---

51. Hamilton, *The Book of Genesis*, 319.

52. Brown, Driver and Briggs says that God's sight here is intentional. "6. *look at, see,* by direct volition: a. subj. men, c. acc. rei, Gn 9:22; 9:23 (J). . . b. subj. God, c. acc. rei Gn 9:16 (P); = inspect 11:5 (J)." (BDB, *r'h*).

God, the Sons of God, and the Man of God

father. Such a contrast highlights the sense of appropriateness in looking or not looking.

This story, immediately following the flood, precedes the giving of the law, (cf. Lev. 18:6–8; 20:11), and yet presumes that there are things which are forbidden for one to look upon. The questions we are concerned with here, are the object of Ham's looking, the nature of such impertinence, and how this relates to divine sight.

The object of Ham's sight has traditionally been his father's genitals. However, according to Leviticus, this "nakedness" could also be construed as Noah's wife. Recent commentary has also suggested that this is euphemistic for homosexual rape. In order to better understand what Ham saw and why it became a cause for offense, we must examine these hypotheses.

A recent article by John Sietze Bergsma and Scott Walker Hahn reviews the main views and suggests an alternative. The four views revolve around the nature of Ham's sin, and of the subsequent curse by Noah of Ham's son Canaan. The first view is the traditional view, held both in antiquity and in the present. It concludes the sin was simply that of voyeurism. As Bergsma and Hahn comment, "The strength of this position is its conservatism: it refuses to see anything in the text that is not explicit. Yet, in a sense, voyeurism is a non explanation, since it fails to elucidate either the gravity of Ham's offense or the reason for the curse of Canaan. It also requires the interpreter to assume the existence of a taboo against the accidental sight of a naked parent that is otherwise unattested in biblical or Ancient Near Eastern literature."[53]

The second view is the traditional rabbinic view that Ham castrated his father in order to gain dominion over him. Though this is attested in the ANE, it does not appear elsewhere in the Hebrew Bible. Hahn and Bergsma comment, "It also provides some rationale, albeit complex, for the cursing of Canaan: Noah curses Ham's fourth son since Ham deprived Noah of a fourth son. What is lacking, however, is any lexical hint in the text of Gen 9:20–27 that would suggest castration."[54]

The third view is that of paternal incest, which in recent years has gained a substantial following, most substantially and recently defended in Robert Gagnon's *The Bible and Homosexual Practice*. "As Hermann Gunkel, Gagnon, and many others have pointed out, the way the text describes Noah as realizing 'what his youngest son *had done* (אשׂה לי) to him' suggests some action more substantial than passive viewing."[55]

---

53. Bergsma and Hahn, "Noah's Nakedness," 27.
54. Ibid., 28.
55. Ibid., 29.

Westermann, quotes Gunkel, saying, "This cannot be all because v. 24 presumes that Canaan[sic] had done 'something to him.'"[56] However, this, according to Westermann, refers to H. Holzinger's view, who presumes that Ham had removed the garment completely."[57] Thus, for Westermann, "Ham's outrage consists in not covering his father."[58]

Finally, Bergsma and Hahn follow F. W. Basset, in deeming Ham's offense as that of incest with His mother. Many of the arguments for paternal incest apply here, yet the change from paternal to maternal has some distinct advantages. "To uncover nakedness" is explicitly used in Leviticus (18 and 20) to describe (hetero)sexual intercourse, and in Ezekiel (16:36–37; 22:10; 23:10, 18, 29), even promiscuity and violence. In Lev 18:6–19; 20:11, 20–21, we see that "to lie with" one's (step)mother, aunt or sister-in-law, is to "uncover" (Heb. גלה) the nakedness of one's father, uncle, or brother, respectively. Bergsma and Hahn conclude, "Thus, from an intertextual perspective, the description of Ham's act as 'seeing his father's nakedness' implies more than a literal 'seeing.'"[59]

Bassett concludes that on the strength of the explicit idioms in Leviticus identifying the uncovering of a man's nakedness as sleeping with his wife, that this is what Ham must have done. This is strengthened by other cases such as Absalom, where this was used in an attempt to supplant the father (David, 2 Sam 16:20–23. Also cf. Reuben and Israel, Gen 49:3–4; 35:22). This has the distinct advantage of leaving the genealogy of Noah intact. Commentators like von Rad[60] had sought to reconcile the curse on Canaan and not Ham by postulating an earlier tradition of Noah's sons as Shem, Canaan, and Japheth. Bassett's solution leaves the text as it is, explaining the curse on Canaan as due to being the offspring of an illicit union between Ham and Noah's wife. This also explains why the curse did not extend to the entirety of Ham's progeny. Bassett admits only one weakness of the theory. "One has only to view v. 23, which tells how Shem and Japheth covered their father's nakedness, as a later addition by someone who did not understand the idiom."[61]

It is this which Westermann objects to, saying, "Bassett, like H. Gunkel, begins with the argument that v. 24 says that the son had done

56. Westermann, *Genesis 1–11*, 488.
57. Ibid., 488.
58. Ibid.
59. Bergsma and Hahn, "Noah's Nakedness," 29.
60. E.g., von Rad, *Genesis*, 131–32.
61. Bassett, "Noah's Nakedness," 237.

God, the Sons of God, and the Man of God

something to his father . . . the narrative makes it perfectly clear that the sentence 'when Ham saw his father's nakedness' can only be meant literally."[62] This is primarily based upon the subsequent actions by Shem and Japheth in covering their father's nakedness with a garment (v. 23) with their faces turned away. Bergsma and Hahn respond to this objection saying, "Proponents of the theory of paternal incest are correct to equate ראה עדוה with גלה עדוה, 'to uncover nakedness' via Lev 20:17, understanding both as euphemisms for sexual intercourse. However, one may take this valid insight one step further by recognizing that in all the relevant texts גלה/ראה עדוה is associated with heterosexual activity and 'the nakedness of the father' (עדוה אב) actually refers to the mother's nakedness."[63]

However, it must be noted that the sexually related idiom seems to be "to uncover X's nakedness" (גלה ערוה) not "to *see* X's nakedness." These two expressions do not seem equivalent in meaning across the board, and to "see X's nakedness" seems to indicate a literal meaning of viewing. In several passages we see the usage of these different terms. In Gen 42:9, 11, we have the idiom, "to see" the (nakedness), but this time, it is of the land, (לִרְאוֹת אֶת־עֶרְוַת הָאָרֶץ) not someone's wife. This is Joseph, accusing his brothers of having come to Egypt as spies (מרגלים). His accusation cannot be that of metaphorically committing "incest" against the land, as the act of spying is one of vision, not destruction, defilement, possession or use.[64] In Lev 20:17, a man seeing his (presumably unmarried) sister's nakedness refers only to her own, not his father's. It is further added, "and if she sees his nakedness . . ," implying that one act could conceivably happen without the other, thus not implying a conjugal act, which by definition, involves both parties.

An example where God is the subject of ראה is found in Deut 23:14. In the preceding verse, the Israelites are commanded to cover their excrement. The reason, given in verse 14 is so that God who walks in the camp to protect you, "may not see among you anything indecent" (i.e., naked, וְלֹא־יִרְאֶה בְךָ עֶרְוַת דָּבָר). Obviously, there are no sexual overtones here. Isa 47:3, referring to the exile, says that Israel, portrayed as a woman, will have her nakedness uncovered, and exposed (ראה). However, it then specifies, "I will not spare a man" (וְלֹא אֶפְגַּע אָדָם). Thus, even here, the metaphor

---

62. Westermann, *Genesis 1–11*, 488.

63. Bergsma and Hahn, "Noah's Nakedness," 34.

64. Especially cf. v. 12, and the infinitive use of ראה with the ל preposition meaning "with the purpose of." In regard to the brothers' coming it yields—"coming *in order* to look." Thus, the idiom cannot be a sexual metaphor.

refers more to degradation than illicit sex. Lam 1 refers to the nations seeing Israel's nakedness, and mocking. Again, it seems degradation is more prominent than sexual molestation. Certainly, incest is out of the picture as these are foreign nations seeing her nakedness.

Ezekiel 16:8, on the other hand, does refer to sexual intercourse. However, here Yahweh metaphorically spreads his skirt over young virgin Israel, and covers her nakedness. He also enters into a covenant with her. In verse 36, however, her nakedness has been uncovered through her harlotries. In the next verse, Yahweh *uncovers* Israel's nakedness so that the nations will *see* her nakedness.

> And [I will] expose your nakedness to them that they may see all your nakedness.

> וְגִלֵּיתִי עֶרְוָתֵךְ אֲלֵהֶם וְרָאוּ אֶת־כָּל־עֶרְוָתֵךְ׃

It seems unlikely that these two idioms are identical. One act is that of shaming exposure, whilst the other is that of illicit intercourse. The following verse speaks of Israel being so exploited that she will be judged like those who commit adultery (וּשְׁפַטְתִּיךְ מִשְׁפְּטֵי נֹאֲפוֹת). She will be given into the hands of her lovers (v. 39) where she will be stripped and abused and laid bare.

Thus, Ham's "seeing" of his father's nakedness would seem to have less to do with an improper conjugal act and more to do with a shaming or disgracing. This act is distinguished in both its object and intention. The object is a forbidden one—the genitals of another family member. In so seeing, one dishonors them. This is no accidental "seeing," however, for Ham spreads the news of the impropriety. Thus, human sight here is not generic knowledge, but an intentional trespass against cultural boundaries of privacy and respect.

This contrasts with God's viewing of Noah as righteous within his generation (7:1). That is, instead of looking to trip him up or publicize his indiscretion, He looks at Noah's way of life in general. It is notable that God does not judge Noah in this episode for his drunkenness, as Ham evidently does. Again, we see that human usage of a term can be pejorative and not a static, generic definition. Hence, "human" applications of terms like "sight" are as context-specific as the divine metaphor.

Conclusion

It would seem, then, that there are two ways of "seeing" things, but these are not fixed to the divine and human realms. Divine beings can see things in the utilitarian sense, observing outer beauty and usefulness for their own purposes, or they can see things for their inherent, created value. Humans as well have a choice as how to see, whether to recognize the goodness *sui generis* of creation, or to find value in it according to selfish ambition. Thus, it is somewhat misleading to simply speak of anthropomorphic language, as it implies a static definition of human sight which is then applied metaphorically to the divine. What we find in Gen 6:1–4, is a further example of the fact that such terms are, as Stern said, "non-constant." They are context-dependent in their meaning.

In Gen 6:5ff, the objects of this sight, the violence and rebellion of mankind against God, are set against the righteousness of Noah. This highlights the detailed accuracy and comprehensive nature of God's sight, in that He sees the needle in the haystack, even the solitary righteous man amongst the corruption of the rest of the world. This motif also highlights the differences in "divine sight," between the sight of the sons of God and God himself. Where the sons of God see the outer goodness (or beauty) of the daughters of men, God sees the evil in the inner world of the thoughts of mankind (cf. 1 Sam 16:7) and the trajectory of these thoughts. The sons of God see these women as useful (טֹבֹת) to further their rebellious schemes, but God saw that "every purpose" (וְכָל־יֵצֶר) of the men's (and women's) hearts was only evil (רַע). Hence, even for 'spiritual' beings, such as the sons of God, sight is a contextually-defined concept. It is not simply a borrowing of the human realm in order to speak of the divine, but a specifically nuanced usage of a term which may even be used metaphorically for humans themselves.

Often this sort of language had been explained using the recourse of source criticism. The earlier J source was assumed to have been full of theologically more naive language for the deity, whilst the later P source came from a later more "sophisticated" school which did away with such "early language." However, as Hamilton notes, the occasion of God's sight in Gen 9:16, presents us with an anthropomorphism typically attributed to P.[65] Von Rad explained the phenomenon as a "personalization." He says,

---

65. Hamilton says, "Commentators who accept the JEDP theory of the Pentateuch have frequently segmented P's account of creation and the Flood from J's by appealing to J's more crass anthropomorphisms from which P is supposed to be relatively free. But what are we to make of this most conspicuous anthropomorphism right in the

In the Eyes of God

"So far as the human description of God is concerned (in terms of pleasure, anger, aversion, zeal, love, etc.), the Old Testament (especially the prophets) reveals scarcely any attempt to 'spiritualise' the picture of God. It was apparently easier in Old Testament faith to tolerate the danger of lessening God's greatness and 'absoluteness' by human description than to run the risk of giving up anything of God's lively personalness and his vital participation in everything earthly."[66] As we have seen here, though, it is not simply "personalness" that is at stake. The descriptions of divine sight play key roles in delineating the nature of what is seen, how it is seen, how that sight differs from other key characters in the story, and the effect of that sight upon God's subsequent actions.

---

middle of a pericope that all source critics attribute to P?" Hamilton, *The Book of Genesis*, 318. (Also cf. Exod 12:13). Westermann also says Zimmerli says, "Here, where it is a question of God's fidelity to his covenant promise, P does not shy away from crass anthropomorphism." Westermann, *Genesis 1–11*, 474.

66. Von Rad, *Genesis*, 117–18.

6

A View to Judgment
Genesis 11:5

*The LORD came down to see the city
and the tower that the sons of men had built.*

We have seen that God's sight can incur many different connotations, from receiving aesthetic pleasure, transferring authority, judgment of sin, acknowledgment of righteousness, and active commitment to a covenant. In this narrative, we find sight expressing irony as well as discrediting the builders of the tower, again demonstrating the context-sensitivity of the metaphor.

In the middle of the Tower of Babel story, we find God going down "to see" the city and the tower that the sons of men had made. When we look at the structure of this short story, we find that this instance of God "seeing" is again placed at the crux. This can be seen in the chiasm Wenham finds in the pericope:

v. 1	Introduction
v. 2	Scene 1: The travels of mankind
vv. 3–4	Scene 2: Human plans to build a city and a tower
v. 5	Scene 3: Divine inspection visit
vv. 6–7	Scene 4: Divine plans to frustrate mankind
v. 8	Scene 5: Mankind is scattered: building stopped
v. 9	Conclusion: What Babel means[1]

As he further observes, "Scene 3, God's inspection visit, is the turning point in the sequence."[2] Hence, we again find this theme in a place of prominence within the story.

---

1. Wenham, *Genesis 1–15*, 235.
2. Ibid.

Visual Capability

Most commentators also detect a note of satire in Gen 11:5. Hamilton says, "It is difficult to miss the irony in this verse. The builders' intention is to erect a tower whose top will be 'in the heavens,' that is, among the gods. But even though they build the tower, it is so far from the heavens that God must *come down* to see it."[3] Matthews views this irony as a commentary on the divine perspective, coming from the divine abode: "The necessary descent of God and the humanness of the enterprise, 'that the men were building,' shows the escapade for what it was—a tiny tower, conceived by a puny plan and attempted by a pint-sized people. God's lofty viewpoint ('see') must be related to the previous reference to the tower's reach for the 'heavens,' where the divine abides."[4]

Wenham also finds this simply a colorful manner of expressing the puniness of the men of Babel and their tower.

> With heavy irony we now see the tower through God's eyes. This tower which man thought reached to heaven, God can hardly see! From the height of heaven it seems insignificant, so the LORD must come down to look at it "He sits above the circle of the earth, and its inhabitants are like grasshoppers" (Isa 40:22). God's descent to earth to view the tower is no more proof of the author's primitive anthropomorphic view of God than is God's asking Adam and Eve where they were hiding in the garden an indication of his ignorance. It is simply a brilliant and dramatic way of expressing the puniness of man's greatest achievements, when set alongside the creator's omnipotence.[5]

However, Hamilton notes the limits on such an interpretation,

> We suggested in our exposition of v. 5 that it is ironical that God must come down to bring into focus, so to speak, what was supposed to be a building invading celestial heights. But v. 6 indicates that we need not press that irony too far. God does not scoff at the building and consider it much ado about nothing. There is no suggestion that he views it as a joke. He does not laugh at them or ridicule them. Rather, he takes the scheme quite seriously. In fact, if something is not done to abort the project, the consequences can be far-reaching. It is God's judgment that any other scheme the human mind could entertain

---

3. Hamilton, *The Book of Genesis*, 354.
4. Matthews, *Genesis 1:1—11:26*, 483.
5. Wenham, *Genesis 1-15*, 240.

would pale into insignificance by comparison with this enterprise. His concern is also that such a hubris-motivated scheme will become a precedent and stimulation for other schemes.[6]

The assumption of many commentators is that the irony of the story is found in the fact that it was "necessary" for God to come down to see the tower that was supposed to be so high it reached heaven. This is what places the joke squarely on the builders. And yet, as Hamilton suggests, God apparently takes this futile project quite seriously.

Yet, this hardly seems justified if the tower is so puny. This would imply that there are indeed things so small God needs to come down to see them, as if He were divinely near-sighted! Von Rad (following Procksch) denies this implication saying,

> On the Yahwistic idiom, Procksch comments correctly: "Yahweh must draw near, not because he is near-sighted, but because he dwells at such tremendous height and their work is so tiny. God's movement must therefore be understood as a remarkable satire on man's doing." God's eye already sees the end of the road upon which mankind entered with this deed, the possibilities and temptations which such a massing of forces holds. A humanity that can think only of its own confederation is at liberty for anything, i.e., for every extravagance. Therefore God resolves upon a punitive, but at the same time preventive, act, so that he will not have to punish man more severely as his degeneration surely progresses.[7]

Though von Rad (and Procksch) deny any problem with God's sight, they remain convinced that the irony lies in the (close) distance God must be at in order to make out the tower. However, this would still require there to be a limit to God's visual capabilities. However, the tower would obviously have been bigger than the men building it, whom God had no trouble "seeing from heaven" and of whose deeds He is already fully aware (Gen 11:5; Ps 33:13; cf. also Ps 14:2; Job 28:24). Cassuto makes this point, saying,

> This "coming down" does not mean that God descended in order to find out what was happening, which is the view of many commentators, who see in the passage a primitive conception of the Deity, as though God does not know what He does not see with His eyes. On the contrary, if we say that He came down to view the city and the tower that the sons of men had built,

---

6. Hamilton, *The Book of Genesis*, 354.
7. Von Rad, *Genesis*, 149.

In the Eyes of God

> it follows that He was already aware of what had taken place. The expression *came down* is only one of the corporeal phrases commonly found in the Pentateuch, and it means that God, as a righteous Judge, wished to investigate the matter thoroughly. As I have explained in the introduction, there is a satiric allusion here: they imagined that the top of their tower would reach the heavens, but in God's sight their gigantic structure was only the work of pigmies, a terrestrial not a celestial enterprise, and if He that dwells in heaven wished to take a close look at it, He had to descend from heaven to earth.[8]

Though Cassuto acknowledges the contradiction in making God come down to learn the extent of the men's activities, he too ends up making this a matter of God's visual capabilities. Like von Rad and Procksch, to establish such an irony (Cassuto's "satiric allusion"), one is required to infer a limit upon God's own vision. If this is so, then how is it, as Cassuto notes, that God was aware of the tower? Could He just barely make it out, but without detail? Furthermore, how should we reconcile this apparent mockery of the Babelites' work with the seriousness with which God meets it (v. 6)?

Indeed, Westermann denies a sense of mockery altogether, saying, "The event described here is of such proportions that mockery and irony are out of place."[9] In fact, upon closer inspection, it does not necessarily say that God *needed* to go down (ירד לראה) in order to see the tower, but simply that He went down for the purpose of[10] (*lamed* preposition)

---

8. Cassuto, *A Commentary on the Book of Genesis*, 244–45.
9. Westermann, *Genesis 1-11*, 550.
10. Gesenius comments on this use of the *lamed* preposition, "The original meaning of the ל is most plainly seen in those infinitives with ל which expressly state a purpose (hence as the equivalent of a final clause, e.g., Gen 11:5." Gesenius, *Gesenius' Hebrew Grammar*, §114g.

seeing it.[11] Just two verses later, He[12] makes his descent (ירד) in order to[13] confuse the builder's language. Are we to infer He could not have done this from heaven either? This seems to be yet another residual effect of improper views of anthropomorphic language. Rather than reflecting a naive, human view of God or a colorful or artistic manner of expressing a propositional statement, the metaphor for divine sight is not a commentary on God's ability to see, but rather, on the nature of the human project and His reaction to it. This can be seen in God's chosen vantage point and the precise object of His sight.

Vantage Point

By examining the contextual entailments of the perspective or vantage point of God's sight, it's object, and its implications, we find that there is more going on than simple irony at the expense of a limited anthropomorphic view of God's sight. Significantly, it seems the builders had already finished the tower. In verse 5, God goes down to see the city and the tower that the sons of men had built. (qal perfect בנה) Then, when He plans to scatter them (v. 6), the emphasis is put on what they have begun (חלל)

---

11. In Hebrew, there are ways to express an inability to see, as for example, if one's eyesight becomes faulty. It is said of Isaac in his old age that literally, "his eyes have faded from seeing" (וַתִּכְהֶיןָ עֵינָיו מֵרְאֹת, Gen 27:1). This verb (כהה) is also used negatively of Moses, whose eyes had not grown dim even in his advanced years (Deut 34:7). In Job's case, the dimness of his eyes was due to grief (Job 17:7), and perhaps the constant tears flowing from them. (cf. v. 8) Thus, the inability to see, for a variety of reasons, can be described if desired. Another manner of describing this is in conjunction with the verb, 'to be able' (יכל). Genesis 48:10 describes Jacob's eyes as so, "heavy from age so that he could not see" (וְעֵינֵי יִשְׂרָאֵל כָּבְדוּ מִזֹּקֶן לֹא יוּכַל לִרְאוֹת). This expression demonstrates that the use of יכל and ראה can also be used to describe the ability to see (or lack thereof). (Cf. 1 Sam 3:2). Thus, it seems unlikely that this inability is in view here.

12. Lit. "We." Von Rad thinks the Hebrew, "let Us" refers originally to a pantheon, which Israel saw as the heavenly council (von Rad, *Genesis*, 149). However, this does not seem the case in terms of divine actions, as in Gen 1:28, mankind was not made in the image of the entire heavenly council, as seen by the use of the masculine singular in the rephrase in v. 27. "God created man in *His* own image, in the image of God *He* created him; male and female *He* created them" (emphasis added). More plausibly, Cassuto calls the plural forms the 'plural of exhortation.' Cassuto, *A Commentary on the Book of Genesis*, 246.

13. Heb. "אשר" According to Koehler-Baumgartner, this can indicate purpose or result. Koehler and Baumgartner, *HALOT*, "אשר," B.

to do.¹⁴ When He confuses their language, they stop (חדל) building the city, but there is no mention of the tower. Though this could simply be a case of hendiadys,¹⁵ as cities often had towers for defense (Heb. מגדל), the change in verb tenses, and the use of verbs emphasizing the continuation and subsequent cessation of the work, make it seem more likely they had finished the tower, but not the city. They had made their mark and were in the process of settling down in this place, in defiance of God's command to "fill the earth" (Gen 1:28, 9:1). So, in going down, God demonstrates that the "tower whose top is in heaven," has in fact not quite made it up to the level where He resides (to look *across* at). It was not that God couldn't see it from heaven, but that the tower (unsurprisingly) simply didn't extend to heaven and therefore, could be descended upon from heaven. God's choice of vantage point reflects more about the men's failed enterprise than it does His visual capabilities.

Furthermore, as in Gen 18, there is a sense in which God is going down for an inspection,¹⁶ which requires, not a closer look for better information, but His presence.¹⁷ Westermann notes, "the intervention of God, which is the thrust of the narrative, is the intervention of the descent. The same 'descent so as to punish' occurs in a Babylonian text; cf. E. G. Kraeling, JAOS 20 (1920) 279f.: The descent of the deity for punitive purposes

---

14. This could also refer to what they have done in rebelling and attempting to make a name for themselves apart from God's mandate to fill the earth.

15. Westermann observes, "Sam and Gk add 'and the tower' so as to harmonize." Westermann, *Genesis 1–11*, 534. According to Westermann [following Speiser], "'City and tower' can be a sort of hendiadys according to E. A. Speiser (see Comm.), and so can mean a city crowned with a tower or a city with a tower." Westermann, *Genesis 1–11*, 534. However, this again does not seem to take into account the change in verb tenses from perfect to imperfect, nor the inclusion of verbs specifically highlighting the continuation or cessation of work.

16. Koehler and Baumgartner, *HALOT*, ראה.

17. Cassuto sees this as a literary counterbalance to the ascent of the men. "The dissection of the narrative into two strata does not resolve the difficulty, for it is still a matter of surprise that the redactor should have left the incongruity in his revised recension. In order to find a solution to the problem a number of varied and fantastic suggestions have been advanced, such as, that the Bible refers to a gradual descent, to begin with up to a certain distance—to the point at which the structure would be visible, or as far as the top of the tower—and subsequently down to the earth; or that in the original form of the tale, the subject of *came down* was not the Lord but one of His angels; or that after *v.* 5 a paragraph, which related that the Lord returned and ascended again to heaven, has been omitted; or that we should read, *But the Lord saw* instead of *But the Lord came down to see*. But not one of these interpretations seems plausible." Cassuto, *A Commentary on the Book of Genesis*, 246. Whilst this is probable, there seems to be more involved than simple literary artistry.

A View to Judgment

(v.7) finds an analogy also in a passage of the so-called Kedar-laomer texts. 'If the king does not speak righteousness, inclines toward wickedness, then his *shêdu* will descend from Esharra, the temple of all the gods' (Jeremias AT, p. 180)."[18] His descent is not to get a better look at something He cannot see, but to bring His role as Judge to bear in a personal and present manner. The effect of this is both to demonstrate His knowledge of the scheme to the builders, as well as the error of their ways. They have neither made it to heaven nor escaped heaven's notice.

The Object of Yahweh's Sight

Though God goes down to inspect the city and tower (v. 5), what He actually sees is found in verse 6.

> The LORD said, "Behold, they are one people, and they all have the same language. And this is what they began to do, and now nothing which they purpose to do will be impossible for them."

Put in His own mouth, we again find the "behold" (הנה) clause, indicative of His personal viewpoint. However, the problem He finds is not an imposing edifice, but rather, a people unified, in speech and purpose, against His mandate to "fill the earth" (1:28, 9:1). Not only this, but He sees the implications of this confederacy. Through their unity of purpose, heritage, and speech, these rebels will use this tower as a springboard for living life and shaping their identity and their world according to their own efforts and rules, completely apart from their Creator.

In their hubris, they seek to make a "name" (Heb. *shēm* [שֵׁם]) for themselves (cf. Eph. 3:14–15). However, in a clever and illuminating wordplay, we find God going down in verse 7, and "there" (Heb. *shām* [שָׁם]) confusing their speech. This locative indexical is not only given prominence in the word order, placed right after the verb, but is also mentioned again in the following verse as, "The LORD scattered them abroad *from there* . . ." (וַיָּפֶץ יְהוָה אֹתָם מִשָּׁם). Yet again, it is emphasized in the etiological statement about Babel in verse 9. Evidently, it was significant that God should not smite the builders *from heaven*.[19] To do so might have implied

---

18. Westermann, *Genesis 1–11*, 550.
19. Westermann notes the unique location of Yahweh in this pericope,

> "Then Yahweh came down to look at . . ." This sentence, like the corresponding one in v. 7, presumes that God is not among people on earth, but above in heaven. This is something different from Genesis 2–3; 4; 6–9. Nevertheless the talk is still that of primeval time inasmuch as God's

171

that the men had indeed invaded and trespassed upon the exclusively divine domain, admitting some measure of success to their venture. Instead, God goes down to execute the builders' punishment from the very place that they had attempted to establish their independent identity. The site in which they sought to make a name for themselves became the very place of their undoing.[20]

Conclusion

Hence, God's sight is often misconstrued in this pericope, precisely because its meaning is not sought within the context. If, with Stern, we find the metaphorical meaning by drawing the entailments of the metaphor from its particular context of use, we find that His seeing in Gen 11:5 is particularly significant in its object and location. Because God sees both the builders' hubris as well as its future implications, His vision is presented as far-sighted rather than near, reaching both into the hearts of men and the future. This reflects the same awareness of the trajectory of their actions as with the antediluvians (Gen 6:5). Furthermore, the fact that He chooses to view them and their work from a particular vantage point demonstrates not a limited human conception of His abilities in service of mocking the builders, but a judicious application of punishment. As seen in the seriousness with which God treats the offense and its potential for harm, as well as in the wordplay on "name" and "there," God comes down to see the tower, *from its location on earth*. This approach not

descent from heaven is not presented as "revelation." Even when God comes down to look at what the people have built and to proceed against it, he is as it were in the same sphere as the people. Nothing happens which corresponds in any way to "revelation"; it is but an intimation of the other dimension to which God belongs. The fact that this is the only place where God descends (11:5 and 7) proves that the talk is still of primeval time. Later, from Gen 12 on, when it is presupposed that God is in heaven or speaks or acts from heaven, it is always a question in some way or another of a revelation. Westermann, *Genesis 1–11*, 550.

Though we agree with Westermann that placing God in heaven, is a unique move in the early Genesis narratives, we contend that it is indeed revelatory and not "primeval" talk at all. It is key to the narrative that God come down to punish the people from the tower, thereby revealing His knowledge of their plans, their ineffectiveness, and His true sovereignty. Any other move would have been at the least less poignant, and at most leaving room for the builders to interpret events much differently.

20. It is amusing to think that in addition to failing in their purpose to remain unified, settled and create their own name, after the "mixing of speech," the people most likely now don't even use the same "name" for the place they were!

only fits the crime but also serves as a definitive statement about the utter failure of their attempt to breech the gates of heaven[21] and subvert His divine decrees.

---

21. *Babel*, though a wordplay on the Hebrew *balel* "to confuse, confound," means in Akkadian, "Gate of God."

7

Status and Blessing in the Sight of God
Genesis 16

WE HAVE SEEN IN OUR PREVIOUS DISCUSSIONS THAT DIVINE SIGHT CAN involve aesthetic and moral appreciation, a transfer of authority, an acknowledgement of moral uprightness, and a judgment fitting the crime. In our next context, we find yet another function and meaning for divine sight—establishing worth. A disconcerting and yet pivotal chapter in the story of Abraham, Gen 16 has traditionally been assumed to recount a failed human attempt to build a legacy. Many clues, however, indicate that more is happening than meets the eye. Not only are the patriarch and matriarch of the people of God, the models of faith, portrayed as desperate and defensive, but even as vindictive in character. God Himself appears suspect, sending an abused runaway slave back to certain persecution. If the story is merely a detour on the road to God fulfilling His promise of a son to the aged couple, this move is unnecessary. More perplexing still is the slave girl's return; something about her encounter with the divine convinces her to go back, yet in her reply, God's promises are conspicuously absent. In fact, though God characterizes Himself as "One who hears," by naming her unborn child, Ishmael (lit. "God hears"), she responds rather surprisingly, calling Him, "A God of Seeing." Furthermore, despite being a "wrong solution" to Sarai's infertility, Hagar is nevertheless heavily associated with Abram (cf. vv. 10–16), with no mention of the matriarch in the last half of the story (vv. 10–16). All of these factors indicate that Hagar is more than merely a foil for elucidating Sarai's struggle with faith.

As the story culminates with Hagar's exclamation and the naming of the well, both revolving around God as seeing her, divine sight is again found to be a lynch pin for understanding the narrative. In this study we will examine the function of the pericope within the Abrahamic metanarrative, the nature of the women's sight and struggle, the object of God's sight, and the effect of seeing in the narrative. In all of these aspects of the

Status and Blessing in the Sight of God

context of Genesis 16, we aim to distill the distinct nature of the metaphor "divine seeing" and its central role in interpreting the story.

Greater Context: Genesis 12:1–3

In the previous chapter (15), God has specified that Abram's promised descendants will come from his own body and will inherit the land. Though this further delineates the original covenant between God and Abram in Gen 12:1–3, it leaves the nature of both his wife's role, and the channel of blessing to the nations through Abram, unspecified. These questions, originally posed at the beginning of the generations of Terah (cf. 11:30, 12:3), begin to take shape in the story of Hagar. Only in its greater[1] contexts, both the story of divine interaction with the world, and with Abraham and Sarai in particular, can the function and meaning of this chapter be seen.

---

1. In its wider context, Garrett sees striking similarities between the two Hagar scenes (16:1–16; 21:1–21).

A	1	Sarai's infertility
B	2–3	Sarai's response: "Sleep with my maidservant"
C	4	Hagar pregnant, abuses Sarai
D	5–6	Sarai complains and drives out Hagar
E	7–9	Angel of the Lord speaks, sends Hagar back
F	10	Promise: "I will ... increase your descendants"
G	11–14	Second word from angel: "Ishmael will be lone wanderer in the desert"
H	15	Ishmael born to Abraham
I	16	Ishmael born of Hagar
A'	1–5	Sarah's fertility
B'	6–8	Sarah's response: praise and laughter
C'	9	Ishmael older, abuses Isaac
D'	10	Sarah complains: "Drive out Hagar"
E'	11–12	God speaks: "Send Hagar out"
F'	13	Promise: "I will make the son of your maid a nation"
G'	14–18	Hagar and Ishmael alone in the desert; second word from God
H'	19–20	Ishmael saved
I'	21	Hagar gets Ishmael a wife

Garrett, *Rethinking Genesis*, 144.

Though the plot may contain similar elements, (Sarai's grievance to Abram, Hagar's expulsion and need, God's provision), Van Seters points out that the two chapters involve different motives and resolutions. While Sarai and Hagar wrestle over respect in 16, inheritance is at stake in 21. Hagar is sent back in 16, but away in 21. Hence, though the form may be related, this is not simply a duplet. This means, however, that it has less significance for our study, as chapter 21 has differing primary concerns.

In the Eyes of God

Genesis 12:1–3 marks the beginning of Abraham's journey with God with promises to reconcile a world that has strayed from Him and His ways. Verse one establishes the human condition of obedience "Go forth," upon which the following blessings will take hold, such as the promise to Abram of a land of his own. Verses 2–3, however, expand to include Abram's relationship with the world under the rubric of blessing. Gerald Janzen observes the implications of this framework,

> In identifying Genesis 12–25 as "Abram's story," it is essential never to let the last clause of 12:3, "by you all the families of the earth shall bless themselves," quite fade from view. For it places Abram's story in its proper contect[sic], and gives his story final significance. That proper context is the manifold story of the whole human community. For if Abram's life under God moves "all families of the earth" to bless themselves by the use of his name, the clear implication is that the stories of those families have an end and meaning in their own right, and that Abram's story finally serves theirs.[2]

However, the middle voice translation, "find blessing" (cf. Proksch, Wenham, etc.) seems preferable to the reflexive "bless themselves" used by Janzen."[3] The progression from Abram being blessed, to having his name used as a blessing, to his blessers being blessed, climaxes if all families are said to have found blessing in him.[4] Thus, Abram's story serves others only as they *derive* blessing from him, situating the meaning of their stories *within* his. The import of this passage is that God reinstitutes His original blessing (Gen 1:28ff.), only by incarnating its agency. Though He is still the source of all blessing, He no longer requires people to deal with Him directly in order to receive a blessing (cf. 4:3, 4, 26; 5:22–24; 6:9). Rather, He reaches out to a humanity that is estranged from Him by establishing a man, Abram, as the agent of blessing. Though human beings may be

---

2. J. G. Janzen, "Hagar in Paul's Eyes and in the Eyes of Yahweh," 18 n. 5.

3. As Wenham notes, "The basic sense of the niphal is medio-passive, that is, it may either be translated as a middle ("find blessing," as here), or as a passive, "be blessed." . . . However, since the pual or qal passive participle is usually employed for the passive of ברך, a middle sense is more likely here. Furthermore, a middle sense here complements and completes the earlier remarks. Already it has been stated that Abram will be a blessing, which presupposes both the passive sense, 'Abram has been blessed,' and the reflexive sense, men will use his name in blessing each other. Then it was stated that all individuals who bless Abram will themselves be blessed. Finally, this clause brings the passage to a triumphant and universal conclusion: 'all the families of the earth will find blessing in you." Wenham, *Genesis 1–15*, 277–78.

4. Wenham, *Genesis 1–15*, 278.

unable to discover this incorporeal God on their own, or may even ignore Him, they can neither ignore nor miss this most human of men, beset with all the desires and frailties they share, yet who is inexplicably blessed in their midst. The manner in which others treat this patriarch and his seed determines the level of divine favor they will enjoy. However, God remains the source of this blessing, not Abram. So one who can find neither God nor blessing, may now be able to find a man, and through him, may ultimately find not only blessing, but its Source. This is the context to which Gen 16 is set, and the truths that the story of Hagar illustrates.[5]

Brodie notes the function of chapter 16 within the framework of Abraham's call, "This diptych brings a new awareness of inclusiveness. To some degree Abraham's original call (12:1–3) was inclusive of all people, but now the idea becomes clearer . . . the covenant, given new depth and moral strength, now explicitly includes the weakest—the foreigners and slaves. Hagar at one stage is a foreign woman slave refugee."[6] Thus, Genesis 16 has a central role to play in fleshing out the themes introduced at the beginning of the Abrahamic cycle.

However, against this, Ralph T. Klein sees that Hagar "is a representative of all the families of the earth (Gen 12:3)," but contends that she is one from whom Abraham and Sarah withheld blessing.[7] Following Klein, Turner points out, "Abraham feels no burden to be a blessing to anyone (except himself)."[8] He puts both Pharaoh and Sarai at risk to save his own

---

5. If, with Wenham, we follow Alexander's analysis of the structure of the Abraham story, we find that chapter 16 is at the crux:

A			Sarah endangered; Abraham in Egypt	12:10—13:1
	B		Lot episodes I	13:2—14:24
		C	Covenant with Abraham	15:1–21
			D Birth of Ishmael	16:1–6
		C¹	Covenant with Abraham	17:1–27
	B¹		Lot episodes II	18:1—19:38
A¹			Sarah endangered	20:1–18

Alexander, "A Literary Analysis of the Abraham Narrative in Genesis," 24, in Wenham, *Genesis 16–50*, 263. Thus, it is likely to make especially poignant comment on the main thrust of the Abrahamic narrative in 12:1-3 which is fulfilled in the rest of the cycle.

6. Brodie, *Genesis as Dialogue*, 234.

7. Klein, "The Yahwist Looks at Abraham," 46, in Lawrence A. Turner, *Announcements of Plot in Genesis*, 108.

8. Lawrence A. Turner, *Announcements of Plot in Genesis*, 105.

neck. He saves Lot, but the Sodomite coalition benefits only obliquely, and Lot only serves Abram's self-interest as a potential heir. Turner adds, "The aged couple are certainly no blessing to Hagar."[9] In any case, no nation has either blessed themselves by or "found blessing in," Abram.[10]

However, Turner's translation of וֶהְיֵה בְּרָכָה as "Be a blessing," (12:2), overlooks that this simply means Abram's name will be part of a blessing *pronounced* by others[11] ("May you be blessed as Abram," cf. Zech 8:13). Furthermore, in 12:3, it is clearly God who is providing the material substance to the blessing and cursing in accordance with how people treat Abram, making the lack of Abram's personal defense or endowment of Hagar (cf. 21:14) irrelevant in light of Yahweh's blessing her (16:10). Though Abram may not do so himself, Hagar nonetheless "finds blessing," and that, in connection with him (16:16).

Genesis 16, then inaugurates the fulfillment of the divine promises to Abram, not solely in 12:2, but especially in 12:3 (also cf. 12:7; 13:16; 15:4–5). It serves to illustrate not only that the promise of the seed will not come through human means and manipulation, but how the "families of the earth will find blessing" in Abram.

The first scene (vv. 2–6) is borne of Sarai's attempt to assuage the shame of her childlessness. However, the story looks beyond merely confirming that divine promises require divine fulfillments. In the second scene (vv. 7–14), God begins to unfold the last part of the original covenant with Abram. It is no accident that Hagar's Egyptian heritage is emphasized from the start (16:1, 3), and that she later becomes the matriarch of twelve nations (Gen 17:20), both lending weight to her being the symbolic representative of the nations. Nor is it an endorsement of patriarchal systems of authority that causes the Angel of Yahweh to command Hagar to return to an abusive mistress. Rather, it is due to the loss of respect she has incurred (*qillēl*, pi.) against Sarai, which evokes the blessing and cursing formula found in 12:3, "he who *dishonors* (*qillēl*) you, I will curse." If the point of the story is simply to illustrate a conflict between women (Westermann), or the naming of the well (Kilian), or even the

---

9. Ibid., 108.

10. Turner also observes that, "The king of Salem pronounces a blessing over Yahweh and Abraham[*sic*] (14.19–20). According to 12.3a this should result in blessings coming to Melchizedek but the story breaks off without giving any sequel. . . . We cannot even be certain from the MT who pays tithe to whom (14.20c)." Lawrence A. Turner, *Announcements of Plot in Genesis*, 107. Either way, a tithe would be to the deity and not the nation. The blessing was clearly over Abram, not Salem.

11. Wenham, *Genesis 1–15*, 276.

proper mode of the fulfillment of the promised seed, then there remains no reason to send Hagar back.[12] She may not be the proper answer to the question of Sarai's barrenness (11:30), but neither is she a throw-away character, serving only to facilitate the development of Sarai's character and crisis of faith. In fact, the close similarities in the blessings bestowed on Hagar (16:10) and Abram (15:5) coupled with the conspicuous emphasis in verses 15–16 on Hagar and Abram establish her blessing from the *mal'ak yhwh* on the grounds of her relationship to Abram. Indeed, Ishmael himself finds blessing due to his father as well (17:20, 21:13). Finally, the naming of God by Hagar (16:13–14) without respect to the content of His previous blessing shows that she cares more about the God she has found to be real and caring. This reflects the ultimate sense of what it means for Abram to be a conduit of blessing to the nations. They find blessing "in him" (cf. 12:3),[13] because it is through him that they find his God—the source of all blessing.

It is against the background of Abraham's role in blessing the nations that the present narrative is set and the meaning of divine sight is found. God's seeing Hagar is motivated by His covenant with Abram, and her association with him.[14] Thus, the covenant provides a particular lens

---

12. Philip Drey says, "Following Hagar's conception, discord entered the household, leading to Hagar's flight. Following these events, one would expect Hagar to disappear and the biblical text to resume the story." Drey, "The Role of Hagar in Genesis 16," 180.

13. That this theme remains important is seen in its frequent repetition (18:18, 22:18; 26:4; 28:14; Acts 3:25; Gal 3:8).

14. This is both a direct and indirect association. Though she is initially Sarai's handmaid, she becomes Abram's wife, though a secondary wife. It is only by his decree that she is then re-transferred to Sarai's authority (v. 6). Thus, her connection with Sarai comes under her association with Abram. How she treats her mistress affects how she respects Abram's decision to delegate his authority to Sarai.

Furthermore, the divine promise itself apparently includes Sarai, as she was mentioned as barren just before it, all attempts by others to appropriate her into their harem are foiled, and in this episode, even surrogacy is ruled out as a fulfillment. (This is much clearer in the parallel passage in chapter 21.) Furthermore, in chapter 18, it is made clear that the promised seed will come through Sarai/Sarah. Thus, Hagar's connection with and treatment of Sarai do fall under the rubric of the blessing formula in 12:1–3. That is, by lightly esteeming Sarai (*qillēl*) she incurs a curse upon herself. This explains why the angel sends her back—as she is carrying Abram's child under a curse. She needs to be in right relationship with the conduits of blessing.

Finally, it should be noted that when the pericope resolves, she is associated directly with Abram a highly-marked four times in the last two verses, all without mention of Sarai.

through which God sees and acts towards people. However, the nature of this sight can be further defined by looking at its object.

The Object of Hearing and Seeing

Although the *mal'ak yhwh* is never recorded as having seen (*rā'â*) Hagar before 16:13–14, he does find (*māṣā'*) her by the well (v. 7). However, there are some unique collocations involved in the angel's focus. Genesis 16:11 is the only occasion in the Hebrew Bible where "affliction" (עֳנִי) is the object of hearing. It reads,

> The angel of the LORD said to her further, "Behold, you are with child, And you will bear a son; And you shall call his name Ishmael, because the LORD has given heed to your affliction."

As Sarna observes, "this constitutes a unique phrase in the Hebrew, being an amalgam of two distinct idioms. Generally, God 'sees *(r-h)* suffering,' as in Genesis 29:32 and Exodus 4:31, and 'heeded *(sh-m-ʿ)* their outcry,' as in Exodus 3:7 and Deuteronomy 26:7."[15] In chapter 16, Hagar is never recorded as saying anything about her affliction, whereas in 21:16, she "lifts her voice and weeps" (וַתִּשָּׂא אֶת־קֹלָהּ וַתֵּבְךְּ:). Hence, the naming of Ishmael, ('God hears') is situated where there has been nothing audible to hear.[16] The absence of sound casts the angel's statement to Hagar in naming her son more as a *heeding* of rather than simply hearing her affliction, a common nuance contained in שָׁמַע.[17]

The explanation of Ishmael's name also points to the nature of Hagar's affliction, to which God has responded. In the immediate context, affliction (ענה) points to the vengeance of her mistress (v. 6) to which no form is given, only its force felt—in Hagar's flight. By using the general ANE epithet for God, *'ēl*, the author is saying that the God of the nations (including Egyptians and Ishmaelites) hears affliction, and that this same God is actually Yahweh, the personal covenantal God of Israel. By naming her son Ishmael, God transforms him from a false measure of status into a constant reminder of his mother's value.

---

15. Sarna, *Genesis*, 121. Also cf. Exod 4:31; Ps 22:24; Neh 9:9, etc.

16. This would seem to suggest it would fit better in the similar expulsion narrative in chapter 21 with Hagar's weeping. However, verses 11–12 obviously belong in this context, as the naming of Ishmael belongs before his birth, not after he is seventeen years old, as in chapter 21.

17. Koehler and Baumgartner, *HALOT*, s.v. "שׁמע."

Though the object of God's hearing/heeding is Hagar's affliction, it is herself that she claims He sees (v. 13). However, the two are linked in that it is *within* the context of her affliction that this 'seeing' is defined. That is, how God sees Hagar is elucidated only in the context of her suffering. Thus, by examining the nature of her suffering, we hope to better understand the contextually relevant parameters for God's sight.

Violence Perpetuated

We may further understand what it is that Hagar claims God to have seen (v. 13) by examining the flip side of her affliction—Sarai's oppressive behavior. Her harshness is echoed in her protest to Abram. She says in verse 5,

> My abuse is your fault! I personally gave my handmaid into your embrace, but when she saw that she had conceived, I lost respect in her eyes. May the LORD judge between you and me!

Sarai's cry, "My abuse (*ḥāmās*)" is often seen as a flagrant violation of the law (see 6:11). Haag defines it as, "the cold-blooded and unscrupulous infringement of the personal right of others, motivated by greed and hate and often making use of physical violence and brutality."[18] Sarai may feel an over-inflated sense of the seriousness of the offense due to the perspective she gained in Egypt. Sarai has previously been described as a beautiful woman (12:11) (יְפַת־מַרְאֶה), so much so that Abram fears for his life, for when the Egyptians see (*rāʾâ*) her, he anticipates that they will kill him to get her (12:11-12). Truly, the Egyptians see her as beautiful (12:14) and the officials see her and praise her to Pharaoh (12:15). Abram is treated well and among other things is given female servants (וּשְׁפָחֹת), one of whom might even have been Hagar (cf. 16:1, 2, 3, 5, 6, 8).[19] In light of the previous emphases on her perilous beauty, and the high praise she received in Pharaoh's court, Sarai takes the highest of exceptions to the loss of respect (*qillēl*) she now finds *in the eyes of* her Egyptian maid. According to Brodie, "Her fall is now complete. She has gone from being admired by Egyptian high society to being looked down on by an Egyptian slave."[20]

---

18. Botterweck, *TDOT*, s.v. "חמס."

19. Though the rabbis call Hagar a daughter of Pharaoh, this is unlikely and unsubstantiated in the text, where such a fact would have served well to heighten the tensions between the two women.

20. Brodie, *Genesis as Dialogue*, 237.

Because Hagar's status has become unclear, at least to the maid-come-wife, Sarai questions whether this might not derive from a change of view *within Abram*. Thus, she not only implicates Hagar in her personal grievance brought before the family court, but incriminates Abram in the court of heaven. In a society where such marital practices were accepted,[21] and no promise had yet specified Sarai as mother of the promised seed, the potential for Abram's complicity with Hagar explains Sarai's unusual demands. It also clarifies his uncharacteristically passive[22] response in v. 6. He is denying culpability in Hagar's over-inflated esteem by affirming her place under Sarai, as per the original agreement.

This affliction is possibly due to an unmentioned implication of Hagar's pregnancy: it demonstrates that Sarai, not Abram, is infertile. Sarna claims, "In ancient times barrenness was imputed to the woman, not the man, although God was seen to be its ultimate cause."[23] Thus, Sarai may have intended to drive out the living reminder of her own infertility or divine disfavor.

Hence, the wrong done to Sarai is steeped in the manner in which she felt valued, both in terms of status, and regard. Prized in Egypt by all who saw her, she is 'looked down' upon by her Egyptian slave. Infertility laid squarely upon her, she seeks to reestablish her place in the eyes of her husband and slave. Thus, our narrative makes a strong connection between sight and value, which we will see later impacting the meaning of divine sight.

Affliction Passed

The violence done to Sarai is now redirected at Hagar. As Westermann aptly observes, "the oppressed when liberated becomes the oppressor."[24] The severity of her vengeance is seen both in Hagar's flight and that this

---

21. E. A. Speiser mentions one of the most well-known of ANE texts pertaining to this practice from Nuzi, "If Gilimninu bears children, Shennima shall not take another wife. But if Gilimninu fails to bear children, Gilimninu shall get for Shennima a woman from the Lullu country (i.e., a slave girl) as concubine. In that case, Gilimninu herself shall have authority over the offspring." Speiser, *Genesis*, 1, 120. This basically amounted to a practice of legal adoption of the concubine's child by the first wife.

22. This is in contrast with his pre-emptive scheme against Pharaoh, quick military resolve for Lot, tithe to Melchizedek, and forwardness towards God about His as yet unanswered promise in chapter 15.

23. Sarna, *Genesis*, 119.

24. Westermann, *Genesis 12–36*, 241.

Status and Blessing in the Sight of God

is the same verb (ענה) for the Egyptian mistreatment of the Israelites in 15:13 (cf. Exod 1:12, 3:7). This resonates conversely with Hagar's story, as she is an Egyptian slave being afflicted (ענה) in Canaan. The affliction God has heeded in 16:11 (cf. Exod 3:7) hence, refers to Hagar's status, in terms of human social standing and value, and corresponding treatment at the hands of Abram and Sarai. As Sarai is threatened in her position as first wife, she belittles and demeans Hagar to the point of making her flee. This is the very thing that would bring affliction upon the Israelites in Egypt—fear of being supplanted, (Exod 1:8–10) and it now plagues Hagar in Hebron.

According to ANE law codes, there were provisions and limits to the discipline allowed towards a concubine. One law in the Code of Hammurabi (number 146) is often compared with these customs:

> When a seignior married a hierodule and she gave a female slave to her husband and she has then borne children, if later that female slave has claimed equality with her mistress because she bore children, her mistress may not sell her; she may mark her with the slave-mark and count her among the slaves.[25]

Furthermore, The Law of Ur-Nammu said, "If a man's slave-woman, comparing herself to her mistress, speaks insolently to her (or: him), her mouth shall be scoured with one quart of salt."[26] As previously mentioned, codes from Egypt and Nimrud also prohibited abuse of the slave-surrogate wife (cf. v. 3, p. 12).

Hence, Sarai's "affliction" of Hagar, the object of God's hearing, seems to have gone beyond normally accepted measures, as Hagar flees to the wilderness (cf. Israel fleeing mistreatment in Exod 14:5). "The narrator's sympathies now are on the side of the oppressed maidservant."[27] In a context full of legal imagery, the author describes Sarai as "afflicting" (ענה) Hagar, which is a homonym for, "giving answer, or evidence." In a case of double entendre, Sarai uses violence to settle the question of her handmaid's position. However, as Hagar too will see, status does not come through self-promotion, but from God's own blessing within human

---

25. Pritchard, *Ancient Near Eastern Texts*, 172 n. 146. A "seignior" refers to a free male, and a "hierodule" to a priestess.

26. "The Laws of Ur-Nammu," Pritchard, *Ancient Near Eastern Texts*, 525, par. 22.

27. Waltke, *Genesis*, 253. Waltke observes further that, "The Mosaic law assumes that a runaway slave has been mistreated. This is evidenced by the stipulation in Deut 23:15: "If a slave has taken refuge with you, do not hand him over to his master." Waltke, *Genesis*, 253 n. 120.

relationships, and at times, despite them. As Waltke says, "Hagar's deliverance does not lie in returning to Egypt, her native land, but in submitting to the mother of Israel and not despising her."[28]

The object of God's 'hearing' has been the affliction of Hagar. However, this affliction has as much to do with its perpetrator as its victim. Sarai felt the sting of a socially-based shame in knowing that her childlessness was not her husband's fault. Added to this was the fall in her esteem from that of being prized among Egyptian royalty to being disdained by her Egyptian slave. All of this becomes subsumed in the "violence" she claims is done to her by Abram in not clarifying the relationship to her maid. In laying the issue back in her lap, Abram allows justice to be miscarried, in that all of Sarai's rage is meted out upon Hagar, well beyond measures typical of surrounding cultures.

Hence, we learn that the 'affliction' that God heard was unjust,[29] even by the standards of other nations. It is driven ostensibly by Sarai's own struggle for status in her world, a pain made more poignant by her maid's fertility. Furthermore, the great wrong she feels in her maid having "looked down" on her, she blames on her husband's lack of establishing the boundaries of the two women's status within the family. Hence, the source of this "afflicting" is a desire on both women's part to be seen as valued within their culture. This is partially related to childbirth, which causes Hagar's false presumption of raised status. It is also facilitated by Abram's initial failure to confirm that the first wife is so by reason of chronology, not the one who has the first or most children. Hence, in Sarai's subsequent vehemence, Hagar is not only stripped of what she thought was a promotion in the eyes of her society and her husband, but she falls even further than she had started, as she is now an abused slave, and then a runaway.

Titles and Descriptors

As we have seen, vision is constructed as a prominent theme in the story of Hagar and Sarai, especially as related to personal status. This can be further elucidated in the titles and descriptors given the main characters. The high density of these titles gives the narrative a consequent emphasis on status, a factor that will affect the interpretation of Yahweh's sight.

---

28. Waltke, *Genesis*, 253.

29. Waltke states, "the narrator judges Sarah's actions against Hagar in the direct statement, 'Sarah mistreated Hagar.'" Waltke, *Genesis*, 252.

Wife

The opening verse confronts the reader not simply with the problem of childlessness, but with an emphasis on the hierarchy of relationships. Sarai is conspicuously re-presented as Abram's wife (אשה, vv. 1, 3), emphasizing her rightful standing as Abram's first and primary wife. It also hints that fulfillment of the blessing is to come through her.[30] Not only is her status stressed, but her own desire for it is as well. Sarai offers her maid to Abram remarking, "Perhaps I will be built up through it." Gerhard von Rad says, "There was no greater sorrow for an Israelite or Oriental woman than childlessness. Even today among the Arabs the barren woman is exposed to disgrace and even grievous wrongs."[31] However, the fact that Sarai does not mention fulfilling God's promise to Abram of an heir, shows that she is concerned with improving her own standing.[32] She seeks to be built up in the eyes of her society.

Egyptian

Hagar is introduced as both a foreigner—an Egyptian—and as Sarai's handmaid.[33] Reis sees the mention of her national origin as having retributive implications for the subsequent punishment of Abram and Sarai's descendants[34] in Egypt. Janzen, too, argues for an ethical comparison, "these two points in the larger narrative, Genesis 15 and Exodus itself, frame Sarai's and Abram's treatment of Hagar and invite the reader to compare their treatment of this Egyptian maid with Egypt's later treatment of the Hebrews."[35] However, in light of the greater context of the

---

30. Waltke, *Genesis*, 251.

31. von Rad, *Genesis*, 97.

32. Also see Antion Jaussen, *Coutumes des Arabes au pays de Moab* (Paris: Libraire d'Amérique et d'Orient, 1948) 35–36; Roland de Vaux, *Ancient Israel: Its Life and Institutions*, trans. John McHugh (London: Darton, Longman & Todd, 1961) 41. From Sharp, "On the Motherhood of Sarah," 6 n. 14.

33. Wenham considers it likely that she was acquired under Pharaoh's patronage (12:16) by Sarai in Egypt rather than as part of her dowry. (cf. Bilhah and Zilpah 32:23(22); 33:1, 2, 6). Wenham, *Genesis 16–50*, 6. (Contra, Sharp, "On the Motherhood of Sarah," 6–7).

34. Reis, "Hagar Requited," 106.

35. J. G. Janzen, "Hagar in Paul's Eyes and in the Eyes of Yahweh," 7. However, it should be noted, there are several points of *discontinuity*. The people ruling Egypt during Abraham's life constituted an entirely different race of people from the inflictors of Israel's slavery (Exod 1:8). Up till this point, Egypt is pictured honorably, even

Abrahamic narrative, it seems more likely that this connects her with the promise of blessing to the nations, as Egypt has not made itself notorious yet (cf. also Gen 12:20—13:1). If anything Abraham has made himself so in their eyes. She is distinguished as foreign, but specifically in terms of a well-known nation, in order to highlight his relationship with the nations. This can also be seen in the other designation used for Hagar.

Handmaid

For several reasons, it is significant that Hagar is called a maid (שפחה) rather than a slave girl/concubine (אמה). Firstly, it establishes lines of authority from which the plot may develop, as the former is a "servant companion of a rich woman (Ps 123:2),"[36] who is owned and answerable to the mistress, not the master (cf. vv. 2, 3, 6). The אמה is connected directly with the master, often acting as a concubine (second-class wife) if her family was too poor for a dowry, or if the master had a previous wife (Exod 21:7-11). However, based on Jacob's referrals to Bilhah and Zilpah as slave-girls (*āmāh*), though they are concubines who have borne him children (33:23 [22] and 31:1, 2, 6), "Cohen" (Shnaton 5-6 [1978] xxv–liii.) argues that there is no difference in meaning between the terms: אמה "slave-girl" is used in legal texts whereas, שפחה "maid" is used more colloquially in narrative."[37]

More importantly, this designation cements her relationship to Sarai, as seen not only in the eyes of the narrator, but in the eyes of God (v7, and 25:12). Though some see it as demeaning, it is actually the factor that connects her to the family of promise, and ends up winning her a great

---

sympathetically, as the victims of Abram's deception. Even the Exodus Era Egyptians, who are infamous for the punishment they endured for the subjugation of Israel are not analogous with the patriarchal couple, because Abram and Sarai are never so much as chastised for their treatment of their Egyptian slavegirl. The Israelites never 'lose respect' (*qillēl*) for their Egyptian lords. Nor were they commanded to return and submit to them by the Angel of YHWH. In fact, they were led *out* of captivity by the Angel of YHWH. (Exod 23:20) Furthermore, Israel's slavery was never treated as a punishment deserved, such as retribution for abuse of Hagar, but as unjust cruelty.(Exod 1:10-22) Thus, the "Egyptian" connection here is not meant to implicate Abraham's later descendants, whose slavery was promised before Hagar ever even enters the picture (15:13). Rather, coupled with the term for maid *šipḥāh*, it functions to establish Hagar as a foreigner, even a mother of nations, one of the *mišpāḥāh* of the earth who will find blessing in Abram.

36. Wenham, *Genesis 16–50*, 6.
37. Ibid.

blessing (cf. 16:9). This can be seen in a related form, the מִשְׁפָּחָה, found in 12:3. Drey explains,

> A better understanding may come from the Ugaritic verb *s-f-ḥ*, which means "being together" and is related to the Hebrew *mišpaḥah* ("clan"). This connection between *s-f-ḥ*, and *mišpaḥah* has been questioned, resulting in the translation of *s-f-ḥ* as "to join" or "attach oneself to." "In other words, *shifḥah* could mean 'someone who joins or is attached to' a person or a clan." If Hagar was a gift to Sarai from Pharaoh, this interpretation would be the best fit.[38]

In any case, this is yet one more echo of Gen 12:3, where all of the families—"*mišpāḥāh*"—will find blessing in Abram and his seed.

Progression

Hagar is subsequently raised in status from a שִׁפְחָה (handmaid), to a אִשָּׁה (wife), but is still treated like property. However, according to Hartley, "The term "wife" indicates that in becoming Sarai's surrogate, Hagar received elevated status in the household. The authority over her passed from Sarai to Abram."[39] Trouble brews as Hagar becomes Abram's wife, as lines of authority are blurred, and boils when her fertility incites a lower view of her mistress. Consequently, she is demoted back to handmaid in her husband's eyes, and to an object of vengeance in those of her mistress. She hits bottom, becoming a fugitive in the desert.

Adele Berlin observes a similar important progression in her exegesis of Ruth. She says, "Both Naomi and the narrator view Ruth's identity as a constant, but the most interesting insight into her identity comes from the way it shifts in the appellations that Boaz and Ruth use. There is a progression in both, from lower to higher, but they are in different classes. Ruth uses three terms to refer to herself when speaking to Boaz: נָכְרִיָּה "foreigner" (2:10), שִׁפְחָה "maidservant," and אָמָה "handmaid" (3:9). These reflect a change of status from a foreigner, i.e., one without a relationship at all, to a gradually ascending relationship of servitude or dependency."[40]

---

38. Drey, "The Role of Hagar in Genesis 16," 184. Drey quotes S. J. Teubal, *Sarah the Priestess: The First Matriarch of Genesis* (Athens, OH: Swallow, 1984), 58. Cf. also C. U. Wolf, "The Terminology of Israel's Tribal Organization, " *JBL* 65 (1946) 47.

39. Hartley, *Genesis*, 165. Furthermore, this underscores the fact that Hagar has not attained the status of a full wife, but shows that giving her to Abram was an official act, not a case of illegitimate relations, and that it was for a prescribed purpose.

40. Berlin, *Poetics*, 88.

A similar progression can be noted in Boaz's choice of referents to Ruth (young woman, my daughter, worthy woman, wife).

Likewise, the titles used for Hagar also reflect her rise and fall, but they also frame the renewal of her sense of identity. Janzen notes, "while Sarai and Abram refer to the Egyptian only in terms of her role as maid, the narrator never refers to her only that way, but always includes her name Hagar and sometimes uses only it."[41] This sets up a play on the value of different characters within each other's eyes that he calls horizons. "Given the importance of 'seeing' in the Hagar story, we may say that part of the atmosphere within which a given individual lives is the settled perceptions of that individual by others . . . 'to be is to be perceived.'"[42]

Hence, we see that status is part of the context in which divine sight is situated. This is first seen in the proliferation of titles and in Sarai's reference to being built up rather than fulfilling divine promises. Furthermore, we see an emphasis on the nations in Hagar's heritage, as well as the allusion in her servitude to the *mišpāḥāh* "families" which are promised to find blessing in Abram. In emphasizing Hagar as the *šiphāh*, she is clearly representing these nations/families of the earth. Thus, divine sight is presented as seeing her *as* a representative of those affected by His promise to bless Abraham through her connection with him. Finally the progression of Hagar's rise and fall illustrates her foremost need, and the primary context for her appellation of God as "One who Sees"—valuation. This theme is further developed in terms of the human sight in the narrative.

Human Sight

This emphasis on valuation is found not only in terms of status, but also in the way the human characters are said to view things. In verse 4, Hagar becomes pregnant, and we read, "*And when she saw (rāʾà)* that she had conceived"—Janzen perceives in this a certain sense of agency based on the first active verb to which Hagar is the subject, "she sees that she has conceived. She emerges finally not just as an object of other perceptions or instrument of other wills, but as a percipient and evaluating subject in her own right."[43] This first glimpse of Hagar in action defines her entire struggle in terms of how she sees herself.

---

41. J. G. Janzen, "Hagar in Paul's Eyes and in the Eyes of Yahweh," 5.
42. Ibid., 3.
43. Ibid., 5.

Status and Blessing in the Sight of God

The emphasis on sight continues, *"and her mistress lost respect in her eyes."* Many versions, have skewed both the direction and force of this by making Hagar the subject, Sarai the object, and using a transitive verb, thus, "Hagar despised her mistress."[44] Wenham softens this to, "looked down on her mistress." However, because of the presence of the phrase, "in her eyes," and the normally passive sense of the verb, it should take "her mistress" as subject rather than Hagar (cf. also v. 6). Thus, it indicates less an active despising and more a raising of Hagar's own status as a child-bearing woman.[45] In fact, Westermann sees contempt being inappropriate as, "the writer was referring . . . to Sarah's having lost status, because of the new standing which Hagar had acquired . . ."[46] He notes that due to the widespread nature of the practice and "natural maternal pride," (O. Procksch), "The meaning is not that she behaves insolently towards her barren mistress."[47] Rather, she is just acting *naturally*.[48]

Despite this tempering of intention from Hagar, Waltke remarks that the narrator, "confirms Sarah's evaluation of the situation by using the same vocabulary as Sarah."[49] According to Meir Sternberg, the narrator establishes objectivity with respect to character. "The reader infers from the equivalence in language an equivalence in vision where the character's involvement might otherwise cast doubt on her objectivity."[50] Thus, though Sarai herself might be biased, the narrator confirms that her statement reflects reality—she has been disdained (*qillēl*) in Hagar's eyes.

Waltke concludes, "Because Hagar treats Sarah with disdain, she is alienated from the family of blessing, as is Lot (See Prov 30:21–23)."[51] Though it is questionable whether either of these characters is ever completely "alienated," as they are later saved (16:9–13; 19:20; 21:13, 17) and Lot is never recorded as despising (*qillēl*) Abraham, they are certainly blessed due to their associations with the "family of blessing." Janzen, too, connects the issue of respect in Gen 16 with the promises in 12:3

---

44. Cf. NIV, NLT, NET, RSV, ESV vs. KJV, NASB.

45. Trible, *Texts of Terror*, 12.

46. Westermann, *Genesis 12–36*, 240. Westermann quotes J. Skinner, *Vetus Testamentum*, 22 (1972) 199.

47. Westermann, *Genesis 12–36*, 240.

48. Jenni and Westermann, *Theologisches Handwörterbuch Zum Alten Testament*, s.v. "קלל."

49. Waltke, *Genesis*, 253.

50. Sternberg, *The Poetics of Biblical Narrative*, 402.

51. Waltke, *Genesis*, 252.

that govern all of the Abrahamic narratives. He says, "such belittling also brings Hagar under the interdiction uttered in Gen 12:3, where God said to Abram, 'I will bless those who bless you, and the one who makes you of no account (*qillel*) I will curse.'"[52] He connects "blessing" with childbirth, and thus interprets this to mean that Hagar had endangered the life of her unborn child by disrespecting Sarai.

However, though 12:3 says God will curse those who belittle or demean (*qillēl*) Abram, there are two key differences in what Hagar has done here. Firstly, though Sarai is included in the promise in 12:3 concerning the cursing and blessing, it is not simply on her own account, but as "Abram's wife"[53] (cf. 12:17, 20:18). Thus, though Hagar views Sarai disrespectfully, she nonetheless maintains some relation to Abram directly as wife, (v. 3) which may moderate any curse she incurred. Secondly, the verb [*qillēl*] in 12:3 is in the pi'el, which according to Koehler-Baumgartner means, "declare cursed, accursed." In fact, "the pi[el] has an (exclusively) declarative sense," and, "clearly has both a declarative and a factitive function, for in קלל pi. (pu.) the declarative is identical with the factitive; to declare someone as insignificant or contemptible also means to make that person insignificant and contemptible."[54] With Hagar in 16:4–5, however, this same verb is in the qal stem. Thus, while Sarai may have lost Hagar's respect for the moment, it was only, "in her eyes," and not her mouth.

---

52. J. G. Janzen, "Hagar in Paul's Eyes and in the Eyes of Yahweh," 6.

53. It might be queried why Hagar has a special relationship with Sarai/Abram over against Keturah, Abram's last wife. In fact, Westermann sees something of the divine promise in Keturah saying, "The author is saying something about the significance of Abraham, the father; he is the father of many peoples, not only of Israel." Westermann, *Genesis 12–36*, 245. Similarly, Drey connects Abraham's covenant with all of his sons, "A Son of Abram is, nevertheless, a son of Abram, and, therefore, part of the covenant. The biblical writer is illustrating that by the covenant of Gen 15 God is willing to bless *any* descendant of Abram." Drey, "The Role of Hagar in Genesis 16," 193.

Yet, though Keturah was also a wife of Abraham, she is not given as great promise as Hagar, nor are her children described as being blessed in any way. In fact, they are listed as her sons, while Isaac and Ishmael are listed as the "sons of Abraham." (1 Chr 1:28) Waltke observes, "although both Keturah (cf. 1 Chr 1:32) and Hagar are concubines, the narrator gives the genealogy of Abraham's children through Hagar a separate book (25:12–18), suggesting the esteemed status of Sarah and God's grace to Abraham and Hagar. The differences[*sic*] between Hagar, an Egyptian slave concubine, and Keturah, a concubine, is Hagar's unique relationship to Sarah as a surrogate mother, Abraham's devotion to Ishmael, and God's promises to Hagar." Waltke, *Genesis*, 335.

54. Koehler and Baumgartner, *HALOT*, s.v. "קלל." This is as opposed to the qal, which simply means, "to be insignificant in the eyes of, to count as nothing." The difference seems to be between viewing someone and treating them poorly.

Status and Blessing in the Sight of God

Again, this evidence underscores the theme of valuation which informs divine seeing. Not only does Hagar found her worth upon her child-bearing ability, but her consequent 'looking down' upon her mistress puts her in jeopardy of coming under the curse of Gen 12:3. If the one who blesses Abram and his seed will be blessed, and the one who despises him will be cursed, then it could be said that this is a sort of lens through which Yahweh approaches humanity. Yahweh sees according to one's relationship to His covenant partner.

The Meaning of Divine Sight

We have established the wider context as dealing with the Abrahamic promise of blessing, and specifically to the nations. These nations find blessing in him as they bless him, but are cursed if they so much as despise him. As the titles used of Hagar (Egyptian, handmaid [šiphāh]) demonstrate, she, as representative of the nations, falls into this paradigm. She is evaluated on the basis of her connection with and treatment of Abram and his family.[55] This is complicated both in her rise in status to Abram's wife, and her carrying his child, as she also 'looks down' on Sarai. This causes her to be treated abusively to the point where she is driven from the family. She is both connected and disconnected, and on the wrong side of the blessing formula.

Pamela Tamarkin Reis postulates that Hagar required a significant dose of incentive to return to what would be almost sure persecution. Evidently, what Yahweh does is enough for in verse 16 we find Abram naming her child, confirming him as his own. So how is it that Yahweh convinces her to return? He[56] announces that He has heard her affliction, and will

---

55. That the blessing applies to his family is seen later in 22:18. However an oblique reference is made in Abram's dream in 15:13-14, for as his seed is to be enslaved, God will judge those who enslave them. That Sarai is also included in this promise is only made clear in 17:16.

56. Actually, the text speaks of "the Angel of the LORD" as speaking with Hagar. Technically an angel or messenger, there is continuing debate over the identity and distinction of this being with regard to the deity. H. Gunkel proposed that the earlier concept of God allowed Him to walk amongst humans, while later conceptions required a substitute. However, Westermann observes that this doesn't explain the occurrence of both the terms Yahweh and His messenger in stories such as Gen 16 and 18. In his own extensive treatment, Westermann denies that *mal'ak yhwh* refers to either a named messenger, such as Hermes as he functioned for the Greek pantheon, nor is there an identification with God Himself, concluding that, "God is present not in the messenger, but in the message." Westermann, *Genesis 12-36*, 244. Also see,

prosper the son she is to call Ishma'el "God hears." Reis finds the dealmaker in the revenge she sees promised for Ishmael in verse 12.[57] Hagar's return to slavery will buy her son's freedom, which he will use to contest with Sarai's son. And yet, this seems anachronistic, as Sarai is still barren. Furthermore, the command was not simply to return, but to submit to her mistress[58] (v. 9). This is not the position for revenge, and certainly Yahweh does not send her back in order to get such on His covenant couple.

Rather, we find the answer in Hagar's reply. She responds to the revelation of God's having heard her rather obliquely in verses 13-14:

> And she called the name of the LORD, the One Who spoke to her, 'You are a God Who Sees,' for she said, 'Indeed here, I have truly seen, just as the One Who sees me.[59]

R. Ficker, מלאך, "Bote," THAT 1, 900-908, Commentaries by Gunkel and von Rad, and "Engel" in RGG, EKL, BHH, cited in Westermann, *Genesis 12-36*, 242. However, it seems Westermann's own observation of the angel—that he never is said to come from or return to God, indicates that he actually is God (as per Procksch, Wenham). All the characters in the Old Testament who encounter him seem to conclude this, (cf. Exod 3:3, 4, Jdg 6:22-23; 13:16-22). Furthermore, the encounters with the Angel of the LORD in Judges also imply a certain fear of death, usually associated with seeing God. (Exod 33:20)

Waltke argues plausibly for a representative ambassador (cf. E. A. Speiser "a distinct class of spiritual beings). "Like all angels, he is a heavenly being sent from the heavenly court to earth as God's personal agent. In the ancient Near East the royal messenger was treated as a surrogate of the king (Judg. 11:13; 2 Sam 3:12-13; 1 Kings 20:2-4). So also the Lord's messenger is treated as God and yet as distinct from God, as God's angel." Waltke, *Genesis*, 254. The church fathers equate him with the second person of the Trinity, but, as Waltke observes, the "NT never makes this connection. Instead, *angelos kyrios is associated with* Gabriel. (Luke 1:11, 19; Matt. 1:20, 24; Luke 2:9)." Waltke, *Genesis*, 254.

However, in Gen 16:13, Hagar explicitly names Yahweh as, *the One who spoke to her, 'ēl-rŏ'î*. She does not mention the angel (*mal'ak*). Thus, at least in this instance, the *mal'ak yhwh* was a manifestation of God Himself, speaking *in person*, not a separate divine being relaying a message. As Moberly says, this is a character, "who is virtually indistinguishable from YHWH himself. (22:11)" Moberly, *Genesis 12-50*, 20.

57. Reis, "Hagar Requited," 90-91.

58. Lit. "afflict yourself" or "humble yourself" beneath her hand. The term for humbling oneself (hitpa'el, ענה) is the same root used of Sarai's affliction of Hagar in v. 6. The implication is that Hagar is can expect no different treatment than she left.

59. On this exceedingly problematic passage, see Appendix: Exegesis of Genesis 13-14. The advantages of this translation include not having to emend the MT, and lending a sense of sight that is commensurate with the motif of sight within the passage. The repeated mention of Hagar "looking down" (*rā'â*) on her mistress, as well as Sarai doing to her, "as was good in her eyes," casts seeing in the realm of status and power. Here, Hagar claims that in seeing her, God has seen her worth despite her

The disparate descriptors of God used by the *mal'ak yhwh* and Hagar thereby create a literary "gap,"[60] designed to encourage the reader to explore the issue exposed by a disjunction in the unfolding of the narrative. The gap is what informs the meaning of a "God who sees."

Why does she respond to a God who hears by calling Him One who Sees? Hagar's response to the prophecy is revealing; she does not mention the *content* of the promises, only the One who gave them. Waltke notes, "She responds to the person, not to the promise. She no longer gloats that she is pregnant but marvels at the Lord's care for her."[61] Though her son will be a constant reminder of God's care for her, she sees beyond the meeting of her needs. She calls God the One who sees and helps her see, rather than the One who merely hears of and fixes her situation. In light of the status motif, rife with visual language, the shift within divine epithets from hearing to seeing demonstrates it is her value in God's eyes that is paramount, not the health of her unborn son, or some potential revenge on her mistress.

This can also be discerned in the way God addresses her. Phyllis Trible observes, "For the first time a character speaks to Hagar and uses her name. Thus the deity acknowledges what Sarai and Abram have not: the personhood of this woman."[62] Somewhat inconsistently, Trible also sees the same God who acknowledged Hagar's personhood as demeaning her, "Yet the appositive, 'maid of Sarai', tempers the recognition, for Hagar remains a servant in the vocabulary of the divine."[63] However, the term "maid" is neither derogatory (cf. I Sam. 1:18, Luke 2:38), nor a permanent designation (cf. 21:17), in the mind of God. Rather, it functions here to highlight Hagar's bond to the promised line that the LORD is preserving. It reflects the designation that Abram has chosen, when he relegated Hagar directly under Sarai's authority, for as his wife, she had come only under his own.

Thus, because of the low value her mistress places on herself, she used her slave for her procreative agenda,[64] unintentionally raising Hagar's status, and thus enabled her to see herself (and Sarai?) with better eyes.

60. Sternberg describes gapping: "From the viewpoint of what is directly given in the language, the literary work consists of bits and fragments to be linked and pieced together in the process of reading: it establishes a system of gaps that must be filled in." Sternberg, *The Poetics of Biblical Narrative*, 186.

61. Waltke, *Genesis*, 255.

62. Trible, "The Other Woman," 226.

63. Ibid.

64. Interestingly, this foreshadows the failed power play of insecure Egyptians (Exod 1:10) on Hebrew midwives.

status. Hagar's realization (*rāʾâ*) of this (v. 4) gave way to her own disdain,[65] leading to her husband's absent defense and the affliction by her mistress. So it is finally in verses 13–14 that the one who is seen as a tool, finds self-worth inappropriately, is dismissed by her husband, and abused by her mistress, is finally encountered by the One Who sees, and thereby truly values her.

Janzen, however, contends that Hagar gains freedom by taking this situation into her own hands—"subjecting herself."[66] But according to Hagar, it is Yahweh who ultimately provides her with a safe grounding for her self-perception (vv. 13–14). It is His blessing and acknowledgement of her in "seeing her" truly,[67] that provides her with the worth she had misguidedly sought in raising her status at the expense of her relationships (v. 4). Yahweh has given her a blessing through her relationship with Abram and Sarai—the knowledge of the One who Sees her. It is this that is expressed in her exclamation in verse 13 and the naming of the well.

Conclusion

What we have seen in this narrative is that God's sight is greatly influenced by the both the major motifs of the story as well as the themes of the wider context. As Hagar's connections with Abraham are established in becoming his wife and bearing his child, and the allusions to Abraham's original call are drawn in her titles, we find her to be seen in terms of this call. She represents the nations who will find blessing in Abram. As such she is evaluated according to her treatment of the blessed couple. In her quest for esteem, she oversteps this boundary. This explains why Yahweh intervenes to send her back. She is Abram's wife, carrying his child, and yet on the road to being cursed. This is part of the lens through which Yahweh sees. He evaluates her standing upon her relationship with Abram and Sarai.

However, the story does not end there. In demonstrating that He has heard her affliction at the hands of Sarai, Hagar becomes convinced that He is a "God Who sees." In addressing her by name, promising her a

---

65. Note the previous use of *rāʾâ* in verses 4 and 5. Hagar becomes aware (*rāʾâ*) of her situation (pregnancy), resulting in a change of her view (*qillēl*) of the relative status between her mistress and herself.

66. Janzen makes a case for the significance of the middle voice of the hitpaʿel of in verse 9.

67. For this translation, see Appendix A: Exegesis of Gen 16:13–14.

future in a multitude of descendants, and hearing her affliction, He sees who she is. She is neither the result of her (mis)deeds in slighting her mistress, nor the sum of her various and changing titles. Despite falling to the lowest rung of the social ladder as a foreign, female runaway slave, she finds herself valued in God's sight. This is neither based on her fertility nor her pride, but her connection with Abraham. Hence, we see that divine sight here amounts to valuation despite class, gender, role, or even moral history. It is colored by the contextual themes of titles, the struggle to be valued, and connection with the promised blessing. These themes shape divine sight in that they set up the problem for which divine sight becomes the answer. Though God honors titles (16:9) and the relationships they represent, He does not value people according to role, but connection to the covenant. Neither is value to be found in performance, for He is the one who brings success, in this case, fertility. Nor is perfection key, as He is seen to forgive the repentant,[68] and still bless them. In seeing Hagar, God imbues her with a sense of worth beyond all societal status or title. He sees her as one intimately connected with His covenant people, and, true to His word, He blesses her, not only with a child and a future, but with the realization of her worth—in His eyes.

---

68. The verb in 16:9 "return" (שׁוב) is the same as to repent, or turn from one's ways, thus hinting at the relational aspect of Hagar's return.

8

A Second Look at Sodom
Genesis 18:1—19:29

> *"I will go down now, and see if they have done entirely according to its outcry, which has come to Me; and if not, I will know." (Gen 18:21)*

IN OUR PREVIOUS CHAPTER, WE FOUND DIVINE SIGHT TO BE INFORMED by the primary themes of status and blessing. It thus functioned as both an affirmation of Hagar's worth as well as motivation for her to return to the conduits of God's covenantal blessing, Abram and Sarai. The story of Babel laid emphasis on God's vantage point in looking at the city and the tower, and thus commented on the project as well as its future ramifications. In our next text, Gen 18 and 19, we find a narrative in which the act of "seeing" plays both a structural and pivotal role.

The pericope is bounded by seeing.[1] Initially, Abraham *looks* up and finds himself some house (tent?) guests. As their meal concludes, the men *look down* toward Sodom. In Gen 18:21, Yahweh Himself expresses a desire to go down to Sodom *to see*, "if they have done all according to its outcry, and if not, I will know." Later, Lot too, *sees* the angelic visitors and rushes to welcome and protect them. When the Sodomites assault Lot, the angels strike them with a form of *blindness*. Lot then pleads with his sons-in-law to take advantage of the divine reprieve, but *in their eyes*, he seems to be joking. As Lot and his family are rushed out of the city, his wife takes one final tragic *look*. We end the story with Abraham also *looking* back, much as he had done years earlier when he separated from Lot, and as the angels had done when they left him, but instead of a fertile plain, he surveys the cities' smoking remains.

---

1. "To 'appear' and 'see' is a key of this scene (18:1, 2 [2x], 21; see also 19:1, 28)." Waltke, *Genesis*, 266. Note that it is commonly agreed that 19:30–38 is an addendum concerned with the etiology of Moab and Ammon.

All of these instances of seeing serve not only to structure the pericope, but also to draw contrasts between the main characters, highlighting their character and desires. In the following, we shall look at some of the main issues in this narrative and how "sight" plays a key role in their interpretation. In each instance of "seeing," beginning with Yahweh's (18:21), we shall examine the agent's intentions in performing the act, the object(s) of their sight, and the ramifications of their seeing for the narrative as a whole. Finally we shall compare the meaning of sight in these instances, how they differ, and how they interact. In so doing, we hope to further expand the notion of supernatural sight as one that can overlap with the natural, performing functions unique to its context. Rather than a monolithic definition, we seek to illustrate how Stern's metaphorical meaning can yield different denotations as it is applied *in context*, thus freeing us from the usual problems of human language being inadequately and somewhat rigidly applied to the divine.

Motive and Need for Seeing: Why Is Yahweh Going Down "to See"?

We have seen Yahweh come down before. "That the LORD describes the outcry as great and the sin as very serious is ominous, especially in the light of the similar phraseology in 6:5, which presaged the flood. 'I want to go down' (coh of ירד) sounds like the 'let us go down' (11:7) that preceded God's judgment at Babel."[2] In chapters 18–19, as in chapter 11, Yahweh's "seeing" follows "to go down" (ירד) in the volitive mode,[3] "I want to (must) go down and I will see . . . ," and consequently it derives its significance as a revelation to the patriarch of Yahweh's intentions (v. 17). However, even Yahweh's intended purpose is illuminating with respect to the objects, motive, and effects of His sight. In the following, we will investigate what Yahweh was up to in "going down to see."

---

2. Wenham, *Genesis 16–50*, 50.

3. Joüon, *A Grammar of Biblical Hebrew*, Joüon says that the *"na"* particle here indicates desire.

In the Eyes of God

Judicial Inquiry

Many commentators, like Claus Westermann, find this to be a "fact-finding" mission. He says, "God decides to step in as judge ('I must go down,' as in Gen 11:5 and 7); the intervention begins with a verification, a judicial inquiry, whether the situation is in accord with the cries of lamentation."[4] God is going down to clarify the facts of the situation, to see if the outcry was accurate. This interpretation lends to the idea that Sodom and Gomorrah's fate was undecided. Nahum Sarna says, "As the wickedness of the city appears to reach intolerable proportions, God personally investigates the situation. The fate of the inhabitants of Sodom is not yet sealed. At this point, the humanity of Abraham is put to the test."[5]

Nathan MacDonald compares this episode with Babel, in that in each case, there is no foregone judgment.

> In vv. 20–21, the divine soliloquy ends, and Yhwh speaks directly to Abraham about his plans. Yhwh is going to go down and see (ארדה נא יראה) whether the outcry that has come up to him is true or not. The attentive reader would recognize an allusion to the story of the Tower of Babel in Gen 11:5: "Yhwh went down to see" (וירד יהוה לראת) judgment is not presupposed by these verses. Instead, Yhwh's words suggest an investigation with no definite decision about Sodom and Gomorrah's guilt or innocence; Yhwh has heard an outcry, and he will investigate the charge before passing judgment.[6]

These views see Yahweh as seeking to "discover" something He does not already know. However, as Victor Hamilton observes, Yahweh is keenly aware of Sodom's situation.

> Thus Yahweh intends to set out on a mission of verification. Will what God sees confirm what he has already heard? Again, we have in this section a bold anthropomorphism— Yahweh will reconnoiter Sodom as investigator. . . . The modern reader may think it strange that Yahweh knows what he is about to do with Sodom (v. 17), he knows about its sin (v. 20), yet he announces his intention to make a judicial inquiry into the state of affairs in the city (v. 21). Is Yahweh fully informed about Sodom's turpitude or is he not? Had vv. 20–21 been a further soliloquy by Yahweh, then we would have no recourse but to suggest that vv.

4. Westermann, *Genesis 12–36*, 290.
5. Sarna, *Genesis*, 132.
6. MacDonald, "Listening to Abraham," 29.

20–21 are intrusive in the narrative. Yet this is not a soliloquy but a speech made to Abraham. Later in the narrative Abraham will raise the issue of whether God is always and consistently just. Almost in anticipation of that interrogation, seemingly almost on the defensive, Yahweh informs Abraham not only of Sodom's state but of his intention to buttress that observation with a fact-finding mission. Thus, already Yahweh dilutes some of Abraham's concerns by letting the patriarch in on the thoroughness of his analysis of the situation at the two cities.[7]

Hamilton also feels this is a fact-finding mission, despite there being strong indication that Yahweh already knows about the sin of Sodom and the rest of the Pentapolis. Had Yahweh's proclamation to "go down and see" been part of His self-talk, this might have indicated a gap in His knowledge. However, as this expressed intent comes in verses 20–21, where Yahweh speaks to Abraham,[8] it expresses His intentions to the patriarch, and not the need to rectify some ignorance on His own part. Yet, Hamilton here seems conflicted, for while he admits Yahweh's prior knowledge, he concludes that Yahweh goes down to see, in order to allay some of Abraham's fears.

MacDonald also defends a fact-finding mission in view of an open-ended and thus genuine dialogue between Abraham and Yahweh over Sodom's fate. "But even judgment is not presupposed by these verses. Instead, Yhwh's words suggest an investigation with no definite decision about Sodom and Gomorrah's guilt or innocence; Yhwh has heard an outcry, and he will investigate the charge before passing judgment."[9]

---

7. Hamilton, *The Book of Genesis*, 20.

8. Though speaking can be to oneself, this is usually expressed as "said to one's heart." Robert Alter notes, "The verb *'amar*, 'say,' is sometimes used elliptically for *'amar belibo*, 'said to himself,' and that seems clearly the case here. With the two divine messengers about to be sent off on their mission of destruction, God will be left alone with Abraham, and before addressing him, He reflects for a moment on the nature of His covenantal relationship with the patriarch and what that dictates as to revealing divine intention to a human partner. Abraham is in this fashion thrust into the role of prophet, and God will so designate him in chapter 20." Alter, *Genesis*, 80, note 17; Alter, *Genesis*, 80, note 17 (cf. Gen 8:21. Also Gen 17:17; Isa 47:8; Pss 10:6; 14:1; Est 6:6; Hos 7:2). In the present case, the end of the soliloquy is determined by the content of the speech and by context. In 17–19, Yahweh is either speaking to Himself, or to his (what turn out to be) angelic companions and not Abraham ("Shall I hide from Abraham . . . ?"). The subsequent repetition of "and Yahweh said" indicates He now speaks aloud to Abraham. This is confirmed by Abraham's response in verse 23 which makes no sense without knowledge of the spoken material in 20–21.

9. MacDonald, "Listening to Abraham," 29.

This openness is based on the absence of a spoken judgment by Yahweh. As Westermann notes, "one difficulty that arises is that there is no actual announcement of the destruction of Sodom in vv. 17–21; there is only an indication of it in v. 17 while in vv. 20–21 Yahweh decides to inquire whether the situation is such as to warrant the outcry."[10]

Whilst these observations have merit in that the judgment is not stated explicitly until 19:13, there are indications of Yahweh's pre-judgment of Sodom, not the least of which is the discussion with Abraham. He apparently understood God's intent to destroy the cities, and on this basis he questions Yahweh. However, it seems that all of these interpretations are dependent on a sense of "knowing." That is, how much Yahweh "knows" affects why He is going down to "see."

Omniscience

One of the primary theological strictures on the interpretation of divine sight is the concept of omniscience. MacDonald comments on the effect of the concern to protect God's omniscience by early Christian writers on the interpretation of Gen 18:21. He says,

> Thus, early interpreters worked with a different set of assumptions, and the non-negotiable affirmation of God's omniscience has two significant effects on the interpretation of the dialogue. First, it seems to minimize any genuine divine responsiveness, since God was already aware of the two cities' wickedness (Josephus *A.J.* 1.11.3 §199; Ephrem the Syrian *Comm. in Gen* 16.1). God's condescension to the human need of discovery is justified in a number of ways: as a divine example to human judges (Ephrem the Syrian *Comm. in Gen* 16.1), or for the purpose of a final offer of forgiveness if Sodom and Gomorrah should repent (Origen *Hom. in Gen* 4.6; *Gen Rab.* 49:6; *T. Neof.* 18:21; *Tg. Ps-J.* 18:21). Second, divine omniscience excludes the possibility that God might learn from Abraham.[11]

According to MacDonald, ancient Christian writers felt this "anthropomorphism" of God's coming down to see was a condescension to human understanding. It was therefore either meant as a thinly-disguised manner of teaching human judges how to investigate crimes before

---

10. Westermann, *Genesis 12–36*, 285.
11. MacDonald, "Listening to Abraham," 42.

rendering judgment, or as a last token offer of mercy to the cities about to be overthrown.

MacDonald, however, finds that this notion of omniscience precludes the intent of the text, which is that Abraham actually taught God. He theologically contrasts his approach with that of Walter Brueggemann with respect to the harsh implications of omniscience: the Scylla of Divine non-responsiveness and the Charybdis of God's ignorance.

> Brueggemann seems to me to present a modified version of the first consequence of God's omniscience in such a way as to dispense with the second consequence altogether. The God of the dialogue cannot be fully responsive, because the God of the earlier tradition is already determined to destroy the cities. However, the lesson that Abraham teaches God mitigates this harsh portrayal. My reading attempts to present a modified version of the second consequence of God's omniscience, but with the loss of the first consequence. That is, God teaches Abraham about divine mercy in a dialogue in which, since Abraham is a prophetic mediator, the fate of Sodom and Gomorrah is genuinely at stake.[12]

MacDonald would have it that either Yahweh knows all and is thus unresponsive—to Abraham's pleas, or He does not and can genuinely react to creatures. So, is Yahweh in the dark here, or at least, "near-sighted," requiring He take a closer look?

Though the concept of omniscience may have guided many exegetes[13] in the past, we find that it is not essential for interpreting this passage. While many commentators contend that the issue for Yahweh is a "judicial inquiry" into the facts of the case against Sodom, we find that this is unlikely the case for several reasons: contextual proof of Yahweh's prior knowledge of Sodom's sin, the outcry itself, Yahweh's proposed plan of action, His staying with Abraham, and His orders to the angels. Let us

---

12. MacDonald, "Listening to Abraham," 42.

13. For example, Nahum Sarna says of Gen 11:5, "The LORD came down. God does not react capriciously; he investigates man's doings. The identical anthropomorphism, or depicting of God in human terms, appears again in 18:21 in connection with the divine scrutiny of the situation at Sodom and Gomorrah. This figurative usage implies no limitation on God's omnipotence, for the divine 'descent' presupposes prior knowledge of human affairs from on high, and God's subsequent counteraction unqualifiedly exhibits His absolute sovereignty. Rather, there is subtle irony here. Man builds a tower 'with its top in the sky,' where God is popularly thought to dwell. Scripture emphasizes God's infinite transcendence and incomparable supereminence by having God 'go down' in order to scrutinize the scene." Sarna, *Genesis*, 83.

examine these contextual clues to determine what God already knew of Sodom.

Prior Knowledge of Sodom's Sin

To interpret Yahweh's seeing as an "investigation" implies that He doesn't already know the facts. But, even without bringing dogmatic issues such as omniscience into the narrative, the reader already knows of Sodom's wickedness and its eventual downfall (Gen 13:10, 13). While the downfall (v. 10) is an anachronistic explanatory interjection, the city's wickedness is highlighted immediately after Lot separates from Abraham (v. 13) as part of the narrative. As such, it is not simply the result of a future judgment, but a fact already presented as relevant within the metanarrative. However, although the destruction of Sodom is foretold in Gen 13:11, 13, MacDonald notes, "there is no prescription for how or when it should occur. Already in the invasion of the four kings (14:1–12), the reader was drawn to expect the imminent end of Sodom and Gomorrah, but on that occasion Abraham successfully intervened. The reader might wonder whether Abraham will again mediate salvation in the face of this new threat."[14] Thus, though the judgment of the sin remains potentially open, the knowledge of the sin itself is already established.

Outcry

Secondly, God has already heard the outcry. This outcry is itself both confirmation of the Sodomites' sin and evidence of its seriousness. When we look at other instances of outcry in the Bible, we find both Yahweh's direct knowledge of its cause as well as its nature. Wenham holds that, "'outcry' refers to the protests of those offended (cf. Prov 21:13). Like the blood of Abel, unpunished sin cries out to heaven for vengeance (cf. 4:10)."[15] Timothy Lytton adds, "They also serve as technical legal terms for a claim

---

14. MacDonald, "Listening to Abraham," 29.
15. Wenham, *Genesis* 16–50, 50.

of injustice linked to a demand for redress."[16] Thus, the cry itself (18:20) has alerted Yahweh to the need for justice.[17]

More than simply an audible sound, this cry of injustice comes straight to Yahweh's ears. Von Rad says,

> The word "outcry" (*ze'āqā*) is a technical legal term and designates the cry for help which one who suffers a great injustice screams. (We even know that the cry was, namely, "Foul play!" *hāmās*, Jer 20.8; Hab 1.2; Job 19.7.) With this cry for help (which corresponds to the old German "*Zeterruf*"), he appeals for the protection of the legal community. What it does not hear or grant, however, comes directly before Yahweh as the guardian of all right (cf. ch. 4.10).[18]

That Yahweh has heard this outcry sets the scene as a judicial case, and establishes that something very serious is wrong in Sodom, as this type of cry is not uttered by those unafflicted. Though the outcry itself does not establish all the facts, awareness of one seems to include cognizance of the other.

In fact, as we see in other instances of the "outcry," there is no need for God to confirm the facts. God knew of Cain's murder simply from the "witness" of his brother's blood "crying out" (4:10). Similarly, the bondage in Egypt needed no "confirmation." God came down not to investigate, but "to deliver" the people (Exod 3:8). As we have discussed earlier, even the "coming down to see" at Babel (11:5) served as the stamp of irony to show

---

16. Lytton, "Shall not the Judge of the Earth Deal Justly?" 36. On note 18 he refers to "Joseph Blenkinsopp, *The Judge of All the Earth: Theodicy in the Midrash on Genesis 18:22–33*, 41 of Jewish Stud. 1, 2 (1990); von Rad, *Old Testament Theology* 207. . . Bruckner, *supra* n. 14, at 143. For another well known example, *see* Genesis 4:10, where the verbal form of *tsa'akah* is used to describe how the blood of Abel, murdered by his brother Cain, 'cries out' (*tzoakim*) to God from the earth. *Supra* n. 11 (New JPS translation)."

17. Though some have compared the cry here to that of the noise which the lesser gods/humanity were making in Enuma Elish and the Atrahasis epic (cf. also T. Jacobsen, "The Eridu Genesis," 520), Hamilton notes some key differences. "Genesis does not refer to the deity's problem with insomnia; on the other hand, the non-biblical accounts do not have any moral overtones connected with the noise. To be sure, one would not be able to discern any moral understanding of the use of 'cry' per se in verse 20. But its juxtaposition with 'sin,' in v. 20, and Abraham's later plea that Yahweh not destroy the innocent (*ṣaddîq*) with the wicked (*rāšāʿ*) would indicate that Yahweh's concerns reach beyond the volume of noise rising from the cities." Hamilton, *The Book of Genesis*, 21.

18. von Rad, *Genesis*, 211.

that the project whose height was to reach heaven, had not quite made it. Again, this instance of "seeing" was not information gathering.

God's Pronouncement

William J. Lyons contends that, "YHWH's words end with 'if not, I will know' (וְאִם־לֹא אֵדָעָה), raising the possibility that the outcry may be unjustified and indicating that as yet no guilty verdict has been handed down."[19] However, as Hamilton alluded, in 18:20, Yahweh makes two assertions: Not only is the outcry of Sodom great, but, "*its sin* is exceedingly grave." Hence, Yahweh has already judged the sin, and found it very serious.

Yahweh's Own Stated Course of Action

Yahweh's own actions indicate He knew of Sodom's sin. He asks Himself (v17) if He should hide from Abraham *what He is about to do* (or doing, אֲשֶׁר אֲנִי עֹשֶׂה). Now, this could be either that He will go down and investigate, or that He will bring judgment upon Sodom. It cannot refer to His plans to speak with Abraham, as that is the content of what He thinks He should reveal. Yet, after stating his intention to go down, Abraham embarks on a dialogue to dissuade Yahweh from an action that would let the righteous suffer the fate of the wicked. Abraham, at least, understands Yahweh to have already found the city condemned. It is the righteous (*ṣaddîq*) for whom he pleads[20] (v. 23). Hence, Yahweh cannot be going down to determine the cities' guilt.

Pre-ordered Destruction

The angel entourage tells Lot that the LORD *sent* them "to destroy" the place (19:13). There is no conditionality in this order, "If you find it totally

---

19. Lyons, *Canon and Exegesis*, 182.

20. Alternatively Lytton notes a Rabbinic interpretation as a dispute over the grounding of the accusations. "The Rabbinic commentator Rashi notes that the metaphor of God going down to investigate teaches that judges should not decide capital cases without adequately clarifying the facts. Yet, as important as factual clarification is to good judging, God sends the two men down to investigate the facts while He Himself remains with Abraham to discuss the governing legal principles. The ensuing dialogue between God and Abraham is not a dispute about facts, but a discussion about law. Thus, we may view Abraham's objections as a challenge to the legal grounds of God's judgment." Lytton, "Shall not the Judge of the Earth Deal Justly?" 37–38.

A Second Look at Sodom

corrupt, then wipe it out." They were simply sent on a mission to seek and destroy. Significantly, this destruction is a result of the previous outcry, not what the angels discovered.

Hence, for a variety of reasons, we find God knowledgeable of the facts of Sodom's sin. The sin has been established earlier in the metanarrative as a generally known fact. The outcry itself is by its nature, evidence of a serious injustice. Yahweh has pronounced the sin "grave" (כבד) before going down. His statement of purpose is taken by Abraham at least, as an indication of His imminent judgment upon the cities. And, finally, Yahweh sends what turn out to be two angels "to destroy" the place—and this is based on the outcry He has already heard. Hence, Yahweh's descent to see "if they have all done according to the outcry that has come to Me," cannot be a mission to discover what He already knows.[21]

Performative Perception Acts: A Witness

So, if God wasn't seeking information, what was He doing? To answer this, we first note that seeing, like speech, can be performative. As J. L. Austin demonstrated,[22] by speaking, we can perform other acts such as promising, threatening, questioning, naming, etc. By uttering the words, "I hereby name this ship, the *Ellen*," given the context of a boat launch and the proper authority, I perform another action—that of *christening* the ship.

Similarly, we contend, perception can also be performative. The question then, is not whether or not God sees, but what He is *doing* by seeing. He is not "gathering information." But, what then? As Gordon Wenham observes, 18:21 is a statement of intent rather than inquiry. "It is not that God needs to go down to confirm what he knows, but that he is visiting it with a view to judgment."[23] In this decidedly judicial context, God's act of coming down and seeing performs the act of a legal witness.

How do we know this? In this narrative, God declares his intent to teach Abraham in the "way of the LORD" by doing righteousness and justice, so that He might bless him and make him a blessing (18:18–19, cf. 12:1–3). It is immediately following this that we hear the LORD talking to

---

21. This is not to rule out this sort of mission *a priori*. We are simply saying that *this* story is not an example of God discovering new information.
22. Austin, *How to Do Things with Words*.
23. Wenham, *Genesis 16–50*, 50.

Abraham[24] about Sodom and Gomorrah's sin, strongly implying that this shall be a test case to instruct Abraham in righteousness and justice. Soon thereafter, we find two of the men heading off to Sodom, while Abraham and Yahweh debate the extent of punishment. Later in the Torah, we find that a witness must be established on the basis of at least two eye-witnesses (Deut 17:6; 19:15). Hence, the mystery of why Abraham encountered three men—Yahweh's two emissaries are going down (19:1), not to determine the righteousness of the place, but to provide a legal witness of its guilt. Though Yahweh Himself does not go down, He does so by proxy.[25] Just as an author can dictate a letter to an assistant, or head of state can send an ambassador to speak on his behalf, so here, Yahweh appropriates the sight of the two angels. They see, and by seeing, they act as witnesses for Yahweh.

In a related passage in Gen 4:10, God again hears an outcry. Although Yahweh doesn't "go down," it is evident that after warning Cain of his impending fall, Yahweh leaves, for Cain is subsequently under the impression that he could lie to God about murdering his brother. However, immediately upon committing murder, God is there questioning him. Yahweh has displayed his knowledge of the outcry (*ṣāʿaq*) of his brother's blood (v. 10). Hence, though He was not around when Cain committed the murder, God does not need to come down to learn of it. Rather, His presence is to confront the offender with this knowledge.[26]

As with Cain, part of the reason for God's personal inquiry in our present passage may be for confrontation. God goes down not to augment his knowledge, but to make the offender cognizant of His awareness of the situation. The closest verbal parallels are with the Babelites and the Hebrew slaves. In each case, God goes down (*yārad*) "to see" a situation He has already described (Gen 11:5; Exod 3:7). With Babel, as we have mentioned previously, the emphasis is on where the punishment is executed.

---

24. As Wenham notes, "The Lord said" suggests that the following words were spoken aloud so that Abraham heard them." Wenham, *Genesis 16–50*, 50.

25. Though He announces this intent in 18:20–21, Yahweh Himself is never said to personally go down (ירד)—He merely "departs" (Heb. 18:33 הלך). It is the two men who look down (שׁקף) towards (16) and eventually go (הלך) to Sodom.(22).

26. Cain responds somewhat obliquely to his banishment. He adds, "and from Your face I will be hidden." God does not correct him, and so we assume this to be the case. And yet God preserves him through a protective "mark." It is as if God is indicating that the offense was a personal one against Himself (cf. Gen 9:6; Ps 51:4[6]). Cain's punishment is that he will not live in God's immediate presence, where He at least had dialogue with God. This indicates that God's presence (face) was the key issue, not knowledge of Cain's sin.

God demonstrates the folly of their hubris in that the tower with its top in heaven is actually quite a way short of its goal. The punishment is not given from heaven, but from [down]"there" (*šām*, Gen 11:7, 8). Similarly in Exodus, God hears the Israelites' cry for help (2:23), groans (2:24), and outcry (3:7). However, in this case, He then sees (ראה) their affliction, and upon that basis, He goes down (ירד) to deliver them from the power of the Egyptians (3:8). Interestingly, Yahweh goes down to Moses and assures him, "I know" (ידע). Yahweh already is aware, before He descends, either to meet with Moses or to deliver the Israelites. His descent then, is "to deliver" (נצל, Exod 3:8), and He proceeds to confront Pharaoh (e.g., 4:22, 23).

But why provide a legal witness to a doomed city? Abraham queries, "Shall not the Judge of the whole earth do what is right?" God is here demonstrating to Abraham, that He does. It is not important simply that Abraham teach his heirs to do righteousness and justice, but that they know it is "the way of Yahweh" (18:19). What does this tell us about the "way of Yahweh"? That He not only corroborates the evidence, but provides proof in confronting the guilty. Though the godless may say of the Judge of the earth (Ps 94:2. cf. Gen 18:25), "The LORD does not see, Nor does the God of Jacob pay heed" (Ps 94:7), the psalmist answers, "Pay heed, you senseless among the people; And when will you understand, stupid ones? He who planted the ear, does He not hear? He who formed the eye, does He not see?" (Ps 94:8–9)

We have seen that it is unlikely that Yahweh was going down to investigate the depth of Sodom's sin. He has already demonstrated knowledge of it, condemnation of it, and ordered his angels to bring judgment because of it. In fact, Yahweh never actually goes down. By sending two emissaries, however, we find He is providing a legal eyewitness as proof of Sodom's sin, as well as demonstration of Yahweh's knowledge. Yahweh's sight then is performative, and in this case, appropriated sight. And yet, to be a performative act, it must be a real act. By going down the emissaries provide both a witness and confront the offenders personally. In so conducting His judgment, Yahweh teaches Abraham more of His way—that of righteousness and justice. He does not hand out sweeping judgments from on high, but confronts the offenders with His knowledge of their deeds.

Object of Yahweh's Sight

There are two primary issues involved in determining the object of Yahweh's sight. The first is where exactly He intends to go down "to see." Is it Sodom, or the surrounding area? Secondly, there is some question as to whether this sight is of the depravity or extent of Sodom's sin. These questions inform the focus and nature of Yahweh's sight in Genesis 18:21.

Location

Von Rad asks,

> What did Yahweh go down to see? (Deut. 29.23; Isa. 1.9f.; 13.19; Jer. 49.18; 50.40; Ezek. 16.46 ff.; Hos. 11.8; Amos 4.11; Zeph. 2.9; Ps 11.6; Lam. 4.6). In these references Sodom and Gomorrah are always mentioned together[27] as though identical. In contrast to them, it is striking that our narrative scarcely mentions Gomorrah and especially that it can give the reader not the least idea of this city and its conditions. It too was simply destroyed. But what were the findings here regarding the wicked and the blameless? The assumption, therefore, that the words "and Gomorrah" in chs. 18.20; 19.24 f., 28 are a later addition is justified.[28]

As Von Rad observes, if God was truly going down to see if they had "done according to the outcry," then why did he not visit the other cities? Von Rad concludes that this anomaly must be a textual addition, but we find this unnecessary.

As Lot represents the category of the "righteous"[29] in Abraham's discussion with Yahweh (18:23–33), Yahweh need only go where Lot dwells. That is, Lot represents the only righteous person in the cities of the plain, and hence, there is no need to search all of the cities. This fact, as we shall see, informs our understanding of Yahweh's going down to see, as Lot becomes the primary focus of Yahweh's mission to, "see if, according to her

---

27. Robert Letellier, notes, "The Gk adds 'and Gomorrah' but through Gen 18–19 Sodom alone is mentioned, perhaps metonymically, for all the cities of the area, the so-called pentapolis. Only in 18,20 and 19,24.28 is Gomorrah also specified, but always coupled with Sodom." Letellier, *Day in Mamre, Night in Sodom*, 109, note 29. Gerhard von Rad adds, "The book of the Wisdom of Solomon even speaks of a pentapolis (ch. 10.6), and therefore includes Zoar too." Von Rad, *Genesis*, 221.

28. von Rad, *Genesis*, 221.

29. See Appendix "The Righteousness of Lot."

outcry, the one coming to me, they have done, all of her, and if not, I will know" (18:21). But first, we must understand what is it "they" have done, and what is meant by "completely/all of her"?

The Extent of Sodom's Sin

One of the keys to understanding the object of Yahweh's sight in 18:20 is the difficult Hebrew term, *kālā* (i.e., "Whether according to the outcry that has come to me, they have done *kālā*"). John Calvin sees this as indicative of the depth of the Sodomites' sin.

> The Hebrew noun כלה, (*cala,*) which Moses here uses, means the perfection, or the end of a thing, and also its destruction. Therefore, Jerome turns it, "If they shall have completed it in act." I have, indeed, no doubt but Moses intimates, that God came down, in order to inquire whether or not their sins had risen to the highest point: just as he before said, that the iniquities of the Amorites were not yet full. The sum of the whole then is; the Lord was about to see whether they were altogether desperate, as having precipitated themselves into the lowest depths of evil; or . . . if by any method, their wickedness was curable.[30]

Calvin sees the reason for Yahweh's descent as the depth of the Sodomite's depravity. He says, "In saying that the 'cry was great,' he indicates the grievousness of their crimes."[31] However, this interpretation does not seem in accord with the rest of the narrative which speaks of the number of righteous in the city, not the level of wickedness or righteousness.

Some other options are noted by Hamilton, "MT *kālā* is difficult. As a substantive it means 'destruction, annihilation.' That meaning may be retained here: 'whether (the) destruction they have done is like the cry that has reached me.' Or it may be taken as an adverb, 'thoroughly, completely,' with the emendation of *kālâ* to *kulâ*. See *HALAT*, 2:455a."[32] In order to decide how *kālâ* should be rendered, let us take a look at some parallel passages.

> Jeremiah 30:11 "For I am with you," declares the LORD, "to save you; For I will destroy *completely* (*kālâ*) all the nations where I have scattered you, Only I will not destroy you completely.

---

30. Calvin, *Genesis*, 585.
31. Ibid., 483.
32. Hamilton, *The Book of Genesis*, 15, note 3.

> But I will chasten you justly And will by no means leave you unpunished."
>
> Jeremiah 46:28 "O Jacob My servant, do not fear," declares the LORD, "For I am with you. For I will make a *full end* (*kālâ*) of all the nations where I have driven you, yet I will not make a *full end* (*kālâ*) of you; but I will correct you properly and by no means leave you unpunished."

In these passages, the verbal phrase has a direct object, and thus, is transitive.[33] However, in Gen 18:21, if *kālâ* is read adverbially, i.e., "completely," or, more literally, "to make an end of," it oddly omits mention of the object of the Sodomites' destructive behavior. Furthermore, though these examples, like 18:21, have God as a subject, MacDonald argues, "a human subject is not unattested (Jer 5:10), and I can see no justification for translating כלה (qal) עשׂה as 'deserve destruction,' except the assumption that Yhwh must have mentioned destruction."[34] Hence, it seems unlikely that Yahweh is coming down to see the extent of the Sodomites' ruinous ways.

A third option is found in the BHS textual notes, which gives an unsupported suggestion that 'completely' (*kālâ*) should be repointed "all of them" (*kulâ*). There is, however, a close parallel to this wording in the first passage to mention these cities. In Gen 13:10, Lot is surveying the land in order to choose which direction to separate from his uncle to accommodate their competing flocks.

> Lot lifted up his eyes and saw all the valley of the Jordan, that it was well watered everywhere—*this was* before the LORD destroyed Sodom and Gomorrah—like the garden of the LORD, like the land of Egypt as you go to Zoar.

Here, Lot lifts up his eyes and sees (*rāâ*) "all of the valley of the Jordan, that all of it (*kulâ*) was watered, before the LORD destroyed Sodom and Gomorrah, as the garden of the LORD, like the land of Egypt as you go to Zoar." In the first passage to mention Sodom, we have Lot seeing the valley that 'all of it' was watered. When Yahweh goes down to Sodom in 18:21, He will see whether they have done, all of it (i.e., the city), according to the

---

33. (Cf. Nah 1:8–9. One possible exception is Jer 4:27, but the subject of the first clause is poetically placed at the end of the clause allowing it to serve double duty as the object of the second clause. A rough literal translation would read:

For thus says the LORD, A desolation will be the whole land, Yet (the whole land) I will not completely destroy.

כִּי־כֹה אָמַר יְהוָֹה שְׁמָמָה תִהְיֶה כָּל־הָאָרֶץ וְכָלָה לֹא אֶעֱשֶׂה:

34. MacDonald, "Listening to Abraham," 29, note 15.

A Second Look at Sodom

outcry that has come to Him. In each case, we have Sodom as the object of sight, and the issue is whether all of it is good (watered) or corrupt.

Thus, the author of Genesis would be making a comparison between how Yahweh sees versus how Lot saw. While Lot saw the potential for good pasture, God sought the heart conditions of those dwelling there. In both cases, the issue is the extent, whether of the watering, or the sin. Thus, because of this parallel within the same set of stories and the sense this makes in our present context, the option to repoint *kālâ* (make destruction) as *kulâ* (all of it) seems the most reasonable.

The issue for Yahweh, then, is the connection between the outcry of Sodom's (*her/its*[35]) sin which He has heard, and how many (all of *her/it*) of the Sodomites have committed it. Thus we find the passage to read:

> I want to go down and see if they have done, all of her, according to her outcry, the one coming to Me.[36]

Furthermore, Abraham's subsequent discussion with Yahweh concerns the number of righteous, not the type or degree of their sin. Hamilton says,

> It appears that Abraham's concern is twofold. His first concern, as expressed in v. 23, is whether Yahweh would indiscriminately kill the innocent along with the guilty. Thus, in v. 23 the emphasis is on the preservation of the *ṣaddîq*. But in vv. 24ff., Abraham expands his concern to include the preservation of the city/the place (*hā'îr/lammāqôm*) because of the presence of a remnant of *ṣaddîq*. Nowhere does Abraham challenge God's evaluation of Sodom's moral turpitude . . . nor does he at any point turn to Sodom to urge repentance.[37]

---

35. Hamilton notes, "MT *hakkeṣa'aqātāh*, lit., 'like her outcry,' is problematic, for the fem. pronominal suffix has no antecedent unless it be Sodom and Gomorrah, which are treated as fem. in the previous verse. Several ancient mss., including LXX and Targ. Onqelos, read final *m* for *h*, hence 'their outcry.' D. Irvin (*Mytharion*, AOAT 32 [Neukirchen-Vluyn: Neukirchener, 1978], p. 21) understands the *k-* after the interrogative as the 'K *veritatis*'—'the especially loud cry which has come to me.'" Hamilton, *The Book of Genesis*, 15, note 4. If we treat these as referring to Sodom as a collective for the towns, then the feminine singular pronoun "her/its outcry" makes sense.

36. Kenneth Mathews notes a possible double meaning, "It is not clear if the NIV renders כָּלָה (n.f.), 'completely, altogether' (cf. EVs); the unusual use of the term adverbially here (also Exod 11:1) has encouraged the emendation כֻּלָּה, 'all of it,' or כֻּלָּם, 'all of them,' (BDB 478 and *BHS*). But כָּלָה may be a double entendre, since its typical usage describes annihilation (by God; e.g., Isa 10:23), thus anticipating the verdict to come." Matthews, *Genesis 11:27—50:26*, 226, note 425.

37. Hamilton, *The Book of Genesis*, 24-25.

Abraham's pleas to spare the righteous, and the city as a whole on their account, would go along well with this interpretation of *kulâ* if God was investigating not the nature of the sin, but its extent.

Implications for Divine Sight

So, what does this mean for the object of Yahweh's sight? Von Rad interprets this passage as an exposition on the idea of collective guilt. Westermann, however, critiques this idea:

> The concept "collectivism" is too general and as a criterion is inept. The question is rather, what is the relationship between God's action towards the individual, whereby he punishes the impious and rewards the pious, and his action in history, his action towards wholes (collectives)? There was no problem in describing God as judge as long as the reference was to individuals, distinguishing the צדיק from the רשע (v. 23); the problem arose when God was described as judge of the world (v. 25), or of cities, countries, or peoples.[38]

In other words, justice becomes a more complex issue when dealing with societies and social systems as opposed to individuals. Abraham's dialogue with Yahweh addresses this complexity. Should the righteous be treated as the guilty in order to punish the guilty community?

This theme of the extent of the sin is echoed in chapter 19, where we find Yahweh's emissaries actually encountering the townspeople. An odd collocation of terms referring to the assembled mob underscores this theme. Janzen also observes this emphasis on the extent of the guilt in the context, "In 19:4 the action of the men of the city involves 'young and old, all the people to the last man.' Such a triple emphasis on the all-inclusiveness of the assembly suggests the 'altogether ' that is still in doubt in 18:21."[39] This emphasis on the whole population being present is confirmation of what Yahweh sought—are there any innocent here? Lot is the only one.

Summary

Hence, we find that the object of Yahweh's sight is the extent of the sin in the Sodomite area. He goes down not to see if they had sinned or how

---

38. Westermann, *Genesis 12–36*, 293.
39. Gerald Janzen, *Abraham and All the Families of the Earth*, 61–62.

A Second Look at Sodom

egregious the sin was, but to provide witness to the fact that there was but one untainted by it. This explains why the visitors head straight to Sodom, bypassing the other four towns. Yahweh is looking for someone specific, and He knows where to look. This also accounts for the (unlikely) emphasis on the entire population gathering at Lot's house, as well as Abraham's concern with the number of the righteous within the community. When communities are being judged, Yahweh takes account of the righteous, though this may have no affect on the judgment of the guilty (cf. Jer 15:1; Ezek 14:14, 20). So all of Sodom has sinned egregiously, save Lot, whom God sees and knows (cf. 18:21).

Sodom's Incorrigibility

Though this is not stated as part of God's knowledge initially, another object of Yahweh's sight is that Sodom was beyond hope. They were presented not only with the salvation of God's chosen one in chapter 14, and with God's justice and kindness in Lot, but also now with God's power and imminent judgment. Thus, God sees in Sodom a people past the point of no return. This is illuminated in several examples of contrasting sight: the crowd, Lot's sons-in-law, and his wife.

The Crowd's Blindness

The crowd at Sodom continue to look for Lot's door after having been temporarily physically *blinded*. Thomas L. Brodie says, "In a narrative that emphasizes seeing, blindness is particularly significant. In this case, it is associated with disordered sexual desire, as though such desire blocks seeing. Sexual obsession blurs one's vision of reality."[40] Though we are not convinced that this is the cause of the blindness, Brodie does bring up the point that there is more than one kind of visual impairment involved. Calvin says, "Whereas, Moses says, that the men were smitten with blindness, we are not so to understand it, as if they had been deprived of eye-sight; but that their vision was rendered so dull, that they could distinguish nothing. This miracle was more illustrious, than if their eyes had been thrust out, or entirely blinded; because with their eyes open, they feel about, just like blind men, and seeing, yet do not see."[41] The irony is poignant and clear—those who cannot see their own guilt or the

40. Brodie, *Genesis as Dialogue*, 251.
41. Calvin, *Genesis*, 502.

righteousness of their visitors, can now not even find the way to the door. Von Rad defines it, "The word in question, which has not yet been etymologically explained, apparently does not mean complete blinding, but rather to be dazzled, to 'see falsely' (Jac.), cf. II Kings 6.18."[42]

This blinding, though temporary, affected more than simply their eyes. As Wenham notes, "Further, it is unexpected that no one in the large mob, even if blind, found his way to the door and summoned others there. Supernatural agency was manifested not simply in the blinding but also in the continued protection of the house until the mob dispersed."[43] Brian Doyle, observing the importance of the 'opening' and the 'door' says,

> The term פתח as access thus comes to parallel the notion of sight as knowledge or vision as cognition which also plays a significant role in the narratives. The blindness of the people of Sodom serves to illustrate their fundamental inability to have access to the divine. Their lack of "sight" echoes their lack of "knowledge." Vision is cognition for the righteous Abraham in Gen. 18.2—"He looked up and saw . . ."—but blindness is the only possible fate of the wicked people of Sodom.[44]

Thus, just as divine agency can be used to illuminate the vision (2 Kgs 6:17, 20), it can take it away, in both natural and spiritual realms. These men could not find the door right in front of them (19:4, 6, 10, 11). Though they sought the visitors inside, they were not only unable, but prevented from seeing, both physically and spiritually. Contrasted with Yahweh, who is witnessing something of which He already has knowledge, these men have no knowledge of their visitor's identity, and despite experiencing their supernatural power, never will.

---

42. Von Rad, *Genesis*, 219. Westermann expounds, "In our idiom too this way of speaking does not mean actual blindness, but a temporary inability to see. This is described here by one word, סנורים, derived by E. A. Speiser from the Akk. *sunwurum*, by A. Ahuvia, *Tarbiz* 38 (1968–69) 90–92, from Hebr. סנר; as it occurs only here and in the same context in 2 Kings 6:18, it points to an old narrative way of speaking, the equivalent of our 'to strike with blindness,' to which the word, later fallen into desuetude, belonged. This narrative trope—threatening foes are struck with blindness at the critical moment—is very common and widespread; it occurs in folktales and in other forms of narrative. For examples and further literature see T. H. Gaster, *Myth, legend . . .* (1969) 158f." Westermann, *Genesis 12–36*, 302. Waltke adds, "The Hebrew term here occurs elsewhere only in the similar context of 2 Kings 6:18. To judge from Jewish Aramaic and these two texts, it means 'to dazzle' and/or 'to deceive,' suggesting they were blinded temporally by a blazing light." Waltke, *Genesis*, 277.

43. Wenham, *Genesis 16–50*, 56.

44. Doyle, "Knock, Knock, Knockin,'" 447.

The Sons-in-Law's Eye for Jesting

Incorrigibility is also found in the eyes of Lot's sons-in-law, who thought he was joking when he pleaded for them to leave with him. Hamilton notes that these were most likely men *betrothed* to Lot's daughters, as other daughters are not mentioned, it is unlikely that they had kept their wives virgins.[45] This fact, however, serves to demonstrate their hardness of heart, for they too must have been part of the crowd (19:4). Despite the earlier events of the evening, including their own experience of temporary physical blinding, they remain unable (unwilling?) to see Lot as one who speaks truth, or has their best interests at heart. Perhaps they, like their compatriots, felt Lot was abetting foreign spies. Despite the display of mercy offered by the angels via Lot (19:12), they could neither see their guilt, their impending doom, nor their salvation, though it stared them in the face. Their sight is perverted, twisting their salvation into a joke.

Lot's Wife's Final Look

Lot's own wife, though dragged out of the city with Lot (19:16), and commanded not to look back, still risks the abominable for one last *look* at her home. Why did she do this? Brodie conjectures, "By looking backward on what is destroyed, gone, dead, Lot's wife herself becomes dead. Her transformation is a further example of the importance in this narrative of seeing. She is like someone who, instead of looking forward, spends life pining about tragedy and about the past—about a former life or love or church ('When I . . .'; 'When we . . .'). At some level such people are dead, dead pillars."[46] However, Hamilton notes, "We are not told why she looked back. The text nowhere suggests that her affection for the city had a stranglehold on her, and that she now entertains a wistful thought toward Sodom. Perhaps she looked back simply because of the noise and the bright horizon of the city behind her. But if that is the case, why does she lose her life? The action seems to be more than simple curiosity. She lost her life for only one reason: because she overtly ignored the directive of v. 17."[47] Whatever her unstated reasons, Lot's wife is inexorably drawn to the city. She neither desires to leave nor to leave it behind.

---

45. Hamilton, *The Book of Genesis*, 40. As Wenham observes, this possibility is more likely than "had married" which would have kept the daughters behind in Sodom. Wenham, *Genesis 16–50*, 57.

46. Brodie, *Genesis as Dialogue*, 252.

47. Hamilton, *The Book of Genesis*, 48.

In the Eyes of God

It was the direction of her sight that seems to have mattered most. She looked *back*.[48] To do so is to show concern of some sort for where one has come from, and not where one is going. Rather than obeying the obviously divine visitors, making sure her own family gets to safety, she looks back to her past, and ultimately, remains in it.

One thing that is notable is that Abraham, like Lot's wife, views the same object, the destruction of the cities. Brodie notes,

> But his vantage point is different. Instead of looking back he looks down, and does so from the place, many miles from Sodom, where he had stood facing Yhwh, insisting on justice. The implication is that instead of seeing the overthrow of the cities as purely destructive, he has some sense of a larger context and of a larger justice. Besides, the smoke from the overthrow is somehow familiar: "and he saw, and behold, the smoke of the land went up like the smoke of a furnace"—effectively like the smoking oven, the smoke and fire which first made the covenant (15:17–18). This covenant was connected with the first rescue of Lot (14:13–16). Amid the fire and smoke, therefore, Abraham saw something more—a presence which in his own time of crisis had made him aware of another dimension.[49]

But Abraham also saw differently.

> The verb that is used for Lot's wife "looking (back)" (*nāḥaṭ*) to Sodom differs from the one used for Abraham's looking to Sodom (*šāqap*). But the verb used here with Abraham was used earlier in connection with the three visitors he entertained (18:16). In fact, both the visitors and Abraham looked "over the face of Sodom" (*'al penê seḥōm*), they before its destruction, he after its destruction. Upon seeing the columns of smoke rising from the city, Abraham can conclude only that the loss of life has been total. He has no personal revelation that his nephew and his two great-nieces are alive. Nobody has lived through this conflagration.[50]

Thus Abraham shares a similar manner of looking and vantage point to the angels, and hence, to Yahweh.

---

48. Lit. "from behind him" (מֵאַחֲרָיו). This presumably absolves Lot of any responsibility for her actions. Had she been looking forward, she would have seen Lot's back, or even Zoar, but as he was headed out of the city and she, behind him looked at the city, by definition she was looking *back* towards it.

49. Brodie, *Genesis as Dialogue*, 252.

50. Hamilton, *The Book of Genesis*, 49.

A Second Look at Sodom

The downfall of Lot's wife is not an inability to see, but the object of her sight, especially in light of divine imperatives to the contrary. Her looking directly reflects the command of the angels not simply to avoid *seeing* (ראה), but not to *look* (נבט), implying intentionality rather than simple visual perception. Notably, she is turned into a "pillar" which is elsewhere a 'garrison, post' ("נְצִיב"cf. 1 Kgs 4:19). She looked back and was ironically set as a permanent watchman over the place. Whilst Yahweh looked for the righteous among the wicked, she only had eyes for the latter.

Summary

In these three examples, we find that Yahweh's sight, vicariously through the two angels, served to offer warning, mercy and salvation to the inhabitants of Sodom. Not only has God provided witness to the comprehensive nature of the cities' guilt, such that there are no righteous whom He will leave behind or for whom he will spare the city, but there is no possibility left for bringing about Sodom's repentance. Even the offers to the sons-in-law and Lot's wife were mocked or challenged. This implies that Yahweh's sight was performative in that it confronted the inhabitants with Yahweh's knowledge of their sin, but also offered His mercy. In blinding the men of Sodom, God's power to exercise judgment is displayed, and the coming doom established. This threat is taken lightly, as evidenced by Lot's sons-in-law.[51] Hence, Yahweh's sight not only establishes guilt through a legal witness, but also confronts through the act of presenting that witness, and yet, in so doing, offers, at the very least to some, God's mercy.

Conclusion

So, what do we know then about divine sight in this pericope? It is not necessarily omniscience. God may know all, but His sight does not function in that capacity within the story. And yet, its function here does not undermine omniscience (*contra* Brueggemann), in that it does not imply a lack of knowledge. Secondly, it is not information-gathering. As we found, sight, like speech, can be performative. In this case visual perception serves the role of a legal witness. More than that, the (appropriated) act of going down and seeing the righteous is how Yahweh offered mercy. He does this by physically going (though via a proxy), so that He makes

---

51. That is, sons-in-law (to be, or . . . not to be), as was the case. The daughters still living with their father evidently had not consummated their marriages.

known His own knowledge (and impending judgment based on it). The Sodomites can see that He sees them and their deeds. They can hide in ignorance no longer. Furthermore, Yahweh's sight serves to show knowledge of the righteous. Yahweh sees not only Lot's heroic hospitality, but his compromised situation. He sees firsthand the difference between Lot and his neighbors, and makes a distinction between them (cf. Exod 11:7). And yet, Lot's salvation is not solely based on his righteousness, but on Abraham's plea for the righteous. It is Yahweh's covenant with him, that all nations would find blessing in him that is upheld by Yahweh's sight. Indeed, the nations eventually springing from Lot, Moab and Ammon, were spared through the efforts of Abraham.

Finally, this instance of "seeing" is vicarious through the angels. They go on Yahweh's behalf. It is a natural use of sight in that it uses the act of visual perception for other purposes. What is more, as this is the "way of Yahweh," this is part of what Yahweh desires for Abraham and his heirs to do, and is thus within the realm of human possibility. Hence, this use of divine sight is not supernatural in its scope—that would apply more to His hearing of the outcry of an entire city from heaven. Rather, Yahweh's seeing is distinctly supernatural in its concern for justice to be properly carried out. Not simply that offenders get their due, but that they know of their Judge, His awareness of them, and His offer of mercy—conditional upon their repentance. Without a confrontation and the promise of judgment, there can be no repentance. Furthermore, Yahweh's sight does not operate simply in panoramic view, but in seeing the details—even the righteous few amongst the many. It is this way of seeing complex problems of justice, which comprises the "way of Yahweh": Confrontation demonstrating an awareness of the offenders and the offense, a view to the genuine repentance of the offenders, and the differentiated application of justice to the righteous and the wicked. These things are supernatural in essence, and Yahweh desires they become the practice of his covenant partner, Abraham and his heirs.

9

The Mountain with a View
Genesis 22

IN OUR LAST CHAPTER, WE FOUND GOD'S SIGHT ACTING IN BOTH A performative manner and by proxy. It performed actions through the use of sight, such as witnessing, confronting, and extending mercy. This accords with Stern's context-based approach to metaphor, which expects to find differing meanings within each individual instantiation' of a particular metaphor like divine "sight." Furthermore, it demonstrates a distinct overlap in divine and human abilities. Although the *modus operandi* might be different, God is still using sight in a manner that humans use it.

In this next pericope, we find just such an instance of metaphorical sight. In 22:8, Abraham asserts God will "see to" the sheep for the sacrifice He has commanded. Though this may entail visual apprehension of the sheep, the primary thrust of the metaphor has traditionally been interpreted that He will "provide" the sacrificial victim. However, though this meaning is often transferred to the statements in 22:14 that God will see, and the ensuing proverb, "On the mount of the LORD it will be seen," we find a different meaning as we examine the context of this pericope as a test of Abraham.

In Genesis 22, according to Phyllis Trible, "references to sight, especially the verb *see* (*rāʾâ*), are proleptic, anticipating a major motif."[1] However, this theme is often hidden by its problematic translation. Many interpreters find this usage of "to see" (ראה) in 22:8, 13, 14 to mean "provide."[2] This is mainly derived from its usage in 22:8, when Abraham

---

1. Trible, "The Sacrifice of Sarah," 174.

2. For example, Walter Brueggemann comments, "The term 'provide' (vv. 8, 14) is difficult. It is an unusual translation of the term *rāʾâ*, otherwise rendered 'see.' Karl Barth (*Church Dogmatics* III, 3, pp. 3, 35) helpfully links the term to *pro-video*, 'to see before,' 'to see to,' 'to see about.' Thus the Latin rendering nicely makes the connection between 'see' and 'provide.' Barth appeals to our text as the ground for his entire

responds to Isaac's question, "Where is the one of the flock?" by saying, "The LORD will see (ראה) to it."

As Walter Moberly acutely observes,

> The context seems to require that "see" here has the sense not merely of sight but of sight leading to corresponding action—a sense which is certainly in keeping with general Hebrew idiom; for *shama'* regularly means not only to hear but also to act in accordance with what is heard, that is, to obey, and *zakar* regularly means to remember not only as a mental process but as an awareness that initiates action.... It is customary to render this "seeing about/seeing to" as "provide." The sense of the verb thus determined in verse 8 is then transferred to verse 14, where the place name chosen by Abraham enunciates a theological principle of considerable importance (though only here within the Old Testament is divine provision formulated in an axiomatic way).[3]

However, as this unusual usage is only seen potentially one other time for a verb occurring 1,324 times in the Hebrew Bible, we must inquire if this heuristic understanding is the most accurate. To determine if this is indeed the sense of the Hebrew *rā'â* in this passage, we begin with an investigation into its context—in what realm are we speaking? We will examine each usage in its immediate context, noting the actor, the object, and the result or effect on the narrative. In doing so, we aim to deduce the intersection of the metaphorical meaning with its individual context, and thus understand the meaning of the verb *in situ*.

Divine and Human Sight in Genesis 22

In looking at the nature of testing,[4] we find it to primarily be a situation intended to elucidate the state of the heart in terms of covenant loyalty to

---

understanding of providence, the doctrine of God's full provision of what is needed for his creatures. Theologically, the difficulty with God as provider may be understood in two ways. First, the notion is problematic for our modern reasonableness with reference to specific gifts. Quite concretely, the visible emergence of the ram is credited to the "seeing for" which God did. Second, to link our word "see" generally to the affirmation of providence makes the broadest claim possible that life is held in the purview of God and that we are destined to live according to his good will." Brueggemann, *Genesis*, 191–92.

3. Moberly, *The Bible, Theology and Faith*, 107–8.
4. See Appendix C: "Testing."

Yahweh. Often the provision has already been given (protection, water, food, etc.) and the test is determining whether or not God's people will remain loyal to Him, having received what they needed from His hand. Similarly, God has already provided Abraham with a sacrifice at the outset of this "test"—Isaac. Yahweh is now examining what Abraham will do in light of this provision. Will he cling to it, or will he obey God? With this context in mind, let us now examine the usage of sight in the chapter.

Abraham's Vision (v. 4)

Abraham's sight is portrayed as primarily physical, as he "lifts his eyes" and the object of his sight is the mountain to which he is being sent on an horrific mission. However, there may be more to his vision than this. JoAnn Davidson comments,

> "and Abraham lifted up his eyes and saw the place": possibly suggesting the height of the mountain that God revealed to Abraham. The more common OT description of "seeing" is "he looked ... and saw." Thus, the author, by describing Abraham's "seeing" by "lift[ing] up his eyes" perhaps hints of Abraham's inner struggle, underscoring his deep mental anguish by implying his head was bowed down. Or, is the use of this particular expression possibly suggesting more than just physical sight?[5]

Not only does this foreboding verse have Abraham perceiving the place that God has directed him to, but it also comes loaded with other connotations. It has much[6] in common with the initial call upon Abraham's life where he is commanded to go to a land "which I [Yahweh] will cause you to see" (אֶל־הָאָרֶץ אֲשֶׁר אַרְאֶךָּ:). Here he is going to a "land of seeing" [Moriah][7] (22:2, אֶל־אֶרֶץ הַמֹּרִיָּה), though it is still Yahweh who directs

---

5. Davidson, "Eschatology and Genesis 22," 237.

6. There are many parallels between this passage and Gen 12:1–3. For example, in 12:2, God commands Abraham to לֶךְ־לְךָ "Go to yourself" which appears only here and in 22:2. As Herschel Shanks observed, the first command severs Abraham's ties with his past, while the second command cuts his ties with his future. Shanks, "Illuminations: Abraham Cut Off From His Past and Future by the Awkward Divine Command 'Go You!'".

7. Fokkelman treats "Moriah" as a mythical place, and says, "I would not change one character or vowel and I interpret the name as the nominal sentence *mori Yah* = 'the Lord (Jahu) is my teacher.'" Jan P. Fokkelman, "On the Mount of the LORD There is Vision," 52. However, though the word as it stands can be derived from several verbs such as teaching *yārâ*, or fear, *yārē*, Moberly points out the connection with sight as emphasized in the etiological comments in verse 14. He says, "This providence, however,

In the Eyes of God

his path (22:1, 12:1). In following Yahweh's orders, he is promised to be made into a great nation, and a blessing to other nations. But here, he is being deprived of his own blessing, and robbed of his sole heir.[8]

The majority of all the occurrences of the idiom, "lifting the eyes," in the OT are found in Genesis.[9] As Wenham notes, "To 'look up' before seeing usually intimates that what is to be seen is of great significance."[10] Jan Fokkelmann notes the progression of the idea within the passage. "The uncertain, painful, and loaded looking up becomes the relieved looking and finding; the identical clause וישא אברהם את עיניו וירא occurs in vv. 4 and 13."[11] In addition to a progression from anxious looking to relieved finding, we also see a parallel in intimacy. As mentioned earlier, Exodus

---

is not just expressed as a general principle, as in 22:8, but it is also explicitly linked to one particular place, where the climax of the story occurs, as the name of that place (22:14a). Although the identity of this place has been much disputed, there can be little doubt that as the story stands the place is none other than Jerusalem, as rabbinic tradition has always recognized. There are three main reasons for this identification. First, the use of the verb ראה is probably to be connected with the name Moriah, understood as a noun from the verbal root ראה with the regular nominal preformative מ. Moriah thus means "place of seeing." If one asks in the light of the rest of the Old Testament where is the place of seeing, where God both sees (22:14a) and is seen (22:14b), the answer is either Sinai (Exod 24:9–11) or Zion (2 Sam 24:15–17; Isa 6:1; Ps 84:5, 8 [Heb. 6, 9]). Since the story envisages the site as three days' journey from Beersheba (22:4), which is appropriate for Jerusalem, but too short a journey for Sinai, it is therefore Jerusalem which is indicated." Moberly, "Christ as the Key to Scripture," 157. Robert Crotty notes ancient attestation for this, "In this vein, *Gen Rabbah* 55:7 suggested that *môrîyāh* referred to 'the place of vision' (*yh' mr'h*)." Crotty, "The Literary Structure," 33.

8. Ishmael has been in effect "disinherited" in 21:10, 12, 14.

9. The others being: Num 24:2; Jos 5:13; Jdg 19:17; 2 Sam 13:34; 18:24; and 1 Chr 21:16. JoAnn Davidson lists those within Genesis, saying, "Texts include: 1) Gen 13:10, Lot 'lifting eyes' and seeing Sodom (hinting that he was seeing more than just the fertile valley, but was also considering what advantages there would be to living there). Also, he was in a position enabling him to look down into the valley and thus didn't need to 'lift' his eyes in a physical sense; 2) Gen 24:63–64, used *twice* in two verses, as Isaac and Rebekah first encounter each other (possibly denoting deep emotions both might have been experiencing at this 'arranged' marriage); 3) 33:1, when Jacob 'lifted his eyes' and saw Esau approaching, thereby suggesting the anxiety he was experiencing (remembering his elder brother's fury at loosing the birthright); 4) Gen 43:29, Joseph 'lifted' his eyes and saw Benjamin as his brothers *bowed* before him (with complex emotions seeing his brother again plus remembering his past dreams and present fulfillment) he certainly didn't need to raise his eyes to view prostrate people; 5) Num 24:2, Balaam 'lifts his eyes' to view the Israelite camp in the valley *beneath* him." Davidson, "Eschatology and Genesis 22," 241, note 30.

10. Wenham, *Genesis 16–50*, 107.

11. Fokkelman, "On the Mount of the LORD There is Vision," 50.

20 is a strong parallel with this passage due to the mention of testing (נסה) to bring about fear (יראה) of Yahweh. In verses 18 and 21 we see the Israelites worshipping God on mount Sinai from afar (מרחק). Here Abraham sees from afar (מרחק), but continues on towards the mountain leaving the people—his servants behind. He explains that he and Isaac will go to worship (נשתחוה) and return to them. In light of the close ties between these passages, this move represents an extraordinarily daring act, as in contrast with Israel in Egypt, Abraham intends to press on closer to God, regardless of the cost.

Abraham's sight here, though physical, seems to invoke other qualities, such as the contemplation of the pain involved in his journey, along with steadfast purpose and hope. These entailments are found in the physical descriptions of the mechanics of his viewing, as well as in the distance of the object on which he is focusing. His lifting of the eyes, as Davidson observes, indicates an initial downward gaze. Conversely, despite the unmentioned turmoil within, he looks up toward the place that God shows him. His purpose is resolute, as he chooses to view this journey as an act of worship, not simple ritual, and as a journey whose completion requires a drawing near to God. His view from "afar" is thus an example of human action which is more than a function of its physical mechanics. Abraham's sight here reveals his heart, both its pain and purpose. As his sight reflects his inner being, it becomes part of the object of God's own sight (cf. v. 12) and informs the meaning of it in verse 14.

God "Seeing" the Sheep (v. 8)

Isaac's question, however, is left hanging, over the characters' heads, and in the readers' minds, "Where is the burnt offering?" Abraham responds in kind, that God will "see" for Himself a member of the flock for the burnt offering. This raises two questions concerning this instance of divine sight; What is it that He sees, and what does it mean for Him to see?

The Object

The Hebrew term הַשֶּׂה is a generic word for (the) one of the flock, which is only later specified in verse 13 as איל "ram." This object of Abraham's claim about God's sight seems to indicate God's provision for the requested offering. However, Phyllis Trible notes another possibility:

> Nevertheless, the meaning of "my-son" remains indeterminate. Its juxtaposition to *'olāh*, burnt-offering, allows the horrendous reading of apposition. "God will see to the lamb for a burnt-offering," namely, "my-son." The language functions on two levels. "My-son" is both speech to and speech about, direct address and direct reference. What it gives in poignancy, it retracts in cruelty.[12]

By taking this appositionally (along with midrashic readings), she reads Abraham's response as a statement of how he understands God to view Isaac—as a sacrifice. Of course, this postulates that God will see (imperfect of ראה) Isaac as a sacrifice, rather than that He already does.

Seeing as Provision?

The first instance of divine sight in the chapter, this verse is also translated in various manners. Moberly says,

> Another important emphasis in Genesis 22 is that God "provides"/"sees" (ראה, 22:8, 14). The somewhat ambiguous use of the verb ראה is not without parallel elsewhere (e.g., 1 Sa. 16:1), but has particular significance in Genesis 22. The general theological point is well captured in English by the notion of providence, whose etymological basis in God's foresight is closely connected to its meaning in terms of God's practical care.[13]

However, using 1 Sam 16:1 as a parallel passage to demonstrate the nature of God's sight in Gen 22:8 actually tends to turn it away from the idea of "provision." This verse has God saying, "I have seen for Myself a King among the sons of Jesse." To take this use of "seeing" as meaning "chosen," ignores the context. The author quite explicitly uses the typical verb for choosing (בחר) in verses 8, 9, and 10 when the Lord says he has not chosen the older sons of Jesse. There is no need to use "see" in an unusual way here for that verb. In verse 7, however, God highlights some of the specific differences between divine and human sight, commanding Samuel not to look on the appearance of a man to determine his right to rule, "for man sees (*rāʾâ*) according to the eyes, but God according to the heart." Thus, this is not about provision, but discernment. In this case, God has not provided a king, but seen the heart of one whom He desires

---

12. Trible, "The Sacrifice of Sarah," 176.
13. Moberly, "Christ as the Key to Scripture," 157.

The Mountain with a View

to make king—David. This also reflects the narrative tension that has been built up earlier in chapter 13, where God announces He is tearing the kingdom away from Saul. Samuel tells Saul,

> But now your kingdom shall not endure. The LORD has sought out (בקש) for Himself a man after His own heart, and the LORD has appointed him as ruler over His people, because you have not kept what the LORD commanded you. (1 Sam 13:14)

Provision involves the meeting of needs by God, whereas here, we find God searching for the right person. Though this person would certainly be God's solution to the issue of filling Israel's throne, the emphasis here is more on God discerning this solution than creating or giving it. Thus, this verse does not serve as a parallel for the notion of ראה as providing.

The Manner of Sight: Provisional, Reflexive, or Intensive

The next issue concerns the particle לֹו, which can be rendered in various ways. Hamilton translates, "Lit., 'God will see for himself the sheep,' if one understands *lô* as reflexive ('for himself') rather than intensive ("God himself")."[14] Still a third option is to read it as altering the sense of the verb from "see" to "see to (it)." For example, Trible comments, "If the narrator has Abraham seeing (*r'h*) the place from afar off, Abraham has God seeing (*r'h*) to the sacrificial lamb before the place is reached. So God dominates the reply in this sentence where syntactic order reverses with subject preceding verb: 'God, indeed God, will see to it . . .'"[15] Hamilton's reflexive option emphasizes God's interest in seeing the "sheep," whereas the intensive option, lends emphasis to the fact that it is God seeing it (in person) and not Abraham or someone else. Trible's approach adds to this a stress on the responsibility for getting the sheep, rather than "seeing" anything.

Ultimately, all of these options are viable. The important thing to note is that the vagueness in the wording, combined with the odd use of verbs lends to the likelihood of this being a double entendre. Abraham says to Isaac, "God will see for Himself a sheep, my son" as well as, "God Himself will see a burnt offering—my son." This openness in the language allows for Abraham to be honestly answering his son, and yet cryptically alluding to God's own view of what is transpiring. Abraham is not asserting that God will provide the sheep, but, as in 1 Sam 16, that He will find

---

14. Hamilton, *The Book of Genesis*, 98, note 8.
15. Trible, "The Sacrifice of Sarah," 176.

225

it. But not just an animal for immolation, God will see Isaac himself on the altar as evidence of Abraham's loyalty and obedience.

Abraham's Hindsight (v. 13)

In verse 13 we have the same rare construction that we found in verse 4, as Abraham "raises his eyes and sees." Phyllis Trible notes the immediate connection of this action with the central dialogue, "Fear of God also brings vision. 'Abraham lifted up his eyes and saw (*r'h*) . . .' Whereas earlier these words introduced 'the place from afar' (22:4), this time Abraham sees differently: not afar off but, at hand, behind him an animal. Freed of attachment, he beholds an answer to Isaac's question, 'Where is the lamb for a burnt offering?' (22:7d)."[16] She contends that Abraham's test concerned his "attachment" to the gift of Isaac, and only after releasing this, was he able to see the lamb.

In contrast, Barry L. Bandstra notes the conjunction of seeing with *hinnēh*.

> The unexpected nature of this sight is indicated first of all by complementation with *hnh* rather than with *ky*. Normally a subordinate *ky* clause follows *r'h*, but here a coordinate *hnh* clause is the complement of *r'h*. The construction *hnh* + noun phrase introduces a highly discontinuous element into the narrative. Indeed, the ram is a new and highly unexpected participant in the story. Characteristic of such new topics, this phrase is indefinite when here first introduced, *'yl 'ḥd* "a certain ram." When referred to in v. 13e, it is definite.[17]

Hence, we note the element of surprise in this instance of Abraham's sight.

Whereas before, we found that Abraham's raising of the eyes indicated a previously downward gaze, hinting at a heavy heart, we now have something slightly different. His eyes were (presumably—v. 10) looking down upon his son whom he was preparing to slay. In fact, the text says the ram was "behind."[18] Thus, the raising of the eyes at the heavenly interruption reflects a shift in attention from the task at hand.

---

16. Trible, "The Sacrifice of Sarah," 179.
17. Bandstra, "Word Order and Emphasis," 118.
18. Moberly comments, "Hebrew *aḥar* is difficult. *BHS* (ad loc.) prefers a strong MSS tradition which reads *'eḥad*, seeing *'ḥr* as a corruption of *'ḥd*, because of the ease of scribal confusion of *resh* and *dalet*. I fail, however, to see the point of *'ayil 'eḥad*, for the *'eḥad* is redundant if "a ram" is the sense of the Hebrew. I therefore retain the

As it is specified as אחר, "behind,"[19] we might presume that Abraham passed it on his way to the place of sacrifice. Jan Fokkelman says,

> I feel that the sentence regarding seeing is the central or most important of the ternary phenomena, with *v. 14d as the climax*. The use of this line as a saying "to this day" breaks through the frame of narrated time and draws the reader's today into the text—this in itself is an invitation to reader-oriented interpretation. The choice of the *nif'al* of ראה is striking after the transitive qal-forms of *v.* 4b//13a and 8b//14b. The passive voice dissuades us from looking for an unambiguous interpretation and fixing on one specific agent (as the one who sees). I therefore appreciate the translation of the new JPS version here: "On the mount of the LORD there is vision." This translation has a very gnomic or proverbial ring and almost merits the label "enigma"—a genre designation which follows well on the mysterious *hintergründig* quality of this story as a whole. I interpret *v.* 14d as the juncture where two trios are tied together: the series concerning Abraham's seeing (4–13a–14d) and the series of God's seeing (8b–14b–14d). Abraham's despair and faith tell us that God's seeing surrounds and leads to the mortal's seeing.[20]

Fokkelmann acutely observes the interplay between divine and human sight. It is only the divine intervention which causes Abraham to look away from his intended task and see the alternate victim for his sacrifice.[21]

---

consonantal text. If *'ḥr* is pointed as in MT then it is an adverb, 'behind' as in Psalm 65:26, which makes good sense. (A possible alternative would be the pointing *'aḥer*, 'other', with the sense that Isaac is regarded as a sacrificial sheep, and the ram is the alternative, 'another ram'; but this seems to me rather forced.)" Moberly, *The Bible, Theology and Faith*, 108, note 55. Another possibility is presented by Wenham, who renders it as 'just caught.' He says, "אחר sometimes occurs in the OT with the meaning 'with' or 'immediately after' (e.g., Jer 25:26; Ruth 1:16; Ecc 12:21; cf. Gen 18:5) and also in Ugaritic (Pope, *BA* 49 [1986] 115–17). Hence our rendering." Wenham, *Genesis 16–50*, 99, note on 13a.

19. Von Rad says, "It is doubtful that the narrator considered the existence of the ram, caught in a thicket, as a miracle (see at ch. 21.19). A more likely assumption is that of a definite mitigation of the miraculous, i.e., that Abraham now sees the ram which perhaps was already there and that it is thus obviously available to Abraham." von Rad, *Genesis*, 237. Cf. also Kant, "Restorative Thoughts: Part 2," 169.

20. Fokkelman, *Narrative Art in Genesis*, 51.

21. Moberly notes the parallel with Samuel's anointing of King David, "Although one need not suppose that Genesis 22 is making the same point about seeing that is made in 1 Samuel 16, there is the striking similarity that each time God initially 'sees' something which is not apparent to the human agent, each time the human agent is enabled to see that which God has seen, and each time there is a general principle

In the Eyes of God

Thus, at least in one sense, his sight was divinely enabled. This too, comments on Abraham's obedience. He took upon himself to do what was asked without looking for a way out (cf. 16:3; 17:18; 18:23–33). He was single-mindedly devoted to the task.

The Mount[22] of Vision (v. 14)

In this verse, there are two mentions of sight. The first is the naming of the place by Abraham, "Yahweh sees" (יְהוָה ׀ יִרְאֶה). The second, contains a proverb based on Abram's name for the place, "On the mount of the LORD, He/It shall be seen (יֵרָאֶה)." Many commentators, reading this verse in conjunction with verse 8, conclude that the "vision" of Yahweh concerns his provision, both of the ram for Abraham, and his people in general. For example, Phyllis Trible says,

---

about divine seeing." Moberly, *The Bible, Theology and Faith*, 107, note 53.

22. There has been much controversy over where *Moriah* is located, though Jewish tradition and 2 Chr 3:1 identify it with the Temple mount. Though Gunkel, and those who follow him (e.g., Killian) find this story to be an etiology for a cult site at Jeruel which practiced child sacrifice, Levenson observes, "The chief deficiency of the theory that Gen 22:1–19 was, in its original form, an etiology of the worship at Jeruel is the total absence of any indication that this obscure place, mentioned exactly once in all of Scripture, ever served as a cult-site. . . . Gunkel and those who follow him err not in drawing our attention to the wordplay on *rā'â* and *yārē'*, but in resorting to the obscure place-name Jeruel to explain it. As I have noted, the paronomasia in question can just as easily have the name Moriah in view, as has been recognized since rabbinic times. This does not establish the traditional Jewish equation of Moriah with Jerusalem; it does argue that Moriah need not be deemed secondary within Gen 22:1–19." Levenson, *Death and Resurrection of the Beloved Son*, 117. Levenson also observes that it is actually not the name which is preserved at all. "Often overlooked in the discussion is that for which the name served as an etiology—not the spot, but 'the present saying, "On the mount of the lord there is vision."' (v 14). Once again, if verse 14b is seen as a late gloss, as Kilian wishes, then the point is lost, and we are back to guessing the location to which Adonai-yireh in verse 14a refers. But if, with Reventlow, we see verse 14 as a unity—the first half giving the name, the second half, its meaning—then we should be less troubled by the absence of any location with the name Adonai-yireh. The narrative tells us that Abraham called it so, but not that it has this name 'to this day,' in the words of many other etiologies. What survives from Abraham's experience, according to verse 14 (if taken as a unity), is not the name of the mountain, but the vision of yhwh that takes place there." Levenson, *Death and Resurrection of the Beloved Son*, 122. Regardless, as Moberly notes, "although the place where God sees and provides is intended to be Jerusalem, the notion of God seeing and providing remains intrinsically meaningful without reference to Jerusalem." Moberly, "Christ as the Key to Scripture," 160.

The Mountain with a View

> As substitute for Isaac (and for the lamb), the ram vindicates Abraham's prediction that "God will see to" the sacrifice (22:8). The ram symbolizes the successful completion of the test. Accordingly, an appropriate etiology concludes this unit of section three.
> So Abraham called the name of that place
> "The Lord will see"
> As it is said to this day,
> "On the mount of the Lord it will be seen" (22:14).
> What is seen is that God provides. To be a God-fearer is to have this vision.[23]

In line with verse 8, Trible concludes that here, God has "seen to" the ram. However, while this context necessarily impinges upon the meaning of Yahweh's sight, there is more than a simple transfer of meaning. Syntactically, in verse 14, there is no לו following the verb "to see." Even the translators of the Vulgate recognized this difference, for though they translated the Hebrew *rā'ă* as *provideo* in verse 8, here, they rendered it *video*, "to see."[24]

Several other issues arise in the translation of this verse. The first concerns the subject of the verb "to see." Sarna notes that with the verb, "יֵרָאֶה [is rendered] literally 'He/it shall be seen.'" The subject of the verb is unclear, although the apparent reference to verse 8 would favor the impersonal rendering, referring to the sheep. A different exegetical tradition is represented by the Septuagint, which renders, 'On the mount the Lord appeared.'"[25] As the verb is in the passive (niphal) stem of ראה (to see), this translation is a distinct possibility.

However, several factors mitigate against translating this as "the LORD appeared." Firstly, in contrast with the LXX, in chapter 22 of the

---

23. Trible, "The Sacrifice of Sarah," 180.

24. Moberly observes this difference between verse 8 and verse 14 in the Latin rendering of the verbs, "It should be noted, however, that the Vulgate uses not *provideo* but *video* in verse 14; that is, the translator reverts to the more common rendering of *rā'ă* by *video* when the context no longer requires an unusual rendering. This suggests that the Vulgate itself does not attribute to *provideo* the significance which it later came to acquire." Moberly, *The Bible, Theology and Faith*, 108, note 54; Moberly, *The Bible, Theology and Faith*, 108, note 54.

25. Sarna, *Genesis*, 154. Kenneth Matthews adds, "The Greek reading (and *Tgs. Ps.-J., Neof.*), however, interprets the subject of 'he saw' (*wayyar'*) as 'the Lord': 'On the mountain the Lord was seen.' In this case the naming of the site indicates a theophany occurred, as the Lord commonly 'appeared' (*wayyērā'eh*) to Abraham (12:7; 17:1; 18:1) and to Israel at Sinai ('the mountain'; e.g., Exod 3:1–2.16; Lev 9:4, 6)." Matthews, *Genesis 11:27—50:26*, 297.

MT, Yahweh is never explicitly said to appear. In verse 1, He merely *speaks* to Abraham at Beersheba.[26] If the saying in verse 14 were concerned with an appearances, it would have occurred on the mountain (cf. v. 14, "it is said to this day, 'On the mountain of the LORD . . .'"). On the mountain, though, it is not Yahweh (or *ĕlōhîm*), but the "angel of the LORD" (מלאך יהוה) who speaks (v. 11). Though it is well known that this being has a close relationship with Yahweh and is often used almost interchangeably with Him,[27] in Abraham's case, Yahweh has always appeared without such a mediating being (cf. 12:7; 17:1; 18:1[28]). Hence, it would seem odd if the only time the writer employs the "angel of the LORD" in a meeting with Abraham is the very time he is highlighting Yahweh's appearing.

Secondly, we note, the angel himself is not mentioned as "appearing." Rather, he "called to him [Abraham] *from heaven*" (vv. 11, 15. cf. 21:17; Exod 20:22; Deut 4:36, etc.). This explicit reference to the non-earthly realm from which the voice originated does not convey the idea of a visual theophany, but rather creates a distance between Abraham and the angel. One recalls a parallel with Sinai, where God's voice was heard (*from the heavens,* Deut 4:36) but no form was seen[29] (v. 15). Similarly in our present case, though there is certainly a divine encounter, neither Abraham's exclamation nor the proverb in 22:14 refers explicitly to a visible manifestation of Yahweh. Thus, it is unlikely that the phrase commemorating the occasion would emphasize an appearance that otherwise goes unmentioned in the narrative.

Furthermore, if, with Westermann, we translate the phrase, "Yahweh appears," to mean that "Yahweh reveals himself!,"[30] what exactly is it that He reveals? If it is His provision, then both instances of *rā'â* in this verse ought to be translated that way, due to their mutual proximity and that the

---

26. For locating the beginning of the narrative, see 21:33. Furthermore, they return to Beersheba in verse 19.

27. Westermann notes, "In v. 11, on the contrary, the word that comes to Abraham intervenes in the course of an action, a critical situation like 21:11 (see *ad loc.*). It is in such situations that the patriarchal stories speak of the messenger of God (the early narratives too). When he is mentioned, something has always already taken place." Westermann, *Genesis 12–36*, 360–61.

28. Though Abraham sees 3 men, it later becomes apparent that two of them are "angels," (19:1, 15) as they leave for Sodom and the LORD remains with Abraham (18:22) to speak with him.

29. Though fire was present, the emphasis in the passage is that Yahweh's personal form was not visible.

30. Westermann, *Genesis 12–36*, 365.

proverb in 14b is based on Abraham's proclamation in 14a.³¹ But the first instance is not in the niphal, and not reflexive ("appears").

If verse 14 highlights God's bodily manifestation, why is there no celebration in the similar, but much more explicit event in Genesis 18? Here there is a feast prepared for Abraham's three visitors, but there is no altar built, no name ascribed. In fact, we find a closer parallel in Genesis 16 where the angel of the LORD again meets with the main character, reverses her action,³² blesses her with descendants, incurs a reaction of proclaiming that God sees, and has a place named for the event. However, as we have already shown, it is not God's appearance, but His esteeming of her which is celebrated. Thus, despite ample opportunity, the celebration of God's appearance alone is without direct parallels within the Abrahamic narrative.

Finally, the proverb in 14b, "On the mountain of the LORD, [it] will be seen (יראה)," is based on Abraham's earlier exclamation, *Yahweh yireh* (יהוה יראה) in 14a, which means "Yahweh sees," not "will be seen."³³ Thus, it makes little sense for Yahweh to be the implied subject in 14b (Yahweh "is seen/appeared"). Though some like von Rad and André Lacocque opt for a dual statement where Yahweh "both sees and is seen,"³⁴ this ignores the result clause, (אשר יאמר היום "with the result that it is said to this day

31. I.e., "Yahweh provides" in 14a, and "On the mount of the LORD, it will be provided" in 14b.

32. I.e., of running away from her mistress. (16:9). Here, he restrains Abraham's hand, reversing his own command and Abraham's action. (22:2, 12)

33. Waltke and O'Connor note that, "In positive clauses אשר alone can introduce . . . a result clause . . . 'He called . . . the place . . . so that (i.e., with the result that) to this day it is said . . .')" Waltke and O'Connor, *Introduction to Biblical Hebrew Syntax*, 638–39. Similarly Joüon, Joüon, *A Grammar of Biblical Hebrew*, 598, 169f. (contra Westermann, 363). Hence, the passive verb in the proverb, "It is seen," (niph. *r'h*) is based on the imperfect of the earlier "Yahweh sees." It follows, then that the subject of what 'is seen' is the object of what Yahweh sees.

34. Von Rad says of the author, "He gives no place name at all, but only a pun which at one time undoubtedly explained a place name. But the name of the place has disappeared from the narrative; only the pun is left, and it now lends itself all the more to a subtle playful change of the supposedly basic word 'see' from active to passive (God sees, God is seen, i.e., he appears). The thoughts are not precise (What does God see? Abraham's obedience? Or does he 'look with favor on the true sacrifice"? Or in general, does he see the man and what benefits him?). The reader is here to be summoned to give free reign to his thoughts. (See at ch. 16.13f.)" von Rad, *Genesis*, 237. Lacocque adds, "What is etiologically prefigured in Genesis 22 is the Temple as the locus for the seeing of Yhwh and the being seen by Yhwh [*ra'ah*], as well as for the human awe [*yara'*] before Yhwh (both verbal roots are decisive in the Aqedah story)." Lacocque, "About the 'Aqedah," 196.

In the Eyes of God

...").³⁵ It is nonsensical to say that Yahweh is seen (14a) *as a result of* His seeing (14b), but rather, what is seen on the mount (14b) is seen because Yahweh sees it (14a). Thus, because of the use of the angel, the lack of mention of or parallel reaction to Yahweh's appearing, and the relationship between the two uses of sight, we conclude that it is not Yahweh who is the subject of this passive verb, but the object of His previous sight.

If it is not Yahweh who will "be seen," then who or what will be seen? As this is a gnomic saying, ("To this day it is said,") the generic subject "it," is most appropriate (hence, "It will be seen." Cf. Gen 10:9; Num 21:14; Hos 1:10). Furthermore, the issue is not Yahweh's presence, but Abraham's response to the test (cf. vv. 1, 12). This "test," comprised of the command to sacrifice Isaac, is reversed in verse 12, and hence brought to a conclusion. The reason given is that Yahweh now knows Abraham's fear of him. Apparently, it is this which the test hinged upon. Thus, the object of *Yahweh yireh*, and thus the subject of the passive "it shall be seen," is Abraham's fear of Him. This included both obedience³⁶ to Yahweh (Moberly, cf. 22:18), while counting the entire covenantal promise itself as the sacrifice (von Rad). Furthermore, the emotional cost of this test is taken into account as well, as fear of Yahweh outweighs Abraham's love for Isaac (22:2, 12). It is this that will be both tested and revealed on Mount Moriah.

In light of the more general focus of a "saying," "it" basically refers to the heart of the worshipper (v. 5). God has tested Abraham to know (cf. Wenham "confirm") whether his obedience to Yahweh's words is more important even than His promises and blessings. Thus the proverb in 14b indicates that the heart of the true worshipper should be fixed on one object alone: Yahweh for Yahweh's sake. This mountain, which 2 Chr 3:1 connects with the site of Solomon's temple, signifies not only the future location of ritual sacrifice,³⁷ but of the proving of cultic and covenantal loyalty. In this holiest of places, worshipers will be tested, to see if, like Abraham, loyalty to Yahweh reigns in their hearts.³⁸

Thus, we find the occasions of *rā'ā* in 22:14 not to be concerned with provision, or appearance, but the condition of the heart. Syntactic

---

35. See Joüon, *A Grammar of Biblical Hebrew*, 598. Also, Waltke and O'Connor, *Introduction to Biblical Hebrew Syntax*, 639.

36. Here, this is expressed as 'hearing/heeding my voice" (22:18).

37. Cf. 2 Chronicles 3: 1. See also, Wenham, "The Akedah: A Paradigm of Sacrifice".

38. Moberly sees this as making the story paradigmatic of Israel's worship. "Thus, Abraham's sacrificial worship on Moriah is readily seen as the archetype of Israel's worship in the Temple in Jerusalem, and is presumably to be understood as ultimately the basis for it." Moberly, "Christ as the Key to Scripture," 158.

differences with verse 8, along with the context of the testing of Abraham's fear, argue against provision alone. A lack of appearance, combined with a unique use of the angel, and the speaking from heaven, among other factors, mediate against an appearance of Yahweh. Rather, it seems that Yahweh sees Abraham's heart. He acknowledges this by stopping the test, providing a substitute, and blessing Abraham for his extreme loyalty.

Conclusion

It seems the key to understanding God's seeing in Genesis 22, is the context of testing in which it is set. Many commentators focus on the object of sight in verse 8 translate *rā'ā* there and in 14 as "provide." For example, James McKeown, who says, "The name of the place encapsulates the significance of the story as God's provision and is very significant for biblical theology: God makes demands but then provides his worshipers with what is needed to fulfill those demands."[39] However, this places the focus on Isaac and his question, rather than the question of Yahweh which concerns Abraham. Isaac seeks to know where the sheep for the sacrifice is, but Yahweh seeks to know if Abraham will obey.

As we have seen, it is unlikely that provision was the foremost concern. It was not that God required a sacrifice and provided the necessary ram. Had He needed a ram, He could have asked Abraham, possessor of many flocks (13:5–7), to bring one. Unlike with Isaac's question, the ram was not the focus. God was testing Abraham's covenant loyalty, and so asked him to sacrifice the fulfillment of those promises—his son, not a ram. It was this loyalty which was seen on the mountain, and so the theological message is that God tests and sees the hearts of his worshipers. That He provides for his worshipers is a different point entirely, and not the primary one the narrative is making. On Yahweh's part, there is no hint or promise of provision, only a chilling command. The door is not even left open for such a substitutionary provision, as the victim is specified by a four-fold address, "Your son, Your only one, the one whom you love, Isaac."

Actually, the "need" itself is artificially created. Though there are some similarities, this is not fully comparable to the trek through the desert in which God enabled the Israelites to follow through His provision of food and water (Exod 15:25; 16:4; Deut 8:2). In each case God commands the person/people to do something that creates a crisis, and God

---

39. McKeown, *Genesis*, 118.

does "provide" for their needs. However, with Israel's trek through Sinai, the "need" was already present by reason of the promise of the land. For the people to receive the promise, they had to follow God through the desert and trust His provision. With Abraham, however, God had already fulfilled His promise, and was threatening to take it away. According to T. D. Alexander, however, this covenant had not been fully ratified.[40] Thus, God required a sacrifice to complete the transaction.

In chapter 22, we have two metaphors for divine sight, both with slightly different entailments. In verse 8, we have a prediction by Abraham that Yahweh will find a sheep for the sacrifice. His wording is intentionally ambiguous, and hence, full of meaning. To Isaac, he indicates a provision of a sacrificial victim, which can simply mean that God will conduct His own successful search for an animal (cf. 1 Sam 16). This instance of sight is akin to provision, as God sees the sheep both physically and in terms of responsibility. He will "see to" the sheep. However, the appositional reading indicates that Abraham also refers to Isaac himself. In this case, the emphasis is both on God's personal attentiveness (He will "see Himself"), as well as the victim. Here Abraham is expressing his hope that God will see the victim of the sacrifice he is obediently making, and by extension, his own loyalty.

It is this second sense which is often muted in verse 14 by reading the first sense alone as its context. The "provision" of the substitute does not happen until after the test is completed (v. 13). God has discovered that for which He had put Abraham to the test. Hence, it is not Abraham's faith in God's provision, but his fear of God with which God was concerned (v. 12), and which He sees. In verse 14 then, sight is more akin to insight, based not simply on words (v. 8) but on a viewing of physical actions. As Abraham held the knife above his son, Yahweh indeed sees both Abraham's hand, as well as his fear of Him, and it is enough.[41] Isaac's sacrifice is not required.

---

40. See Appendix C: Testing.

41. This begs the question of whether or not Yahweh knew of Abraham's heart condition. Though this issue lies somewhat outside the purview of this thesis, I might suggest an answer. We must see Abraham's heart not with a fixed predeliction towards obedience, but one which is shaped by his experience. The test at hand involved discerning the depth of his obedience—i.e., whether or not it was greater than his love for Isaac. This, by nature, can only be determined when Abraham is faced with this dilemma. For this reason, this could not be 'seen' by God before the test, even if He foreknew what Abraham would do, as it was only completely formed in his heart during the test. "Seen" in this sense would refer to a first-hand experiencing of Abraham's pivotal decision to obey and an intentional regarding of this decision as proof positive of Abraham's "final answer" in the matter.

Yahweh has also experienced the agonizing choice Abraham has made within himself, even though he did not go through with the act. Thus, in exclaiming, "Yahweh sees," Abraham proclaims God's knowledge of his heart, not just that he loved his son, (v. 2) but feared Yahweh even more. In viewing Abraham's lack of withholding his son from God (vv. 12, 16), God both views his reaction and discerns his loyalty. All of this is apparently done from the heavenly realm (v. 11), confirming it is not Yahweh's appearance which is celebrated here, but His spiritual discernment of the oft-hidden states of the heart. It is this fact which is commemorated about the place in which God is worshipped, prefigured here by the "mount of the LORD." Rather than limiting God's sight to the mountain, this speaks to the nature of worship, exemplified by that at the temple. In worship, God will see not only the cultic act, but discern the loyalty of His worshipers, not only in terms of ethical norms, but ultimate obedience.

10

Conclusion

ANTHROPOMORPHIC LANGUAGE HAS PROVIDED A CONUNDRUM FOR exegetes and theologians for millennia. Attempting to use human language to describe the divine presents ontological and epistemological problems that push our speech to the breaking point. Initially, we looked at several different modes of speech, the univocal, equivocal, analogical, and metaphorical, looking at their approach to speaking of a transcendent being. The univocal approach treated language for God and for humans as having the same sense. This immediately runs into problems, however, as God is a non-created Being and His attributes are neither contingent nor finite in nature. Process theologians attempt to retain this way of speaking of God, but end up redefining His nature and relationship to creation and wind up with a form of panentheism that makes the world part of God, rather than a traditional theism which defends a greater Creator/creature ontological distinction.

Equivocal ways of speaking lose any ground of meaning as the term for a divine attribute has no relation to its use for humans. Recognizing this, scholars such as Maimonides promoted the *via negativa*, in which attributes are only denied of God (i.e., He is *in*-finite, *im*-mutable, etc.). Although this method continues to inform our theology, it remains quite limited in what it can assert. In order to say as much as most theologians and people in faith traditions would desire, this method simply does not take them far enough.

Furthermore, it requires other means to explain the assertions of the biblical text that God *is* a Shield, Shepherd, King, Rock, Savior, etc. This usually involves some form of accommodation, that can be used to explain various ideas from shifts in Old Testament laws to provisions for divorce or even the new covenant. However, this approach lacks a principled guide to its application, and often runs the risk of muting the sense of individual texts. Furthermore, it struggles under the burden of explaining how we *know* that something is accommodated.

Analogical language, especially as developed by Aquinas, is a valiant attempt to correlate the language of humanity with that of the divine whilst acknowledging the ontological differences between the two. However, while it grapples appropriately with both the nature and relationship of its objects, it fails to find proper epistemic grounds upon which to establish this relationship. We simply do not know the relationship between God and His attributes, and cannot therefore say in what way they relate to the relationship between humans and their own descriptors.

Metaphorical approaches, and specifically that of Josef Stern, have provided a way of speaking of God in human language that points at the divine attribute without defining it. And yet, it can say more than the *via negativa* for, within a particular context of usage, through the intersection of the metaphorical character and the contextually-determined metaphorical content it can make truth conditional propositions. This is especially helpful in referring to transcendent divine qualities, which by their very nature are not definable in created human language. At the same time, this approach allows the contextual usage of these terms to come into play in the interpretations of their various instantiations. This comes close to the functional approaches of Alston, Ferré, and Aaron, in highlighting the function of the divine attribute, and hiding its mechanics. However, Stern's metaphorical approach is ultimately superior in that it does not require a divine trait to function in the same way across all contexts. Rather, the predicate is allowed to be informed by the motifs, structure, and thrust of a given text. Furthermore, this allows for an interplay and commentary upon the corresponding human predicates within the narrative.

In addition to the nature of speech, we also examined the philosophical ground for making truth claims about the divine. Though Barth proposes an "analogy of faith," we feel we must press further. Though we too must begin with God's own self-revelation, we feel Wolterstorff's conception of divine speech acts allows us to see human language, not as broken, but as divinely appropriated. Furthermore, our approach to metaphors allows us to make use of human language in a manner which avoids the problems of literal speech, which ran Barth's program aground, leading to his heuristic analogy of faith.

We found that Nicholas Wolterstorff's conception of divine discourse allowed for both divine grounding of assertions about the divine, as well as accessible and (potentially) understandable human language. He builds this model upon the idea of appropriated speech acts in which one agent accomplishes something by means of the speech of another agent. This model seems to furnish us with the accuracy of divine knowledge (located in the God who appropriates things to Himself), as well as the accessibility of human language. This left us with the task of interpreting the language itself, to which we turned to metaphor theory.

Metaphors themselves we found to be superior descriptive tools, as, according to the conceptual domain theories of Cognitive Linguistics, they are able to convey whole structures and networks of information, rather than being reduced to unsubstantial literary flourish or to singular more "literal" paraphrases. Furthermore, we found that these metaphors, despite being irreducible to literal language, are yet able to convey propositional statements, and thus make truth claims. This is highly important for biblical theology, as we now find there to be a plethora of claims about the deity which lie not in the more straightforwardly didactic sections of the Old Testament, but within the metaphorical descriptions within narrative and poetry.

This constitutes one of the major thrusts of this book, and it promises more rewards in filling out the biblical picture of God and His activity. Not that this material was not there before, but this understanding of metaphor may prove helpful for exegetes in excavating these nuggets or making bolder truth claims about the divine picture they previously sensed was present.

In our third chapter, we noted the direction that the transfer of meaning took between the divine and human terms. As humans were made in the image and according to the likeness of God (Gen 1:26), it was they who were actually defined in "theomorphic" terms. Although there are several texts which observe differences in the divine and human usage of terms such as (seeing, repenting, thinking, changing the mind), these were found to reflect differences in choice rather than strictly ability. In fact we found that, as with 1 Sam 16:7, humans are implored, if not commanded, to see as God sees, i.e., according to the heart. The implication is that there is an ability which lies within the purview of the divine, but that can be employed by humans, if divinely enabled. What this says for our interpretation is that terms should be considered not only in view of their primary actors, but in their contexts as natural and supernatural functions of the term. For occasionally, humans can "image" the divine in the sense in which they act. Furthermore, God remains free to act in a "natural" manner if the occasion requires it. Terms that both the deity and humans share include some leeway in the senses in which they can be taken.

Conclusion

Roger White gave us a framework to describe this phenomenon in terms of *primary* and *derivative* senses of a term. The primary sense, in this case the divine, is not simply the chronologically or numerically first term, but the one on which all others depend. The derivative sense requires the primary for its sense. It is not identical, but is known *in relation to* the primary. For example, if pure white is a primary concept, then all derivative "whites" are known in relationship to this primary concept. Similarly, God's attributes are primarily spoken of him and only derivatively of humans.

However, this left us with an undefined primary sense. As Ricoeur observed, however, "possession" is the flip side of reference. If A refers to B, then B "possesses" A-ness. Hence, the definition of the divine attributes lies in their examples. This is where Stern's approach to metaphors is helpful. He allows us to point to the quality or action, without fully defining it using *de re* metaphors. And yet, when that quality is spoken of in a particular context, we are able to speak more specifically. It is here that the divine attribute or action is exemplified, and those traits of the same name which are derivatively applied to humans, defined.

The true test of an interpretive approach is in its exegesis, and so we examined the case of divine sight throughout Genesis. What we found was that, as Stern's approach had emphasized, this metaphor took on varying content within its different contexts. In Genesis 1, God's sight demonstrated the aesthetic pleasure God received from the reflection of His creativity in creation. In chapter 2, however, God observes man's naming of the creatures, and in so doing, His seeing marks a transferal of His authority—though limited in context to ruling and not valuation. This is contrasted with human sight in chapter 3, where the woman adopts the view of the serpent in seeing herself as deficient and the forbidden fruit as more than simply good in its own right, as God had seen. Rather, she adopts a utilitarian stance, evaluating creation according to how it might benefit her. Though the couple's eyes were opened, this marks the beginning of their *inability* to see as God does. This is echoed in the similar view of the sons of God who see the daughters of men as "good" (*tôb*) for their subversive schemes. In sharp and immediate contrast, God's sees the thoughts of mankind as the opposite of its state at creation—continually evil, all the time. And yet he also sees the needle of righteousness in the haystack of corruption—Noah. He also looks upon the rainbow, an intentional act of diligence toward keeping the covenant He has made. Divine sight functions as an impartation of worth to Hagar, and as a legal witness of Lot's righteousness and Sodom's incorrigibility. Finally, it looks at Abram's heart, testing it to see if He will choose the Giver over the gift in the *Aqedah*.

God's sight differs not only in function, but in emphasis on different elements. For instance, in Gen 1, it served to supply the reader with an "internal" view of God's perspective on His creation, both its parts and as a sum greater than these elements. Though often it is assumed God has seen "from heaven," there are occasions where this is not the case. In Gen 11:5, it is emphasized that God came down to see, in order to underscore the failure of Babel's builders to reach heaven. In other cases, sight is contrasted with other faculties, such as in Gen 16:13, where the contrast with hearing alerts the reader to a different idea behind Hagar's ascription of Yahweh as, "A God Who Sees." Furthermore, in the Sodom narrative, God's sight is appropriated from that of the two men/angels sent down as a witness against Sodom.

This also points to the differing perlocutions which divine sight causes in the narrative. In the case of Sodom, the sight acted as a witness, but this was in service of teaching Abraham the "way of Yahweh"—a manner of upholding justice which confronts personally, presents evidence, and offers mercy before enacting punishment. With Hagar, divine sight functioned to imbue worth, but in turn, gave her the confidence to return to an abusive relationship with due respect for the couple through whom "all the families on the earth shall find blessing." Hence, divine sight not only functions differently and contains varying elements, but serves differing narratival purposes. For these reasons, it requires a context-sensitive approach to illuminate these effects.

What have we accomplished? We have attempted to throw yet more light upon an age-old problem. While this treatment follows in a long line of theological work on the topic of religious language and metaphors for God, it also does not promise to be the last. However, what we hope to have shown is that instances of divine action, at least, should not automatically be reduced simply to theological categories such as omnipotence, omniscience, omnipresence, immutability, etc., nor to criteria such as personhood, life, and approachability. Rather, we hope to have incorporated two unique approaches to these "anthropomorphic expressions."

First, as metaphors are both full of descriptive potential, able to make truth-claims, and yet are irreducible to singular statements, these should be evaluated in context. Josef Stern's semantic theory of metaphor allows for the expression to contain information that any competent user of the language would possess. Thus, when the metaphor is placed in a particular context, its meaning becomes identifiable and even articulatable, while at the same time being able to handle the subtleties of a divine-human gap. That is, the concept of metaphorical character allows us to point at an entity without having to fully define it. This creates the necessary space for us to speak of a transcendent God, without falling into univocity or equivocation. Furthermore, it allows us to say more than the *via negativa* and yet remain more contextually sensitive than Alston's functionalist approach. Finally, it does not fall over the unstable foundation of analogy, for it does not ground its truth in an analogy that either does not exist or is not quantifiable.

Secondly, this also allows us to take into consideration the nature of the biblical conception of the primary and derivative senses of its descriptions of God. According to Gen 1:26, the divine is presented as primary and humanity as its derivative, the understanding of the divine can only come through its samples and contexts, rather than by crass definition. What this requires us to do is to draw out more contextually-specific significance and function for these divine actions. Noting how they function in the narrative can shed more light on the narrative as well—especially highlighting contrasts with employment of the same term by human or other agents.

Another area which we presented was the idea of perception acts, analogous to the Speech Acts described by James L. Austin, and developed by John Searle. The idea is that acts of seeing, like those of speech, can perform other actions, what Austin would call *illocutionary acts*. These second order acts have effects called perlocutions. For example, by seeing Hagar, God imparts a sense of worth to her which then enables her to return to what will surely be more affliction at Sarai's hand. This is what is needed however, for her to be rightly related to the couple to whom God's salvific covenant has been made. This concept seems capable of enabling a better understanding of divine actions by elucidating their place and effects within the narrative.

There are several potential areas in which this research could be developed. Obviously, there are other divine actions to which this method of referral and defining could be applied. More importantly however, are other areas of anthropomorphic language itself. This study focused on verbal predicates, but there are nominal and attributive ones as well. How does this approach work in terms of the primary metaphors of Kingship, Shepherding, and Warrior? What about the inanimate metaphors such as rocks and fountain? How does this apply to the attributions of body parts?

Another area of application could be the idea of perception acts. This could conceivably be transferred to other verbs to produce "repentance acts" or "hearing acts," etc.

Furthermore, this approach to divine metaphors can have many implications for theological discussions, such as divine immutability and the nature of His response to creation. If the metaphors describing God's actions are seen as truth-conditional propositions, defined within the context, and as playing pivotal roles in the narrative, this could enter into the debate on whether or not God is immutable, or in what sense He is. Related to this would be the discussion of whether or not God is outside of time and history. In any case, if these terms can be shown to carry more meaning and import for our understanding of God, it seems unwise to keep them muted.

Appendix A

Exegesis of Genesis 16:13–14

A KEY PASSAGE IN TERMS OF DESCRIBING A "GOD WHO SEES," THIS VERSE is widely acknowledged to be one of the most difficult passages in the Old Testament, with nearly every term being contested. Part of this involves the flexibility of the term *r'oi*, a participle which can mean "the One Who sees me" or simple "seeing." Secondly, the term *halom* usually means "hither," which seems out of place in an etiological phrase. The term *'ahare* can have either temporal or spatial meaning and thus the collocation with "I have seen" and the "One Who Sees Me" can have multiple interpretations.

Although this has led interpreters since Wellhausen to amend the text, we find this to be unnecessary. By reading this in line with the themes of status and worth which are already tied to visual terms in the pericope, we find this verse can actually add significance to the primary thrust of the narrative. In the following, we shall take the translation phrase by phrase, discussing its difficulties and how it may best be interpreted in the context of the narrative.

Genesis 16:13

וַתִּקְרָא שֵׁם־יְהוָה הַדֹּבֵר אֵלֶיהָ אַתָּה ה אֵל רֳאִי כִּי אָ רָאִי כִּי אָ מְרָה הֲגַם הֲלֹם רָא יתִי אַחֲרֵי רֹאִי׃

> *And she called the name of the LORD, the One Who spoke to her, "You are a God Who Sees,"[1] for she said, "Indeed[2] here, I have truly seen, just as the One Who sees me."[3]*

---

1. Sam. Pentateuch simply has האר, "A God who has seen," (Hamilton, *Genesis*, 455.), which itself does not remove ambiguity, where LXX (followed by the Vulgate), reflects a participle with 1st common singular ending. "the One Who Sees me."

2. The Hebrew text is framed as a rhetorical question, expecting a positive answer, which in English requires either the addition of a negative- "Have I not seen . . ." or recasting as a positive affirmation.

3. Or, The One Who sees me.

In the Eyes of God

And She Called the Name of the LORD

Hamilton observes that Hagar is not *invoking* God's name, but using the traditional formula for naming. "The text does not state that she 'called upon the name [*qārā' bᵉšēm*] of Yahweh,' an expression we saw in 4:26 and 12:8 (and 19 more times in the OT). Rather it states, *she called the name* [or named] *Yahweh who spoke with her (wattiqrā' šēm-yhwh haddōḥēr ēlêyhā)*."⁴ In fact, Waltke says, "This is the only instance in the Bible where a human being is represented as conferring a name on God."⁵ Westermann says, "That is not to say that Hagar gives to a hitherto nameless divine being a name that sticks to him everywhere and always . . . but Hagar says: 'For me he is whatever else he may be called, the God who sees me,' i.e., the one who came to my aid in my distress."⁶

The One Who Spoke to Her

This phrase serves to connect the *ml'k yhwh* with the One she names *'lohim r'y*, "a God who sees." Thus, at least here, the angel is virtually indistinguishable from the deity.

You are a God (El) of Seeing.

The MT is pointed as a noun, "Sight, Vision." However, many⁷ have re-pointed it to match the participle with the first person pronoun at the end of the verse often rendered, "The One Who sees me." Booij resists this move, "In not identifying *r'y* at the end of *v.* 13a with *r'y* at the end of *v.* 13b, the Masoretic vocalization appears to have contributed to a pure transmission of the text. To the narrator the words *'l r'y* ("God of seeing", "God of sight") left room for both moments: man's searching for God, the Living One (cf. Ps Xlii 3, lxxxiv 3, 8) and God's looking after man."⁸ Waltke adds, "The name is a pun, meaning either 'the God who sees me' (so NIV), which fits the context, and/or 'the God I see,' which fits her explanation. The former speaks of his care for her; the latter, of her experiences of God's manifestation."⁹ Sarna expands this, noting that *El Roi* can mean either

---

4. Hamilton, *The Book of Genesis*, 455.
5. Waltke, *Genesis*, 255.
6. Westermann, *Genesis 12–36*, 247.
7. Cf. von Rad, *Genesis*, 194, Sarna, *Genesis*, 121.
8. Booij, "Hagar's Words In Genesis XVI 13B," 6.
9. Waltke, *Genesis*, 255.

"God of seeing," "God of my seeing," or "God who sees me." "Most likely, the several meanings are intended to be apprehended simultaneously. When God 'sees,' it is, of course, that He shows His concern and extends His protection; when Hagar 'sees,' she experiences God's self-manifestation."[10] However, this attention does not simply afford protection, but value and inner strength. Hagar, the slave that found both "self"-esteem and status in pregnancy but ran from authority and affliction, now finds her worth not in the promise of God, but simply in His sight. This provides the fortitude and resolve to face the situation she left, itself potentially unchanged.

Mark Brett contrasts this view of God's sight with Sarai, who did what, "was good in her eyes," "Whatever Sarai's construction of the good, *El Roi* sees things differently."[11] Hence, the name speaks not merely of physical sight, but of seeing relationships correctly. This involves all the allusions to sight in the chapter; after seeing (*r'h*) she was with child, Sarai lost all respect in Hagar's eyes. Apparently, *El Roi* sees this differently as well, and while blessing her pregnancy, sends Hagar back to honor her mistress.

Indeed, (Have I not ...?)

Koenen sees this question as rhetorical—"Have not I seen here . . ."—expecting a positive answer. He says, "The Interrogative particle must rather like in Gen 27:36, serve the emphasis of the following thoughts and is to be translated in the sense of "Indeed.""[12] Waltke concurs, adding that, "her question, which demands an emphatic affirmative, probably entails both that she has looked at God and he has seen her."[13]

I Have truly Seen

The motif of sight is emphasised by the particle *gm*. Though generally translated, "also, even," Waltke and O'Connor observe, "The second major coordinator *gm*, though it is used as an item adverb, generally has more distinctly logical force than *'p*, though it can be used as an emphatic . . . often with a pronoun following"[14] (cf. Isa 66:3 as it intensifies the verb,

---

10. Sarna, *Genesis*, 121.
11. Brett, *Genesis: Procreation and the Politics of Identity*, 59.
12. Koenen, "Wer Sieht Wen? Zur Textgeschichte von Gen 16:13," 468.
13. Waltke, *Genesis*, 255.
14. Waltke and O'Connor, *Introduction to Biblical Hebrew Syntax*, 663, 39.3.4c.

"They have *plainly* chosen their paths"[15]). According to Muraoka, though it is typically thought to serve an additive function, in some places, such as Gen 16:13 and Num 13:27, 1 Sam 22::7, "the particle can be translated in its asseverative meaning 'certainly, surely.'"[16] Labuschagne finds in the etymology of the Ugaritic equivalent its meaning preserved as, "with voice, aloud."[17] Thus, he postulates that *gm*, in some cases like Gen 16:13, "implies emphasis, force, stress, explicitness."[18]

The particle can intensify a verb such as *r'h*, even if it does not immediately follow the particle. According to Koehler and Baumgartner, "*gm* often occurs at the beginning of the clause and not where it belongs logically"[19] (e.g., Hos 9:12; Zech 9:11; Gen 17:16). גַּם שׁוֹנֵא actually to impose a fine Pr 17$_{26}$, HALOT '*gm*' shows how *gm* can intensify a verb, here in the case of relating it to reality, similar to *r'yty* in Gen 16:13b. Thus, the translation is rendered: "Indeed, I have *seen truly* . . ." One interesting parallel with Gen 16:13 is Exod 3:9:

וְעַתָּ֕ה הִנֵּ֛ה צַעֲקַ֥ת בְּנֵי־יִשְׂרָאֵ֖ל בָּ֣אָה אֵלָ֑י וְגַם־רָאִ֙יתִי֙ אֶת־הַלַּ֔חַץ אֲשֶׁ֥ר מִצְרַ֖יִם לֹחֲצִ֥ים אֹתָֽם׃

> Now, behold, the cry of the sons of Israel has come to Me, and I have *truly* seen the oppression with which the Egyptians are oppressing them.

Here, the particle *gm* also modifies the verb *r'h*, and functions more than simply in an additive function, as a waw is serving that purpose. Rather, it intensifies the verb, assuring Moses that God is acutely aware of the situation, rather than simply having heard of its effects. Thus it should be translated, "Now, behold, the cry of the sons of Israel has come to Me; I have truly [מג] seen the oppression with which the Egyptians are oppressing them." This can also be compared with Gen 18:21, where God has also heard the outcry (*tsaqah*) but is coming down to see (*r'h*) the extent of the Sodomites' sin. The general situation is known, but firsthand, detailed, personal, and even legally verifiable knowledge is shown (A similar

---

15. Waltke and O'Connor, *Introduction to Biblical Hebrew Syntax*, 663, 39.3.4d.

16. Muraoka, *Emphatic Words and Structures in Biblical Hebrew*, 145.

17. However, both he and Muraoka reject Dahood's proposal to actually translate *gm* in the Hebrew, "aloud," due to lack of convincing examples.

18. Muraoka, *Emphatic Words and Structures in Biblical Hebrew*, 144.

19. Koehler and Baumgartner, *Hebrew and Aramaic Lexicon of the Old Testament*, s.v. "מג".

function is possible with Exod 33:12 with *gm* and *mts'*, "I have known you by name and you have *truly found* favor in my sight." Once again, the phrase is intensified by the particle *gm*, building upon the first clause). This is also seen in 1 Sam 24:12 where David's cry to Saul is intensified through *gm* and repetition, "See, my father, see . . ."(*r'h gm r'h*). Other potentially "intensifying" occurrences of *gm* with *r'h* include: Neh 13:23; Ps 95:9; Eccl 2:4; 9:13; Isa 47:3; Jer 7:11. Thus, Gen 16:13 would read, "Indeed, I have *seen truly* after He saw me." God has corrected her vision—not only of authority, but of the source of her worth, and her future.

Brodie observes the particular use of the motif of seeing; "The issue, however, is not only that she has seen God and lived, but—as indicated by the preceding phrase (16:13a, 'God of Seeing') and by the earlier seeing motif (12:1, 7; 13:14-15; 15:1, 5; 16:4-6)—that God is a God of seeing; and she now knows that God sees her and makes her see. The result is a new sense of reality and of herself."[20] In addition to his list, many other verses in Genesis reflect a focus on God's seeing (1:4, 10, 12, 18, 21, 25, 31; 2:19; 6:2, 5, 12; 7:1; 11:5). Unfortunately, Brodie defines this in terms of salvation, "For with seeing comes life; 'see' has the sense of see and rescue."[21] Unlike chapter 21, where Hagar has run out of water and despairs that she and the boy will die (21:14-15), there is no danger mentioned in this scene, no rescue made, save that of a relationship between Hagar and Abram/Sarai. Rather, due to the heavy emphasis on the motif of status in the chapter, "to see" in this context takes on the sense, *to value correctly, to assign proper worth*.

Here

Westermann finds *hlm* untranslatable, which he says cannot mean "here," but only "hither."[22] Therefore, he emends it to *'elohim*, along the lines of Wellhausen's own emendations. Thus it explains the element *lhy* in the name of the spring by the later concept that one who sees God must die (Gen 33:20). White, emphasizes the location of the theophany by reading *hlm* in its usual allative function of "hither" rather than "here."[23] However,

---

20. Brodie, *Genesis as Dialogue*, 239. Brodie cites Richard J. Clifford, "Genesis [1:1—25:18]."

21. Brodie, *Genesis as Dialogue*, 239.

22. Westermann, *Genesis 12-36*, 248.

23. H. C. White, "The Initiation Legend of Ishmael."

as Seebass,[24] and Schoors have shown, though it usually means "hither," *hlm* can mean "here." In defense of this, Schoors cites the dictionaries (BDB, 30 and HAL, 34, Zorell, 35.), Judg 20:7, the lack of distinction between *šm* (there) and *šmmh* (thither), and some examples in Ugaritic and Phoenician.

After

Schoors adopts the LXX[25] "face" over the MT *'ḥry* "after". He sees it as a *tiqqune sopherim*, one of eighteen attested "emendations of the scribes," to keep the text from saying certain things about God. (e.g., Gen 18:22—God standing before Abram could imply subservience) translating it, "She called the name of Yahweh who spoke to her: 'Thou art a God of vision'; for she said: 'Have I here really seen the face of him who sees me?'"[26] Similarly, Janzen simply repoints "אַחֲרֵי" to be the substantive "אֲחֹר," "back," (cf. Hamilton—citing 2 Sam 2:23 "the hinder end of a spear,") and thus sees it as a euphemism for "face," based on the proscription against human viewing derived from Exod 33:20, 23). However, in 33:23 when God tells Moses he will see His back instead of His face, a direct object marker is used, and the pointing is different (אֲחֹרָי). Thus, it is not likely to refer, as Janzen suggests, to God's back, as a euphemism for His face.

In a different approach, White, combines the verb *r'yty* ("I have seen"), with *'ḥry* ("after") resulting in "looked after." For him, this refers to the after-effects of God's presence (cf. J. Lindblom, "Have I really here seen the back of him who has seen me?"[27]). Booij makes a similar move, but focuses on the action of the verb, "look after or search." Thus he renders, "Would I have gone here indeed looking for him that looks after me?" However, this is untenable in light of verse 8, which clearly shows Hagar is not searching, but fleeing.

Arnold and Choi however, note another use of *'ḥry:* metaphorical. In this function, it is translated as,

> Denoting a behavior patterned after or according to that of another, or in support of another: . . . and both you and the king

---

24. Seebass, "Zum Text Von Gen. XVI 13B."

25. LXX is followed by Peshitta and Vulgate. Sam. Pent. Has a simple finite form, "He has seen."

26. Schoors, "A Tiqqun Sopherim in Genesis XVI 13B?," 495.

27. Lindbom, "Theophanies in Holy Places in Hebrew Religion," 103, note 21, in H. C. White, "The Initiation Legend of Ishmael," 285–86.

who reigns over you will *follow* [literally: *be after*] YHWH your God" (1 Sam 12:14).²⁸

This is also attested in 2 Kgs 13:2, (lit."*went after*"= *followed*), and Job 31:7. Joüon notes, "אַחֲרֵי,» is probably a pseudo-plural (by analogy with the antt onym לִפְנֵי *before*).²⁹ Thus, Hagar is claiming to be able to see *according to the manner of,* the One Who sees her. She now values herself, not on the societal bases of marriage or fertility, but because she knows that the God of Abram and Sarai, also has His eye on her, and His blessing as well.

The One Who Sees Me

Sarna notes that *El Roi* can mean either "God of seeing," "God of my seeing," or "God who sees me." "Most likely, the several meanings are intended to be apprehended simultaneously. When God 'sees,' it is, of course, that He shows His concern and extends His protection; when Hagar 'sees,' she experiences God's self-manifestation."³⁰ In context though, it has further implications. God's attention does not simply afford protection, but value and inner strength. The slave who found 'self-esteem' and status in pregnancy, but flouted authority and fled affliction, now finds her worth in God's promise, but His view of her. This alone provides the fortitude and resolve to face the situation she left, which was potentially unchanged.³¹

Genesis 16:14

The translation of verse 13 is then reflected in that of 14, the naming of the well. This well commemorates not merely Hagar's encounter, but the nature of the God she met, and its affect upon her.

עַל־כֵּן קָרָא לַבְּאֵר בְּאֵר לַחַי רֹאִי הִנֵּה בֵין־קָדֵשׁ וּבֵין בָּרֶד׃

> Therefore the well is called "Well of the Living One Who sees me." As anyone can see,³² it is between Qadesh and Bered.

---

28. Arnold, *A Guide to Biblical Hebrew Syntax*, 97. Cf. also Waltke and O'Connor, *Introduction to Biblical Hebrew Syntax*, 192–93, 11.2.1a.

29. Joüon, *A Grammar of Biblical Hebrew*, 346, 103.B.n.

30. Sarna, *Genesis*, 121.

31. 16:15 assumes Hagar's return, as Abram names his son the name given to Hagar in the wilderness.

32. Being in the voice of the narrator, (cf. 2, 6, 11) and "Behold," being a bit archaic, a more current English idiom, (centered around drawing attention to something), was used.

In the Eyes of God

The Living One Who Sees Me

This word has been translated as an obscure reference (Wellhausen, "jawbone"), but more often treated as an allusion to Exod 33:20, emphasizing *Hagar's* life, *after* seeing God. (Cf. Judg 13:22. So Manoah said to his wife, "We will surely die, for we have seen God"). Sarna says, "lahi to the Arabic *chayy* means 'a clan,' and Roi could be a proper name."[33] Though Zimmerli thinks the real etymology of the place is not "contained here," and suggests dependency on an older name that was, "no longer understood," (cf. Wellhausen's "jawbone,") the significance is more certain. Several suggested meanings include, "Spring of the living one who sees me" (many exegetes), "Spring of the living one whom I saw" (R. Killian), "the well to the living sight" (O. Procksch), "well of the living sight" (E. A. Speiser, H. C. White), "the one who sees me lives " (J. Wellhausen).[34]

However, in light of the previous discussion, the name of the well in Gen 16:14 is actually about God. J. Gerald Janzen says, "from being related to the God of her owners through her relations to her owners, Hagar is now related to Yahweh directly and in her own right."[35] Thus the name, "Well of the Living One Who sees me" commemorates Hagar's discovery that the god of her owners, the one she has heard so much about, really lives. She knows this now because she has seen Him for herself. This god is One who truly sees her situation, her future, and her worth.

---

33. Sarna, *Genesis*, 122.
34. Westermann, *Genesis 12–36*, 248.
35. J. G. Janzen, "Hagar in Paul's Eyes and in the Eyes of Yahweh," 13.

Appendix B

The Righteousness of Lot

It is often assumed that, because of Lot's choice to live in Sodom, and his offering of his daughters to the mob, that Lot is not righteous. However, T. D. Alexander defends a different reason for Yahweh's descent,

> In 19:29 it is suggested that Abraham's prolonged discussion with God in 18:22–33 was due to his concern for Lot. This is also implied by the fact that Sodom, and not the cities of the valley, is the focus of attention throughout the dialogue in chapter 18. However, if Abraham is primarily concerned for Lot, he feels obliged to posit his case for Lot's deliverance not on the grounds of kinship but rather on the grounds of righteousness—a fact highlighted by the recurrence of the term *šaddiq* ("righteous") in verses 22–28. Yet such an approach would have been extremely futile unless Lot could be truly regarded as righteous. Here also the Genesis narrative would seem to support the position adopted in 2 Pet 2:8–9 and elsewhere.[1]

Thus, God was not really looking for the wicked, for He already knew they were there. He is seeking out the righteous, and the angels head straight for Lot's city.

But why Lot? Brevard Childs contends that Lot was remembered on account of Abraham (19:29). Though MacDonald acknowledges, "this would have the virtue of explaining why Abraham, rather than Lot, is remembered,"[2] he feels the "remembering" deals more with the dialogue in 18:22–32. But, these are not necessarily mutually exclusive. Though He sends them to destroy the cities (19:13), Yahweh, on account of Abraham's plea *for the righteous*, causes his emissaries not only to provide witness against Sodom, but to attest to Lot's righteousness. That Abraham assumes God is threatening the imminent destruction of the cities is seen in his line of questioning, but it is Lot's lot which hangs in the balance. Hence, Westermann says, There is not a sentence that so much as hints that Abraham was imploring God's mercy to avert a disaster from the peo-

---

1. Alexander, "Lot's Hospitality," 291.
2. MacDonald, "Listening to Abraham," 40–41.

ple (against F. Delitzsch, Komm. ad loc., J Ruwet and J. Sharbert, lit. to 18:16b33; J. Schreiner, BZ [1962] 1–31). Such is the concern of Jon. 3:4 where the wording is quite different. One could turn the whole dialog into the form of a hypothetical condition: "Would you destroy Sodom if . . . ?"[3] Despite the fact Abraham does not mention Lot by name, Jack Lundbom says,

> It is really kinsman Lot and his family who are uppermost in Abraham's mind, for they are settled in Sodom and a destruction of the city will mean their destruction. Abraham rescued them once before (Genesis 14). Any anxiety over Lot is entirely unexpressed, however, but it is there and must not be overlooked or judged peripheral in the dialogue. The fate of Lot and his household stands behind the very first question Abraham asks of Yahweh, "Will you indeed sweep away the righteous with the wicked?" (18.23).[4]

But many have claimed that Lot was not righteous. Scott Morschauser summarizes,

> Commentators often state that Lot comes out poorly in comparison to Abraham. For example, Lot is in the "category of a buffoon" (Coats, *Genesis*, pp. 143–44). It is further stated that the reason for Lot's deliverance is solely due to his relation to Abraham (Gen 19.29; cf. James L. Kugel, *The Bible as it Was* [Cambridge: Belknap Press; Harvard: University Press, 1997], pp. 181–83). There is an element of truth to this observation: the bond between Abraham and Lot is surely a factor in the divine protection of the younger man. Nevertheless, I would argue that Lot is not an irrelevant cipher in the whole drama of Sodom's destruction. The author of Genesis 19 (vv. 16, 19, 21) utilizes covenant-like language (חמל, "compassion/mercy"; מצא עבד חן בעיני, "a servant has found favor in one's eyes" נשא פן לדבר, "to give approval to a request") expressing divine regard for Lot for his risking himself on behalf of the messengers. Indeed, Lot's actions are wholly characteristic of the *arad kitti*. The patriarch's stance is extraordinary within an otherwise lawless/law-rejecting society. For this reason, Lot is rewarded with the grant of life (cf. Moran, *Biblical and Related Studies*, pp. 180–81). In addition to the examples cited by Moran, the same pattern is to be discerned in the rescue of Rahab (Josh 6.25),

---

3. Westermann, *Genesis 12–36*, 292–93.
4. Lundbom, "Parataxis," 141.

the collaborators at Bethel (Judg 1.24–25), and the elevation of Ittai the Gittite for his loyalty to David during Absalom's revolt (2 Sam 15.19–21)—strikingly enough, all in situations in which a city or society is *in extremis*.[5]

In order to determine whether Lot was indeed righteous, and thus on Abraham's mind and in God's sight, we need a working definition. Von Rad defines it, "Righteousness in Old Testament thought does not consist in the perfection of action, in the sense of approximation to an ideal, absolute norm. Rather, 'righteous action' is always defined by a communal relationship which has been predetermined according to some form (cf. at ch. 15.7)."[6] It is this that Lot possesses via his relationship with Abraham and his hospitality to those whom Yahweh sent. However many commentators still claim Lot is unrighteous. Let us examine their complaints.

Hospitality

Some have claimed evidence for Lot's unrighteousness in his paltry meal, his offer of his daughters to the Sodomite mob, and his later drunkenness resulting in incest. However, as Alexander notes, "By caring for the needs of others he resembles Abraham, and since Abraham is commended for his generosity Lot is therefore also to be viewed in a favorable light. Lot's hospitality is a mark of his righteousness."[7] It should also be noted that the difference in the meals offered the visitors is overrated. While Abraham orchestrates the preparation of bread and a fatted calf, Lot prepares unleavened bread and a banquet with wine (מִשְׁתֶּה cf. Gen 21:8; 26:30; 29:22; 40:20). Though the bread seems paltry, it is part of a feast, which is typically quite grand. The difference in meal description may also simply have been a difference between that of a rancher and a city-dweller. Again, the time of day (midday vs. evening) may have dictated the type of meal that Abraham and Lot served.

As to the quality of Lot's hospitality, Brian Doyle identifies a unique element of his guests; "The primary characters of Genesis 19 are Lot, his

---

5. Morschauser, "'Hospitality', Hostiles and Hostages," 479–80, note 63.

6. Von Rad, *Genesis*, 213 NIDOTTE adds, צָדַק terminology indicates right behavior or status in relation to some standard of behavior accepted in the community. It also entails the adjudication of such behavior or status as well as the more abstract sense of some claim to it. Nowhere, however, is this standard made explicit, nor is covenant invoked as a ground or basis for צֶדֶק. If a special notion like covenant is assumed, it remains firmly in the background." VanGemeren, *NIDOTTE*, "צדק" OT e.

7. Alexander, "Lot's Hospitality," 290.

visitors (ambiguous, unrecognized then recognized divine presence) and the people of Sodom gathered en masse outside the door of his house."[8] It would seem that if Lot didn't recognize the identity of the visitors immediately, then his sense of hospitality is augmented all the more. He sits at the gate, not only attempting to bring about justice, but intervening for any visitors who might come by—*regardless* of status. This borders on the heroic.[9] Whereas Abraham pleaded for His visitors to stay for a meal, Lot insists (וַיִּפְצַר־בָּם מְאֹד, "pressed them hard") on their staying in his house and *not* the city square, perhaps knowing the foul treatment they would likely encounter there. However, it may be significant that these were not just any "sojourners." These were emissaries sent by Yahweh. To receive them (even unwittingly) was to receive Yahweh Himself (Matt 10:40; John 13:20; Gal 4:14). Hence, Lot's hospitality is comparable to Abraham's and rules out any unrighteousness in this realm of life.

Offering His Daughters

The heaviest accusation against Lot, however, comes from his offer to the Sodomite mob of his virgin daughters, "to do to them as is good in your eyes." Though his offer is rejected, it horrifies the modern, if not ancient audience. What sense of righteousness could possibly drive hospitality to such a barbaric level? Gerald Janzen sees Lot's daughter—offer as a shock tactic and not sincere. "Lot in Gen. 19:8 seeks to shock the men of the city to their senses, by apparently offering for gang rape two young women whom they as 'my brothers' would recognize and treat as the daughters of a neighbor. In that case, if vv. 4–5 establish the quantitative measure of the city's wickedness, v. 8 suggests its qualitative measure."[10] However, he concludes, "Lot may hope to awaken his neighbors to the common humanity they share with those whom they view only as strangers, therefore enemies, and therefore fit objects of their power."[11] Though the angels certainly possess no "common humanity," they were perceived as men (18:2, 16, 22; 19:5, 8, 10, 12, 16).

8. Doyle, "Knock, Knock, Knockin'," 441.

9. Hamilton says, "He essentially did obeisance, *bowing down with his face to the ground!* Such action by Lot toward the newcomers who approach him would be strange. It is the new comer who is expected to genuflect, as does Abraham the outsider when he approaches the sons of Heth (Gen. 23:7, 12). Here Lot actually outdoes his uncle in his show of welcome to the newcomers." Hamilton, *The Book of Genesis*, 32.

10. Gerald Janzen, *Abraham and All the Families of the Earth*, 64.

11. Ibid.

Another intriguing possibility is that the daughters are offered as collateral, a surety that the visitors Lot is housing are not spies. Scott Morschauser suggests that Lot's position at the city gate was not that of a judge, but watchman. In taking the guests under his roof, he was in a sense, placing them under house-arrest, in order to deny them unrestricted access to the city. The officials of the city come to Lot and demand the guests in order to interrogate them, to discern if they were spies. Citing the recent wars in Gen 14 as background for this episode, Morschauser explains the reasoning behind the procedure,

> The women—technically, legal detainees/captives—are to be held safely overnight, and are to be released, unharmed, when the two visitors vacate the premises in accordance with Lot's assurance.[12]

Thus, the mob's reaction is seen as one of paranoia and suspicion of Lot as a traitor, and their issue is not unbridled sexual desire, but the interrogation of potential spies. Lot's offer is thus not a *carte blanche* for the abuse of his daughters, but a diplomatic means of ensuring the safety of the visitors and the Sodomites themselves from treachery. Presumably, the visitors would have left in the morning and the daughters been returned unharmed. Morschauser suggests that it is just such an abuse of this cultural practice that occurs in Judg 19 with the Levite and his concubine visiting Gibeah. However, though she was to be held unharmed as collateral, she was raped and murdered.

Drunkenness

As to Lot's drunkenness, Alexander responds, "It is difficult not to see some connection between the present account of Lot's drunkenness and that of Noah in 9:10–27. If Noah can be designated "righteous" (6:9), why should Lot be viewed differently? Concerning the events in Sodom we should not judge too harshly a man placed in an extremely dangerous and apparently impossible situation. Faced with the demands of the crowd Lot had few options. How easy it would have been for him to let the mob have its way. Yet rather than yield to their wishes he is prepared to protect his guests at the cost of dishonoring his own daughters. Lot's predicament calls for a sympathetic understanding rather than a harsh condemnation."[13]

---

12. Morschauser, "'Hospitality', Hostiles and Hostages," 477.
13. Alexander, "Lot's Hospitality," 291.

Hence, to answer von Rad's contention that this must be a later addition to the text, it was not about the basis of Yahweh's decision but about the righteous Lot. We don't know about the other cities, simply because Lot wasn't there. Apparently they shared the same attitudes and practices for which Sodom itself was condemned, and therefore participated in her judgment. Yahweh is looking for the righteous, not the unrighteous, and He knows where to find them.

Appendix C

Testing

To understand what it is Yahweh "sees" in Genesis 22, we must understand that for which He is looking. The opening verse describes the following events as a test of Abraham by Yahweh (v. 1), and hence, the pericope concerns a somewhat artificial situation. The crisis is manufactured. Instead of Abraham trusting his son to Yahweh's protection from other dangers, it is Yahweh Himself ordering his death. All of this comes under the framework of a divine "test." Though Abraham proclaims (presumably in faith) that God will 'see for Himself' a sheep, there is no hint or promise on Yahweh's part that this will be the case. Yahweh is placing Abraham in a quandary—will he obey an horrific command of God's, or will he refuse and try to save his son? What exactly is Yahweh testing in Abraham and why? In order to better understand this context of "testing," let us now look at some intertextual parallels to divine testing [נסה][14] in the Old Testament to discern any common threads. After this, we shall look at the ethics of testing to attempt to establish a framework in which to grasp how such a gruesome command of Yahweh can be understood, and to grasp in what sense He sees in this passage.

Testing for Provision

The first parallel to Gen 22 is found in Exod 15:25 as the Hebrews wander through the Sinai desert encountering only bitter water.

> Then he [Moses] cried out to the LORD, and the LORD showed him a tree; and he threw *it* into the waters, and the waters became sweet. There He made for them a statute and regulation, and there He *tested* [נסה] them.

At Marah, God tests the Israelites as a collective whole. Upon their grumbling, He provides water for them, but in verse 26, challenges them with a conditional promise. If they obey His commandments, He promises not

---

14. Though there are more common verbs for "testing," namely, בחן "try, test" and צרף "refine," we seek a more exact parallel with Gen 22, in which only נסה appears.

to bring any of the plagues of the Egyptians upon them, as He is their Healer. This test is one of Yahweh's provision, though contingent (at least in the future) upon the obedience of His people. Similarly, we find another episode where provision is at issue in Exod 16:4:

> Then the LORD said to Moses, "Behold, I will rain bread from heaven for you; and the people shall go out and gather a day's portion every day, that I may *test* them, whether or not they will walk in My instruction."

Here also we find God testing the Israelites in the desert, this time to see if they will obey His instruction concerning the manna. They do not, and find that what they had stored had festered by morning (16:20). In these instances, provision does seem to be a significant part of the test. Will the people trust that God will provide them food and water as they follow Him through the desert? However, we may note that in each case, the provision is given first, and obedience required afterward (cf. also Deut 8:16).

In Deut 8:2, we again find testing by God to include the aspect of provision in the form of manna, but with a twist.

> You shall remember all the way which the LORD your God has led you in the wilderness these forty years, that He might humble you, *testing* you, to know what was in your heart, whether you would keep His commandments or not. [3] He humbled you and let you be hungry, and fed you with manna which you did not know, nor did your fathers know, that He might make you understand that man does not live by bread alone, but man lives by everything that proceeds out of the mouth of the LORD (cf. also 8:16).

In this instance as well, the manna serves to impart the knowledge that God's words are more important for life than the provision itself. Furthermore, we note that here, like Gen 22, the test also appears to be one of God discerning the heart motives of those being tested, and these seem to be summed up in 'whether you would keep His commandments or not.'

As in Deut 8:2, the test in 8:16 centers around provision and humbling, but this time, it mentions—"to do good for you in the end." So too, Abraham received a much stronger confirmation and expansion of the blessing upon passing the test of Yahweh in Genesis (cf. 15–18).

These occurrences of divine testing all involve provision, but this provision is often given initially with a view to the people's response. It is not a "reward" for obedience, but an incentive for faith. The test emphasizes obedience and loyalty to Yahweh, because He has *already* provided for them.

Testing Loyalties

However, in other passages, "testing" (נסה) seems to be used in an entirely different sense. For example, Exod 20:20 says,

> Moses said to the people, "Do not be afraid; for God has come in order to *test* you, and in order that the fear of Him may remain with you, so that you may not sin."

Perhaps the closest parallel to our passage (Gen 22:8, 14), Moberly notes the unique connection,

> The two primary words for interpreting the story are "test" in 22:1, the narrator's explicit guide to the nature of the story, and "fear" in 22:12, the eliciting of Abraham's fear (in the sense of obedience, *cf.* Dt. 5:29, Jb. 1:1, 28:28) being the purpose of the test. A conceptual linkage between divine testing and the obedience of Israel as a nation is well attested elsewhere (Exod 15:25, 16:4, Dt. 8:2, 13:3 [Heb. 4], Judg. 2:22, 3:4), and the specific juxtaposition of "test" and "fear" comes in only one other passage, Exodus 20:20, in which Moses explains to Israel the purpose of God giving to Israel the Ten Commandments, the heart of Torah. The verbal and conceptual parallel between Genesis 22:1, 12 and Exodus 20:20 is hermeneutically suggestive.[15]

Upon seeing and hearing the theophany at Sinai, the people cower back in fear. They promise obedience to Moses as their mediator, but do not deal with God directly. Notably, God comes to test them, "*so that the fear of Him may remain with you*, and so you may not sin" (italics mine). As with Abraham in Gen 22, the issue is fear, only here the people demonstrate an emotional fear (נוּעַ). However, as von Rad notes, "Where the phrases 'fear of God' and 'fearing God' occur in the Old Testament, they refer not to a particular form of strong emotions but rather to their consequence, i.e., to obedience (Gen 20.11; 42.18; II Kings 4.1; Isa. 11.2; Prov. 1.7; Job 1.1, 8). It would be more correct to interpret the phrase 'fear of God' simply as a term for obedience to the divine commands."[16] Hence, here again we find

---

15. Moberly, "Christ as the Key to Scripture," 155.
16. Von Rad, *Genesis*, 241–42. Claus Westermann says, "In Genesis 22:12 it[the fear of God] is Abraham's perfect obedience, demonstrated in the severest of tests. Gen. 22:12 and Ex. 20:18b–21 seem to be close to each other; in both cases God tests

a divine test whose purpose is to instill in its subject a fear leading them to obey Yahweh. However, in this case, there is no "provision." God has given the torah, but no food, water, land, fertility, blessing, etc.

A related sense of testing [נסה] arises in Jdg 2:22 (cf. also 3:1, 4), where Canaanites and Philistines are left in the land God had promised to the Israelites. As punishment for Israel's disobedience, these peoples were allowed to remain

> . . . in order to *test* Israel by them, whether they will keep the way of the LORD to walk in it as their fathers did, or not.

Again, it is the obedience that is being tested, and no provision is given. Similarly, in Deut 13:3, false prophets are left to test the love of Israel for her God.

> You shall not listen to the words of that prophet or that dreamer of dreams; for the LORD your God is *testing* you to find out if you love the LORD your God with all your heart and with all your soul.

Yahweh is testing the love of the people, if they love Him more than the signs and power of false prophets. This also connects with Abraham, as Isaac too was a fulfillment of prophecy—Yahweh's own, (12:3, 15:5, 17:2ff., [esp 16] 18:10, 14). The question here is whether the people being tested are more loyal to the gift or the Giver.

Finally, we find the only other test of an individual, that of Hezekiah in 2 Chr 32:31 (cf. 2 Kgs 20:12, Isa 39:1).

> Even *in the matter of* the envoys of the rulers of Babylon, who sent to him to inquire of the wonder that had happened in the land, God left him *alone only* to *test* him, that He might know all that was in his heart.

In this case, God actually leaves the subject of His testing, in order "to *know* all that was in his heart." This echoes Gen 22:12 (cf. also Deut 8:2 and 13:3), where, upon completing the test, Yahweh announces, "Now, I know that you fear God" (cf. also Exod 20:20). The purpose is also similar—to know the heart (fear) of the test subject. Again, loyalty seems the crux of the matter.

(נסה), and it is a question of proving the fear of God." Westermann, *Genesis 12–36*, 362. See also, H. P. Stähli, *Theologisches Handwörterbuch zum Alten Testament* 1, 765–78.

Testing

This example highlights the danger of using "test" to imply that it is "*only*[17] a test." That is, this (mis)use takes the fact that the narrative was a test meant it was a sort of game, and not a real situation. However, Walter Breuggemann notes,

> It is not a game with God. God genuinely does not know.[18] And that is settled in verse 12, "Now I know." There is real development in the plot.... The narrative will not be understood as a flat event of "testing." It can only be understood if it is seen to be a genuine movement in the history between Yahweh and Abraham. The movement is from "take" (v. 2) to "you have not withheld" (v. 12), and from "test" (v. 2) to "now I know" (v. 12). The move in both forms is accomplished by the affirmative in verse 8, an enigmatic statement of unqualified trust. It is only verse 8 that permits the story to move from its problem to its solution.[19]

In order to prove anything, the test must be real. As seen in Numbers, Deuteronomy, and Judges, these tests can be failed with dire consequences.

---

17. Cf. the New American Standard version of 2 Chr 32:31 above, as the italics ("*alone only*") are the translator's explanatory additions.

18. This could mean Yahweh does not have experiential knowledge of something He already knows to be in Abraham's heart, or that He is genuinely not cognizant of the fact of Abraham's fear. Or, it could be that the test itself brought Abraham's fear into being. Moberly notes, "Issues about God within the Old testament are never posed in separation from the relational dynamic through which Israel knows God. The most explicit raising of the issue of divine omniscience, Ps. 139, raises the issue entirely within the context of the psalmist's relationship with God. It would be a mistake to construe God's 'knowing' in relation to his 'testing' any differently. The concern of the texts is for a deepening of the encounter between God and people. Although the primary emphasis falls upon the appropriate human response, this response is relational at the same time as being moral, and (107) this relationship is not conceived as one-sided but rather God is engaged within the encounter in such a way that the outcome is a genuine divine concern. When Abraham is depicted as 'one who fears God', the divine pronouncement 'now I know', rather than 'now people will know', indicates that the deepened relationship is in some way an intrinsic concern of God even as it also constitutes the nature of mature humanity." Moberly, *The Bible, Theology and Faith*, 106–7. However, whether or not God is omniscient, or in what sense He is, is an issue beyond the scope of this work.

19. Brueggemann, *Genesis*, 187.

Summary

What we see from this brief overview is that, with some notable exceptions (Exod 15; 16; Deut 8), divine testing does not necessarily entail provision or providence. For example, Hezekiah's testing involves no withholding of blessing or material lack on his part. The same goes for the discerning of a false prophet in Deut 13, and the giving of the law in Exod 20. In these cases at least, the test is to "know the heart" of the group or individual under scrutiny. This often includes a loyalty beyond a dependence for provision. In fact, in those instances where the provision is given, it is given *before* the test, not as a reward. More specifically, nearly every occurrence of a divine test [נסה] concerns whether or not the people will follow the "ways" or keep the "commandments" of Yahweh. Hence, there does not always seem to be a *quid pro quo* understanding in divine tests. That is, sometimes, the test simply brings out the nature of the relationship between God and those being tested for its own sake, and not necessarily with a view to their material gain (though cf. Deut 8:16).

Similarly, in Genesis 22, we find no promise of blessing at the outset, nor any lack in Abraham, either for food or protection. Indeed, Abraham does gain an increase to his blessing, but this cannot be construed as a lack at the beginning of this episode, as he is in quite good shape financially (cf. chapter 13). In fact, he has been given his heir and the fulfillment of the divine promises, and, as with these other cases of testing [נסה], a test ensues. Furthermore, this very real test concerns the fear of Yahweh (v. 12), which is tantamount to his obedience.

The Ethics of Testing

In addition to the issue of what is being "tested" (trust in providence, loyalty/fear, etc.) is the nature of the test itself. Many commentators have been seriously disturbed by the implication of the text that God could make such a request. For instance, following writers such as *Genesis Rabbah*, Rashi, Ibn Ezra, Gersonides, Bahya, Aaron ben Elijah, Abravanel, Joseph Herman Hertz, and W. Gunther Plaut, Laurence Kant claims that,

> Abraham misinterpreted God's instructions. God simply told Abraham to **bring Isaac up** the mountain. God may have mentioned a sacrifice, but God does not name the victim. God never told Abraham to kill Isaac, but simply asked him to make an

offering, presumably an animal. **Abraham** (not God) decided to identify Isaac as that animal.[20] (Bold original)

He asserts that God had asked him to take Isaac along to the sacrifice, but not as victim. In this way he attempts to relieve God of an unethical command.

However, though this would seem to get God off the proverbial hook, André Lacocque counters,

> It nullifies not only the *Wirkungsgeschichte* of Genesis 22, but the tense drama conveyed by the text.... But one simple "detail" in the story suffices for silencing such copping-outs: the presence of Isaac, Abraham's son, his only son, his beloved son. Is Isaac just accompanying his father for an outing to the country side? The term "son" occurs nine times in the narrative (Kant, Part II, p. 175). Besides, Gen 22:18 is unmistakably condoning Abraham's interpretation of the divine order.[21]

For this reason, as well as the narrative dissonance with the promised heir, this attempt to get God out of the ethical bind is unsatisfactory.

Conversely, Søren Kierkegaard explains this as the, "teleological suspension of the ethical."[22] By this, he means that faith, as a re-

20. Kant, "Restorative Thoughts: Part 2," 174.
21. Lacocque, "About the 'Aqedah," 198–99.
22. Kierkegaard explains, "The ethical as such is the universal, and as the universal it applies to everyone, which may be expressed from another point of view by saying that it applies every instant. It reposes immanently in itself, it has nothing without itself which is its *telos*, but is itself *telos* for everything outside it, and when this has been incorporated by the ethical it can go no further." Kierkegaard, *Fear and Trembling*, 64. In applying this notion to our current text, Kierkegaard says, "The story of Abraham contains therefore a teleological suspension of the ethical. As the individual he became higher than the universal. This is the paradox which does not permit of mediation. It is just as inexplicable how he got into it as it is inexplicable how he remained in it. If such is not the position of Abraham, then he is not even a tragic hero but a murderer ... A man can become a tragic hero by his own powers—but not a knight of faith." Kierkegaard, *Fear and Trembling*, 77. The reason Abraham's actions were not explicable, is that they do not conform to the pattern of the ethical. A tragic hero is one whom, because of circumstance, must choose between two evils. This choice is made based on a heirarchy of ethical norms which everyone understands and to which they all are applied. This is the universal. However, Abraham is not acting on this basis, but on that of faith. He is responding to God and not a universal ethic. This fact confounds the ethic, as it would judge Abraham to be a murderer. However, he is acting in a very precarious manner, one which is not staid and buttressed by a universal ethic. He is actually entering into the absurd (another of Kierkegaard's terms) and by so doing he transcends the universal, becoming the father of faith.

lationally-oriented system, by nature supersedes that of the ethical. According to Kierkegaard, Abraham was not following God's commands out of adherence to an ethical system to which all adhere, but *faithfully*, as an appropriate response to a personal God.

However, Jon Levenson claims that it is Kierkegaard's "Pauline-Lutheran" heritage that guides his interpretation.

> It is not just that Abraham acts according to an inward faith that offers exemption from legal norms; the basis of that faith may even be an expectation of bodily resurrection: if he is slain, Isaac will be recalled to life. The influence of the New Testament could not be more obvious:
>
> By faith Abraham, when put to the test, offered up Isaac, and he who had received the promises was ready to slay his only son, of whom it was said, "it is through Isaac that offspring shall be continued for you" [Gen 21:12]. He reasoned that God was able to raise even from the dead, and he received Isaac back as a symbol (Heb 11:17–19).[23]

Levenson attributes this influential interpretation to a Christian bias in reading the text of which he claims are too cryptic to be an accurate interpretation.

> These alternative construals of Abraham's words and actions would not have come to be, I submit, if Kierkegaard's Christian view of Abraham as a paragon of faith were self-evident, or even reasonably clear. All to the contrary, it is precisely the narrator's technique in telling the tale of the aqedah that keeps us in the dark on the issue of Abraham's subjectivity, the very point about which Kierkegaard claims so much information.[24]

Levenson cites Erich Auerbach's famous passage on the Aqedah, which vividly articulates the very nebulous wording which the biblical writer uses.

> The externalization of only so much of the phenomena as is necessary for the purpose of the narrative, all else left in obscurity; the decisive points of the narrative alone are emphasized, what lies between is nonexistent; time and place are undefined and call for interpretation; thoughts and feelings remain unexpressed, are only suggested by the silence and the fragmentary speeches;

---

23. Levenson, *Death and Resurrection of the Beloved Son*, 131.
24. Ibid., 131–32.

the whole, permeated with the most unrelieved suspense and directed toward a single goal (and to that extent far more of a unity), remains mysterious and "fraught with background."[25]

In sum, Levenson sees Kierkegaard as reading too much into an intentionally vague text. To claim that Abraham was being prophetic by his statement in verse 5 that the boy and he would return to the servants is unjustifiable. Rather, Levenson claims, "Abraham's statement in verse 5 was to keep the servants from interfering, or Isaac as well, or with Bachya ben Asher, that "Abraham intended to bring [Isaac's] bones back with him, and therefore he said 'we will return to you' in the plural.'"[26]

Gottverlassenheit

Gerhard von Rad contends that as Genesis 22 was merely a test, God never intended Isaac any harm. He points not to the test itself, but to the promise which forms its context.

> Above all, one must consider Isaac, who is much more than simple a "foil" for Abraham, i.e., a more or less accidental object on which his obedience is to be proved. Isaac is the child of the promise. In him every saving thing that God has promised to do is invested and guaranteed. The point here is not a natural gift, not even the highest, but rather the disappearance from Abraham's life of the whole promise. Therefore, unfortunately, one can only answer all plaintive scruples about this narrative by saying that it concerns something much more frightful than child sacrifice. It has to do with a road out into Godforsakenness, a road on which Abraham does not know that God is only testing him.[27]

Von Rad insightfully labels Abraham's trek up Moriah the "road to Godforsakenness" (*Gottverlassenheit*), because the gravity of God's command lies not simply in Abraham's love for Isaac, but Isaac as embodying Abraham's past and future. More than just child sacrifice, this is a sacrifice of the promises upon which he has built his entire life and relationship with God. It is God's own plan to save the world, His *Heilsgeschichte*, which rides on Isaac.

---

25. Auerbach, *Mimesis*, 11–12.
26. Levenson, *Death and Resurrection of the Beloved Son*, 131.
27. Von Rad, *Genesis*, 244.

However, Moberly feels that though von Rad says he will avoid a psychological interpretation of Abraham's experience, his road to God-forsakenness is just this. It plays upon a presumed mental turmoil within Abraham, which goes unmentioned in the text. Hence, Moberly says, "Von Rad's central concept relates more readily to a subjective state of feeling than to an objective act of obedience, and so again is subtly moving away from concerns of the Genesis text."[28] In contrast, Moberly claims that the text focuses on outward acts of obedience. He observes the paradigmatic nature of the text,

> It is a characteristic note that obedience is a real possibility. "This commandment which I command you this day is not too hard for you, neither is it far off. . . . But the word is very near you; it is in your mouth and in your heart, so that you can do it" (Dt. 30:11, 14). This possibility of obedience is what Abraham supremely exemplifies; obedience can be a reality even when it takes its most demanding form.[29]

However, in attempting to read only what is explicit in the text, Moberly's approach seems a bit cold to the emotive nature of the subject of the text. As Auerbach noted, this text is especially lacking in detail. As Meir Sternberg is so ubiquitously quoted for, a text such as this one with so many details left out, requires the reader to fill the "gaps." However, Sternberg cautions that this "gap-filling" must be done with a view to the text's own rules and content.[30]

In our current text, though the psychological emphasis is not explicit, it is certainly implicit from clues in the text itself. Firstly, the very nature of such a test requires there to be a draw away from obedience which is to be overcome. This presents us with a gap asking to be filled—what is the nature of this "pull" for Abraham? Furthermore, it is this pull which gives obedience its significance within the narrative, for it answers why Yahweh says, "*Now* I know that you fear God." Abraham had been obedient to Yahweh before. He had commanded him to leave his country and family,

---

28. Moberly, "Christ as the Key to Scripture," 170.

29. Ibid., 172.

30. Sternberg says, "Illegitimate gap-filling is one launched and sustained by the reader's subjective concerns (or dictated by more general preconceptions) rather than by the text's own norms and directives. A case in point is the readings to which the rabbis subject biblical stories. The hypotheses they frame are often based on assumptions that have no relevance to the world of the Bible (e.g., that Jacob and Esau went to school), receive no support whatever from the textual details, or even fill in what the narrative itself rules out." Sternberg, *The Poetics of Biblical Narrative*, 188.

and "go to a place where I will show you," and unhestitant, Abraham left (12:1, 4). God told him of the promise of an heir, and Abraham believed (15:5–6). He even brought Yahweh a sacrifice upon His request (15:9–10). So why is it only now that Yahweh knows Abraham's fear/obedience?

In part, it is the psycho-emotional nature of the request. However, this does not constitute indiscriminate gap-filling, but is derived from the text itself. As Yahweh repeatedly says, "you have not withheld your son, your only son, from Me" (vv. 12, 16). This repetition echoes the original request in verse 2, where Yahweh commands Abraham to, "Take now your son, your only son, *whom you love*, Isaac," and sacrifice him. Hence, there *is* psycho-emotional content here, even by Yahweh's account. We don't know how Abraham felt precisely during his trek to Moriah, but we know he loved Isaac and yet was willing to relinquish him to Yahweh. Though Moberly correctly observes that this willingness is obedience, it should be stressed that this obedience comes at a high emotional and psychological price. It is this price which makes the sacrifice significant in Yahweh's eyes.

Hence, so far we have determined that attempts such as Laurence Kant's to reread the narrative in order to extricate Yahweh from this unethical command are unacceptable for they contradict facts presented in the text (Isaac's presence 22:8, God's approval message 22:18) and the very *Wirkungsgeschichte* of the text. Kierkegaard presents us with an out—that this represents a "teleological suspension of the ethical" whereby the relationship between Abraham and God supersedes ethical systems. Levenson argues this is reading New Testament interpretations into the text.

Von Rad argues that this is not about human sacrifice, but about the divine promise, and giving up the gift to the Giver of gifts. Moberly finds this approach also "reads" psycho-emotional content into the text, and opts for obedience as the ultimate aim of the test. Whilst we agree that obedience is paramount, Sternberg's emphasis on gap-filling allows us to answer questions the text leaves open, but only within textual constraints. Hence, the presence of Abraham's love for Isaac, acknowledged by Yahweh, along with the unique result of *this* instance of Abraham's obedience, lead us to conclude that Abraham is indeed being asked not just to do something unethical, but to walk the road of *Gottverlassenheit*, to give up the culmination of God's own promises, which just happens to lie in a human being—his son Isaac.

In the Eyes of God

Only a Test?

Though von Rad accurately notes the significance of the cost to Abraham, he mitigates it by claiming it is 'only a test.' Jon Levenson, censures him on this point, saying,

> The announcement that "God put Abraham to the test" cannot, however, be interpreted as von Rad takes it, as a signal to the reader (though not to Abraham) that the aqedah is only a test. Nothing in the verb used (*nissâ*) implies that the act commanded will not be carried to completion, that Isaac will be only bound and not sacrificed on the altar.[31]

As Levenson observes, it would not be much of a test if Abraham knew for certain that God would not allow him to complete his orders—it would be a meaningless exercise.

However, the narrator saw fit to inform the *reader* that this was a test. That is, God's actions required some justification, as they were not commands in line with His character (cf. Gen 9:6). Though we are skeptical about Levenson's contention that child sacrifice was not always the abomination it later became,[32] even if he were correct, this command would still contradict the *promise* of Yahweh that Isaac was the fulfillment of His promise to make many nations out of Abraham (12:2; 17:4–6; 18:18). Thus, there is a disjunction in the narrative, if not an ethical one.

The use of the verb *nsh* tells us that God was not seeking the sacrifice itself, but, as we have noted from our brief review of the verb, he sought to determine the level of Abraham's loyalty by noting his obedience. As Levenson himself says, "What is tested in Gen 22:1–19 is not Abraham's knowledge, as knowledge is generally understood today, but his devotion to God, the God who now demands the ultimate sacrifice."[33] However, this devotion is not simply relative to others, but in contradistinction with ethical norms (as per Kierkegaard). Lacocque says,

---

31. Levenson, *Death and Resurrection of the Beloved Son*, 126.

32. However, Lacocque points out that this would contradict the very cultural norms within which Genesis was written. Lacocque, "About the 'Aqedah," 197–98. Furthermore, Ed Noort says, "However, the idea that the firstborn son belongs to YHWH appears in the Hebrew Bible almost always together with the possibility of substitution (Exod 13:13.15, exception: Ex 22:29). To presuppose that at one time the reality was that every new firstborn had to be sacrificed, contradicts everything we have learned about the history of religion in the Levant." Noort, "Human Sacrifice and Theology," 9.

33. Levenson, *Death and Resurrection of the Beloved Son*, 130.

> I do not understand Levenson's statement that "[Abraham is] placing obedience to God not above ethics, as Kierkegaard would have it, but above his love for Isaac" (p. 128). True, on the issue of preferences, Abraham loves Isaac more than Ishmael and less than God; Isaac loves Esau more than Jacob; and Jacob loves Rachel more than Lea—but to kill one for the love of the other is clearly another matter altogether. It so happens that Abraham's readiness to commit murder places him at odds with ethics, not just within a scale of preferences. The *nissah* (testing) of Abraham is precisely due to its monstrosity—Levenson stresses this point himself."[34]

As Lacocque aptly observes, any attempt to mitigate the effect of God's commands misconstrues its purpose. No reading of misunderstanding, psychological musings, or relativized loyalties, will absolve God of this most heinous command. Neither will mitigating its force by relegating its status to that of "only a test." Though Isaac is more than just human—he is the embodiment of God's promises—how can God make such a command?

Covenant Ratification

T. D. Alexander,[35] makes an interesting case that chapter 22 is a ratification of the covenant specified in chapter 17. He compares this with the covenant between God and Noah in chapters 6–9, finding the following (common) structure:

> (a) The promise of a covenant (6:18)
> (b) The obligations of the covenant (6:14–16, 19–21; 7:1–3)
> (c) The fulfillment of the obligations (6:22; 7:5)
> (d) The offering of a sacrifice (*'ōlāh*) (8:20)
> (e) The establishment of the covenant (9:9–17)[36]

These parallels establish the sign of the covenant (rainbow, circumcision), that the party walk before God and be blameless (6:9, 17:1), etc. Based on the form of the covenant with Noah, Alexander claims that the covenant

---

34. Cf. also Bachya ben Asher, whom both Lacocque and Levenson cite: "this trial was not like any other, and nature cannot bear it, nor the imagination conceive it." *Commentary on the Torah* [Hebrew], Jerusalem: Mossad Harav Kook, 1966, I.193.

35. This thesis is further developed in a doctoral thesis supervised under Alexander, and published as: Williamson, *Abraham, Israel and the Nations*.

36. Alexander, "Genesis 22 and the Covenant of Circumcision," 20.

described in Gen 17 is incomplete, as there is no sacrifice ratifying the covenant. This, he claims is found in Gen 22. Hence, the covenant is left on the table unsigned, as it were, until Abraham demonstrates his loyalty and offers the required sacrifice to seal the deal. Alexander claims four benefits of this view:

> First, it explains why Abraham is tested. God wants to determine whether or not Abraham has kept the conditions of the covenant promised in chapter 17. By his obedient response to such a searching demand, Abraham shows his loyalty to God. He is quite prepared to put God before his family. Secondly, by viewing chapter 22 as part of a conditional covenant we have an explanation as to why Abraham is considered in chapter 26 to have merited by his obedience the divine guarantee of the promises.... Thirdly, if chapter 22 parallels in part the covenant with Noah, then the apparent secondary nature of 22:15–18 need no longer trouble us. The divine oath could not have been given sooner in chapter 22. The sacrifice of the ram was required before God could confirm with an oath the promises he made earlier.[37]

If this is correct, then it would seem that God's "test" in chapter 22 concerns not child sacrifice, nor Abraham's psychological state, but the loyalty (fear) demanded by the covenant and demonstrated through extreme obedience. That this is a test, as Levenson notes, makes it no less real, and yet, we see that the narrative incongruity alerts us to the fact that God's purposes, though "fraught with background," are other than they might at first seem. Yahweh is not a blood-thirsty deity, callously demanding human sacrifice. Rather, within the context of a covenant promise, He seeks a covenant partner who will walk with Him for His own sake, and not simply for the benefits of the covenant. It is precisely because the command lies outside of typical ethical boundaries, or at least narrative values (such as the promised heir) that it qualifies as a proper test. To have remained within those boundaries would have been to follow those sets of behavioral rules (Kierkegaard's *universal*) rather than to follow God Himself.

---

37. Alexander, "Genesis 22 and the Covenant of Circumcision," 21.

Conclusion

We have seen in our brief survey of testing (נסה), that the object of testing is most often a member of the covenant people's obedience to Yahweh's commands. Though there are occasions where provision is the focus, most often, this has already been given at the outset, and the response of faith is tested in its light.

This, of course, both squares with and conflicts with our present pericope. If Isaac is the provision of the promised seed, then the provision has been given. Abraham is being tested as to his obedience having already received the fulfillment of the promise. However, if the sheep is in view, obviously there has been no provision given. However, as the test ends upon Abraham's obedience, and not upon His finding the sheep, it seems that the former is more likely the case. Furthermore, this loyalty on trial is a 'test' in which not just a human child, but the embodiment of all the promises upon which this narrative, and indeed God's own *Heilsgeschicte*, have now come to a head. It is this crucial moment which is ultimately the ratification of God's covenant with Abraham.

Bibliography

Aaron, David H. *Biblical Ambiguities: Metaphor, Semantics, and Divine Imagery.* Leiden: Brill, 2002.
Alexander, T. D. "Genesis 22 and the Covenant of Circumcision." *Journal for the Study of the Old Testament* 25 (1983) 17–22.
———. "A Literary Analysis of the Abraham Narrative in Genesis." Ph.D. diss., University of Belfast, 1982.
———. "Lot's Hospitality: A Clue to His Righteousness." *Journal of Biblical Literature* 104 (1985) 289–91.
Alston, William P. "Being-Itself and Talk About God." *Center Journal* 3.3 (1984) 9–25.
———. *Divine Nature and Human Language.* Ithaca, NY: Cornell University Press, 1989.
———. *Illocutionary Acts and Sentence Meaning.* Ithaca, NY: Cornell University Press, 2000.
Alter, Robert. *Genesis: Translation and Commentary.* New York: Norton, 1996.
Aquinas, Thomas. *Summa Theologiæ: A Concise Translation.* Translated by Timothy McDermott. Notre Dame, IN: Christian Classics, 1989.
———. *Summa Theologica.* Translated by Rev. Daniel J. Sullivan and the Fathers of the English Dominican Province. Chicago: Encyclopedia Britannica, 1952.
Arnold, Bill T., and John H. Choi. *A Guide to Biblical Hebrew Syntax.* Cambridge: Cambridge University Press, 2003.
Auerbach, Erich. *Mimesis: The Representation of Reality in Western Literature.* Edited and translated by Willard R. Trask. Princeton, NJ: Princeton University Press, 1953.
Austin, James L. *How to Do Things with Words: The William James Lectures Delivered at Harvard University in 1955.* Oxford: Clarendon, 1962.
Baloian, Bruce E. "Anthropomorphism." In *New International Dictionary of Old Testament Theology and Exegesis,* edited by Willem A. VanGemeren. Pradis, version 5.13.0025. No pages. Grand Rapids: Zondervan, 2002.
Balserak, Jon. *Divinity Compromised: A Study of Divine Accommodation in the Thought of John Calvin.* Dordrecht, The Netherlands: Springer, 2006.
Bandstra, Barry L. "Word Order and Emphasis in Biblical Hebrew Narrative: Syntactic Observations on Genesis 22 from a Discourse Perspective." In *Linguistics and Biblical Hebrew,* edited by Walter R. Bodine, 109–23. Winona Lake, IN: Eisenbrauns, 1992.
Barr, James. "Theophany and Anthropomorphism in the Old Testament." In *Congress Volume: Oxford 1959,* edited by G. W. Anderson, De Boer, et al., 31–38. Leiden: Brill, 1960.
Barth, Karl. *Church Dogmatics* Vol. II, Part I: *The Doctrine of God.* Edited by G. W. Bromiley and T. F. Torrance. Translated by T. H. L. Parker et al. Edinburgh: T. & T. Clark, 1957.

Bibliography

Bassett, Frederick W. "Noah's Nakedness and the Curse of Canaan a Case of Incest?" *Vetus Testamentum* 21 (1971) 232–37.

Benin, Stephen D. *Footprints of God: Divine Accommodation in Jewish and Christian Thought.* Albany, NY: State University of New York Press, 1993.

Bergsma, John Sietze, and Scott Walker Hahn. "Noah's Nakedness and the Curse on Canaan." *Journal of Biblical Literature* 124 (2005) 25–40.

Berlin, Adele. *Poetics and Interpretation of Biblical Narrative.* Sheffield, UK: Almond, 1983.

Black, Max. "Metaphor." In *Models and Metaphors: Studies in Language and Philosophy*, 63–82. Ithaca, NY: Cornell University Press, 1962.

Booij, T. "Hagar's Words In Genesis XVI 13B." *Vetus Testamentum* XXX (1980) 1–7.

Botterweck, G. Johannes, Helmer Ringgren, and Douglas W. Stott. *Theological Dictionary of the Old Testament.* Grand Rapids: Eerdmans, 1975.

Brett, Mark G. *Genesis: Procreation and the Politics of Identity.* London: Routledge, 2000.

Brodie, Thomas L. *Genesis as Dialogue: A Literary, Historical and Theological Commentary.* Oxford: Oxford University Press, 2001.

Brueggemann, Walter. *Genesis.* Atlanta: John Knox, 1982.

———. *Theology of the Old Testament: Testimony, Dispute, Advocacy.* Minneapolis: Augsburg Fortress, 1997.

Burrell, David. *Analogy and Philosophical Language.* New Haven: Yale University Press, 1973.

Calvin, John. *Genesis.* (Original, 1554.) Translated by John King. Edinburgh: Banner of Truth, 1965.

———. *Institutes of the Christian Religion.* Edited by John T. McNeill. Translated by Ford Lewis Battles. The Library of Christian Classics, vol. 21. Philadelphia: Westminster, 1960.

Cassuto, Umberto. *A Commentary on the Book of Genesis: Part I From Adam to Noah.* Translated by Israel Abrahams. Jerusalem: Magnes, 1961.

Cherbonnier, E. LaB. "The Logic of Biblical Anthropomorphism." *The Harvard Theological Review* 55 (1962) 187–206.

Childs, Brevard S. *Biblical Theology of the Old and New Testaments: Theological Reflection on the Christian Bible.* Minneapolis: Augsberg Fortress, 1992.

———. *Old Testament Theology in a Canonical Context.* London: SCM, 1985.

Clark, W. Malcolm. "The Righteousness of Noah." *Vetus Testamentum* XXI (1971) 261–80.

Clements, R. E. *Old Testament Theology: A Fresh Approach.* Marshall's Theological Library. London: Marshall, Morgan, and Scott, 1978.

Clines, D. J. A. "The Image of God in Man." *Tyndale Bulletin* 19 (1968) 53–103.

———. "The Significance of the 'Sons of God' Episode (Genesis 6:1–4) in the Context of the 'Primeval History' (Genesis 1–11)." *Journal for the Study of the Old Testament* 13 (1979) 33–46.

———. "The Tree of Knowledge and the Law (Ps. XIX)." *Vetus Testamentum* 24.1 (1974) 8–14.

Collins, C. John. "What Happened to Adam and Eve? A Literary-Theological Approach to Genesis 3." *Prebyterion* 27.1 (2001) 12–44.

Cooper, John W. *Panentheism: The Other God of the Philosophers.* Grand Rapids: Baker, 2006.

Croft, William, and D. Alan Cruse. *Cognitive Linguistics.* Cambridge: Cambridge University Press, 2004.

Bibliography

Crotty, Robert. "The Literary Structure of the Binding of Isaac in Genesis 22." *Australian Biblical Review* 53 (2005) 31–41.

Culver, Robert Duncan. "Anthropomorphism, Analogy and Impassibility of God." Paper given at the Midwest meeting of ETS, Taylor University, Fort Wayne, IN, 1996.

Davidson, JoAnn. "Eschatology and Genesis 22." *Journal of the Adventist Theological Society* 11.1–2 (2000) 232–47.

Doyle, Brian. "'Knock, Knock, Knockin' on Sodom's Door': The Function of פתח/דלת in Genesis 18–19." *Journal for the Study of the Old Testament* 28 (2004) 431–48.

Drey, Philip R. "The Role of Hagar in Genesis 16." *Andrews University Seminary Studies* 40.2 (2002) 179–85.

Eichrodt, Walther. *Theology of the Old Testament*. Philadelphia: Westminster, 1961.

Eslinger, Lyle. "A Contextual Identification of the Bene Ha'elohim and Benoth Ha'adam in Genesis 6:1–4." *Journal for the Study of the Old Testament* 13 (1979) 65–73.

Ferré, Frederick. "In Praise of Anthropomorphism." *International Journal for Philosophy of Religion* 16 (1984) 203–12.

———. *Language, Logic and God*. London: Eyre & Spottiswoode, 1962.

Fokkelman, Jan P. *Narrative Art in Genesis: Specimens of Stylistic and Structural Analysis*. Amsterdam: Van Gorcum, 1975.

———. "'On the Mount of the LORD There is Vision': A Response to Francis Landy Concerning the Akedah." In *Signs and Wonders: Biblical Texts in Literary Focus*, edited by J. Cheryl Exum, 41–57. Decatur, GA: Scholars, 1989.

Garrett, D. *Rethinking Genesis: Sources and Authorship of the First Book of the Pentateuch*. Grand Rapids: Baker, 1991.

Gesenius, W. *Gesenius' Hebrew Grammar*. 2nd ed. Edited by E. Kautzsch and translated by A. E. Cowley. Oxford: Clarendon, 1910.

Goldingay, John. *Old Testament Theology: Israel's Gospel*. Downer's Grove, IL: InterVarsity, 2003.

Grelot, Pierre. *The Language of Symbolism: Biblical Theology, Semantics and Exegesis*. Peabody, MA: Hendrickson, 2006.

Hamilton, Victor P. *The Book of Genesis: Chapters 1–17*. Grand Rapids: Eerdmans, 1990.

———. *The Book of Genesis: Chapters 18–50*. Grand Rapids: Eerdmans, 1994.

Hamori, Esther J. *"When Gods Were Men": The Embodied God in Biblical and Near Eastern Literature*. Berlin: de Gruyter, 2008.

Hartley, John. *Genesis*. New International Biblical Commentary. Peabody, MA: Hendrickson, 2000.

Helm, Paul. *John Calvin's Ideas*. Oxford: Oxford University Press, 2004.

Hendel, Ronald S. "Of Demigods and the Deluge: Toward an Interpretation of Genesis 6:1–4." *Journal of Biblical Literature* 106 (1987) 13–26.

Henry, Carl C. F. *God, Revelation, and Authority*. Waco, TX: Word, 1979.

Heschel, Abraham. *The Prophets, II*. New York: Harper & Row, 1962.

Hess, Richard S. "Splitting the Adam: The Usage of 'Adām in Genesis I–V." In *Studies in the Pentateuch*. Vetus Testamentum Supplement Series 41, 1–16. Leiden: Brill, 1990.

Hre Kio, Stephen. "Revisiting 'the Sons of God' in Genesis 6.1–4." *The Bible Translator* 52 (2001) 234–39.

Humphreys, W. Lee. *The Character of God in the Book of Genesis: A Narrative Appraisal*. Louisville: Westminster John Knox, 2001.

Bibliography

Janzen, J. Gerald. *Abraham and All the Families of the Earth: A Commentary on the Book of Genesis* 12–50. Grand Rapids: Eerdmans, 1993.

———. "Hagar in Paul's Eyes and in the Eyes of Yahweh (Genesis 16) A Study in Horizons." *Horizons in Biblical Theology* 13 (1991) 1–22.

———. "Kugel's Adverbial *Kî Tôb*: An Assessment." *Journal of Biblical Literature* 102 (1983) 99–106.

Jenni, Ernst, and Claus Westermann. *Theologisches Handwörterbuch Zum Alten Testament*. München: Gütersloher, 1976.

Joüon, Paul. *A Grammar of Biblical Hebrew, Vol. 2. Part 3, Syntax, Paradigms and Indices*. Edited and translated by T. Muraoka. Roma: Editrice Pontificio Istituto Biblio, 1991.

———. *A Grammar of Biblical Hebrew*. Revised English. Edited by Takamitsu Muraoka. Subsidia Biblica. Rome: Editrice Pontificio Istituto biblico, 2006.

Kant, Laurence A. "Restorative Thoughts on an Agonizing Text: Abraham's Binding of Isaac and the Horror on Mt. Moriah (Genesis 22): Part 2." *Lexington Theological Quarterly* 38.3 (2003) 161–94.

Keel, Othmar. *The Symbolism of the Biblical World: Ancient Near Eastern Iconography and the Book of Psalms*. Translated by Timothy J. Hallett. Winona Lake, IN: Eisenbrauns, 1997.

Kierkegaard, Søren. *Fear and Trembling and the Sickness Unto Death*. Translated by Walter Lowrie. New York: Doubleday, 1942.

Kittay, E. F. *Metaphor: Its Cognitive Force and Linguistic Structure*. Oxford: Oxford University Press, 1987.

Klein, Ralph T. "The Yahwist Looks at Abraham." *Concordia Theological Monthly* 45 (1974) 43–49.

Kline, Meredith G. "Divine Kingship and Genesis 6:1–4." *Westminster Theological Journal* 24 (1962) 187–204.

Koehler, Ludwig, and Walter Baumgartner, editors. *Hebrew and Aramaic Lexicon of the Old Testament*. Leiden: Koninklijke, Brill NV, 1994–2000. CD-ROM Edition.

Koenen, K. "Wer Sieht Wen? Zur Textgeschichte von Gen 16:13." *Vetus Testamentum* 38 (1988) 468–74.

Kövecses, Zoltán. *Metaphor: A Practical Introduction*. Oxford: Oxford University Press, 2002.

Kraeling, Emil G. "The Significance and Origin of Gen. 6:1–4." *Journal of Near Eastern Studies* VI.4 (1947) 193–208.

Lacocque, André. "About the 'Aqedah' in Genesis 22: A Response to Laurence A. Kant." *Lexington Theological Quarterly* 40 (2005) 191–201.

Lakoff, George, and Mark Johnson. *Metaphors We Live By*. Chicago: University of Chicago Press, 1980.

Letellier, Robert Ignatius. *Day in Mamre, Night in Sodom: Abraham and Lot in Genesis 18 and 19*. Biblical Interpretation Series. Leiden: Brill, 1995.

Levenson, Jon D. *The Death and Resurrection of the Beloved Son: The Transformation of Child Sacrifice in Judaism and Christianity*. New Haven: Yale University Press, 1993.

Lindbom, J. "Theophanies in Holy Places in Hebrew Religion." *Hebrew Union College Annual* 32 (1961) 91–106.

Bibliography

Lundbom, Jack R. "Parataxis, Rhetorical Structure, and the Dialogue Over Sodom in Genesis 18." In *The World of Genesis: Persons, Places, Perspectives*, edited by Philip R. Davies and David J. A. Clines, 136–45. Sheffield, UK: Sheffield Academic, 1998.

Lyons, William John. *Canon and Exegesis: Canonical Praxis and the Sodom Narrative*. London: T. & T. Clark, 2002.

Lytton, Timothy D. "'Shall not the Judge of the Earth Deal Justly?': Accountability, Compassion, and Judicial Authority in the Biblical Story of Sodom and Gomorrah." *Journal of Literature & Religion* 31 (2002-3) 31–55.

MacDonald, Nathan. "Listening to Abraham—Listening to Yhwh: Divine Justice and Mercy in Genesis 18:16–33." *Catholic Biblical Quarterly* 66 (2004) 25–43.

Macquarrie, John. *God-Talk: An Examination of the Language and Logic of Theology*. London: SCM, 1967.

Matthews, Kenneth A. *Genesis 1:1—11:26*. Nashville: Broadman and Holman, 1996.

———. *Genesis 11:27—50:26*. Nashville: Broadman and Holman, 2005.

Mauser, Ulrich. "God in Human Form." *Ex Auditu* 16 (2000) 81–99.

McFague, Sallie. *Metaphorical Theology: Models of God in Religious Language*. Philadelphia: Fortress, 1982.

McKeown, James. *Genesis*. Grand Rapids: Eerdmans, 2008.

Meyers, Carol. *Discovering Eve: Ancient Israelite Women in Context*. New York: Oxford University Press, 1988.

———. "Gender Roles and Genesis 3:16 Revisited." In *The Word of the Lord Shall Go Forth: Essays in Honor of David Noel Freedman in Celebration of His Sixtieth Birthday*, edited by Carol L. Meyers and M. O'Connor, 337–54. Winona Lake, IN: Eisenbrauns, 1983.

Moberly, R. W. L. *The Bible, Theology, and Faith: A Study of Abraham and Jesus*. Cambridge Studies in Christian Doctrine. Cambridge: Cambridge University Press, 2000.

———. "Christ as the Key to Scripture." In *He Swore an Oath: Biblical Themes from Genesis 12–50*, edited by R. S. Hess, Wenham G. J., and P. E. Satterthwaite, 143–73. Carlisle, UK: Paternoster, 1994.

———. "Did the Serpent Get It Right?" *Journal of Theological Studies* 39 (1988) 1–27.

———. *Genesis 12–50*. Old Testament Guides. Sheffield, UK: JSOT, 1992.

Morris, Thomas V. *Our Idea of God*. Downers Grove, IL: InterVarsity, 1991.

Morschauser, Scott. "'Hospitality', Hostiles and Hostages: On the Legal Background to Genesis 19.1–9." *Journal for the Study of the Old Testament* 27 (2003) 461–85.

Muraoka, T. *Emphatic Words and Structures in Biblical Hebrew*. Jerusalem: Magnes, 1985.

Noort, Ed. "Genesis 22: Human Sacrifice and Theology in the Hebrew Bible." In *The Sacrifice of Isaac: The Aqedah (Genesis 22) and Its Interpretations*, 1–20. Leiden: Brill, 2002.

Parry, Robin A. *Old Testament Story and Christian Ethics: The Rape of Dinah as a Case Study*. Milton Keynes, UK: Paternoster, 2004.

Petersen, David L. "Genesis 6:1–4, Yahweh and the Organization of the Cosmos." *Journal for the Study of the Old Testament* 13 (1979) 47–64.

Preuss, Horst, Dietrich. *Old Testament Theology*. Edinburgh: T. & T. Clark, 1991.

Pritchard, J. B., editor. *Ancient Near Eastern Texts*. Princeton, NJ.: Princeton University Press, 1978.

Pseudo-Dionysius. *Pseudo-Dionysius: The Complete Works*. The Classics of Western Spirituality. Translated by Colm Luibheid et al. New York: Paulist, 1987.

Bibliography

Ramsey, G. W. "Is Name-Giving an Act of Domination in Genesis 2:23 and Elsewhere?" *Catholic Biblical Quarterly* 50 (1988) 24–35.

Ramsey, Ian T. *Religious Language: An Empirical Placing of Theological Phrases*. London: SCM, 1957.

Reis, Pamela Tamarkin. "Hagar Requited." *Journal for the Study of the Old Testament* 87 (2000) 75–109.

Rendtorff, Rolf. *The Canonical Hebrew Bible: A Theology of the Old Testament*. Translated by David E. Orton. Leiden: Deo, 2005.

Richards, I. A. *The Philosophy of Rhetoric*. London: Oxford University, 1936.

Ricoeur, Paul. *From Text to Action: Essays in Hermeneutics, II*. Evanston, IL: Northwestern University Press, 1991.

———. *The Rule of Metaphor: Multi-Disciplinary Studies of the Creation of Meaning in Language*. Translated by Robert Czerny with Kathleen McLaughlin and John Costello. Toronto: Toronto University Press, 1975.

Sailhamer, John. *Genesis Unbound*. Sisters, OR: Multnomah, 1996.

———. *The Pentateuch as Narrative: A Biblical-Theological Commentary*. Grand Rapids: Zondervan, 1992.

Sarna, Nahum M. *Genesis*. Philadelphia: Jewish Publication Society, 1989.

Schoors, A. "A Tiqqun Sopherim in Genesis XVI 13B?" *Vetus Testamentum* 32.4 (1982) 494–95.

Searle, John. *Speech Acts*. Cambridge: Cambridge University Press, 1969.

Seebass, H. "Zum Text Von Gen. XVI 13B." *Vetus Testamentum* 21 (1971) 254–55.

Shanks, Herschel. "Illuminations: Abraham Cut Off From His Past and Future by the Awkward Divine Command 'Go You!'" *Bible Review* 3.1 (1987) 8–9.

Sharp, Donald B., S. J. "On the Motherhood of Sarah: A Yahwistic Theological Comment." *Irish Biblical Studies* 20 (1998) 6–7.

Speiser, E. A. *Genesis*. The Anchor Bible. Garden City, NY: Doubleday, 1964.

———. "*YDWN*, Gen. 6:3." *Journal of Biblical Literature* 75.2 (June 1956) 126–29.

Stern, Josef. *Metaphor in Context*. Cambridge: MIT, 2000.

Sternberg, Meir. *The Poetics of Biblical Narrative: Ideological Literature and the Drama of Reading*. Bloomington, IN: Indiana University Press, 1987.

Stiver, Dan R. *The Philosophy of Religious Language: Sign, Symbol and Story*. Malden, MA: Blackwell, 1994.

Swinburne, Richard. *The Coherence of Theism*. Oxford: Clarendon, 1977.

Tarski, Alfred. *Logic, Semantics, and Metamathematics: Papers from 1923 to 1938*. Translated by J. H. Woodger. Oxford: Oxford University Press, 1956.

Thisleton, Antony. *A Concise Encyclopedia of the Philosophy of Religion*. Grand Rapids: Baker, 2002.

Tracy, David. *The Analogical Imagination: Christian Theology and the Culture of Pluralism*. New York, NY: Crossroad, 1981.

Trible, Phyllis. "Genesis 22: The Sacrifice of Sarah." In *"Not in Heaven": Coherence and Complexity in Biblical Narrative*, edited by Jason P. Rosenblatt and Joseph Sitterson, 170–91. Bloomington, IN: Indiana University Press, 1991.

———. "The Other Woman." In *Understanding the Word: Essays in Honour of Bernhard W. Anderson*, edited by J. T. Butler, E. W. Conrad, and B. C. Ollenburger, 221–46. Sheffield, UK: JSOT, 1985.

———. *Texts of Terror*. Philadelphia: Fortress, 1984.

Turner, Denys. *The Darkness of God: Negativity in Christian Mysticism*. Cambridge: Cambridge University Press, 1995.
Turner, Lawrence A. *Announcements of Plot in Genesis*. Journal for the Study of the Old Testament Supplement Series. Sheffield, UK: JSOT, 1990.
———. "The Rainbow as the Sign of the Covenant in Genesis IX: 11–13." *Vetus Testamentum* XLIII.1 (1993) 119–24.
van der Toorn, Karel, ed. *The Image and the Book: Iconic Cults, Aniconism, and the Rise of Book Religion in Israel and the Ancient Near East*. Leuven: Peeters, 1997.
van Gemeren, Willem A. "The Sons of God in Genesis 6:1–4 (An Example of Evangelical Demythologization?)." *Westminster Theological Journal* 43 (1981) 320–48.
Van Hecke, P. "Conceptual Blending: A Recent Approach to Metaphor. Illustrated with the Pastoral Metaphor in Hos 4,16." In *Metaphor in the Hebrew Bible*, edited by P. Van Hecke, 215–31. Leuven: Leuven University Press, 2005.
VanGemeren, Willem A., general editor. *New International Dictionary of Old Testament Theology and Exegesis*. CD-ROM. Grand Rapids: Zondervan, 2004.
Vanhoozer, Kevin J. *The Drama of Doctrine: A Canonical Linguistic Approach to Christian Theology*. Louisville, KY: Westminster John Knox, 2005.
Von Rad, Gerhard. *Genesis: A Commentary*. 3rd ed. Translated by John H. Marks. London: SCM, 1972.
———. *Old Testament Theology: The Theology of Israel's Historical Traditions*. Translated by D. M. G. Stalker. Edinburgh: Oliver and Boyd, 1962.
Waltke, Bruce K. *Genesis: A Commentary*. Grand Rapids: Zondervan, 2001.
Waltke, Bruce, and M. O'Connor. *Introduction to Biblical Hebrew Syntax*. Winona Lake, IN: Eisenbrauns, 1990.
Weinandy, Thomas, O.F.M. *Does God Suffer?* Notre Dame, IN: Notre Dame Press, 2000.
Wenham, Gordon J. "The Akedah: A Paradigm of Sacrifice." In *Pomegranates and Golden Bells: Studies in Biblical, Jewish, and Near Eastern Ritual, Law, and Literature in Honor of Jacob Milgrom*, edited by David P. Wright, David Noel Freedman, and Avi Huritz, 93–102. Winona Lake, IN: Eisenbrauns, 1995.
———. *Genesis 1–15*. Word Biblical Commentary. Waco, TX: Word, 1987.
———. *Genesis 16–50*. Word Biblical Commentary. Dallas, TX: Word, 1994.
Westermann, Claus. *Genesis 1–11*. Translated by John J. Scullion. London: SPCK, 1983.
———. *Genesis 12–36*. Translated by John J. Scullion. London: SPCK, 1981.
White, H. C. "The Initiation Legend of Ishmael." *Zeitschrift Für Dei Alttestamentliche Wissenschaft* 87 (1975) 267–306.
White, Roger. "Notes on Analogical Predication and Speaking about God." In *The Philosophical Frontiers of Christian Theology: Essays Presented to D. M. Mackinnon*, edited by Brian Hebblethwaite and Stewart Sutherland, 197–226. Cambridge: Cambridge University Press, 1982.
Williamson, Paul R. *Abraham, Israel and the Nations: The Patriarchal Promise and Its Covenantal Development in Genesis*. Sheffield, UK: Sheffield Academic Press, 2000.
Wolff, Hans Walter. *Anthropology of the Old Testament*. Mifflintown, PA: Sigler, 1996.
Wolterstorff, Nicholas. "Unqualified Divine Temporality." In *God and Time*, edited by Gregory E. Ganssle, 187–213. Downers Grove, IL: InterVarsity, 2001.
———. *Divine Discourse: Philosophical Reflections on the Claim That God Speaks*. Cambridge: Cambridge University Press, 1995.

Name and Author Index

Aaron ben Elijah, 262
Aaron, David, 13, 15, 16, 29, 30, 30n88, 57, 65, 66, 80, 80n66, 81, 118, 237, 273
Abravanel, I., 262
Ahuvia, A., 214n42
Albright, W. F., 115n33
Alexander, T. D., 177n7, 234, 251, 251n1, 253, 253n7, 255, 255n13, 269, 269nn35 & 36, 270, 270n37, 273
Alston, William, 12, 12n36, 13, 14, 15, 15n44, 16, 17, 17nn48 & 49, 18, 18n50, 36n101, 57, 237, 241, 273
Alter, Robert, 199n8, 273
Aquinas, Thomas, 4, 8, 9, 9n25, 9n27, 10, 10n29, 10n31, 11, 11nn33 & 34, 12, 17, 19, 20, 55n148, 84, 84n3, 87, 87n13, 97, 237, 273
Aristotle, 6, 14, 18, 20, 60
Athanasius, 53
Auerbach, Erich, 264, 265n25, 266, 273
Augustine, 24
Austin, J. L., 35n101, 36n101, 205, 205n22, 241, 273
Ayer, A. J., 15n43

Baḥya, 262
Baloian, Bruce, 88, 88n16, 273
Balserak, Jon, 26, 26n78, 27, 28, 28n82, 30, 30n89, 32n95, 273

Bandstra, Barry L., 226, 226n17, 273
Barbour, Ian G., 13
Barth, Karl, 13, 34, 34n97, 35n99, 39, 40, 45n120, 56, 96, 97, 219n2, 237, 273
Basinger, David, 2n4
Basset, F. W., 160, 160n61, 274
Battles, Ford Lewis, 274
Baumgartner, Walter, 117nn38 & 39, 169n13, 170n16, 180n17, 190, 190n54, 246, 246n19, 276
Benin, Stephen, 23, 23n65, 24, 25, 26n75, 26n77, 26n79, 27n81, 29n86, 274
Bergsma, John Sietze, 159, 159n53, 160, 160n59, 161, 161n63, 274
Berlin, Adele, 117, 118, 187, 187n40, 274
Black, Max, 17, 18, 60, 60n3, 66, 73, 73n38, 77, 274
Blenkinsopp, Joseph, 203n16
Booij, T., 244, 244n8, 248, 274
Botterweck, G. Johannes, 138n11, 181n18, 274
Boyd, Greg, 2n4
Bratsiotis, N. P., 138n11
Brett, Mark, 245, 245n11, 274
Briggs, 158n52
Brodie, 177, 177n6, 181, 181n20, 213, 213n40, 215, 215n46,

281

Name and Author Index

Brodie (*cont.*)
216, 216n49, 247, 247nn20&21, 274
Brown, R. E., 158n52
Bruckner, 203n16
Brueggemann, Walter, 45, 45n121, 46, 46nn126–28, 47, 49, 51, 52, 52nn142&143, 54, 56, 201, 217, 219n2, 220n2, 261n19, 274
Budde, 142n24
Bultmann, Rudolph, 13, 40, 113n23
Burge, Tyler, 102n43
Burrell, David, 19, 19n54, 274
Butler, J. T., 278

Calvin, John, 22, 23n64, 26, 27, 27nn80&81, 28, 29, 29n87, 30, 30n90, 31, 31nn91&92, 32, 32n94, 53, 209, 209n30, 213, 213n41, 274
The Cappadocians, 53
Cassuto, 113n23, 138n10, 139, 139n16, 148, 148n36, 167, 168, 168n8, 169n12, 170n17, 274
Cavell, S. 78
Cherbonnier, Eduard LaB., 90, 90n21, 92, 92n25, 93n26, 274
Childs, Brevard S., 1, 1n1, 21, 21n63, 44, 45, 45n119, 47, 52, 54, 56, 57, 83, 86, 86n11, 87, 87n12, 87n14, 89, 251, 274
Choi, John H., 248, 273
Chrysostom, John, 22, 24, 27
Clark, W. M., 154, 154n44, 155, 274
Clement of Alexandria, 136

Clements, R. E., 42, 42n113, 44, 49, 50, 50n139, 53, 56, 274
Clines, D. J. A., 88n17, 129n61, 136n4, 137, 137n6, 137n8, 138n9, 139n13, 171, 274, 277
Collins, J., 128n59, 274
Conrad, E. W., 278
Cooper, John, 3n9, 274
Costello, John, 278
Coulson, S., 67n24
Cowley, A. E., 275
Croft, William, 63, 63n10, 64, 64nn15&16, 65, 65n17, 67, 68n26, 69, 70, 70n30, 82, 82n68, 274
Crombie, I. M., 13
Crotty, Robert, 222n7, 275
Cruse, D. Alan, 63, 63n10, 64, 64nn15&16, 65, 65n17, 67, 68n26, 69, 70, 70n30, 82, 82n68, 274
Culver, Robert S., 1, 3n1, 2n6, 275
Czerny, Robert, 278

Damascene, John, 5
Davidson, JoAnn, 70, 78, 78n53, 221, 221n5, 222n9, 223, 275
Davies, Philip R., 277
de Vaux, Roland, 185n32
Delitzsch, F., 252
Dillmann, A., 145n31
Doyle, Brian, 214, 214n44, 253, 254n8, 275
Drey, Philip, 179n12, 187, 187n38, 190n53, 275
Driver, S. R., 158n52

Eckhart, Meister, 5
Eichrodt, Walther, 40, 40n107, 41, 42, 44, 49, 50, 51, 53, 56, 121, 275

Eisenstein, Albert, 95
Eslinger, Lyle, 136n4, 275
Exum, J. Cheryl, 275
Ezra, Ibn, 262
Ferré, Frederick, 9n28, 10, 10n30, 12, 15n43, 57, 237, 275
Ficker, R., 192n56
Fiddes, Paul, 45n120
Fokkelman, Jan P., 221n7, 222, 222n11, 227, 227n20, 275
Forstman, H. Jackson, 27n81
Frege, G., 4, 74
Fretheim, Terrence, 47, 86, 87

Gagnon, Robert, 159
Garrett, D., 175n1, 275
Gaster, T. H., 214n42
Gerson, Levi ben, 26n77, 262
Gesenius, 154n43, 168n10, 275
Glucksberg, S., 65
Goldingay, John, 47, 47n130, 48, 86, 275
Grady, Joseph E., 66, 67, 68, 83
Gregory of Nyssa, 23
Grelot, Pierre, 76, 76n50, 77, 275
Gunkel, Hermann, 131n70, 156, 159, 160, 191n56, 228n22

Haag, H., 181
Hahn, Scott Walker, 159, 159n53, 160, 160n59, 161, 161n63, 274
Hallett, Timothy J., 276
Hamilton, Victor, 108n5, 112, 112n22, 115, 118, 118n41, 131, 131n69, 133, 137, 137n7, 140, 140n18, 143, 143n26, 150, 150n39, 152, 152n40, 153, 154, 154n42, 155, 156n47, 157, 157n50, 158, 158n51, 163, 163n65, 166, 166n3, 167, 167n6, 198, 199, 199n7, 203n17, 204, 209, 209n32, 211, 211n35, 211n37, 215, 215n45, 215n47, 216n50, 225, 225n14, 243n1, 244, 244n4, 248, 254n9, 275
Hamori, Esther J., 2n6, 275
Hartley, John, 110, 111, 111n15, 112, 187, 187n39, 275
Hartshorne, Charles, 3n9, 7
Hebblethwaite, Brian, 279
Helm, Paul, 26, 27n80, 31, 31n91, 32, 275
Hendel, Ronald, 141n20, 275
Henry, Carl, 7, 7n22, 275
Hertz, Joseph Herman, 262
Heschel, Abraham, 83, 84, 84n4, 85, 85nn8&9, 86, 89, 89n19, 275
Hess, R. S., 124n53, 275, 277
Hoag, Gary, 79n60
Holzinger, H., 160
Höver-Johag, I., 119n42
Humphreys, 132, 132n72, 275

Irenaeus, 136

Jackendoff, R., 65, 66
Jacob, B., 157
Jacobsen, T., 203n17,
Janzen, J. Gerald, 114, 114n25, 115, 115n30, 176, 176n2, 185, 185n35, 188, 188n41, 189, 190n52, 194, 194n66, 212, 212n39, 248, 250, 250n35, 254, 254n10, 276

Name and Author Index

Jaussen, Antion, 185n32,
Jenni, Ernst, 189n48, 276
Johnson, Mark, 60, 61n5, 62n7, 62n9, 63, 65, 66, 276
Josephus, 136n4, 200
Joüon, Paul, 116, 116n36, 117n39, 197n3, 231n33, 232n35, 249, 249n29, 276
Jüngel, E., 43
Justin, 136

Kant, Laurence, 227n19, 262, 263, 263n20, 267, 276
Kaplan, David, 72
Kautzsch, E., 275
Keil, C. F., 141
Kidner, Derek 141
Kierkegaard, Søren, 5, 263, 263n22, 264, 265, 267, 268, 269, 270, 276
Killian, R., 228n22, 250
Kio, Hre, 139, 139n14, 275
Kittay, E. F., 21, 276
Klein, Ralph T., 177, 177n7, 276
Kline, Meredith, 136n4, 145n31, 276
Köhler, L., 88
Kövecses, Zoltan, 60n4, 63n14, 72, 72n35, 276
Koehler, Ludwid, 117nn38 & 39, 169n13, 170n16, 180n17, 190, 190n54, 246, 246n19, 276
Koenen, K., 245, 245n12, 276
König, E., 141n20
Kraeling, E., 138n10, 140n20, 142n24, 170, 276
Kugel, James L., 113, 113n24, 114, 114n25, 115, 115n30, 252, 276

Labuschagne, C. J., 246

Lacocque, André, 231, 231n34, 263, 263n21, 268, 268n32, 269, 269n34, 276
Lakoff, George, 60, 61, 61n5, 62, 62n7, 62n9, 63–65, 66, 68, 69, 70, 71, 73, 83, 276
Letellier, Robert, 208n27, 276
Levenson, 228n22, 264, 264n23, 265, 265n26, 267, 268, 268n31, 268n33, 269, 269n34, 270, 276
Lindblom, J., 248
Lowrie, Walter, 276
Lundbom, Jack, 252, 252n4, 277
Lyons, William J., 204, 204n19, 277
Lytton, Timothy, 202, 203n16, 204n20, 277

MacDonald, Nathan, 198, 198n6, 199, 199n9, 200, 200n11, 201, 201n12, 202, 202n14, 210, 210n34, 251, 251n2, 277
Macquarrie, John, 6, 7n19, 40, 277
Maimon, Moses ben, 5, 6, 25, 26, 26n77, 34, 35, 35n98, 59n1, 236
Maimonides, Moses
Marks, John H., 279
Matthews, Kenneth, 110, 110n13, 112, 147, 147n33, 166, 166n4, 211n36, 229n25, 277
Mauser, Ulrich, 88, 88n17, 89n18, 277
McCabe, Herbert, 87n13
McFague, Sallie, 19, 19n56, 277
McHugh, John, 185n32

Name and Author Index

McKeown, James, 233, 233n39, 277
McLaughlin, Kathleen, 278
McNeill, John T., 274
Meyers, Carol, 144n27, 277
Miller, Patrick D., 46, 46n125
Miskotte, C. K. H., 43n116
Moran, William L., 252
Morris, Thomas V., 7, 8, 8n23, 277
Morschauser, Scott, 252, 253n5, 255, 255n12, 277
Muraoka, Takamitsu, 246, 246nn16–18, 276, 277

Nachmanides, 25
Nicholas of Lyra, 32, 32n95
Noort, Ed, 268n32, 277

O'Connor, 231n33, 232n35, 245, 245n14, 246n15, 249n28, 277, 279
Ollenburger, B. C., 278
Origen, 53, 136n4, 200

Parker, T. H. L., 273
Parry, Robin, 140, 140n19, 277
Petersen, David, 138, 138n12, 277
Philo, 136n4
Pines, Shlomo, 35n98
Pinnock, Clark, 2n4
Plato, 14, 95
Plaut, W. Gunther, 262
Pope, Marvin H., 227n18
Preuss, Horst Dietrich, 42, 43, 43n114, 44, 44n117, 50, 53, 54, 56, 277
Pritchard, J. B., 183nn25&26, 277
Procksch, O., 167, 168, 189, 192n56, 250
Pseudo-Dionysius, 5, 5n15, 6n16, 277

Ramsey, Gordon, 121, 121n47, 122, 122n47, 278
Ramsey, Ian T., 13, 14n39, 278
Rashi (Shlomo Yitzhaki), 204, 262
Reis, Pamela Tamarkin, 185, 185n34, 191, 192, 192n57, 278
Rendtorff, Rolf, 44, 48, 48n136, 49, 50, 53, 56, 278
Richards, I. A., 17, 18, 60, 60n2, 278
Ricoeur, Paul, 20, 20n58, 66, 73, 73n39, 75, 75n46, 97, 98, 98n36, 103, 239, 278
Ringgren, Helmer, 274
Rosenblatt, Jason P., 278
Ruwet, J., 252

Sailhamer, John, 105, 105n1, 111, 111n17, 147, 148n34, 278
Sanders, James, 2n4
Sarna, Nahum M., 180, 180n15, 182, 182n23, 198, 198n5, 201n13, 229, 229n25, 244, 244n7, 245n10, 249, 249n30, 250, 250n33, 278
Satterthwaite, P. E., 277
Schneider, Sandra M., 35, 35n99
Schoors, A., 248, 248n26, 278
Schreiner, J., 252
Scotus, John Duns, 7, 11n34
Scullion, John J., 279
Searle, John, 36n101, 241, 278
Seebass, H., 248, 248n24, 278
Shakespeare, William, 95
Shanks, Herschel, 221n6, 278
Sharbert, J., 252
Sharp, Donald B., 185n32, 278
Sitterson, Joseph, 278
Socrates, 7, 14
Soskice, Janet, 19

Name and Author Index

Speiser, E. A., 140n20, 170n15, 182n21, 192n56, 214n42, 250, 278
Stähli, H. P., 260n16,
Stalker, D. M. G., 279
Stern, Josef, 16, 16n45, 18, 21, 21n62, 33, 55, 59, 59n1, 68, 69, 70, 70n31, 71, 72, 73, 73n40, 74, 75, 75nn47&48, 76, 77, 77n51, 78, 78n54, 79, 79nn60&61, 80, 81, 96, 102, 102n44, 103–5, 107, 112, 120, 126, 163, 172, 197, 219, 237, 239, 240, 278
Sternberg, Meir, 189, 189n50, 193n60, 266, 266n30, 267, 278
Stiver, Dan, 7n20, 9, 9n26, 10, 10n30, 11n32, 12, 12n35, 14n41, 18n52, 19, 20, 20n57, 20n59, 278
Stoebe, H. J., 119n42
Stott, Douglas W., 274
Sutherland, Stewart, 279
Swinburne, Richard, 11, 11n34, 278

Tarski, Alfred, 61, 61n6, 68, 69, 278
Tertullian, 136n4
Teubal, S. J., 187n38
Thisleton, Antony, 55n148
Tillich, Paul, 40
Tracy, David, 19, 19n55, 278
Tracy, Thomas F., 52n142
Turner, Denys, 5, 5n13, 64, 64n15, 65, 279
Turner, Lawrence A., 156, 157n48, 177, 177nn7&8, 178, 178n10, 279

van der Toorn, 2n5, 279

Van Hecke, Pierre, 62, 62n8, 67, 67n23, 67n25, 81, 81n67, 279
Van Seters, John, 175n1
VanGemeren, Willem A., 253n6, 273, 279
Vanhoozer, Kevin, 36n104, 279
von Rad, Gerhard, 53, 83, 83n1, 87, 88, 88n15, 89, 93, 121, 121n46, 127, 127n57, 130, 130n66, 131, 131n69, 133, 138n10, 156, 160, 160n60, 163, 164n66, 167, 167n7, 168, 169n12, 185, 185n31, 192n56, 203, 203n16, 203n18, 208, 208nn27&28, 212, 214, 214n42, 227n19, 231, 231n34, 232, 244n7, 253, 253n6, 256, 259, 259n16, 265, 265n27, 266–68, 279

Waltke, Bruce, 111, 111n16, 111n18, 111n20, 145n30, 153, 153n41, 183n27, 184, 184nn28-30, 189, 189n49, 189n51, 190n53, 192n56, 193, 193n61, 196n1, 214n42, 231n33, 232n35, 244, 244n5, 244n9, 245, 245nn13-15, 249n28, 279
Weinandy, Thomas, 85n8, 279
Wenham, Gordon, vii, 85n8, 108n5, 109, 109n7, 112, 112n21, 116nn34&35, 118, 118n40, 119n42, 127, 127n58, 129, 129n62, 130, 131n70, 133, 136, 136n2, 136n4, 139, 140n17, 142, 142n25, 148, 148n35,

Wenham, Gordon (*cont.*)
    154, 155, 155n45, 165,
    165n1, 166, 166n5, 176,
    176nn3–5, 178n11,
    185n33, 186n36, 189,
    192n56, 197n2, 202,
    202n15, 205, 205n23,
    206n24, 214, 214n43,
    215n45, 222, 222n10,
    227n18, 232, 232n37,
    277, 279
Westermann, Claus, 109,
    109n8, 110, 112, 115n33,
    128n59, 136n4, 137,
    137n5, 139, 141, 141n21,
    142, 145, 157, 157n49,
    160, 160n56, 161n62,
    164n65, 168, 168n9, 170,
    170n15, 171nn18&19,
    178, 182, 182n24, 189,
    189nn46-48, 190n53,
    191n56, 198, 198n4, 200,
    200n10, 212, 212n38,
    214n42, 230, 230n27,
    230n30, 231n33, 244,
    244n6, 247, 247n22,
    250n34, 251, 252n3,
    259n16, 276, 279

White, H. C., 247n23, 248, 247, 248n27, 250, 279
White, Roger, 94, 94n28, 95, 97, 279
Whitehead, Alfred North, 3n9
Wiesel, Elie, 46, 46n127
William of Ockham, 11n34
Williamson, Paul R., 269n35, 279
Wittgenstein, L., 4, 15n34, 19, 20
Wolf, C. U., 187n38
Wolff, Hans Walter, 138n11, 279
Wolterstorff, Nicholas, 18n51, 34, 35, 35nn98–102, 36, 37, 37n105, 38, 38n106, 39, 40, 52n144, 56, 57, 76, 92n25, 237, 279
Woodger, J. H., 278

Zimmerli, Walther, 164n65, 250

Scripture Index

Old Testament

Genesis

1–11	58
1–3	105
1	108n6, 111–13, 115, 119, 121, 124–27, 239, 240
1:1	111
1:1ff.	58n149
1:3	121n44, 125
1:4	107, 112–14, 116, 117, 123, 133, 247
1:4f.	109
1:4ff.	98
1:6–8	112
1:7	121n44
1:8	108n5
1:9–10	113
1:9	121n44
1:10	107, 108, 108n5, 110, 247
1:11	121n44
1:12	107, 108, 108n5, 110, 247,
1:14–19	112
1:15	121n44
1:18	107, 110, 247
1:21	107, 110, 121n44, 247
1:25	107, 110, 121n44, 247
1:26–28	128
1:26–27	88
1:26	57, 84, 122, 143, 150, 238, 241
1:27	121n44, 169n12
1:28	97, 121–23, 126, 143, 150, 169n12, 170, 171, 176
1:31	107, 110, 112, 114, 117–19, 129, 147, 147n33, 149–51, 156, 247
2–3	171n19
2	120–24, 126, 143, 149
2:7	124
2:10	187
2:16–17	123
2:17	110, 134
2:18	120, 124, 125
2:18b	124
2:19	105, 120, 123, 124, 247
2:20	124
2:20b	124
2:21	138
2:22	125
2:23	127n56, 138
2:24	125, 138, 140
2:25	127, 128n59
3	127, 129n61, 142–44, 144n27, 145, 146, 149, 239
3:1	127, 260
3:3	134
3:4	260
3:5	107, 110, 126, 132
3:6	115n30, 126, 134, 142
3:7	126
3:8–9	128n59
3:8	50, 51, 128n59
3:9	187
3:15	142, 146, 149

289

Scripture Index

Genesis (cont.)

3:16	144n27
3:17	85n7
3:19	124n55
3:21	27
3:22–23	85n7
3:22	84, 107, 126–28
4	171n19
4:3	176
4:4	176
4:12	85n7
4:26	176, 244
5:1–3	124n53
5:22–24	176
6-9	171n19
6	85n7, 137, 138n11, 140, 140n19, 142, 149
6:1	136n4, 140, 145
6:1–8	136
6:1–4	136n4, 138
6:2	115n30, 116, 135, 142, 145n29, 149n38, 247
6:3	85n7, 136n4, 137, 138, 138n11
6:4	138, 140, 145, 149n38
6:5	55n147, 105, 135, 136, 147–51, 153, 156, 163, 172, 247
6:6–9	269
6:6–7	119
6:6	43, 136, 155
6:7	136
6:8	136, 153
6:9	154, 155, 176, 255, 269
6:11	150, 151, 155, 181
6:12–13	153
6:12	105, 135, 147, 148, 150–53, 155, 156
6:13	151, 155
6:14–16	269
6:17	152
6:18	269
6:19–21	269
6:19	152
6:22	269
7:1–3	269
7:1	105, 135, 147, 153, 155, 247, 269
7:1b	154
7:5	269
7:15	152
7:16	152
7:2	124n54
7:21	152
8:1	32
8:13	150, 178
8:17	152
8:20	269
8:21	199n8
9:1	170, 171
9:2	152
9:3	152
9:4	152
9:5	171
9:6	97, 171, 268
9:7	171, 171n19
9:9–17	269
9:10–27	255
9:13	156
9:14	156
9:16	105, 135, 156, 163
9:20–27	159
9:22	135, 158, 158n52
9:23	158n52, 160
9:24	160
10:9	232
11	98
11:1	165
11:2	165
11:3–4	165
11:5	2n6, 76, 105, 165–67, 168n10, 172, 172n19, 240, 247
11:6–7	165
11:6	84, 167, 169
11:7	172n19
11:8	165
11:9	165
11:30	175, 179

Genesis (cont.)

12–25	58, 176
12:1–3	175–77, 177n5, 179n14
12:1	247, 266
12:2–3	176
12:2	178, 268
12:3	175–79, 187, 189–91, 260
12:4	266
12:7	178
12:8	244
12:10–20	139, 142
12:11	145n29, 181
12:14	116, 145n29, 181
12:17	190
12:20—13:1	186
13–14	192n59
13:10	116, 116n35
13:14–15	247
13:14	116, 116n35
13:16	178
13:18–19	116n35
14	252, 255
14:19–20	178n10
15	175, 182n22, 185, 190n53
15:1	106n2, 247
15:4–5	178
15:5–6	267
15:5	106n2, 179, 247, 260
15:7	253
15:9–10	267
15:13–14	191n55
15:13	148, 186n35
16	144, 174, 180, 191n55
16:1–16	175
16:1	178, 181
16:2–6	178
16:2	181
16:3	178, 181
16:4–6	190, 247
16:5	181
16:6	181
16:7–14	178
16:7	180
16:8	181
16:9–13	189
16:9	187, 195, 195n68
16:10–16	174
16:10	178, 179
16:11	86, 180, 183
16:13–14	179, 180, 243
16:13	86, 98, 105, 122, 192n56, 243, 246, 247, 249
16:14	249, 250
16:15	249n31
16:16	178
16:17	106n2
16:18	106n2
16:20	106n2, 258
16:21	106n2
17	269, 270
17:2ff.	260
17:4-6	268
17:16	246, 260
17:17	199n8
17:20	178, 179
18	98, 106n2, 155, 170, 179n14, 191n55
18:1—19:29	196
18:2	116, 150, 254
18:5	227n18
18:10	260
18:14	260
18:16	106n2, 254
18:17	151
18:18	179, 268
18:20–21	51, 77, 106n2
18:20	141, 189
18:21	2n4, 47, 76, 98, 105, 246
18:22	106n2, 248, 254
18:22–33	251
18:22–32	251
18:22–28	251
18:23–33	151
18:23	252
18:25	207

Genesis (cont.)

Reference	Pages
19	106n2, 252
19:5	254,
19:8	254,
19:10	254
19:12	254,
19:13	251
19:16	252, 254
19:17	106n2
19:19	252
19:21	252
19:26	106n2
19:28	106n2, 150, 151
19:29	251
19:30–38	196n1
20:11	259
20:18	190
21	144, 179n14, 180n15
21:1–21	175
21:8	253
21:12	264
21:13	179, 189
21:14–15	247
21:14	178
21:16	180
21:17	189
21:19	128, 129n61
21:33	84n6
22	98, 257, 257n14, 258, 262, 269, 270
22:1–19	268
22:1	51, 257, 259
22:4	116
22:8	105, 106n2, 259, 267
22:11	192n56
22:12	2n4, 153, 259, 260
22:13	150
22:14	86, 105, 106, 106n2
22:14a	222n7
22:14b	222n7
22:15–18	270
22:18	179, 191n55, 263, 267
23:7	254n9
23:12	254n9
24:16	145n29
24:63–64	222n9
24:63	116, 117, 150
24:64	116n35
25:12–18	190n53
25:12	186
26:4	179
26:7	145n29
26:8	106n2, 150
26:17–21	122
26:30	253
27:1	169n11
27:36	245
28:14	179
29	98
29:2	150, 151
29:17	145n29
29:22	253
29:31–32	105
29:31	148
29:32	180
31:2	150
31:10	150
32:25	105
33:1	150
33:20	247
34	140, 140n19
35:22	160
36:2	140
37:25	150
40:6	150
40:16	113, 115, 115n30
40:20	253
41:16	72
41:25	72
41:45	121n47
42:9	161
42:11	161
42:14	161
42:18	259
42:27	150
43:14	91
48:10	169
49:3–4	160
49:15	116

Scripture Index

Exodus

1:10–22	35
1:10	193
1:12	183
1:8–10	183
1:8	185
2:2	115n30, 116, 145n29
2:23–25	46, 98
2:23	148
2:25	47, 76, 148
3:1–2	229n25
3:3	192n56
3:4	148, 192n56
3:7–9	98
3:7	47, 76, 141, 180, 183
3:8	148
3:9	47, 76, 246
3:10	148
3:14	44
4:31	76, 148, 180, 180n15
11:7	218
12:13	157, 163
12:30	148
13:13	268
13:15	268
13:17	30
14:5	183
15	262
15:25	257, 259
15:26	257
16	262
16:4	258, 259
20	262
20:17	127
20:18b–21	259n16
20:20	259, 260
20:22	230
21:1–6	28
21:7–11	186
22:29	268
24:9–11	222n7
31:3	92n23
31:18	52n144
32	155
33:12	247
33:19	85n8, 91
33:20	192n56, 248
33:23	248
34:6–7	45,

Leviticus

9:4	229n25
11:44–45	90n21
11:44	97
18	160
18:6–19	160
18:6–8	159
19:2	90n21, 97, 128
20	160
20:7	90n21, 97
20:11	159, 160
20:17	161
20:20–21	160
20:26	90n21, 97,

Numbers

	102n42
6:23–27	118
6:28	118
13:27	246
14:30	155
14:38	155
16:22ff.	155
21:14	232
22:31	92n23, 99, 100, 129
23:19	29, 43, 55n147
23:3	26n77
24:2	222n9
32:22	122
32:29	122

Deuteronomy

1:39	130
3:11	145
4:9	158
4:23	158

Scripture Index

Deuteronomy (*cont.*)

4:29	79
4:31	158
4:35	92n23
4:39	92n23
5:21	127
5:29	259
6:12	158
8	262
8:2	258–60
8:11	158
8:16	258, 262
8:19	158
9:13	76
13	262
13:3	259, 260
17:6	206
19:15	206
23:14	161
23:15	183n27
26:7	180
28:29	101n41
28:31	101n41
28:32	101n41
28:34	101n41
29:7	145
30:11	266
30:14	266
31:4	145
32:4	84n6
34:7	169n11

Joshua

5:13	222n9
6:25	252
7:1	155
12:4	145
13:12	145
15:14	145
15:49	141n20
18:1	122

Judges

1:24–25	253
2:22	259, 260
3:4	259
6:22–23	192n56
11:13	192n56
13:16–22	192n56
13:22	250
15:2	145n29
19	255
19:17	222n9
20:7	248

Ruth

1:16	227n18
4:12	144

1 Samuel

1:11	157
1:18	193
3:2	169n11
10:17	154
12:14	249
13:14	99, 99n39
15	32
15:2	32
15:6	32
15:11	32
15:29	43
15:35	32
16	98
16:1	155
16:6	99
16:7	41, 51, 86, 92n23, 98, 99, 99n39, 102n42, 103, 163, 238
16:7b	99
16:12	99
16:12b	102
16:17	106n2
24:12	247
25:29	88

294

2 Samuel

1:20	140
1:24	140
3:12–13	192n56
8:11	122
11	139
11f.	142
11:2	145n29
13	140
13:14	140
13:34	222n7
15:19–21	253
16:20–23	160
18:24	222n9
2:23	248
21:16	145
21:18	145
21:20	145
21:22	145
24:15–17	222n7

1 Kings

4:19	217
8:50	91
9:2	102
20:2–4	192n56
20:3	145n29

2 Kings

	102n42
4:1	259
4:35	129
6:1	99
6:16	100
6:17–20	129
6:17	92n23, 98, 100, 128, 129n61
6:18	100
6:20	101, 128
7:38	158
13:2	249
20:1–11	32
20:12	260
23:34	121n47
24:17	121n47

1 Chronicles

1:28	190n53
1:32	190n53
2:4	144
20:4	145
20:6	145
20:8	145
21:16	222n9
21:27	141n20
22:18	122

2 Chronicles

2:6	51n140
3:1	228n22
6:40	43
9:18	122
30:9	91
32:8	138n11
32:24–25	32
32:25	32
32:31	260, 261n17

Nehemiah

1:11	91
5:5	122
9:9	180n15
9:22	145
13:23	247

Esther

1:11	145n29
2:2	145n29
2:3	145n29
6:6	199n8
7:8	122n51

Scripture Index

Job

1:1	259
1:6	136
1:8	259
2:1	136
6:14	91n22
10:4	86, 138n11
10:4f.	41, 43
17:7	169n11
17:8	169n11
28:24	167
28:28	259
31:7	249
34:14–15	139
36:7	117n37
38:7	136
38:12–13	111

Psalm

2:4	50
8:5	84
9	157
9:12	157
9:14	157
10:6	199n8
10:12	157
14:2	106n2, 167
19:1–6	110n12
22:24	180n15
25	76
25:18	76
32:8	117n37
33:6	48
33:13	167
33:18	117n37
34:7	28
34:15	117n37
35:21	129
44:22	41
51:4[6]	206n26
56:5[4]	138n11
72:1	91
72:13	91
74:19	157
74:23	157
78:39	138n11
82:6	84
84:5	222n7
88:10–12	46
91:8	100n40
91:11–12	28
94:2	207
94:7	43
94:8–9	207
94:9	1
95:9	247
100:5	119n42
103:13	91
115:5	76
119:77	91, 129n61
121:4	41
123:2	186
135:11	145
136:18	145
139	51, 261n18
139:12	116
139:23	41
145:4	110n12
145:6–7	110n12
145:9–10	110n12
146:8	129
148:1–14	110n12

Proverbs

1:7	259
21:13	202
30:21–23	189

Ecclesiastes

2:4	247
2:24	116
3:13	113
8:17	116
9:13	247
12:21	227n18

Isaiah

3:16	140
6:9–10	101
7:14	130
10:23	211n36
11:2	259
14:14–15	90n21
31:3	91
35:5	129
38:1–8	32
39:1	260
40:18	92
40:22	92, 166
40:25–26	92
40:27	92
40:28–31	92, 92n23
40:28	92
42:7	129
42:14	50
43:10	98
44–45	51
44	55n147, 98
44:8	98
45:5	92n23
45:14	92n23
45:21	92n23
45:22	92n23
47:3	161, 247
47:8	199n8
49:15	91, 113, 157
51:9	48
52:8	100n40
55:7–9	90
55:11	141
66:3	245

Jeremiah

4:28	43
7:11	247
15:1	213
17:5	138n11
23:23	43
25:26	227n18
25:31	152
31:20	48
34:11	122
34:16	122
42:12	91

Lamentations

5:20	158

Ezekiel

14:14	213
16:8	162
16:36–37	160
18	155
22:10	160
23:10	160
23:18	160
23:29	160

Daniel

1:9	91
5:23b	1

Hosea

1:10	232
2:23	91
7:2	199n8
9:12	246
11	47
11:7–9	90
11:8–9	32
11:8	43f.
11:8f.	43
11:9	55n147

Jonah

3:4	252

Micah

6:8	91n22
7:19	122n51

Scripture Index

Zechariah

7:9	91
9:11	246
9:15	122n51

Malachi

3:6	43

Pseudepigrapha

1 Enoch

6:2ff.	136n4

Jubilees

5:1	136n4

New Testament

Matthew

1:3	144
1:20	192n56
1:24	192n56
10:40	254
13:10–11	79
19:8	33n96

Mark

10:5	33n96

Luke

1:11	192n56
1:19	192n56
2:9	192n56
2:38	193

John

13:20	254

Acts

3:25	179

Galatians

3:8	179
4:14	254

Ephesians

3:14–15	171

Philippians

2:7	43

Titus

1:2	29

Hebrews

4	259
6:4	92n23
6:10	157
6:18	29
11:17–19	264

1 Peter

1:4	92n23

2 Peter

2:4	136n4
2:8–9	251

1 John

2:16	127

Jude

6	136n4
7	136n4

Revelation

12:12–17	144n28

www.ingramcontent.com/pod-product-compliance
Lightning Source LLC
Chambersburg PA
CBHW061431300426
44114CB00014B/1636